The War Machine and Global Health

The War Machine
and Global Health

A Critical Medical Anthropological Examination of the Human Costs of Armed Conflict and the International Violence Industry

Edited by Merrill Singer
and G. Derrick Hodge

ALTAMIRA
P R E S S

A Division of Rowman & Littlefield Publishers, Inc.
Lanham • New York • Toronto • Plymouth, UK

Published by AltaMira Press
A division of Rowman & Littlefield Publishers, Inc.
A wholly owned subsidiary of The Rowman & Littlefield Publishing Group, Inc.
4501 Forbes Boulevard, Suite 200, Lanham, Maryland 20706
http://www.altamirapress.com

Estover Road, Plymouth PL6 7PY, United Kingdom

British Library Cataloguing in Publication Information Available

Library of Congress Cataloging-in-Publication Data
The war machine and global health : a critical medical anthropological examination of
the human costs of armed conflict and the international violence industry / edited by
Merrill Singer and G. Derrick Hodge.
    p. ; cm.
Includes bibliographical references and index.
ISBN 978-0-7591-1190-5 (cloth : alk. paper)
1. War—Health aspects. 2. World health. I. Singer, Merrill. II. Hodge, G. Derrick,
1968-
[DNLM: 1. World Health. 2. Violence. 3. War. WA 530.1 W253 2010]
RA646.W372 2010
362.1—dc22
                                                                        2009038592

∞ ™ The paper used in this publication meets the minimum requirements of American
National Standard for Information Sciences—Permanence of Paper for Printed Library
Materials, ANSI/NISO Z39.48-1992.

Printed in the United States of America

In memory of two remarkable men
who struggled against murderous right-wing governments:

Oskar Schendler
and his munitions plant workers,
Jews from Krakow, and inmates of Płaszów concentration camp
who never produced usable munitions

and

Archbishop Oscar Romero,
whose struggle on behalf of the poor of Latin America
cost him his life at the hands of a right-wing paramilitary

And in solidarity with the group of remarkable women
led by Leymah Gbowee of the Liberian Mass Action for Peace
who fought peacefully to successfully end the
Liberian Civil War of 1989 to 2003

CONTENTS

CONTENTS

PART THREE
THE WAR MACHINE AND THE MACHINERY OF HUMAN SOCIAL LIFE

INTRODUCTION
The Myriad Impacts of the
War Machine on Global Health
Merrill Singer and G. Derrick Hodge

Painting the Picture of War

Spanish surrealist painter Salvador Dali once quipped, "Wars have never hurt anybody except the people who die." Even were this true, war-related mortality figures alone would be sufficiently staggering to provoke public outcry and public health, medical, and health social scientific engagement. In the twentieth century—by all measures "the bloodiest in human history" (Garfield 2008:25)—the two largest wars alone, World Wars I and II, caused at least 80 million deaths. Since the end of World War II, there have been at least 160 wars around the world with as many as 25 million (and probably many more) people killed, most of them civilians (Levy and Sidel 2008). As Nordstrom (1997:114–115) observes, "Militaries operate on one single truth: the strategic employment of violence." Consequently, when greed or conflict find expression through the mobilization of armed troops, misery always follows. And, as summarized by Kurz (2001:210), it is invariably "grotesque, unspeakable, an abomination, a modern negativity."

While all wars by their nature are brutal, some seem to be especially egregious. A case in point in recent years was the internal war that tore apart Yugoslavia and devastated the disputed city of Kosovo. Despite recognition that causalities were predominantly civilian (possibly as high as 90 percent), the actual mortality rate for Kosovo during the war remains disputed (Toole et al. 1993). Overall, it is estimated that there were at least 200,000 civilian casualties throughout Yugoslavia. A survey of almost

1,200 households in Kosovo found that 64 percent of identified cases of mortality for the period from February 1998 until June 1999 were attributed by family members to war-related injuries. The crude mortality rate for the population increased by 2.3 times compared to the preconflict level (Spiegel and Salama 2000), the death rate being highest during April 1999 at the height of the Serbian genocidal campaign of "ethnic cleansing" against Albanians (Danner 1992).

Another case in point is the one studied by Nordstrom: the Mozambican Civil War that lasted from 1975 to 1994. During this period, close to a million people died (many from starvation), millions became refugees, and brutalities were routinely committed against civilians. A report written for the U.S. State Department by Robert Gersony (1988) titled "Summary of Mozambican Refugee Accounts of Principally Conflict-Related Experience in Mozambique" offers nightmarish remembrances that include having been "raped on [a] frequent, sustained basis" and subsequently suffering with venereal disease, which this practice proliferates. Severe beatings were inflicted on young girls and women who resisted sexual demands. Such punishment may also have been inflicted on the husband or father of the female who resisted. Such punishment reportedly included execution in some circumstances (Gersony 1988:22).

Because combatants confiscated any food they found, starvation ensued. Notes Gersony (1988:23–24), "The refugees' allegations of food deprivation appear to explain the wasted physical condition of the men, women and children arriving by the thousands in asylum countries naked and severely malnourished." To this gruesome list of cruelties, Nordstrom adds her own chilling narratives, including one of a mother who told of being forced to watch her son be sliced up and cooked and then being compelled to eat some of his body.

As the examples above suggest, Dali's peculiar approach to assessing the human costs of war offers far too restrained an accounting of the full measure of harm that is generated. Indeed, directly or indirectly, war touches the lives of most people on the planet, often with enduring and costly health consequences. The carnage produced by contemporary war, including suffering inflicted through sexual crimes, mass displacements, and malnutrition, extend the causalities of war far beyond those who die. For instance, the Spanish Civil War—Dali's most immediate personal encounter with the bloody clash of warring armies—began during the summer of 1936 when General Francisco Franco spearheaded a military coup against the democratically elected government of the Second Spanish Republic. Although Dali fled to a comfortable life in the United States, like Picasso's powerful mural *Guernica*, Dali's painting about the war, *Soft Construction with Boiled Beans*, came to stand as a universal artistic outcry against the enormous brutality, destruction, and suffering of wartime violence. Of the estimated 500,000 deaths during the Spanish Civil War, only about 200,000 died from direct combat-related causes (Jackson 1987; Thomas 2001).) At least another 100,000 to 200,000 people were executed, disproportionately by Franco's forces. Thousands more were killed during bombing raids by Franco's German-supplied air force, as occurred at the Basque town of Guernica in April 1937. German high-explosive and incendiary bombs rained on Guernica for over three hours. Townspeople fleeing the aerial assault were slaughtered by machine gun fire. In all, 1,600 civilians were killed or wounded in the brutal attack. Unable to achieve victory through his early use of what later would come to be called "shock-and-awe" tactics, Franco imposed an economic blockage against parts of the country he could not defeat militarily. The result was widespread starvation and malnutrition among civilians, resulting in the immediate death of 25,000 to 50,000 people. Additionally, at least 165,000 people died of diseases spread by the social disorder created by the conflict. All together, over 3 percent of the Spanish population died in the war, and another 7.5 percent sustained injuries (Payne 1987).

Contrary to Dali's statement, suffering did not end with the generation that fought the war. González et al. (2006) have analyzed coronary heart disease data for Spain for the years 1990–2002, finding an increased risk for heart problems for both sexes for persons born during the war, especially among those born during the period when famine was most intense (namely, the years 1937, 1940, 1943, and 1945). They concluded that suffering nutritional stress in utero had long-term health consequences for people born in the war-linked famine-stricken areas. They did not die during the war, but their physical health was never the same, a point developed further in chapter 1 by Clarkin.

Immediate casualties, in short, are only the beginning; war-related deaths and injuries are numerous and insidious and last far longer than active combat (Pedersen 2009). Thus, a simple counting up of the dead—the "body count," to use a morbid expression made popular by the

U.S. war against Vietnam—is never sufficient. Framed by the holistic and ethnographically grounded theoretical perspective of critical medical anthropology and more broadly by the political economy of health, this book of essays by medical anthropologists and other health social scientists examines the full measure of the disastrous global health effects of the war machine in the contemporary world. More important, it provides a political-economic framework for assessing the war machine. In this regard, a primary goal of this book is to increase understanding of the causes of the brutalities that are documented herein, an awareness that is critical if the war machine is ever to be effectively opposed.

The Machinery of War

By using the term "war machine," we seek to draw attention to the whole canvas of war and not simply its most glaring features. The concept of the war machine avoids a narrow focus on the undeniably considerable and complex public health impacts of bullets, bombs, and battles. In addition to the varied forms of direct armed hostility, the concept of the war machine includes vast war industries and their heavy toll on environments and workers, the international weapons trade that reaps great profit while helping to fuel new conflicts, the saber-rattling ideologies and policies that justify and encourage war, and war budgets that rob public treasuries of funds needed for pressing health and social needs.

During 2008, for instance, the United States officially spent almost $700 billion on "defense," although other war costs are known to be hidden in the budget under intentionally obscure headings (Sweetman 2000). This amounts to more than double the combined cost of the next five largest military budgets in the world. At the same time, the U.S. economy was falling deeply into recession, its infrastructure was increasingly in tatters, and almost 50 million of its residents lacked health insurance coverage. It has been argued that the failure of the United States to provide universal health care, a feature that separates the country from other developed nations, is a direct consequence of its bloated military budget. At the same time, in 1990, the per capita spending by Ethiopia was $16 for military purposes compared to $1 for health care. Sudan surpassed this disparity, spending $25 per capita on the military and only $1 per capita on health care (Foege 2000). Similarly, the money used to purchase 28 missiles by

South Korea in 2005 could have purchased immunizations for 120,000 people against common diseases, or it could have provided safe drinking water to 3.5 million people for three years. While some have argued that spending on war is the best way to ensure peace and prosperity and hence meet a critical social need, as Albert Einstein aptly retorts, "You cannot simultaneously prevent and prepare for war."

The term "war machine" harkens back to what President Dwight D. Eisenhower in his presidential farewell address on January 17, 1961, called the "military-industrial complex," namely, the "conjunction of an immense military establishment and a large arms industry" (Eisenhower 1968). In what has become a globalized world of interlocked economies, fast-flowing commodities, multinational corporations, and rapid-fire communication technologies, it is possible to speak of a global military-industrial complex (but see Chomsky 2004) that supports a global war machine. Documenting and analyzing its costs, in human flesh and agony, are the goals of this volume.

This global war machine is intimately linked to the global economic system (Baer et al. 2003; Hooks 1991), in which the United States plays a primary role. There are as a result of the U.S. global economic reach approximately 400,000 U.S. soldiers stationed overseas (four times the number of UN troops) in 120 countries (Keane 2003). These vast and widely dispersed armed forces, which the U.S. Army (2004) calls "a land force unmatched in human history," play an important role on the ground that goes far beyond a strictly military mission. This broader mission is articulated by the U.S. Army as "Civil Administration" (CA) operations:

> CA operations play a command support role in all operational environments and across the operational continuum. The U.S. Army organizes, trains, equips, and provides CA units to support all operations where the civilian populace of an FN [Friendly Nation, although CA work occurs in occupied nations as well] is involved. CA missions are dynamic because they are directly affected by politico-military considerations. . . . CA operations encompass the relationship between military forces, civil authorities, and people in a friendly or occupied country or area. CA operations support national policy and implement U.S. national objectives by coordinating with, influencing, developing, or controlling indigenous infrastructures in operational areas. (Department of the Army 2000)

The ultimate meaning of "controlling indigenous infrastructures" would seem to refer to the preparation of a territory for a new round of material exploitation, that is, for the extraction and export of wealth, the control of labor forces, and the opening of new markets. Further, through its CA activities, U.S. Army commanders "are afforded the tools necessary to establish links to the international and local communities" (Department of the Army 2000). In these and other ways, the various branches of the U.S. military (and that of others) plays a role in linking together a world system that while overtly economic in nature—that is, a capitalist system of global production, distribution, marketing, and consumption—is supported by politicomilitary components. For instance, dispersed government, military, and corporate entities like ExxonMobil, Halliburton, the U.S. Army and its Civil Affairs and Psychological Operations Command, the International Close Protections Services of the United Kingdom, Mingnan Huital Technology Corporation of China, the Ava Gostar Company of Jordan, the country of El Salvador, and the Iraqi Parliament are all connected economically by the war in Iraq.

As seen in the ethnographic chapters of this book, while the health consequences of war are best seen at the microlevel of on-the-ground lived experience, they are best understood at the macrolevel that includes pressures of intensified global competition for disperse resources. In various ways, militaries are in fact indispensable tools for the expansion (and survival) of global capitalism. We conclude this volume with a consideration of the intricate connections between dominant economic forces and the apparently endless state of global conflict in which we now find ourselves. The analytical tool of critical medical anthropology supports our ability to identify connections between health, war, and political economy.

In the World of War-Scapes

Nordstrom (1997) introduced the concept of "war-scape" to capture the fluid global features of the war machine in action, especially including a shifting mosaic of local, national, and international relationships and interactions. This approach allows realization that immediate combatants, in all their variability of ideology, motivation, and behavior in local contexts, are inextricably connected to foreign strategists who help in planning, to arms suppliers who provide the fire power, to outside mercenaries and private security forces who assist in and may lead the fighting, to corporate interests in oil or diamonds or other natural resources who spurn war publicly and plan it privately, and to blackmarketeers who know the value of a prolonged conflict.

Moreover, the globalization of the war machine has changed the face and the consequences of war, including the appearance of notable patterns of similarity across local settings. As indicated by the People's Health Movement (2008:112).

> The health impacts of war and conflict have become increasingly important in the context of the changing nature of war and conflict. Rarely do armies wear distinctive uniforms and fight across clearly drawn battle lines. Modern wars and conflict are characterized by aerial bombardment, guerrilla tactics and acts of "terrorism," substantially changing the nature of the primary victims of war. . . . Since World War II, civilians, especially women and children, have constituted the majority of deaths in wars.

The toll of war on children, for example, has been documented by a growing number of researchers (Machel 1996) and is examined further with regard to child conscription by armed groups in chapter 3 by Kohrt and his colleagues. Notably, this toll is not the unique expression of any particular war but has become a pattern of the modern war-scape writ large. Similar patterning appears in other features of contemporary war, as seen across the chapters to follow this introduction. Hence, it can be argued that there is a dynamic tension between the local and the global in war as in other aspects of the modern world.

Perspective and Focus

Like *Unhealthy Health Policy: A Critical Anthropological Examination* (Castro and Singer 2004) and *Killer Commodities: Public Health and the Corporate Production of Harm* (Singer and Baer 2008), its companion volumes in a series of edited medical anthropological books published by AltaMira, the current volume provides a timely and poignant assessment of an immediate and pressing threat to global health. Further, like the two prior volumes, this book offers a critical analysis of political and economic forces driving the contemporary world scene. The chapters that make up this volume include both thematic analyses of key aspects of the global war machine, in its diverse expressions, as well as case studies of specific conflicts, and provide up-to-date assessment of its staggering public health and social impact as a force shaping the world in these times. In making this assessment, it is necessary to consider (and to document), in addition to military casualties, multiple health-related consequences of the war machine, as itemized and discussed briefly below.

Injuries and Deaths of Civilians

Beginning with the U.S. Civil War—a conflict that was particularly noteworthy for its targeting of civilians, primarily in the South—a body of International Humanitarian Law (IHL) has developed that specifies the minimum protections and standards for the treatment of civilians in times of war. The aim of this set of legal protections is to prevent attacks on noncombatants, limit displacement of civilian populations, and avoid the destruction of civilian property. At the heart of IHL is the demand that belligerents respect the distinction between combatants and noncombatants. Unfortunately, the IHL codes are routinely ignored. It is estimated that during the twentieth century, there were approximately 45 million military deaths around the world compared to 62 million civilian war-related deaths (Sivard 1996). During a speech before the UN Security Council in November 2002, Secretary-General Kofi Annan declared, "The toll of dead and wounded—particularly among innocent civilians—has risen to levels that can be described, without any exaggeration, as appalling." In his talk, Annan drew attention to Darfur, Sudan, stating that international aid workers there have been "dismayed by the recent pattern of attacks on civilians, humanitarian workers and facilities, including the shameful attacks on civilians at or near food distribution sites" (UN Office for the Coordination of Humanitarian Affairs 2003).

Language is also a weapon of war to the extent that it either justifies violence by claiming to be defensive or hides violence by using rhetoric that obscures the reality of suffering. Anthropologist Hugh Gusterson (1995), for instance, has outlined the rhetorical gymnastics played by weapons researchers that serve to distance themselves from the consequences of their work. Using the term "collateral damage," militaries have stressed their inability to protect civilians in many situations. As defined by the U.S. Department of Defense (2001:95), collateral damage refers to "unintentional or incidental injury or damage to persons or objects that would not be lawful military targets in the circumstances ruling at the time. Such damage is not unlawful so long as it is not excessive in light of the overall military advantage anticipated from the attack." Determining what level of collateral damage constitutes "excessive" remains vague, and usefully so, as a means of avoiding war crimes charges.

It is estimated, for example, that between 1969 and 1973, at least 50,000 and as many as 150,000 noncombatant Cambodian peasants were killed by bombs dropped by U.S. airplanes. In *Ending the Vietnam War*, former Secretary of State Henry Kissinger (2003) reports that the Historical Office of the U.S. Secretary of Defense accepted the lower figure as accurate. Fifty thousand people was, apparently, a nonexcessive level of collateral damage "in light of the overall military advantage" that was gained.

From a public health perspective, civilian casualties of the war machine have become, increasingly, a primary issue of concern. Calling for new controls on military activities, however, would confront active efforts to convince the public that civilian casualties are low, as seen in the U.S. war in Iraq. After interviewing over 50 U.S. Iraq War veterans, Hedges and Al-Arian (2008) conclude that the commonly believed and reported civilian death toll of 10,000 is a product of the decision of military authorities to *not* investigate or accurately report the common occurrence of civilian deaths. Dozens of those interviewed by Hedges and Al-Arian witnessed Iraqi civilians dying from American firepower, suggesting a mortality rate that is as much as 100 times higher than popular understanding. Hills and Wasfi's examination in chapter 4 documents that the losses sustained by the Iraqi people go beyond war fatalities and include multiple traumas, some directly at the hands of the U.S. military and some as a result of their encounters with private mercenary forces.

Blackwater Worldwide's employees who have been responsible for civilian deaths in Iraq are similar to the right-wing paramilitaries that decimated civilians all over Latin America throughout the Cold War. Numerous military and paramilitary personnel were trained in "modern war" by the U.S. Army in the School of the Americans in Fort Benning, Georgia. The knowledge gained there in rural guerilla combat, terrorist bombings, and urban "cleansing" has been used by many right-wing leaders to stifle internal dissent. Pine's examination in chapter 8, for example, documents that the losses sustained by the Iraqi people go beyond war fatalities and include multiple traumas, some at the hands of the U.S. military and some as a result of their encounters with private mercenary forces.

Notably, Blackwater has recruited Chilean soldiers, veterans of Augusto Pinochet's reign of terror that on September 11, 1973, overthrew the democratically elected President Salvador Allende, leading to the disappearance of 30,000 civilians (Scahill 2008; for details on the United States sponsorship of terrorism in Chile, see also Kornbluh 2004). Others are foreign-born members of the U.S. military who seek expedited naturalization through military service as described by Adams in chapter 9.

Trauma and Injury to Children

As noted, of special concern in assessing the impact of the war machine on civilians is the case of child victims. Locke and coworkers (1996), for example, investigated the physical and mainly psychological consequences of exposure to war in Central American in a small sample of children who subsequently immigrated to the United States. Of the 22 children they examined, 18 suffered from chronic health problems. Fifteen of the children had observed distressing events, including bombings and homicides, of whom 13 exhibited greater-than-average symptoms of poor mental health. Because the symptoms they suffered were hidden, many of the children's caretakers were unaware of their distress. Such patterns are common among children exposed to war, although the nature and extent of children's torment varies depending on the dynamic interaction of a set of factors, including the child's prior psychobiological status and resiliency, the extent of the disruption caused to the family unit and wider community, the availability of supportive and ameliorative elements in the cultural system in which the child is socialized, and the ferocity, suddenness of onset, and duration of exposure (Betancourt and Khan 2008; Elbedour et al. 1993).

When conditions are especially bad, as occurred in the city of Kosovo during and after the intense conflict in Yugoslavia in 1999, the outcomes for children can be severe. In one Kosovo study, Baràth (2002) used a standardized inventory of coping measurements to assess the health and psychosocial status of over 800 Albanian school-age children in 2000. Most of the children were living in dwellings without electricity or safe drinking water and were surrounded by garbage piled up on the streets (a combination that increasingly around the world is not limited to war zones). Almost half the children were still being exposed to firearms, explosives, and mined fields near home, and most said they did not feel safe. As a result, they suffered from frequent headaches (60 percent), stomach pains (41 percent), high fevers (32 percent), and sleeplessness (18 percent). Three groups of stressors were identified as having the greatest impact on the children: 1) lack of cultural and supportive/security resources at home or in the community, 2) poor physical and mental health conditions, and 3) school-related stressors. Teachers at the children's schools reported high rates of learning and behavioral disorders, and both children and parents expressed grave concerns about the children's mental health. Not surprisingly, in other research on Kosovo children, those who experienced the loss of a family member in the conflict suffered the highest levels of trauma, including high rates of posttraumatic stress disorder comorbid with depression (Hasanović et al. 2006). As the case of Kosovo and the wider conflict that it came to symbolizes affirms, in the twentieth century war or its aftermath became the primary contexts for the perpetuation of genocide. In Darfur, this pattern continues into the twenty-first century.

Of course, the injuries of war for children are not only psychological. Giroux (2009), with specific reference to the Israeli invasion of Gaza in 2008–2009, an offensive known to have caused the deaths of hundreds of Palestinian children, observes that "children no longer serve as an ethical referent against acts of barbarism, they simply become collateral damage, while a ghastly and inhumane act is justified under the pretense of historical necessity and 'surgical strikes.' This language reveals more about a political state that uses such euphemisms than the repugnant strategies it denotes." Bornstein's chapter 7 details the cost that Palestinians, including children, pay for the brutality that surrounds them.

Enduring Injuries

While wars end or at least shift from one geosocial context to the next, the physical and emotional wounds they inflict on survivors, combatants, and civilians alike go on indefinitely (Hashemian et al. 2006). The

People's Health Movement (2005:254) reports that "millions [of people] are psychologically impaired from wars during which they were physically or sexually assaulted; were forced to serve as soldiers; witnessed the death of family members; or experienced the destruction of their communities and even nations. Psychological trauma may be demonstrated in disturbed and antisocial behaviour such as aggression toward others, including family members. Many combatants also suffer from post-traumatic stress disorder on return from military action." Writing in *Internal Medicine* 32 years after the end of the war, Jack McCue (2007), clinical professor of medicine at the University of California, San Francisco, observes that many internists are still seeing "the ravages of the . . . Vietnam War—chronic psychiatric illnesses, drug addiction, and cirrhosis from hepatitis C and alcoholism—that had their roots in Vietnam and are still with us today. Of these, Vietnam War–related posttraumatic stress disorder (PTSD) and its consequences are problems that physicians in public and VA hospitals still treat on a frequent basis."

Of course, most of the suffering caused by the U.S. war in Vietnam was experienced and continues to be experienced by the Vietnamese. Exemplary are the effects of the chemical Agent Orange, used as a defoliant to rob the Vietnamese combatants of the protective cover of their jungles. An Australian nongovernmental organization that is working on the longer-term health effects of exposure to Agent Orange maintains that as many as 1 million Vietnamese suffer from cancers, genetic disorders, and other disabilities (Vietnamese Victims of Agent Orange Trust 2008).

Since the U.S. war in Vietnam, improvements in body armor, such as Kevlar, have significantly increased the likelihood of surviving significant war wounds. Seventy-five percent of American soldiers who suffered traumatic brain injury (TBI) in Vietnam died. Although this is a common injury suffered by blast-exposed patients, there has been a threefold reduction in mortality from TBI in the current U.S. wars in Iraq and Afghanistan. As a result, a higher percentage of current war injury survivors must contend with enduring TBI symptoms of speech and language deficits, loss of cognitive skills and memory, depression and anxiety, and headaches and sleep disturbances in addition to other permanent physical injuries. Additionally, rates of PTSD among veterans of the wars in Iraq and Afghanistan, as discussed in chapter 4 by Hills and Wasfi and in chapter 2 by Harding and Libal, have been notable if for no other reason than the tendency of military physicians to underdiagnose it.

Injuries of war do not necessarily commence during the war itself, as discussed previously in relation to late-onset coronary heart disease in the aftermath of the Spanish Civil War. Significantly delayed onset of PTSD, for example, has been described among elderly war veterans, men who only began to express war-related trauma symptoms following later-in-life unrelated medical complaints, psychosocial stress, and/or cognitive impairment (Ruzich et al. 2005). Late reappearance of earlier PTSD symptoms has been affirmed in meta-analysis (Andrews et al. 2007). Delayed psychosis and posttraumatic epilepsy are further examples of late-onset injuries associated with head wounds. Such injuries are also associated with higher morbidity rates after age 50 among combat veterans (Weiss et al. 1982).

Cancers associated with toxic exposures on battlegrounds have also been suggested by several studies. Bullman et al. (2005) studied the effects of the nerve agent sarin during the March 1991 demolition of weapons at Khamisiyah, Iraq. They compared over 100,000 exposed Gulf War veterans to over 200,000 Gulf War veterans who were not exposed and discovered an increased risk of death due to brain cancer deaths in the exposed group. They also found evidence of a dose–response relationship, by comparing those who were exposed to sarin for one versus two days. An association has also been established after a study of testicular cancer in soldiers who experienced active involvement in the Persian Gulf war zone compared to those in undeployed reserve units, but the sample size of the study was small (Levine et al. 2005). Notably, internal contamination with depleted uranium isotopes has been detected in British, Canadian, and U.S. Gulf War veterans as late as nine years after exposure to radioactive dust during the first Persian Gulf War (Duraković 2003).

Long before active conflict ensues, the mere preparation for war promotes morbidity and mortality. In chapter 6, Vine documents the nearly universal poor health outcomes for people displaced by military strategies. The U.S. and British militaries conspired to forcibly remove the entire Chagossian people from their Indian Ocean island in order to give the United States a military base for future operations in the Middle East. The result was sagren, or "death by sadness." The health consequences of the war machine, then, must include the phenomenal human cost to the countries that host the over 700 United States military bases and those of other countries around the globe (see Johnson 2004a, 2004b). Indeed, as our discussion has already indicated, reports of the immediate casualties of an armed conflict dramatically underestimate the full health consequences of the war machine.

Epidemics and the Enduring Movement of Infectious Agents

In an often-quoted passage about the intimate relationship between war and disease, the renowned bacteriologist Hans Zinsser (2000:153) pointed out that "soldiers have rarely won wars. They more often mop up after the barrage of epidemics. And typhus, with its brothers and sisters—plague, cholera, typhoid, dysentery—has decided more campaigns than Caesar, Hannibal, Napoleon, and all the inspector generals of history." The American Civil War serves as a grim affirmation of Zinsser's observation. One product of this internecine conflict—one that resulted in more deaths (620,000) than any U.S. war before or since—and attesting to its ferocity are a series of photographs taken on the battlefields shortly after the cessation of hostilities. One well-known photograph of this sort was Timothy O'Sullivan's 1863 "The Harvest of Death," an image of fallen Union soldiers after the Battle of Gettysburg (Gardner 1959). It captures a haphazard array of crumpled bodies of soldiers shot as they desperately ran downhill. Only one face is seen in the black-and-white photograph, a soldier lying on his back, his frozen countenance reflecting all the unspeakable horrors of war. Yet while the average Civil War soldier might have feared meeting a similar fate, "disease was the biggest killer of the war" (Civil War Society 2002). Three out of five deaths in the Union army and two of three deaths of Confederate soldiers were caused by disease, not bullets, with typhoid and dysentery being the primary killers of the war (Bollet 2004).

Fifty years later, during World War I, disease again haunted the battlefields, encampments, and other war-scapes of the conflict. The primary disease in this war was influenza, although bacterial infections, in syndemic conjunction with the flu, was a likely cause of the particularly lethal epidemic (Singer 2009). Disease devastated armies on both sides of the conflagration. Half of U.S. military fatalities, for example, were victims of disease (Tice 1997).

More recent wars in developing countries have also been marked by significant loss of life due to disease both during and after hostilities have ceased. Soviet troops in Afghanistan from 1978 to 1989 suffered heavily from hepatitis, typhoid, and paratyphoid fevers; Grau and Jorgensen (1997) estimate that approximately 300,000 Soviet soldiers suffered infectious diseases, contributing to the total of almost 15,000 fatalities in the Soviet army. Similarly, as many as 50,000 Rwandan refugees died as a result of cholera or dysentery (Goma Epidemiology Group 1995). While war continues to spread diseases, old and new, the relationship between these two primary causes of human mortality is in transition. In the past, disease has provided some degree of constraint on war to the extent that it enfeebled armies. This has changed as medical discoveries have been used to protect armies, making the world a safer place for warfare (Coker 2004). Moreover, with the spread of modern biological warfare, disease is not only a *consequence* of war but also potentially an ever more deadly *weapon* in the arsenal of the war machine.

Famine and Malnutrition

The war machine impacts nutrition in multiple ways, including disruption of civilian food production and other subsistence activities, embargoes and blockades that severely hinder the flow of food to populations, and the displacement of people into areas with limited food supply (Santa Barbara 2008). In chapter 7, Bornstein describes chronic food insecurity among Palestinians as a result of Israeli settlements, checkpoints, and the Wall (built by Israeli forces to disrupt and control Palestinian lives). In Palestine and elsewhere, children are highly vulnerable to nutritional deficiencies, particularly when so many were inadequately nourished even before the most recent Zionist expansion. Even into the next generation, war makes itself known through the effects of undernutrition in utero. This is a point convincingly argued by Clarkin in chapter 1.

In wars in Somalia in 1993 and Liberia two years later, moderate to severe malnutrition among children under five years of age was extensive. Jean Ziegler of the UN Human Rights Commission has reported that acute malnutrition among Iraqi children under five years of age doubled in 2004 as a result of the U.S. occupation and the breakdown of social institutions (Carroll 2005). According to Ziegler, more than a quarter of

Iraqi children lacked an adequate diet, while almost 8 percent were acutely malnourished. This in turn leads to weakened immune response, increasing vulnerability to infectious disease. Indeed, producing conditions that lead to malnutrition can be adopted as an intentional weapon of war, as suggested, for instance, by the numerous reports of famine within Gaza since the Israeli blockade.

Undocumented Casualties

Not all causalities of war are displayed in war photographs or on CNN, nor are they counted in UN reports; they are intentionally hidden. This includes those who die or are intentionally murdered in prisoner-of-war camps, civilian concentration camps, or torture rooms or who disappear through paramilitary action. These are also sites of enduring emotional and physical harm for survivors. Michael Kennedy (2009) has recorded the experiences of Palestinian youth whom the Israeli Defense Forces imprisoned and tortured at Al-Fara'a detention center. One of his informants recalls,

> The x's are where they put children in a sort of confinement—they were "put away" for an indefinite amount of time. We went away and didn't know when we were coming back. The x's are about 12 rooms, each one 4 feet by 12 feet, and a tiny window. I stayed there, everyone stayed here at some point, for months at a time, with six to eight even 15 other boys in one room. . . . When a boy would come back from being tortured, we would crowd to one side of the room so he could sleep. . . . This sound [of boys being tortured] we cannot get out of our heads. This was the sound of the x's.

Notable among hidden casualties of the global war machine were the thousands who disappeared in Argentina after the overthrow of the government by a military junta in 1976. In what the junta itself called its "dirty war," civil liberties were suspended, Congress was closed, judges were dismissed, and universities were purged. The military then launched a wave of organized violence against civilians that included abduction, torture, and disappearances. The exact number of people who were never heard from again is unknown, but human rights organizations estimate that 30,000 people disappeared or were known to have been killed by the government during military rule. Included on the list of the "Desapareci-dos" (disappeared) were high school students who protested government abuses (Armed Conflict Events Data 2003; see also Kornbluh 2004). "Young children were also kidnapped with their parents, and pregnant young women were kept alive until giving birth. With changed identities, the children were appropriated by military personnel" (Jelin 2004:407).

The theft of Yemini children after World War II, awarded as a gro-tesque form of compensation to Holocaust survivors, is another example of violent upheavals in family relations introduced by the war machine, using children as both victims and weapons of cultural warfare (Weiss 2003). This practice is reminiscent of similar actions in other contexts involving ethnocide, including the removal of Native American, Native Canadian, and Australian Aboriginal children from their families to be placed either with a white foster family or in an "Indian School," a mechanism that turned indigenous peoples of color into inferior whites (see Robbins 2002:260).

In 2008, Physicians for Human Rights issued its report *Broken Laws, Broken Lives: Medical Evidence of Torture by U.S. Personnel and Its Impact.* While noting that the particular experiences of detainees in Iraq, Af-ghanistan, and Cuba has varied, significant consistencies were found in the treatment of individuals captured and detained by the United States in its wars in Iraq and Afghanistan. As the document (Physicians for Human Rights 2008:113) states, repeated and combined use of techniques, in-cluding beatings, isolation, stress positions, temperature extremes, sensory overload and deprivation, sleep deprivation, and other forms of torture, were reported by all former detainees evaluated. This consistent pattern, especially when considered in conjunction with the many other reports about detainee treatment, including those from official investigations by the U.S. government, the International Committee of the Red Cross, firsthand accounts, and the media, as well as government documents, leads to the conclusion that the United States systematically employed torture and ill treatment against detainees.

As this report makes clear, while there is a tendency to portray the most extreme and hidden war brutalities as the handiwork of rogue na-tions or the product of internal wars of failed states, even the most power-ful and developed nations also are implicated.

Destruction of Health and Social Infrastructure

War impacts human health indirectly through the obliteration of housing, the disruption of health care facilities, and the partial or wholesale devastation of all manner of social and physical infrastructure. The decimation of institutions of education, civil security, and governance, as well as roadways, sewage and water systems, and food distribution structures, produces large numbers of both cross-border refugees (now totaling some 12 million worldwide) and internally displaced persons (20 million to 25 million internally). Both of these groups of refugees suffer long-term poor health outcomes as a result of displacement and destruction of infrastructure. The United Nations found that by the end of the Indochina wars, in 1991, Cambodia had only 30 doctors left (Machel 1996). As a result of the U.S.-funded Contra War against the Sandinista government in Nicaragua from 1982 to 1987, almost a quarter of the country's health centers were partially or fully destroyed or forced to close because of frequent attacks by the right-wing "Contras."

While smallpox had been virtually eliminated in Bangladesh prior to its 1971–1972 struggle for independence, it quickly returned in the midst of hostilities, causing over 18,000 deaths. In the early 1970s, Uganda had achieved immunization coverage of almost three-fourths of all children. By the end of the civil war that brought Yoweri Museveni to the presidency, "coverage declined steadily until fewer than 10 per cent of eligible children were being immunized with antituberculosis vaccine (BCG), and fewer than 5 per cent against diphtheria, pertussis and tetanus (DPT), measles and poliomyelitis" (Machel 1996:35). Losses of this sort extend the impacts of the war machine far into the future and hamper the return to peace. These patterns are analyzed in detail by Harding and Libal in chapter 2 with reference to the impacts of the contemporary U.S. occupation of Iraq.

Health-Related Environmental Damage of War and Its Production

In peacetime and during wars, the war machine causes extensive damage to environments, creating danger zones. For example, minefields (including an estimated 70 million to 100 million antipersonnel explosives that are still active and in place in over 75 countries worldwide) continue to exact a toll in human life and limb—at a rate of 15,000 to 20,000 a year—long after active fighting has ended (Sirkin et al. 2008). Moreover, the military dumping of toxic chemicals—such as perchlorate, a rocket fuel that has leaked into the groundwater used by millions of people—despoil the planet and cause death and disease.

Westing (2008) categorizes the environmental consequences of the war machine into 1) unintentional, 2) intentional, and 3) intentional for amplification (explicitly for environmental warfare). Unintentional damage is the result of the use of weapons, especially high-explosive munitions, on enemy forces. Use of hardened military shells (containing depleted uranium), for example, has impacted the environments of Kosovo and Iraq in recent wars. As a result of military actions such as this, there can be extensive immediate and longer-term air, water, floral, and faunal damage as well. "Ecocide" is also an intentional weapon of war, as seen in the slaughter of entire herds of bison by the U.S. Army in the nineteenth century (see Robbins 2002:210) or the contemporary felling of olive trees in Palestine by the Israeli army (Bornstein, personal communication).

Ecosystems are also decimated by the construction of military sites, fortification, and lines of supply but also by factories that produce arsenals and other equipment for the war machine. We have already mentioned the use of intentional environmental warfare by the United States to devastate agricultural zones and forested environments during its war in Vietnam. Bomb craters in a tropical environment produce pools of stagnant water that promote mosquito breeding and the spread of malaria and other vector-borne diseases.

Additionally, environmental damage is caused by the intentional release of pent-up forces in nature, such as an attack on a dam or forest (with the intention of causing forest fires). These diverse ways in which the war machine can severely damage environments are compounded by interaction with other anthropogenic impacts on the environment, from the use of fossil fuel and the buildup of greenhouse gases to industrial air, water, and land pollution. Interactions of this sort that exacerbate environmental degradation and disruption (e.g., global warming) are beginning to have significant impact on human health, as discussed by Baer in chapter 5. The resulting scarcity of resources necessary for human life, then, give cause for another cycle of warfare.

Conclusion

The French prime minister during World War I, George Clemenso, is credited with uttering the now famous line, "War is much too serious a matter to be entrusted to the military." This is true for multiple reasons, one of which is the severe health costs of modern conflict. Given their horrific toll, war and the machines that drive it are critical public health issues that merit the focused attention of all health workers, health social scientists, and health activists. This point, the primary message of this volume, is affirmed by the chapters that follow across multiple health issues and widely dispersed lands. As these pages detail, while there may be no stopping war at all times and in all places, there are more than enough reasons to try to do so. For those concerned about global health, no lesser objective is sufficient. The chapters that follow challenge the war machine while they document the consequences of war across multiple health issues and widely dispersed geographies. Critical medical anthropology, along with a number of other compatible perspectives in other disciplines, provides the framework for understanding how the damaged bodies described here are but one site of a global conflagration of violent conflict. We anticipate that war is likely to increase in both intensity and number as a result of dwindling global resources and the insatiable quest for profit. If this is true, then the world faces a future of ever-worsening human health catastrophes. In the conclusion to this volume, we analyze the political-economic and geoeconomic processes that drive this trend. We invite readers to critically engage all the claims made in this volume and to use its analyses as a call to both scholarly and political action.

Works Cited

Andrews, Chris, Bernice Brewin, Rosanna Philpott, and Lorna Stewart
    2007   Delayed-onset posttraumatic stress disorder: A systematic review of the evidence. *American Journal of Psychiatry* 164:1319–1326.

Armed Conflict Events Data
    2003   Argentina's "Dirty War" 1976–1983. Online: http://www.onwar.com/aced/nation/all/argentina/fargentina1976.htm. Accessed January 14, 2009.

Baer, Hans, Merrill Singer, and Ida Susser
2003   *Medical Anthropology and the World System.* 2nd ed. Westport, CT: Praeger Publishers.

Baràth, A.
2002   Children's well-being after the war in Kosovo: Survey in 2000. *Croatian Medical Journal* 43(2):199–208.

Betancourt, T., and K. Khan
2008   The mental health of children affected by armed conflict: Protective processes and pathways to resilience. *International Review of Psychiatry* 20(3):317–328.

Bollet, Alfred
2004   The major infectious epidemic diseases of Civil War soldiers. *Infectious Disease Clinics of North America* 18(2):293–309.

Bullman, Tim, Clare Mahan, Han Kang, and William Page
2005   Mortality in U.S. Army Gulf War veterans exposed to 1991 Khamisiyah chemical munitions destruction. *American Journal of Public Health* 95(8):1382–1388.

Carroll, Rory
2005   Iraq War is blamed for starvation. Guardian.co.uk, March 31. Online: http://www.guardian.co.uk/world/2005/mar/31/iraq.united nations. Accessed January 15, 2009.

Castro, Arachu, and Merrill Singer, eds.
2004   *Unhealthy Health Policy: A Critical Anthropological Examination.* Walnut Creek, CA: AltaMira.

Chomsky, Noam
2004   War crimes and imperial fantasies: Interview with David Barsamian. *International Socialist Review* 37(September/October). Online: http://www.isreview.org/issues/37/chomsky.shtml. Accessed January 6, 2008.

Civil War Society
2002   Medical care, battle wounds and disease. Online: http://www.civilwar home.com/civilwarmedicine.htm. Accessed May 14, 2008.

Coker, Christopher
2004   War and disease. 21st Century Trust. Online: http://www.21stcentury trust.org/coker2.html. Accessed January 9, 2008.

Danner, Mark
1992 Five perfected steps. Online: http://balkansnet.org/ethnicl.html. Accessed January 8, 2008.

Department of the Army
2000 *Civil Affairs Operation*. Field Manual 41-10. Washington, DC: Department of the Army. Online: http://www.globalsecurity.org/military/library/policy/army/fm/41-10_2000. Accessed January 7, 2008.

Duraković, A.
2003 Undiagnosed illnesses and radioactive warfare. *Croatian Medical Journal* 44(5):520–532.

Eisenhower, Dwight D.
1968 "Farewell Address." In *The Annals of America: Vol. 18. 1961–1968: The Burdens of World Power*, 1–5. Chicago: Encyclopaedia Britannica.

Elbedour, S., R. ten Bensel, and D. Bastien
1993 Ecological integrated model of children of war: Individual and social psychology. *Child Abuse and Neglect* 17(6):805–819.

Foege, W.
2000 Arms and health: A global perspective. In *War and Public Health*, edited by Barry Levy and Victor Sidel. Washington, DC: 3–11, American Public Health Association.

Gardner, Alexander
1959 *Gardner's Photographic Sketch Book of the Civil War*. New York: Dover Publications.

Garfield, Richard
2008 The epidemiology of war. In *War and Public Health*, edited by Barry Levy and Victor Sidel, 23–36. Washington, DC: American Public Health Association.

Gersony, Robert
1988 *Summary of Mozambican Refugee Accounts of Principally Conflict-Related Experience in Mozambique*. Washington, DC: Department of State.

Giroux, Henry
2009 From Mississippi to Gaza: Killing children with impunity. Counterpunch. Online: http://www.counterpunch.org/giroux01142009.html. Accessed January 14, 2009.

Goma Epidemiology Group
1995 Public health impact of Rwandan refugee crisis: What happened in Goma, Zaire, in July 1994? *Lancet* 345:339–344.

González, L, C. Avarez-Dardet, A. Nolasco, J. Pina, and M. Medranmo
2006 Famine in the Spanish civil war and mortality from coronary heart disease: A perspective from Barker's hypothesis. *Gaceta Sanitaria* 20(5):360-367.

Grau, Lester, and William Jorgensen
1997 Beaten by the bugs: The Soviet-Afghan war experience. *Military Review* 62(November–December). Online: http://wwwcgsc.army.mil/milrev/english/NovDec97/indxnd97.htm. Accessed February 2, 2006.

Gusterson, Hugh
1995 *Nuclear Rites: A Weapon Laboratory at the End of the Cold War.* Berkeley: University of California Press.

Hasanović, M., O. Sinanović, Z. Selimbasić, I. Pajević, and E. Avdibegović
2006 Psychological disturbances of war-traumatized children from different foster and family settings in Bosnia and Herzegovina. *Croatian Medical Journal* 47(1):85–94.

Hashemian, Farnoosh, Kaveh Khoshnood, Mayur Desai, Farahnazm Falahati, Stanislav Kasl, and Steven Southwick
2006 Anxiety, depression, and posttraumatic stress in Iranian survivors of chemical warfare. *Journal of the American Medical Association* 296:560–566.

Hedges, Chris, and Laila Al-Arian
2008 *Collateral Damage: America's War against Iraqi Civilians.* New York: Nation Books.

Hooks, Gregory
1991 *Forging the Military-Industrial Complex: World War II's Battle of the Potomac.* Urbana, IL: University of Chicago Press.

Jackson, Gabriel
1987 *The Spanish Republic and the Civil War 1931–39.* Princeton, NJ: Princeton University Press.

Jelin, Elizabeth
2004 The family in Argentina: Modernity, economic crisis and politics. In *Handbook of World Families*, edited by Bert Adams and Jan Trost, 391–413. Thousand Oaks, CA: Sage.

Johnson, Chalmer
2004a   *Blowback: The Costs and Consequences of American Empire.* New York: Macmillan/Metropolitan Books.
2004b   *The Sorrows of Empire: Militarism, Secrecy, and the End of the Republic.* New York: Macmillan/Metropolitan Books.

Keane, Jack
2003   An Army update. Online: http://www.globalsecurity.org/military/library/report/2003/VCSA_Presentation_as_of_23Jul03.ppt#258,2, Slide 2. Accessed January 7, 2002.

Kennedy, Michael
2009   Whispers from Al-Fara'a. *Anthropology News* 50(1):5.

Kiernan, B.
1989   The American bombardment of Kampuchea, 1969–1973. *Vietnam Generation* 1(1):4–41.

Kissinger, Henry
2003   *Ending the Vietnam War: A History of America's Involvement in and Extrication from the Vietnam War.* New York: Simon & Schuster.

Kornbluh, Peter
2004   *The Pinochet File: A Declassified Dossier on Atrocity and Accountability.* New York: New Press.

Kurz, Donald
2001   *Political Anthropology: Paradigms and Power.* Boulder, CO: Westview.

Levine, P., H. Young, S. Simmens, D. Rentz, V. Kofie, C. Mahan, and H. Kang
2005   Is testicular cancer related to Gulf War deployment? Evidence from a pilot population-based study of Gulf War era veterans and cancer registries. *Military Medicine* 170(2):149–153.

Levy, Barry, and Victor Sidel, eds.
2008   *War and Public Health.* 2nd ed. New York: Oxford University Press.

Locke, C., K. Southwick, L. McCloskey, and M. Fernández-Esquer
1996   The psychological and medical sequelae of war in Central American refugee mothers and children. *Archives of Pediatric and Adolescent Medicine* 150(8):822–828.

Machel, Grac'a
  1996   Promotion and protection of the rights of children: Impact of armed
         conflict on children. United Nations, UNICEF. Online: http://www
         .unicef.org/graca/a51-306_en.pdf. Accessed January 15, 2009.

McCue, Jack
  2007   Enduring injuries to brain and mind: Medical consequences of the
         Iraq War. *Internal Medicine* (May). Online: http://www.imwr.com/
         issues/articles/2007-05_38.asp. Accessed January 9, 2008.

Nordstrom, Carolyn
  1997   *A Different Kind of War Story.* Philadelphia: University of Pennsyl-
         vania Press.

Payne, Stanley
  1987   *The Franco Regime 1936–1975.* Madison: University of Wisconsin
         Press.

Pedersen, Jon
  2009   *Health and Conflict: A Review of the Links.* Oslo: Fafo.

People's Health Movement
  2005   *Global Health Watch 1.* London: Zed Books.
  2008   *Global Health Watch 2.* London: Zed Books.

Physicians for Human Rights
  2008   *Broken Laws, Broken Lives: Medical Evidence of Torture by U.S. Person-
         nel and Its Impact.* Cambridge, MA: Physicians for Human Rights.

Robbins, Richard
  2002   *Global Problems and the Culture of Capitalism.* Boston: Allyn and
         Bacon.

Ruzich, M., J. Looi, and M. Robertson
  2005   Delayed onset of posttraumatic stress disorder among male com-
         bat veterans: A case series. *American Journal of Geriatric Psychiatry*
         13(5):424–427.

Santa Barbara, Joanna
  2008   The impact of war on children. In *War and Public Health*, edited by
         Barry Levy and Victor Sidel, 179–192. Washington, DC: American
         Public Health Association.

Scahill, Jeremy
    2008   *Blackwater: The Rise of the World's Most Powerful Mercenary Army.* New York: Nation Books.

Singer, Merrill
    2009   *Introduction to Syndemics: A Systems Approach to Public Health and Community Health.* San Francisco: Jossey-Bass.

Singer, Merrill, and Hans Baer, eds.
    2008   *Killer Commodities: Public Health and the Corporate Production of Harm.* AltaMira/Rowman & Littlefield.

Sirkin, Susannah, James Cobey, and Eric Stover
    2008   Landmines. In *War and Public Health*, edited by Barry Levy and Victor Sidel, 102–116. Washington, DC: American Public Health Association.

Sivard, Ruth
    1996   *World Military and Social Expenditures.* Washington, DC: World Priorities.

Spiegel, P., and P. Salama
    2000   War and mortality in Kosovo, 1998–99: An epidemiological testimony. *Lancet* 355(9222):2204–2209.

Sweetman, Bill
    2000   In search of the Pentagon's billion dollar hidden budgets—How the US keeps its R&D spending under wraps. *Jane's International Defence Review.* Online: http://www.janes.com/defence/news/jidr/jidr000105_01_n.shtml. Accessed January 3, 2009.

Thomas, Hugh
    2001   *The Spanish Civil War.* New York: Random House.

Tice, D.
    1997   Flu deaths rivaled, ran alongside World War I. *Pioneer Planet*, March 10.

Toole, Michael, S. Galson, and W. Brady
    1993   Are war and public health compatible? *Lancet* 341(8854):1193–1196.

United Nations Office for the Coordination of Humanitarian Affairs
    2003   Special Report: Civilian Protection in Armed Conflict. Online at: http://www.irinnews.org/pdf/in-depth/Civilian-Protection-in-Armed-Conflict.pdf. Accessed January 9, 2008.

U.S. Army
    2004   Press release: "The Army budget—Fiscal year 2005." Army Public Affairs. Online: http://www.globalsecurity.org/military/library/budget/fy2005/army/greentop.pdf#xml=http://www.globalsecurity.org/cgibin/texis.cgi/webinator/search/pdfhi.txt? query=120+countries&pr=default&prox=page&rorder=500&rprox=500&rdfreq=500&rwfreq=500&rlead=500&rdepth=0&sufs=0&order=r&cq=&id=491955f93. Accessed January 7, 2008.

U.S. Department of Defense
    2001   *Dictionary of Military and Associated Terms*. Washington, DC: U.S. Department of Defense.

Vietnamese Victims of Agent Orange Trust
    2008   About the problem. Online: http://www.agentorange.org.au/about-the-problem. Accessed May 14, 2009.

Weiss, G., W. Caveness, H. Einsiedel-Lechtape, and M. McNeel
    1982   Life expectancy and causes of death in a group of head-injured veterans of World War I. *Archives of Neurology* 39(12):741–743.

Weiss, Meira
    2003   The immigrating body and the body politic: The "Yemenite Children Affair" and body commodification in Israel. In *Commodifying Bodies*, edited by Nancy Scheper-Hughes and Loic Wacquant, 93–110. Thousand Oaks, CA: Sage.

Westing, Arthur
    2008   The impact of war on the environment. In *War and Public Health*, edited by Barry Levy and Victor Sidel, 69–84. Washington, DC: American Public Health Association.

Zinsser, Hans
    2000   *Rats, Lice and History*. New York: Penguin Books.

PART ONE

THE WAR MACHINE AND GLOBAL MORBIDITY AND MORTALITY

CHAPTER ONE

THE ECHOES OF WAR
Effects of Early Malnutrition on Adult Health
Patrick F. Clarkin

A Biocultural Approach to War

The direct and indirect mechanisms through which war affects health are numerous. One pathway is the violence of malnutrition, a frequent by-product of war. "High-intensity conflict" (defined, following Cohen and Pinstrup-Andersen [1999], as a war with more than 1,000 deaths per year) regularly leads to severe food insecurity and malnutrition. If this occurs during growth and development in childhood, infancy, or even prenatally, there exists a high likelihood of long-term or even permanent costs to health. The developmental origins of health and disease hypothesis, or DOHaD (Barker 1998; Gluckman and Hanson 2005), within the context of war is well supported by a body of evidence that strongly indicates that physiological stressors, particularly malnutrition, occurring in utero or in infancy predispose an individual to developing chronic diseases later in life, including cardiovascular disease, diabetes, obesity, and osteoporosis. Using examples from World War II and the first and second Indochina wars, this chapter examines how war-induced famine has long-term and possibly irreversible effects on the development of some of the aforementioned chronic diseases.

While it is necessary to incorporate a healthy dose of biology here, the focus will not be physiological. Rather, my aim is to link different levels of analysis by employing a hybrid of critical, biocultural, and evolutionary perspectives to demonstrate that warfare consistently creates a suite of conditions that are harmful to human biology and health. Studies on the health effects of war typically have fallen under the aegis of epidemiology, public health, relief agencies, or human rights groups. Some anthropologists have advocated a greater role for the discipline in investigating the broader impacts of war on human biology and health. For example, Farmer (2003:241) has called for "mak[ing] room in the academy for serious scholarly work on the multiple dynamics of health and human rights, *on the health effects of war and political-economic disruption*, and on the pathogenic effects of social inequalities. . . . By what mechanisms do such noxious events and processes become embodied as adverse health outcomes?" (emphasis added). In order to account for these mechanisms, multiple disciplines are needed, as none is sufficient by itself to describe how ecological and political-economic disruptions, in this case resulting from war, get "under the skin" (Goodman and Leatherman 1998:20). Anthropology, given its multiple subdisciplines, may be uniquely poised to examine war from a biocultural perspective.

While it has been difficult to live up to the ideal of holism in anthropology (Wiley 2004), collaboration is essential if the goal is to not only understand the health costs of war but ultimately to reduce its frequency. It is clear that theoretical overlap toward the study of human biology and health exists among the traditional subdisciplines of anthropology. Critical cultural and medical anthropologists have correctly pointed out the need to account for the role that human agency, political economy, inequality, historical contingency, and wider global forces have on local realities and health (Baer et al. 2003; Singer 1998). Similarly, a number of biological anthropologists have called for a holistic, transdisciplinary approach to human biology that goes beyond looking at single stressors and broadly defines the environment as the totality of its evolutionary, ecological, and social components, including social inequality (Leatherman et al. 1993; Little and Haas 1989; Thomas et al. 1989). Biological anthropologists are particularly well suited to study the effects of stressors on biology, and warfare arguably creates conditions (at least in the short term from an evolutionary standpoint) that rival any of the ecological stressors traditionally studied in the discipline, such as hypoxia at high altitudes, circumpolar temperatures, or infectious diseases in tropical latitudes. They may also address the ways that populations adapt to conditions created by war or whether the concept of adaptation is even appropriate under such circumstances (Bogin et al. 2007; Ellison and Jasienska 2007; see also Singer 1989).

For these reasons, it becomes clearer that a hybrid of approaches to the study of war and health has great utility. Ecological and evolutionary approaches are likely to reveal consistent biological responses to war. However, critical and biocultural perspectives remind us that rather than focusing solely on biological variables and risking overgeneralizations when looking at the health effects of war, it is also necessary to account for local historical circumstances. In some cases, the general health status of a population may already be poor prior to war's inception because of poverty or structural violence exacerbated by inequality or colonialism (e.g., Laos during the first and second Indochina wars). In other cases, the health of a population may be good prior to the onset of war, then rapidly deteriorate once war begins and recover fairly quickly after the cessation of military conflict (e.g., the Netherlands during World War II). In either scenario, what they share in common is that war inexorably makes things worse, and the health effects may reverberate for decades for fundamental biological reasons that will be discussed here.

War, Food Insecurity, and Malnutrition

Throughout history, armed conflict has served as both cause and consequence of food insecurity and famine. In the seminal two-volume study *The Biology of Human Starvation* by Ancel Keys et al. (1950), the forty-fifth chapter was devoted to the effects of famine on childhood growth and development. A meta-analysis conducted for the purposes of this essay reveals that Keys et al. cited eighty-eight studies in the chapter pertaining to famine (after excluding a subsection on seasonality and family), sixty-one of which (69 percent) dealt with famine resulting from war. The fact that the majority of citations pertained to war may be reflective of the historical period, given that most of the authors' research took place during and just after World War II (indeed, much of their research on the effects of starvation was conducted on conscientious objectors to the war). An alternative interpretation is that when conducting a literature review on famine, military conflict reliably provides examples from which to draw.

The reasons for this are many. Food often has been used deliberately as a weapon in war, and its provision has served as a means to win the "hearts and minds" of a population (Macrae and Zwi 1994). Conversely, withholding food through the destruction or theft of crops or through the interception or obstruction of food aid or trade routes has been used to deprive an adversarial military or a civilian population suspected of supporting one's opposition (Levy et al. 2000; Roland 1992; Vincent 1994). Food blockades, sieges of cities, and "scorched-earth" tactics meant to deny food to civilian and military populations have been documented in ancient history from Mesopotamia, Egypt, and the siege of Troy to the "winning of the West," from Native Americans to Leningrad and the Netherlands in World War II, to Ethiopia, Eritrea, Angola, and Mozambique in the 1980s and 1990s (Carmean 2002; Macrae and Zwi 1994; Stein et al. 1975; White 2005). In addition to direct attacks on crops and livestock, food production may be diminished through the reduction of the farming population via targeted killings, genocide, terrorization, forced recruitment, enslavement, and forced displacement or through contamination of farmland by indiscriminant bombing, chemical weapons, or land mines (Cohen and Pinstrup-Andersen 1999; Cuny and Hill 1999).

For refugees, food acquisition is tenuous, particularly for those who have fled their homes but remain "internally displaced" (i.e., remain within their country of origin), since finding sanctuary from nearby military conflict may be difficult and delivery of food aid may be problematic. In fact, in the early 1990s, internally displaced persons had higher mortality rates than did displaced persons who crossed international borders, though, admittedly, reliable data are difficult to collect (Toole and Waldman 1993).

Displaced individuals are at several disadvantages with regard to obtaining adequate food, leading to quantitative and qualitative nutritional deficiencies. First, as involuntary migrants, refugees are often forced to flee without warning or time to plan for evacuation. Second, long journeys to safety, usually on foot, are physically draining. For children who have lost one or both of their parents, the chances of finding food or making the journey are even harder. Third, on reaching safety, displaced persons are often trapped in less fertile areas with fewer natural resources than their former homes. In subsistence economies, agricultural cycles broken by war mean that it could take months to grow crops to fruition. For the poor, there are even fewer options since they have few liquid resources available to exchange for food possessed by nondisplaced local populations, and food prices are often increased during war, making it even harder to acquire adequate nutrition. Fourth, massive displacement during war leads not only to the loss of one's own home but also to the large-scale destruction of social support and trade networks, thus removing any safety net. Fifth, despite the Geneva Convention's call for the protection of civilian victims of war, refugees crossing international borders are often seen as burdens by host countries, possibly affecting the provision of food aid (Toole and Waldman 1997). Sixth, conditions for displaced people are often crowded and unsanitary, promoting the spread of air- and waterborne infectious disease, which has an interactive effect with malnutrition (Yip and Sharp 1993). Finally, food aid rations for refugees, particularly in past decades, have been inadequate in total calories and micronutrients. Mason (2002) traced the history of international food relief efforts and reported that prior to the late 1980s, caloric recommendations were as low as 1,200 to 1,800 kilocalories per person per day, rising to 1,900 kilocalories in 1989, 2,100 in 1997, and then 2,400 in 2000. In effect, more realistic needs of refugees were recognized, causing rations roughly to double over two decades, though refugees from earlier decades likely suffered a cost to their health as a result of the earlier recommendations.

Childhood Growth during War: Adaptation or Accommodation?

Biological anthropologists, epidemiologists, physicians, and humanitarian aid workers have long recognized that physical growth during childhood is to a great extent a reflection of the larger environment, including available nutrition, exposure to infection, and social and economic inequality (Bogin 1999). In the words of the pediatrician and auxologist James Tanner (1986:3), childhood growth is a mirror for "the material and moral condition" of a society. In various populations around the world, anthropometric markers such as height and weight repeatedly have been demonstrated to increase over generations when conditions conducive for health improve. The opposite is also true; wherever the "material and moral condition" is in decline, including during war, childhood growth usually declines as well.

In the study by Keys et al. (1950) mentioned previously, the growth of children living in war-induced famine conditions were compared to those in nonfamine conditions from the same country (e.g., children in postwar conditions vs. prewar conditions or children in war zones vs. those in safe zones). The majority of studies (41 of 61, or 67.2 percent) found that war had a negative impact on either height or weight. Fifteen studies (24.6 percent) found no effect on growth, while just two studies (3.3 percent) showed positive effects, the reasons for which are unclear. Three showed contradictory effects (i.e., some age-groups or sex groups were negatively affected, while others had no effect or even positive effects). Additional studies have shown that during World War II, childhood growth declined sharply in many countries, including China, Japan, the Soviet Union,

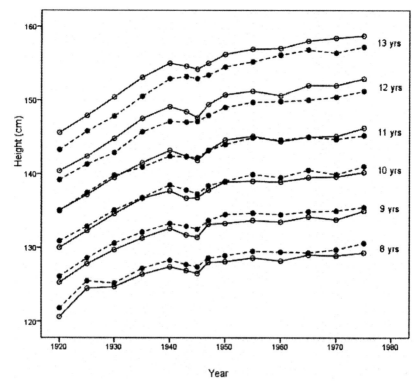

Figure 1.1. Height of schoolchildren aged 8 to 13 years in Oslo, Norway, from 1920 to 1975. Height increased over time but decreased in the mid-1940s during World War II. Boys are solid circles; girls are open circles. Data from Brundtland et al. (1980).

Germany, France, Italy, and Belgium (Kimura 1984; Markowitz 1955; Vlastovsky 1966). For example, data from Brundtland et al. (1980) on Norwegian children reveal that height increased from 1920 to 1940, then declined during the war, after which it began to increase again.

Similar patterns have been found in more recent decades as well, where rates of acute malnutrition ranged from 12 to 81 percent among refugee children from many war-torn countries from the late 1980s to the mid-1990s, including Afghanistan and various African nations (Toole and Waldman 1997).

Military conflict also has had a negative impact on other markers of growth and development. A delay in the age at menarche, or first menstruation, has been observed in Croatia and Bosnia during the 1990s war in the former Yugoslavia and in South Korea during the Korean War, likely because of a combination of nutritional and psychological stress (Hwang et al. 2003; Prebeg and Brali 2000; Tahirović 1998). Admittedly, it is necessary to avoid overgeneralizing the effects of war and to take into account the local circumstances that a given conflict has on any particular population (e.g., the duration and intensity of the war, the prewar political-economic conditions that may exacerbate stresses brought on by war, or whether specific groups fare worse than others). Overall, however, the trend appears to be consistent: war is wanton in its destruction and is detrimental to growth and development and, by extension, health. For example, while the poor and disadvantaged groups may be hit the hardest by war, Bogin and Keep (1999) reported that height declined among Mayan and Ladino children from all social classes in Guatemala from 1974 to 1984, a period that included some of the harshest fighting of the civil war and led to economic instability, a drop in food production, and the targeting of civilians by the military.

A deeper look into the biology of growth and development reveals why they frequently decline during war. Reducing the rate of growth is a predictable mechanism for the body to cope with a shortage of nutrients by forgoing the development of new tissues in favor of maintaining those already present (Bogin 1999). From an evolutionary perspective, natural selection should favor genes that provide an organism some physiological and morphological plasticity as a means of responding to rapidly changing environmental conditions over time scales shorter than a lifetime rather than directing it down a rigid, predetermined genetic pathway with no room for deviation (Piersma and Drent 2003). This has led Ridley (2003:174) to refer to plasticity as natural selection's "master stroke" because it increases an organism's chances for survival and reproduction by allowing genes to "flexibly calibrate" themselves and their protein products by responding to unforeseen circumstances. The process of reducing growth rate, however, should not be viewed as a purely adaptive one. A more appropriate concept may be "accommodation," defined as a biological response that favors the survival of the individual but also leads to significant losses in some important functions (Frisancho 1993:7). For example, children with low weight for their age, even at moderate deficits, have a higher risk of mortality, perhaps because of a reduced immunological capacity to stave off infection (Pelletier 1994).

Similarly, a low height for age, or "stunting," is not innocuous or cost free (e.g., see Pelto and Pelto's [1989] critique of the "small-but-healthy" hypothesis). Stunting typically begins in infancy, when growth rates are rapid, nutritional requirements per unit of body weight (particularly protein) are at their highest, and infection as a result of weaning is common. When the nutritional situation is poor, such as during war or in the case of poverty, a smaller body may have lower absolute caloric requirements and be easier to maintain than a larger body, thereby increasing the probability of survival and, ultimately, the opportunity to reproduce (Bateson et al. 2004). However, stunting is also correlated with compromised immunocompetence and cognitive performance as well as decreases in child physical activity (Martorell 1989). The potential for catch-up growth during childhood does exist, but this prospect decreases significantly when stressful conditions are severe and prolonged, as they often are during war (Tanner 1990:128). Thus, malnutrition's effects may last into adulthood and lead to shorter final height, a reduced capacity for physical work, and possibly impaired fertility and higher infant mortality rates (Martorell 1989). Furthermore, these biological outcomes not only are the result of social disruption but also play an integral role in a vicious circle of perpetuating health inequalities and the reproduction of poverty (Leatherman 1998). In this light, it is clear that biological responses to malnutrition are not adaptive in the strictest sense but rather lead to a costly compromise in terms of health.

The Echoes of War:
The Enduring Effects of Prenatal Malnutrition

The DOHaD model reveals another important mechanism through which war-related malnutrition has enduring effects on health. Evidence from epidemiological studies and experimental studies on animals demonstrates that prenatal malnutrition may predispose the individual to developing various chronic diseases in adulthood, including non–insulin-dependent (type 2) diabetes, obesity, coronary heart disease, stroke, hypertension, and osteoporosis (Barker 1998; Joseph and Kramer 1996; Langley-Evans 2006). Such effects are not limited to prenatal malnutrition experienced at the level of famine and may be triggered by more modest levels of malnutrition (Jackson 2000) or even psychological stress and an increase in stress hormones experienced by the mother during gestation (Seckl and Meaney 2006). This is the result of a fairly consistent series of physiological responses made by the fetus, though the costs to health may take decades to become fully apparent. Thus, it seems that "earlier environmental influences can have an echo throughout life" (Gluckman and Hanson 2005:19). It has been argued that the DOHaD also may be critically important in reducing the burden of chronic diseases in populations with high poverty rates or who face various forms of discrimination (Kramer et al. 2006; Moore 1998). However, it is the intensity and duration of prenatal malnutrition accompanying war and the resulting "echoes" that are of interest here.

A synthesis of biocultural and evolutionary perspectives helps elucidate why prenatal malnutrition increases the probability for health problems later in life. First, as is true of the child, malnutrition has an adverse effect on the physical growth of the fetus. Data from various countries show that war-related food insecurity coincides with significant negative effects on birth weight, sometimes by as much as 1,100 grams (Keys et al. 1950; Markowitz 1955; Skokić et al. 2006; Steckel 1998; Vlastovsky 1966). Importantly, qualitative differences exist between fetal and child responses to malnutrition. Since the organs of the fetus are still in their initial stages of development, the fetus has a much greater degree of plasticity to modify its metabolism on receiving maternal "signals" regarding the external nutritional environment. If the situation outside the womb is poor, fetal muscles may become resistant to the hormone insulin, effectively prioritizing scarce amounts of glucose for the brain and red blood cells and leaving the individual better equipped to deal with nutritional deprivation (Hales and Barker 1992). This "thrifty phenotype" is adaptive in that it increases the probability for survival of the fetus during malnutrition, though it may come at the expense of the development of other organs and also lead to a predisposition for non–insulin-dependent diabetes later in life, particularly if the postnatal nutritional environment improves. Prenatal malnutrition may also elevate the risk for other conditions later in life, including obesity and cardiovascular diseases (Barker 1998; Yajnik 2000). Therefore, it seems more appropriate to view these fetal responses as "making the best of a bad start" rather than as adaptations per se (Jones 2005).

Furthermore, it has been argued that in response to malnutrition, a fetus may alter its growth trajectory and physiology not only to avoid immediate negative energy balance but in expectation of the future nutritional environment as well. According to Bateson et al. (2004:420), "The pregnant woman in poor nutritional condition may unwittingly signal to her unborn baby that it is about to enter a harsh world. If so, this 'weather forecast' from the mother's body may result in her baby being born with characteristics, such as a small body and a modified metabolism, that help it to cope with a shortage of food." Gluckman and Hanson (2005) have referred to this idea as the "predictive adaptive response" model, whereby prenatal metabolic adjustments continue to be adaptive into the postnatal period but only when nutritional conditions remain constant. The implication is that intrauterine malnutrition at critical periods of development may "program" physiology and, as a result, have long-term effects on health (Lucas 1998). It is likely that these long-term adjustments to metabolism would have served our hunter-gatherer ancestors well since nutritional conditions would have changed slowly as a result of natural ecological fluctuations.

Over the past few thousand years, however, humans increasingly have gained a greater ability to induce dramatic environmental and social changes on a very brief time scale, as is the case when a high-intensity war commences and ends within the life span of an individual. In a scenario where a fetus experiences nutritional deprivation prenatally, inducing the development of a thrifty phenotype, there exists the potential for a mismatch should the postnatal social conditions improve and the nutritional situation shift from that of deprivation to one of excess. Although fetal metabolic adaptations may eventually lead to the aforementioned chronic diseases later in life, this is consistent with evolutionary theory and was likely favored by natural selection because genes (in this case those enhancing plasticity in fetal development) that have harmful effects later in life may be favored by selection if they increase the probability of reaching the age of reproduction (Williams 1957).

It is likely that such fetal plasticity was favored by natural selection deep in mammalian history, given that similar patterns have been observed in other species. In addition to humans, prenatal malnutrition has been associated with postnatal insulin resistance, reduced muscle mass (sacrificed in favor of other tissues), and elevated body fat (for enhanced energy storage) in rats, sheep, and guinea pigs (Budge et al. 2005; Kind et al. 2005). With this in mind, it is plain that both genes and environment play a critical role in the development of chronic diseases and that both operate in an inextricably intertwined fashion rather than as oppositional forces (Ridley 2003). Social or environmental factors may create conditions of nutritional deprivation in utero, but the response of the fetus is one that

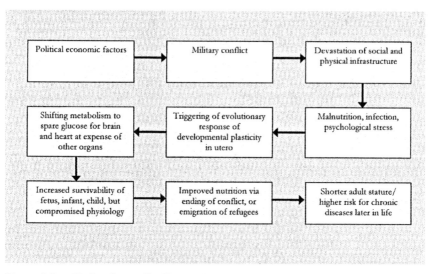

Figure 1.2. Chain of causality illustrating the pathway from war, via prenatal malnutrition and fetal plasticity, to the development of chronic diseases and smaller body size in adulthood.

has been established by natural selection in the distant past. Therefore, it seems appropriate to view the developmental origins of chronic disease as multifactorial, influenced by various levels of causality.

The final sections of this chapter attempt to link different levels of analysis by discussing specific case studies of famine resulting from wars in Europe and Southeast Asia and their long-term effects on adult health.

Famine and World War II

A great deal of research has been conducted on the health effects of pre-natal famine in the Netherlands and in the Soviet Union during World War II, both of which resulted from Nazi food blockades on the civilian population. In the case of the Netherlands, the importation of all food and supplies was restricted in the western part of the country (including the six largest cities of Amsterdam, Rotterdam, Utrecht, Leiden, Haarlem, and The Hague) from October 1944 to liberation by Allied forces on May 7, 1945, a period referred to as the "Hunger Winter" (Stein et al. 1975). The blockades were implemented to break a work strike by Dutch railroad workers who had been urged to resist Nazi occupation by the queen-in-exile, Wilhelmina. In November 1944, the rations per person in the famine region were 1,200 calories per day, but this figure had declined to 580 calories by February 1945. After Nazi withdrawal, the nutritional situation quickly improved, with rations rising to over 2,000 calories a day.

The immediate effects of the Hunger Winter were an estimated 20,000 deaths from famine-related causes, a decline in fertility and birth weight, an increase in perinatal mortality, and an increase in birth defects such as spina bifida and anencephaly (Neugebauer et al. 1999; Smith 1947; Susser et al. 1998). Moreover, given the well-delineated historical and geographical parameters of the famine, it was possible to assess its long-term effects on survivors. By using place and date of birth, researchers have been able to determine not only whether a person was exposed to famine prenatally but also the *timing* of exposure. In one of the earlier studies to look at the impact of the famine on adult health, Ravelli et al. (1976) examined the military draft records of more than 300,000 19-year-old Dutch males, 31 percent of whom were exposed to famine either pre- or postnatally. They found that the cohort exposed to famine during the first two trimesters of gestation had the highest rate of obesity by early adulthood, and a significantly higher rate than unexposed control subjects born outside of the famine area ($p < 0.0005$). Later studies with a smaller sample ($n \sim 740$) reported that the famine had various deleterious effects on health at age 50 years, such as impaired glucose tolerance (a precursor for diabetes), coronary heart disease, hypertension, and higher serum cholesterol (Painter et al. 2005; Roseboom et al. 1999).

Similar patterns were found in Russian adults born during the siege of Leningrad from 1941 to 1944. At that time, food supplies were prevented from reaching the city, leading to the deaths of up to 1 million people (of a population of 2.4 million), mainly from starvation (Stanner et al. 1997). At the height of the siege from November 1941 to February 1942, daily rations provided a meager 300 calories per day, with virtually no protein. In a study of 549 men and women 52 or 53 years old, blood pressure was higher among those exposed to the siege prenatally or in infancy when compared to a control group that was born outside the city limits and thus spared from famine. There was also an interactive effect between prenatal and postnatal conditions in that among women who were prenatally exposed to the Leningrad famine, obesity had a stronger effect on raising blood pressure than in women exposed in infancy or not at all. A larger study of more than 5,000 people found that those who were exposed to the siege as children had higher blood pressure compared to unexposed individuals and that men had higher mortality from ischemic heart disease and stroke (Koupil et al. 2007). This illustrates that both pre- and postnatal conditions can have long-term effects in the programming of cardiovascular diseases, such as during conditions of extreme psychological stress and nutritional deprivation resulting from war.

Wars in Southeast Asia: The Past Is Not Past

The first and second Indochina wars (1945–1954 and 1958–1975, respectively) devastated civilian life in Vietnam, Cambodia, and Laos, with enduring costs to health. Following World War II, France tried to regain control over its former colony in Indochina, which had been disrupted by the war at home and by Japanese military expansion throughout Asia (Stuart-Fox 1997). However, communist-inspired independence movements, in particular the Vietminh and Pathet Lao, mobilized against the French returning as a colonial power. According to LaFeber (2007:36), the United States hoped that France would be able to "recover its colonial hold and milk Vietnam's wealth (notably in food products and rubber plantations)" in order to help it regain its strength and be better able to repel communism in Europe. After France's defeat by the Vietminh in the decisive battle at Dien Bien Phu in May 1954, the United States became more committed to military intervention in the region. This was in the hopes of "containing" communism and preventing its spread from Indochina throughout Asia, which would have meant the loss of potential trading partners, decreased access to raw materials, and significant loss of profits.

The immediate costs of the war, which began in Vietnam but quickly spilled into Laos and eventually Cambodia, were enormous. For the United States, more than 58,000 U.S. military personnel were killed, while roughly 3 million Vietnamese died from war-related causes between 1965 and 1975 alone, representing 7.7 percent of the population (Allukian and Atwood 2000; U.S. National Archives 2007). Additionally, 10 million people were displaced from their homes in South Vietnam alone, while in the North, American air strikes damaged roads and railways, all 29 provincial capitals, and 2,700 of 4,000 villages. In neighboring Laos, of a population of 3 million people, 200,000 died, and 750,000 were made internal refugees (Stuart-Fox 1997), while an estimated 1.7 million Cambodians died during the genocide of 1975–1979 (Kiernan 1996).

Many effects of the war lasted beyond well beyond the official period of conflict. Environmental destruction from conventional bombs and dioxin-containing defoliants such as Agent Orange destroyed rubber tree plantations, mangrove forests, and shrimp and fish stocks in Laos and Vietnam (Allukian and Atwood 2000). These factors, along with unexploded ordnance littering villages and nearby fields, made it difficult to farm both during and after the war (Morikawa 1998). Laos alone was subjected to more than half a million bombing missions that dropped 2.1 million tons of bombs at the cost of $7.2 billion (Stuart-Fox 1997:144). This calculates as two tons for every inhabitant, giving Laos the infamous distinction of being the most heavily bombed nation, per capita, in the history of warfare.

These historical events certainly became embedded "under the skin" in the people of Vietnam, Cambodia, and Laos. As recently as 1995, blood levels of dioxin were 10 times higher in southern than northern

Vietnamese as a result of the spraying of defoliants decades earlier, thus leading to an elevated risk for various cancers (Schecter et al. 1995). There is also some suggestive evidence that prenatal malnutrition or other early biological insults resulting from the wars in Southeast Asia may have increased the risk for chronic diseases in those who remained in the region or elsewhere in the refugee diaspora. In a study of 490 Cambodian adult refugees in California, 99 percent suffered from "near-death due to starvation" under the Khmer Rouge between 1975 and 1979 (Marshall et al. 2005). This illustrates how widespread hunger was during the period and suggests that the DOHaD model might be applicable to the region. In fact, King et al. (2005) found that rates of diabetes among adults in Cambodia's Siem Reap and Kampong Cham provinces were much higher than predicted given the rural agricultural lifestyle of the country, leading the authors to speculate that the period of mass starvation under the Khmer Rouge "may have left a grim legacy" (1639).

Thus far, the only studies that have directly tested the DOHaD hypothesis on the effects of war on early malnutrition and later chronic disease in Southeast Asian populations have been among refugees from neighboring Laos, in particular Hmong and Lao living in the United States or French Guiana (Clarkin 2008, 2009). There is consensus among scholars that food insecurity and human suffering in Laos were most intense in certain areas and among certain populations, namely, rural farmers and highland minority groups (including the Hmong) in the northeast and southern parts of the country, while the towns on the western border along the Mekong River were largely protected (Stuart-Fox 1997:139). For instance, infant mortality rates were as high as 50 percent in war-torn areas, while persons displaced from war-zone areas in the northeast were reported to be starving, with protein, calorie, and micronutrient deficiencies (Weldon 1999:125; Yang 1993:51).

Using birthplace as a proxy for prenatal nutrition, Clarkin (2008, 2009) compared the height and body fat percentage of 378 Hmong and Lao adults (mean age 34.3 and 43.5 years, respectively) who were born between 1945 and 1980 in either a war zone or a safe zone. Birthplaces were categorized as "war zone" if nearby conflict (including fighting from guerilla troops, regular ground troops, or American air strikes) likely led to food insecurity in the nine months prior to birth. Retrospective life history interviews revealed that most Hmong were from the northeast of Laos, while most Lao were from larger towns along the Mekong River, in particular the capital of Vientiane. After cross-checking birthplaces against the historical record, it was determined that 30.5 percent of Hmong were born in a war zone versus just 3.0 percent of Lao. In addition, 38.8 percent of Hmong and 3.0 percent of Lao were displaced from their homes by war during infancy, while the Hmong were displaced from their homes an average of 2.5 times versus 1.0 for the Lao. Finally, the Hmong were also more likely to have a close relative die during their own childhood than the Lao, including a sibling (76.8 vs. 40.4 percent) or a parent (24.2 vs. 11.1 percent). Thus, it was clear that, at least in this relatively small sample, the primarily rural highland Hmong suffered more from the war than did the lowland Lao.

Accordingly, the biological data reveal predicted patterns. After excluding the very small number of Lao who were born in a war zone for purposes of maintaining statistical validity, three groups were compared: 1) Hmong born in a war zone, 2) Hmong born in a safe zone, and 3) Lao born in safe zone. For both sexes, height was greatest among the Lao,

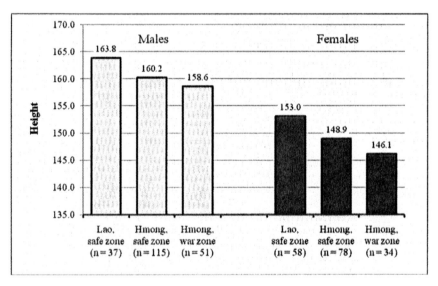

Figure 1.3. Average (mean) height of 373 Hmong and Lao adult refugees by place of birth. Males are represented by light-colored bars, females by dark bars. All Lao adults in this study were born in towns and villages that were generally protected from the war, while the Hmong were more likely to be born in areas in proximity to military conflict. Results indicate that being born in a war zone was associated with significantly shorter adult height (p = 0.009).

then Hmong born in safe areas, followed by Hmong born in a war zone ($p < 0.001$).

This was not due solely to prenatal exposure to malnutrition but was likely the result of the Hmong from war zones having more experiences with malnutrition (or other stressful experiences such as infection or psychological stress) throughout infancy and childhood. Conversely, the Lao in this sample were likely more protected from these stresses, while the Hmong born in safe zones may have been spared at least during the prenatal period of life but likely had intermediate exposure to war-related stressors throughout childhood. The opposite pattern was seen with regard to obesity: namely, Hmong born in a war zone had the highest body fat percentage, followed by Hmong in a safe zone and Lao born in a safe zone ($p = 0.019$, after controlling for age and sex). This finding of higher body fat in adulthood, following prenatal exposure to malnutrition, mirrors the pattern found in Ravelli's (1976) Dutch Hunger Winter study. It is also consistent with the "thrifty phenotype" concept, where a fetus modifies its metabolism in order to cope with postnatal nutritional scarcity. After the war, it is likely that the rapid transition away from food insecurity to one of adequacy or even excess after migrating to French Guiana or the United States has led to a mismatch between expected and actual nutritional conditions, increasing the risk for obesity and its concomitant sequelae, such as diabetes and cardiovascular disease.

Conclusion

More than a decade ago, Leatherman and Goodman (1998) proposed that anthropologists, particularly biological anthropologists, focus their efforts at better understanding how social and economic processes affect human biology, which they termed the "biology of poverty." Similarly, the discipline today may be well positioned to address the "biology of warfare" by delineating the ways that military conflict impacts human health in various societies. One might envision greater collaboration between the various subdisciplines of anthropology on the causes and consequences of war, including the study of growth patterns or infectious disease epidemiology within war zones (modern or historical) or retrospective studies testing whether refugees disproportionately suffer from chronic diseases in comparison to nonrefugees. By illustrating the interplay between evolution, developmental plasticity, and wider social events, biological anthropology can make a unique contribution to the understanding of how warfare contributes to disparities in health. Unfortunately, many opportunities for research exist.

It is possible that dissemination of these findings could cause political leaders considering war a reason to pause, if only briefly, to consider the likelihood that negative health consequences would linger for decades after hostilities have officially ended. In the hierarchy of arguments against war, priority certainly must be given to the immediate loss of life among combatants and civilians. Beyond this, important consideration should be given to the myriad ways that war-induced stressors permanently embed themselves in the biology of survivors of war, often leading to future pathology. This includes not only the more well-known phenomena of physical trauma resulting in injury and psychological distress leading to posttraumatic stress disorder or major depression but also the less cited problem of early malnutrition leading to disruptions in physical growth and development. Such disruptions *predictably* lead to impairments in final adult height, muscle mass, work capacity, immunocompetence, cognitive performance, and fertility as well as elevated risk for chronic diseases in adulthood. Although it could be argued that chronic conditions such as coronary heart disease, stroke, and diabetes are certainly not limited to populations suffering from war or severe malnutrition, the evidence strongly suggests that these greatly exacerbate the problem. Furthermore, chronic diseases are among the leading causes of death worldwide and therefore cannot be considered trivial. Reducing the frequency of war and, by extension, malnutrition is likely to have the side benefit of reducing the global burden of chronic diseases as well as other incalculable benefits to health.

Biological anthropologists (e.g., Thomas 1998) have noted that studies of human adaptability need to make the connections between sociopolitical processes and their downstream biological manifestations more explicit in order to increase the relevance of the subdiscipline. What an adaptability perspective adds to the study of war and health is that it provides an awareness not only that there is a correlation between ecological and economic destruction brought by war and a higher predisposition for chronic disease but also of why that correlation exists. For fundamental biological reasons, developmental plasticity allows the fetus to respond to malnutrition to increase its immediate chances of survival and possibly in expectation of future nutritional scarcity. However, plasticity has limits, and fetal accommodations are suboptimal compromises that become programmed, or "locked in," and made a permanent part of an individual's physiology. It is also important to remember that plasticity is triggered by environmental events and is intertwined rather than separate from larger social forces. Quite simply, our bodies have memories, and events such as war and political-economic disruption trickle down into our cells, leading to the embodiment of war experiences and elevating risk for adverse health outcomes.

Finally, although it is risky to speak in generalities about war, it is a safe conclusion that, regardless of the motives or politics of the participants, warfare is quite efficient at harming human health. Whether its effects are intentional or incidental, war disrupts every facet of a society to such a predictable degree that this must be considered an integral component of armed conflict. Thus far, there are many studies of war leading to a decline in nutrition and physical growth of children, but only a few examples of war-related prenatal famine leading to chronic disease have been documented (the Netherlands, Leningrad, and Laos). It is likely that wars of the past produced similar long-term health effects, though these may be lost to time. According to the historians Will and Ariel Durant (1968:81), "War is one of the constants of history. . . . In the last 3,421 years of recorded history only 268 have seen no war." The importance of the Durants' calculation is not to suggest that war is inevitable or to de-historicize it since it is clear that peaceful societies and periods of history do exist (Fry 2006). Rather, it is significant because historically the calculation of health costs of war have rarely gone far beyond the traditional casualty statistics of deaths and injuries and been expanded to include such things as impaired growth and development or an increase in chronic diseases. It is certain that wars' victors have grossly underestimated the damage done by war over human history.

Works Cited

Allukian, Myron, and Paul L. Atwood
    2000   Public health and the Vietnam War. In *War and Public Health*, edited
            by Barry S. Levy and Victor W. Sidel, 215–237. Washington, DC:
            American Public Health Association.

Baer, Hans A., Merrill Singer, and Ida Susser
2003   *Medical Anthropology and the World System: A Critical Perspective.*
Westport, CT: Praeger.

Barker, David J. P.
1998   *Mothers, Babies, and Health in Later Life.* Edinburgh: Churchill Livingstone.

Bateson, Patrick, David Barker, Timothy Clutton-Brock, Debal Deb, Bruno D'Udine, Robert A.Foley, Peter Gluckman, Keith Godfrey, Tom Kirkwood, Marta Mirazón Lahr, John McNamara, Neil B. Metcalfe, Patricia Monaghan, Hamish G. Spencer, and Sonia E. Sultan
2004   Developmental plasticity and human health. *Nature* 430(6998): 419–421.

Bogin, Barry
1999   *Patterns of Human Growth.* 2nd ed. Cambridge: Cambridge University Press.

Bogin, Barry, and Ryan Keep
1999   Eight thousand years of economic and political history in Latin America revealed by anthropometry. *Annals of Human Biology* 26(4):333–351.

Bogin, Barry, Maria Ines Varela Silva, and Luis Rios
2007   Life history trade-offs in human growth: Adaptation or pathology? *American Journal of Human Biology* 19(5):631–642.

Brundtland, G. H., K. Liestol, and L. Walloe
1980   Height, weight and menarcheal age of Oslo schoolchildren during the last 60 years. *Annals of Human Biology* 7(4):307–322.

Budge, Helen, Mo G. Gnanalingham, David S. Gardner, Alison Mostyn, Terence Stephenson, and Michael E. Symonds
2005   Maternal nutritional programming of fetal adipose tissue development: Long-term consequences for later obesity. *Birth Defects Research. Part C, Embryo Today: Reviews* 75(3):193–199.

Carmean, Kelli
2002   *Spider Woman Walks This Land: Traditional Cultural Properties and the Navajo Nation.* Walnut Creek, CA: AltaMira.

Clarkin, Patrick F.
2008   Adiposity and height of adult Hmong refugees: Relationship with war-related early malnutrition and later migration. *American Journal of Human Biology* 20(2):174–184.

Clarkin, Patrick F.
2009   *Lao Health and Adjustment in Southern New England Three Decades after the Secret War.* Occasional Paper Series. Boston: University of Massachusetts, Boston Institute for Asian American Studies.

Cohen, Marc J., and Per Pinstrup-Andersen
1999   Food security and conflict. *Social Research* 66(1):376–415.

Cuny, Fred, and Richard B. Hill
1999   *Famine, Conflict, and Response: A Basic Guide.* West Hartford, CT: Kumarian.

Durant, Will, and Ariel Durant
1968   *The Lessons of History.* New York: Simon & Schuster.

Ellison, Peter T., and Grazyna Jasienska
2007   Constraint, pathology, and adaptation: How can we tell them apart? *American Journal of Human Biology* 19(5):622–630.

Farmer, Paul
2003   *Pathologies of Power.* Berkeley: University of California Press.

Frisancho, Andres Roberto
1993   *Human Adaptation and Accommodation.* Ann Arbor: University of Michigan Press.

Fry, Douglas
2006   *The Human Potential for Peace: An Anthropological Challenge to Assumptions about War and Violence.* New York: Oxford University Press.

Gluckman, Peter D., and Mark A. Hanson
2005   *The Fetal Matrix: Evolution, Development and Disease.* Cambridge: Cambridge University Press.

Goodman, Alan H., and Thomas L. Leatherman
1998   Traversing the chasm between biology and culture: An introduction. In *Building a New Biocultural Synthesis: Political-Economic Perspectives on Human Biology,* edited by Alan H. Goodman and Thomas L. Leatherman, 3–41. Ann Arbor: University of Michigan Press.

Hales, C. Nicholas, and David J. P. Barker
1992   Type 2 (non-insulin dependent) diabetes mellitus: The thrifty phenotype hypothesis. *Diabetologia* 35(7):595–601.

Hwang, Ji-Yun, Chol Shin, Edward A. Frongillo, Kyung Rim Shin, and Inho Jo

2003 Secular trend in age at menarche for South Korean women born between 1920 and 1986: The Ansan study. *Annals of Human Biology* 30(4):434–442.

Jackson, Alan A.

2000 Nutrients, growth, and the development of programmed metabolic function. In *Short and Long Term Effects of Breast Feeding on Child Health*, edited by Berthold Koletzko, Kim Fleischer Michaelsen, and Olle Hernell, 41–55. New York: Kluwer Academic.

Jones, James Holland

2005 Fetal programming: Adaptive life-history tactics or making the best of a bad start? *American Journal of Human Biology* 17(1):22–33.

Joseph, Kuruthukulangar S., and Michael S. Kramer

1996 Review of the evidence on fetal and early childhood antecedents of adult chronic disease. *Epidemiologic Reviews* 18(2):158–174.

Keys, Ancel, Josef Brozek, Austin Henschel, Olaf Mickelsen, and Henry Longstreet Taylor

1950 *The Biology of Human Starvation*. Minneapolis: University of Minnesota Press.

Kiernan, Ben

1996 *The Pol Pot Regime: Race, Power, and Genocide in Cambodia under the Khmer Rouge, 1975–79*. New Haven, CT: Yale University Press.

Kimura, Kunihiko

1984 Studies on growth and development in Japan. *Yearbook of Physical Anthropology* 27:179–214.

Kind, Karen L., Claire T. Roberts, Annica I. Sohlstrom, Arkadi Katsman, Peter M. Clifton, Jeffrey S. Robinson, and Julie A. Owens

2005 Chronic maternal feed restriction impairs growth but increases adiposity of the fetal guinea pig. *American Journal of Physiology: Regulatory, Integrative and Comparative Physiology* 288(1):R119–R126.

King, Hilary, Lim Keuky, Serey Seng, Touch Khun, Gojka Roglic, and Michel Pinget

2005 Diabetes and associated disorders in Cambodia: Two epidemiological surveys. *Lancet* 366(9497):1633–1639.

Koupil, Ilona, Dmitri B. Shestov, Pär Sparén, Svetlana Plavinskaja, Nina Parfenova, and Denny Vågerö
  2007   Blood pressure, hypertension and mortality from circulatory disease in men and women who survived the siege of Leningrad. *European Journal of Epidemiology* 22(4):223–234.

Kramer, Michael S., Cande V. Ananth, Robert W. Platt, and Kuruthukulangar S. Joseph
  2006   US Black vs White disparities in foetal growth: Physiological or pathological? *International Journal of Epidemiology* 35(5):1187–1195.

LaFeber, Walter
  2007   The United States and Vietnam: The enemies. In *The War That Never Ends: New Perspectives on the Vietnam War*, edited by David L. Anderson and John Ernst, 35–54. Lexington: University Press of Kentucky.

Langley-Evans, Simon C.
  2006   Developmental programming of health and disease. *Proceedings of the Nutrition Society* 65(1):97–105.

Leatherman, Thomas L.
  1998   Illness, social relations, and household production. In *Building a New Biocultural Synthesis: Political-Economic Perspectives on Human Biology*, edited by Alan H. Goodman and Thomas L. Leatherman, 245–267. Ann Arbor: University of Michigan Press.

Leatherman, Thomas L., and Alan H. Goodman
  1998   Expanding the biocultural synthesis toward a biology of poverty. *American Journal of Physical Anthropology* 102(1):1–3.

Leatherman, Thomas L., Alan H. Goodman, and R. Brooke Thomas
  1993   On seeking common ground between medical ecology and critical medical anthropology. *Medical Anthropology Quarterly* 7(2):202–207.

Levy, Barry S., Gurinder S. Shahi, and Chen Lee
  2000   The environmental consequences of war. In *War and Public Health*, edited by Barry S. Levy and Victor W. Sidel, 51–62. Washington, DC: American Public Health Association.

Little, Michael A., and Jere D. Haas
  1989   Introduction: Human population biology and the concept of trans-disciplinarity. In *Human Population Biology: A Transdisciplinary*

Science, edited by Michael A. Little and Jere D. Haas, 3–12. New York: Oxford University Press.

Lucas, Alan
1998   Programming by early nutrition: An experimental approach. *Journal of Nutrition* 128(2 Suppl.):401S–406S.

Macrae, Joanna, and Anthony Zwi
1994   Famine, complex emergencies and international policy in Africa: An overview. In *War and Hunger: Rethinking International Reponses to Complex Emergencies*, edited by Joanna Macrae and Anthony Zwi, 6–36. London: Zed Books.

Markowitz, Stephen D.
1955   Retardation in growth of children in Europe and Asia during World War II. *Human Biology* 27(4):258–273.

Marshall, Grant N., Terry L. Schell, Marc N. Elliott, S. Megan Berthold, and Chi-Ah Chun
2005   Mental health of Cambodian refugees 2 decades after resettlement in the United States. *Journal of the American Medical Association* 294(5):571–579.

Martorell, Reynaldo
1989   Body size, adaptation and function. *Human Organization* 48:15–20.

Mason, John B.
2002   Lessons on nutrition of displaced people. *Journal of Nutrition* 132(7):2096S–2103S.

Moore, Sophie E.
1998   Nutrition, immunity and the fetal and infant origins of disease hypothesis in developing countries. *Proceedings of the Nutrition Society* 57(2):241–247.

Morikawa, Masahiro
1998   Legacy of the Secret War: Medical needs in the UXO-contaminated areas in Laos. *Journal of the American Board of Family Practice* 11(6): 485–486.

Neugebauer, Richard, Hans Wijbrand Hoek, and Ezra Susser
1999   Prenatal exposure to wartime famine and development of antisocial personality disorder in early adulthood. *Journal of the American Medical Association* 281(5):455–462.

Painter, Rebecca C., Tessa J. Roseboom, and Otto P. Bleker
  2005   Prenatal exposure to the Dutch famine and disease in later life: An overview. *Reproductive Toxicology* 20(3):345–352.

Pelletier, David L.
  1994   The potentiating effects of malnutrition on child mortality: Epidemiologic evidence and policy implications. *Nutrition Reviews* 52(12):409–415.

Pelto, Gretel H., and Pertti J. Pelto
  1989   Small but healthy? An anthropological perspective. *Human Organization* 48(1):11–15.

Piersma, Theunis, and Jan Drent
  2003   Phenotypic flexibility and the evolution of organismal design. *Trends in Ecology and Evolution* 18(5):228–233.

Prebeg, Živka, and Irena Brali
  2000   Changes in menarcheal age in girls exposed to war conditions. *American Journal of Human Biology* 12:503–508.

Ravelli, Gian-Paolo, Zena A. Stein, and Mervyn W. Susser
  1976   Obesity in young men after famine exposure in utero and early infancy. *New England Journal of Medicine* 295(7):349–353.

Ridley, Matt
  2003   *Nature via Nurture: Genes, Experience, and What Makes Us Human.* New York: HarperCollins.

Roland, Charles G.
  1992   *Courage under Siege: Starvation, Disease and Death in the Warsaw Ghetto.* New York: Oxford University Press.

Roseboom, Tessa J., Jan H. P. van der Meulen, Anita C. J. Ravelli, Gert A. van Montfrans, Clive Osmond, David J. P. Barker, and Otto P. Bleker
  1999   Blood pressure in adults after prenatal exposure to famine. *Journal of Hypertension* 17(3):325–330.

Schecter, Arnold, Le Cao Dai, Le Thi Bich Thuy, Hoang Trong Quynh, Dinh Quang Minh, Hoang Dinh Cau, Pham Hoang Phiet, Nguyen Thi Ngoc Phuong, John D. Constable, Robert Baughman, Olaf Päpke, J. J. Ryan, Peter Fürst, and Seppo Räisänen
  1995   Agent Orange and the Vietnamese: The persistence of elevated dioxin levels in human tissues. *American Journal of Public Health* 85(4):516–522.

Seckl, Jonathan R., and Michael J. Meaney
2006 Glucocorticoid "programming" and PTSD. *Annals of the New York Academy of Sciences* 1071:351–378.

Singer, Merrill
1989 The limitations of medical ecology: The concept of adaptation in the context of social stratification and social transformation. *Medical Anthropology* 10(4):218–229.
1998 The development of critical medical anthropology: Implications for biological anthropology. In *Building a New Biocultural Synthesis: Political Economic Perspectives on Human Biology*, edited by Alan H. Goodman and Thomas L. Leatherman, 93–123. Ann Arbor: University of Michigan Press.

Skokić, Fahrija, Selma Muratović, and Gordana Radoja
2006 Perinatal and maternal outcomes in Tuzla Canton during 1992–1995 war in Bosnia and Herzegovina. *Croatian Medical Journal* 47(5):714–721.

Smith, Clement A.
1947 Effects of maternal undernutrition upon the newborn infants in Holland (1944–1945). *Journal of Pediatrics* 30(3):229–243.

Stanner, S. A., K. Bulmer, C. Andrés, O. E. Lantseva, V. Borodina, V. V. Poteen, and J. S. Yudkin
1997 Does malnutrition in utero determine diabetes and coronary heart disease in adulthood? Results from the Leningrad siege study, a cross sectional study. *British Journal of Medicine* 315(7119):1342–1348.

Steckel, Richard H.
1998 Birth weights and stillbirths in historical perspective. *European Journal of Clinical Nutrition* 52(S1):S16–S20.

Stein, Zena, Mervyn Susser, Gerhard Saenger, and Francis Marolla
1975 *Famine and Human Development: The Dutch Hunger Winter of 1944–1945*. New York: Oxford University Press.

Stuart-Fox, Martin
1997 *A History of Laos*. Cambridge: Cambridge University Press.

Susser, Ezra, Hans W. Hoek, and Alan Brown
1998 Neurodevelopmental disorders after prenatal famine. *American Journal of Epidemiology* 147(3):213–216.

Tahirović, Husref F.
1998   Menarchal age and the stress of war: An example from Bosnia. *European Journal of Pediatrics* 157(12):978–980.

Tanner, James M.
1986   Growth as a mirror for the conditions of society: Secular trends and class distinctions. In *Human Growth: A Multidisciplinary Review*, edited by Arto Demirjian and Micheline Brault Dubuc, 3–34. London: Taylor and Francis.
1990   *Fetus into Man: Physical Growth from Conception to Maturity*. Cambridge, MA: Harvard University Press.

Thomas, R. Brooke
1998   The evolution of human adaptability paradigms: Toward a biology of poverty. In *Building a New Biocultural Synthesis: Political-Economic Perspectives on Human Biology*, edited by Alan H. Goodman and Thomas L. Leatherman, 43–74. Ann Arbor: University of Michigan Press.

Thomas, R. Brooke, Timothy B. Gage, and Michael A. Little
1989   Reflections on adaptive and ecological models. In *Human Population Biology: A Transdisciplinary Science*, edited by Michael A. Little and Jere D. Haas, 296–319. New York: Oxford University Press.

Toole, Michael J., and Ronald J. Waldman
1993   Refugees and displaced persons: War, hunger, and public health. *Journal of the American Medical Association* 270(5):600–605.
1997   The public health aspects of complex emergencies and refugee situations. *Annual Reviews of Public Health* 18:283–312.

U.S. National Archives
2007   Statistical information about casualties of the Vietnam War. Online: http://www.archives.gov/research/vietnam-war/casualty-statistics .html. Accessed May 10, 2008.

Vincent, Shaun
1994   The Mozambique conflict (1980–1992). In *The True Cost of Conflict: Seven Recent Wars and Their Effects on Society*, edited by Michael Cranna, 81–112. New York: New Press.

Vlastovsky, V. G.
1966   The secular trend in the growth and development of children and young persons in the Soviet Union. *Human Biology* 38(3):219–230.

Weldon, Charles
1999   *Tragedy in Paradise: A Country Doctor at War in Laos.* Bangkok: Asia Books.

White, Philip
2005   War and food security in Eritrea and Ethiopia, 1998–2000. *Disasters* 29(S1):S92–S113.

Wiley, Andrea S.
2004   *An Ecology of High-Altitude Infancy: A Biocultural Perspective.* New York: Cambridge University Press.

Williams, George C.
1957   Pleiotropy, natural selection and the evolution of senescence. *Evolution* 11(4):398–411.

Yajnik, Chittaranjan
2000   Interactions of perturbations in intrauterine growth and growth during childhood on the risk of adult-onset disease. *Proceedings of the Nutrition Society* 59(2):257–265.

Yang, Dao
1993   *Hmong at the Turning Point.* Minneapolis: Worldbridge Associates.

Yip, Ray, and Truman W. Sharp
1993   Acute malnutrition and high childhood mortality related to diarrhea: Lessons from the 1991 Kurdish refugee crisis. *Journal of the American Medical Association* 270(5):587–590.

CHAPTER TWO

WAR AND THE PUBLIC HEALTH DISASTER IN IRAQ

Scott Harding and Kathryn Libal

Public health is directly shaped by war, conflict, and capitalism, yet exploring the connections between these processes remains neglected in scholarship and policymaking arenas. Such inquiry is vital to better understand how public health systems can be rebuilt following the cessation of violent conflict, which is critical to promoting individual well-being and supporting families and communities. Anthropologists have much to offer regarding the interconnections between health, war, and political economy. While the ethnography of war and political conflict are topics of lasting interest to anthropologists (Lubkemann 2008; Nordstrom 2004; Scheper-Hughes and Bourgois 2004), medical anthropology has not deeply examined the connections between war and health (Inhorn 2008). In her presidential address to the Society for Medical Anthropology in 2007, Marcia Inhorn signaled "chagrin over medical anthropology's relative apathy" in the face of ongoing wars in the Middle East (2008:418). She asserts:

> As a discipline, we have been faint of heart and lacking moral courage in this arena. In so doing, we have turned away from the brutal realities, the embodied suffering, the psychological devastation, the sexual violence, and the refugee aftermath of war (2008:421-422).

The history of Iraq illustrates that war is not an episodic and limited phenomenon; rather it is often a long-term, structural process with different phases, some more visible than others. Instead of an event that erupts by accident or as a result of historical enmity, war and other "complex emergencies" must be understood as intentional acts with their own politics, functions, and benefits (Keen 2008; Calhoun 2004). Thus in most cases of war and other "man-made" disasters, global and local interests are profoundly intertwined. In chronic conflict—whether low intensity among local actors or high intensity involving local and international actors—key social institutions and the well-being of ordinary people are compromised in multiple ways. In particular, health outcomes diminish as the impacts of war become embedded in society over time. This is especially so in the case of Iraq, where powerful geopolitical actors, such as the United States, have sought to control local resources and populations.

Tracing the "costs" of war extends far beyond calculating the resources set aside for waging battle or keeping peace. War continues to have negative health consequences long after formal cessation of armed conflict. Aside from immediate destruction, war creates direct and indirect negative effects on health that can take generations to overcome (Inhorn 2008). War diverts resources to the military, fractures local community and creates forced displacement, undermines economic networks, and degrades the physical environment, thus jeopardizing food production and water quality. Violent conflict, by disrupting public health and other basic infrastructure, can create long-term conditions of famine and disease, often killing more people indirectly than who die from direct fighting (Krause and Mutimer 2005). This problem is acute in developing countries: increased military spending in response to conflict typically continues after formal fighting ends, reducing spending on vital services like education and health care (Gupta, et al. 2002). While the health effects of war are profound, they are often disregarded by powerful global actors and obscured by popular media accounts of most violent conflict.

The 2003 U.S. invasion and the ongoing conflict in Iraq have destabilized an already fragile society and worsened social conditions for most people, while a public health disaster has silently unfolded.[1] The war has aggravated social divisions and fueled ethnic/sectarian conflict, fractured communities, undermined social development, and created a massive displaced population. Less noticed, stresses on the Iraqi health care system have increased since 2003, while health and the well-being of

Iraqis have deteriorated.[2] High rates of mortality and morbidity related to the conflict, rising child and infant mortality, and the reliance of almost one third of Iraqis on emergency aid all signal a deepening public health disaster (Medact 2008).

The health crisis in Iraq must be understood in historical context, as Iraqis have experienced three decades of war and isolation from the international community. The Iran-Iraq War in the 1980s, the 1991 Gulf War, and more than a decade of UN-imposed economic sanctions contributed to the current humanitarian disaster. In particular, sanctions and a separate U.S. trade embargo in the 1990s devastated social development, effectively dismantling Iraq's once impressive public health system (Garfield 1999; Medact 2004; Popal 2000; Rawaf 2005). The current armed conflict in Iraq and its attendant effects have further undermined previous social progress and health gains. Moreover, U.S.-backed neoliberal reconstruction policies implemented following the overthrow of Saddam Hussein have intensified these effects.

Since the 2003 invasion, U.S. military operations, ethnic cleansing, and other targeted violence by Iraqis have intensified the scale of suffering and loss of life. Communities which had been ethnically and religiously diverse have been segregated into separate Shi'a and Sunni enclaves controlled by local militia, Iraqi security forces, or the U.S. military. Because of this rising sectarianism, many Iraqis find it difficult to work, attend school, access health care, or obtain services. Despite a drop in violent deaths and large-scale attacks by 2008, human rights violations remain widespread, marked by indiscriminate killings, bombings, and kidnappings.

Although violence has increased in Iraq since the U.S. invasion, Iraqis' well-being is also threatened by external factors. U.S.-initiated neoliberal policies have helped foment the "sectarianization" of public services, including health care, and a continued degradation of key state functions. Hastily implemented privatization and the 2003 decision to "de-Baathify" the government and public sector undermined what weak health infrastructure remained after the sanctions era (Klein 2007; Phillips 2005). Because of ongoing violence and the fragmentation of the state, preventable disease, infant mortality, and "excess" deaths have increased in most of the country. Malnutrition, lack of sanitation and clean water, and limited access to medical services, resulting from pervasive conflict, contribute to these trends (Medact 2008; United Nations Children's Fund [UNICEF] 2008a). The ongoing crisis has also accelerated the dismantling of Iraq's medical system, as health care professionals have become the deliberate targets of insurgent groups as a weapon of war. With these providers increasingly at risk, Iraq faces a "brain drain" of the most qualified medical personnel, including the loss of educators training new doctors and nurses. In the long term this poses significant barriers to the reconstruction of the health care sector. In the short term, access to health care is uneven, with quality increasingly dependent on one's ability to pay for services. Another troubling trend is the closure of "humanitarian space" for UN agencies and international nongovernmental organizations (NGOs) providing medical assistance to Iraqis. Medecins Sans Frontieres and other health-related NGOs have resorted to using mobile clinics in Iraq, creating trauma units in neighboring countries, and training ordinary Iraqis in community health services to compensate for a degraded public health sector. Given the scale of displacement of Iraqis, the limited access to adequate primary health care and mental health services for some 2 million refugees living in Jordan, Syria, and other host countries represents another destructive effect of the war (Harper 2008; International Crisis Group 2008a; Libal and Harding in press).

In short, the conflict in Iraq represents a compelling example of a "man-made disaster" (Harding 2007). Despite formal attention to Iraqis' well-being, humanitarian and health consequences of the war have been lesser concerns of U.S. foreign policy than achieving geopolitical goals. We highlight the systemic effects on health of the U.S. invasion of Iraq and chronic armed conflict that has ensued since 2003. We illustrate how the current conflict represents a continuation of external structural violence initiated in the 1990s in the form of economic sanctions and U.S. foreign policy decisions. Under the rule of Saddam Hussein, and in the wake of his overthrow, internal and external policy decisions have slowly crippled state services, while social conditions in Iraq have deteriorated.[3]

The U.S. Legacy: Political Instability and Violence

The 2003 U.S. invasion of Iraq and overthrow of Saddam Hussein triggered massive internal destabilization in Iraq, which further undermined social development, health, and well-being in much of the country. The social fabric of local communities has been radically transformed, as many members of religious minority groups and families of mixed Shi'a and Sunni backgrounds have fled the country or to "safer" neighborhoods and provinces. As a result of sectarian conflict, much of the central and southern provinces have been transformed into distinctly divided communities along ethnic and religious lines.

The ongoing U.S. military occupation also complicates Iraq's political processes. By late 2008 there was little evidence of fundamental political reconciliation or progress on key policy issues (International Crisis Group 2008b). Despite U.S. pressure to achieve a number of political "benchmarks," several of the most crucial initiatives have stalled. The existence of a civil war, failing state institutions, and deep ethnic, religious, and tribal cleavages thus compromise the future stability of Iraq and suggest that comprehensive social development via a strong government is a distant prospect. One recent analysis of weak and "failed states" ranked Iraq second worst in the world in terms of vulnerability to violent internal conflict and social dysfunction (Fund for Peace and Foreign Policy Magazine 2008).

The enactment of a "Baghdad Security Plan" and an increase ("surge") in U.S. troops in 2007 appears to have helped reduce the level of violence and attacks on civilians and security forces. While more than 5,500 civilians died from violence in Baghdad province alone in the first quarter of 2007, according to government ministries (Susman 2007), by October the number of civilian deaths fell to approximately 1,000 a month (Buckley and Gordon 2007). The level of civilian casualties dropped by late 2008 to their lowest reported level since the war began (Brookings Institution 2008). This reflects a combination of the "surge," an agreement by followers of Moqtada al-Sadr to stop attacks against U.S. forces, reduced armed violence among Shiite factions, and the incorporation of anti-U.S. insurgents into "Awakening Councils" which focused on stabilizing local neighborhoods and targeting al-Qaeda in Iraq (Galbraith 2008). Despite the apparent gains, violence against women and professional groups like academics, rising intolerance against minorities, and sectarian violence in those areas with diverse ethnic and religious groups remain especially problematic (United Nations Assistance Mission for Iraq [UNAMI] 2007a). Moreover, even though violence declined in late 2007, lawlessness remains endemic in central and southern Iraq.

Although levels of violence continued to drop throughout 2008, analysts suggest these gains could be quickly reversed and that instability continues to plague Iraq (Farrell and Oppel Jr. 2008; International Crisis Group 2008b). The United Nations found that "continual fear from violence from all sides, including armed sectarian groups, criminal rackets, various militias, as well as during operations by security and military forces is a daily reality for civilians" (UNAMI 2007c:3). The International Committee of the Red Cross (ICRC) asserted that engaging in the mundane pursuits of everyday life—walking to school, shopping, and riding the bus—were now matters of life and death (ICRC 2007). Fear of everyday violence in Iraq is particularly acute for women and girls, limiting their freedom of movement and ability to go to work or school (Susskind 2007).

Within this context, the rush to embrace lower levels of violence as proof of the "success" of U.S. policy and the legitimacy of the Iraqi government is misleading. In reality, fundamental tensions among tribal, religious, and ethnic groups remain unresolved, while basic municipal services are an empty promise for most Iraqis. The central government remains weak, while heavily armed sectarian militias and insurgent groups bide their time as they consolidate control of different sectors of the government and economy. "Iraq still lacks the formal rules to divide the power and spoils of an oil-rich nation among ethnic, religious and tribal groups and unite them under one stable idea of Iraq. The improvements are fragile" (Farrell and Oppel Jr. 2008:A7). Overall, the political situation in Iraq remains divided on several key issues, including representation in national and provincial governments, proposed legislation related to oil revenue sharing, and the status of Kirkuk. Given the continued political polarization, national elections scheduled for early 2010 offer little hope of resolving these issues.

The Politics of Denial: The Death Toll in Iraq

U.S. forces in Iraq have never provided data on civilian casualties and deaths, a deliberate effort to deflect attention from the human cost of the war and maintain domestic support for military operations. Distancing themselves from "body counts" of the Vietnam War, the Bush administration claimed that counting civilian casualties was not a part of the U.S. mission. While the Iraqi government attempted to count bodies processed through morgues, it ended this practice reportedly under pressure from the U.S. and Iraqi governments (Steele and Goldenberg 2008).

Several organizations and scholars have attempted to estimate Iraqi deaths using different methodologies (Roberts et al 2004). Their estimates of civilian deaths vary widely and each has generated controversy. The UN, using information from the Iraqi government, hospitals, and health care officials, reported that 34,352 civilians died in violence in 2006 alone (UNAMI 2007a). The Iraqi government claimed that some 150,000 civilians had been killed between 2004 and 2006 (Oppel Jr. 2006). The Iraq Body Count, an independent public database of violent civilian deaths derived from media reports in Iraq resulting from the 2003 U.S. military intervention, suggests a death toll (as of April 2009) of approximately 91,000–100,000 (Iraq Body Count 2009). Other research found an ("excess") civilian death toll from 2003–2006 of approximately 600,000 (Burnham et al 2006). The latter estimates, published in *The Lancet*, were based on the second Iraqi household survey conducted by researchers at Johns Hopkins University. At the time this represented a civilian casualty figure of approximately 2.5 percent of Iraq's population, dramatically higher than any other study had found. Somewhat predictably, this publication generated controversy over the findings and methodology used. Both surveys were dismissed by the U.S. and British governments, were criticized by some researchers (Daponte 2007; Hicks 2006), and received minimal media coverage, especially in the United States (Tirman 2008).

In early 2008 the World Health Organization (WHO) estimated that 151,000 violent deaths occurred from March 2003 through June 2006 (Iraq Family Health Survey Study Group 2008). This was more than triple the Iraq Body Count estimates for the same period. The WHO survey, based on a household survey with 9,345 heads of households, found that "violence is a leading cause of death for Iraqi adults and was the main cause of death in men between the ages of 15 and 59 years during the first 3 years after the 2003 invasion" (484).

A much higher casualty figure was produced by a prominent British polling firm in January 2008. The group estimated "that over 1,000,000 Iraqi citizens have died as a result of the conflict which started in 2003" (Opinion Research Business 2008). This meant that some 20 percent of Iraqis had experienced at least one death in their household due to the ongoing conflict, rather than from natural causes. According to the report, in August 2007 the group found that 1.2 million Iraqis had died since 2003, and decided to conduct additional research in rural areas of Iraq to enhance the validity of their research. These findings generated scant attention in the U.S. media or among organizations addressing the Iraq conflict (Tirman 2008).

Although data on violent civilian deaths vary widely, even the lowest estimates reveal a dramatic level of violence in Iraq since 2003. As troubling has been the relative silence by the international community and U.S. media about the loss of life in Iraq. Similarly, little notice has been paid to the changing life expectancy rates in Iraq. The current life expectancy rate at birth is 57 years (WHO 2008). Life expectancy in Iraq dramatically improved in the late 1970s and 1980s, and then began to decline with the onset of economic sanctions. Factoring in gender reveals that life expectancy rates for Iraqi males at birth have now plummeted to 48 years, reflecting their risk of dying prematurely from violent causes (WHO 2008; United Nations Development Program [UNDP] 2008).

The Human Costs of Economic Sanctions and War in Iraq

When considering the dismantling of modern Iraqi society, an historical perspective that includes an assessment of external influences on state capacity illustrates the civilian consequences of war and militarism. The Iran-Iraq War (1980–1988) devastated Iraq's economy and undermined gains in living standards, yet by 1990 Iraq still ranked second highest in human development in the Middle East (Pedersen 2007). Thus the damage inflicted by the U.S. military in the first Gulf War and from UN sanctions (1990–2003), along with the ongoing conflict, bears much responsibility for the shift from an increasingly self-sufficient country to a failed state.

The state of health, nutrition, and well-being under sanctions contrasts with Iraq's relatively affluent status in 1990. Before the 1991 Gulf War, Iraq invested heavily in the health sector, making primary medical care available to most urban residents and some 80 percent of the rural population. Infant and child mortality had been reduced significantly during the 1980s, while water and sanitation treatment services "were well developed" (UNICEF 1998:7). Until the mid-1980s, in terms of social development, Iraq was "fast approaching standards comparable to those of developed countries" (UNDP 2002:11). This perspective was echoed by a European doctor we interviewed, who was involved in humanitarian relief in Iraq during the First Gulf War and participated in international planning teams for health reconstruction following the 2003 invasion. He asserted that Iraq's achievements in primary health had been significant; Iraq had better vaccination rates and was outperforming many European countries.

Much of Iraq's infrastructure was destroyed by U.S. bombing in the Gulf War. This damage, combined with the onset of sanctions, precipitated a public health crisis, as malnutrition and the rate of water-borne diseases erupted in 1991 (Hiltermann 1991; Ascherio, et al. 1992). Sanctions undermined the ability of the public health system and social infrastructure to address health care and nutrition. Iraq's health-care system, formerly among the most developed in the region was seriously degraded (Popal 2000). By the time of the 2003 U.S. invasion, "the public health system was in tatters, it was under-resourced, and the population was economically deprived," noted an interviewee. As Iraq's economy withered, child malnutrition, disease, and infant and child mortality increased sharply in the 1990s, and food self-sufficiency declined (Dobson 2000; Garfield 1999; UNICEF 1998). Sanctions were chiefly responsible for the excess deaths of 300,000–500,000 infants and children during the 1990s (Garfield and Leu 2000). By 2003, the UN found that more than one-fifth of Iraq's population in its most populated areas was "chronically

poor" and that nearly two-thirds of Iraqis were dependent on government food rations (UN World Food Program 2003). Thus, under sanctions, Iraq "experienced a shift from relative affluence to massive poverty"
(UNDP 2002:12).

While obtaining current figures on social indicators is difficult, available data suggest that the overall health of much of the Iraqi population
is precarious (Medact 2008; UNICEF 2008b; UNHCR 2008). Despite
some economic and social progress since 2003, the U.S.-led war has
created a deepening disaster for Iraqis in terms of social development
and public health. A comprehensive household survey in 2004 found
deteriorating physical and social conditions. Electrical, water, and sewer
systems were deeply compromised and unreliable, further endangering
health. Since that study, conditions have declined significantly. More than
half of Iraqis live on less than $1 a day, unemployment ranges from 25
to 40 percent, and more than 8 million people are categorized as "poor"
(UNAMI 2007b, 2007c).

A lack of medicines, equipment, and health care personnel has im-
periled an already fragile health service system. UNICEF reported that
the ongoing conflict and underinvestment in infrastructure have "undermined Iraq's vital social services to the point where many basic family needs are going unmet" (UNICEF 2008a). The UNICEF special
representative for Iraq found that a lack of hygiene and safe drinking
water are "priority concerns for Iraqi families" and that young children
are particularly affected by waterborne diseases and malnutrition. The
International Organization for Migration (IOM) reported that "water
and sewage systems in the country are generally poorly functioning
and dilapidated. In places where water networks/sewage systems exist or connect to areas they are either overstretched . . . or deficient"
(2008a:14). Reflecting the degraded water and sanitation systems, a
cholera outbreak occurred in late 2007 in Baghdad and parts of Kurdish
Iraq (UNAMI 2007c).

Costs for basic (and private) health care in Iraq have also risen, drugs
and other critical supplies are often nonexistent, and an acute shortage of
hospital beds exists. Most hospitals and primary health care centers in the
southern and central governorates are operating in substandard condition.
As one UN official in an interview with us noted,

A lot of the health facilities do not have medications they need. They are overstretched—there are too many people going there and they don't have the simple equipment. Sometimes the equipment is broken down and can't be replaced or it is stolen during the earlier part of the war. So the health conditions are very, very poor.

Thus, as the International Committee of the Red Cross underscores, "five years after the war began, many Iraqis do not have access to the most basic health care. . . . The Iraqi health-care system is now in worse shape than ever. Many lives have been lost because prompt and appropriate medical care is not available" (ICRC 2008:8).

Food security is precarious for Iraqis in central and southern governorates. In 2003 the UNWFP conducted a food security assessment and found that some 11 percent (2.6 million people) were "extremely poor and vulnerable to food insecurity" (UNWFP/Central Organization for Statistics and Information Technology [COSIT] 2006:1). At that time, if the Public Distribution System (PDS) program were eliminated, then another 3.6 million Iraqis would have been food insecure. In a follow-up survey in 2006, the UNWFP found that 15 percent of Iraqis (some 4 million people) were food insecure and "in dire need of different types of humanitarian assistance, including food," despite receiving public food rations (UNWFP/COSIT 2006:2). The survey also found that "a further 8.3 million people (31.8 percent of the surveyed population) would be rendered food insecure if they were not provided with a PDS ration."

Hunger and malnutrition have a devastating effect on children; between 1990 and 2005 the increase in infant mortality in Iraq (150 percent) was the highest in the world (Save the Children 2007). An estimated 19 percent of Iraqi children suffered from malnutrition under sanctions, while 28 percent were malnourished by 2007 (NGO Coordination Committee in Iraq and Oxfam 2007:3). Child mortality rates, which soared in the 1990s, have worsened since 2003. Only 30 percent of Iraqi children are estimated to have access to clean water (UNICEF 2007). One in eight Iraqi children died in 2005 before their fifth birthday; more than half of these deaths occurred among babies less than one month old (Save the Children 2007). Declining school enrollment also reveals the disintegration of social institutions that ensure children's well-being. The Iraqi Ministry of Education reported that 30 percent of elementary school children attended school in 2007, a sharp decline from figures of 75 percent in 2006 (Amnesty International 2008).

Particularly detrimental to the long-term stability of Iraq is the mental health impact of pervasive violence and family and community disintegration, especially on children (UNICEF 2007; Medact 2004). While surveys of children's mental health and the effects of the war have been limited, the World Health Organization found that in areas hard hit by violence up to 30 percent of Iraqi children suffer from a posttraumatic stress disorder (UNICEF 2007). With mental health services already scarce before the 2003 U.S. invasion, those suffering trauma as a result of the current conflict have few viable treatment options (Al-Jadiry and Rustam 2006; Curie 2006). A recent study found that a lack of community support and pervasive stigma toward those with mental illness prevented 65 percent of patients in Iraq's only long-term mental health facility from family and community reintegration (Humaidi 2006). The significance of the gap in mental health services cannot be understated: political and social reconciliation must be seen as linked to the ability to deal with the long-term affects of such trauma on a generation of Iraqis.

The disintegration of key social institutions (especially in the central and southern provinces) and endemic conflict in Baghdad and other cities have forced large numbers of Iraqis to leave their homes. The UN estimates that some 2.2 million refugees have fled to neighboring countries, while 2.8 million Iraqis are considered "internally displaced persons" (IDPs) (IOM 2008b). According to aid workers we interviewed, Iraqi refugees are among the most traumatized they have encountered in recent decades. A recent study of Jordan and Lebanon found that a high percentage of Iraqi families are "undergoing a period of serious emotional and psychosocial threats. These threats create widespread distress in (the) living environment of displaced Iraqis" (IOM 2008a:14). Refugees in Syria reported "a high exposure to distressing and traumatic events" in Iraq, such as being a victim of violence, kidnappings, and torture, as well as displacement itself. Related to this, "high incidences of domestic violence as well as anxiety and depression" have been reported among Iraqi refugees in Syria (ICMC 2008:8). Yet, as in Iraq, mental health services for refugees are severely limited in Jordan and Syria, where the majority of Iraqi refugees reside. Few systematic studies have been done on the mental health needs of displaced Iraqis. A 2004 survey of refugees living in London found high levels of distress and mental health needs, concluding that in general "a high proportion of Iraqi refugee family members constitute a population at risk for adjustment and mental health problems" (Hosin et al. 2006:129). Given that this research predates the period when violence in Iraq escalated, the mental health needs of more recent Iraqi refugees is likely even more profound.

Although refugees have garnered more media attention since 2007, IDPs in Iraq are increasingly vulnerable and lack critical protections and their material conditions are less well documented. The United Nations found that many internally displaced Iraqis cannot access needed medicines, adequate housing, or work (UNAMI 2007c). In one third of Iraq's 18 governorates, more than 25 percent of IDPs lack regular access to water (IOM 2008b). Some relief workers worry that those Iraqis who are too poor to move at all remain the most vulnerable, for they lack the networks and resources to move to safer and better functioning communities. As one UN official working with IDPs told us in an interview in July 2008:

> There are just many, many reasons why being displaced is not an ideal situation. . . . [T]he choice is you and your family members get killed or you leave. . . . But increasingly the conditions for the displaced are deteriorating and I think many Iraqis are realizing that leaving is just not a very good option [either].

The "Brain Drain" and its Consequences on Health Care

While the flow of refugees from Iraq has garnered notice, little attention has been paid to *who* exactly has left the country and its implication for long-term stability and the redevelopment of Iraq. A discernable "brain drain" has emerged, as academics and intellectuals, trained medical professionals, former government workers, entrepreneurs, the middle class, and the wealthy have fled the violence and persecution engulfing much of Iraq (Sassoon 2009; UNAMI 2007a).

The ability of key state institutions to function effectively is threatened by the loss of skilled workers, trained specialists, and administrators. As of late 2007, an estimated 40 percent of professionals have fled Iraq since 2003 (Brookings Institution 2007). Key sectors of Iraqi society have been disproportionately affected. For example, more than half of Iraq's registered physicians are estimated to have left the country (ICRC 2008; Medact 2008). Trained specialists, the backbone of Iraq's health care system, are increasingly in short supply as most have also fled violence and persecution. The head of the Iraqi Doctors' Syndicate estimated that between 60 and 70 percent of physicians with 15 to 20 years' experience have left Iraq, and an even higher percentage of those with more experience have fled (Kami 2008).

Another way the ongoing crisis has accelerated the dismantling of Iraq's medical system is that health care professionals have become the deliberate targets of violence as a "weapon of war." Physicians have been a particular object of violence, while thousands of other health care workers have been subject to kidnapping, violence, and intimidation, helping to fuel this flight of trained medical specialists (Brookings Institution 2007; ICRC 2008; Medact 2008; UNAMI 2007b). An estimated 2,000 Iraqi physicians have been murdered since the 2003 U.S. invasion, with hundreds more kidnapped (Brookings Institution 2008). In an interview, a UN official noted that even monitoring health conditions in Iraq has become dangerous for their Iraqi workers. A humanitarian representative underscored that the health professionals with whom they collaborated in Iraq were at great risk: "Hospitals are targets; patients coming into hospitals are targets; patients inside hospitals are targets." In this climate, "everybody is afraid of everybody."

Attacks against health professionals and their attendant effects are another hidden cost of war. Interviews with humanitarian NGOs underscore that skilled medical personnel are now in short supply in Iraq, while access to adequate health care is inconsistent, especially for those with conflict-related injuries or chronic health conditions. One respondent in our study asserted that any doctor who could leave had already done so: "Everybody's left . . . [We have] got a country which was functioning in pre '91 on a European level—let's say Kuwait in the Middle East. [Now] we've gone to an Afghanistan level." The return of medical professionals following reconciliation between factions will be essential to the revival of health care in Iraq as well as the training of a new generation of physicians and other health professionals.

Teachers and academics have also been persecuted, as Iraq's education sector has been similarly undermined. According to Medact (2008:5), the current crisis has created a "poorly trained, overworked, demoralized, fearful, underpaid health workforce." While this development has been neglected in U.S. debates about the Iraq War, the short- and long-term impact on health seems clear: "Iraqis describe their health system as 'beheaded,' because many of its brightest and best have already migrated, while the practitioners, managers, and teachers of the future are not being developed or supported" (Medact 2008:5).

While some professionals fled beginning in the late 1960s, a process which continued in the 1980s and 1990s, the current refugee flow suggests the creation of a new Iraqi Diaspora. This development highlights the barriers to return migration of Iraqi refugees and the impact on long-term reconstruction efforts. Many of those fleeing Iraq today represent the best hopes for the creation of a vibrant, nonsectarian civil society and strong government. Based on a recent survey of Iraqi refugees (UNHCR 2008), as well as historical examples of other civil wars and refugee flows, it is unlikely that most Iraqi refugees will return without a drastic shift in the political and security environment. This assessment was shared with us by NGO and UN representatives working with Iraqi refugees in Jordan and Syria.

Although the likelihood of migration by professionals differs by occupation, the negative impact on key social institutions like health care is significant (Chikanda 2006). Thus, the ability to rebuild the Iraqi health care system faces a number of challenges. A culture of medical migration to the west already exists in other developing countries, with many physicians and skilled health personnel fleeing conflict and political violence (Hagopian, et al. 2005). Without addressing militarism and fundamental political conflict, Iraq risks falling prey to similar institutional factors that have undermined public health elsewhere in the developing world.

In the interim, the larger political disputes dividing Iraq are evidenced in the structure and governance of the current health system. Health care provision and policy planning are managed through the patchwork efforts of the Ministry of Health, UN organizations, and international NGOs. A weak, fractured government has been unable to overcome its differences and promote development that addresses the decline in public health. Indeed, in many respects political and military conflict in Iraq has fueled the division of key services and government ministries among competing and sectarian groups (Marfleet 2007). The Ministry of Health has struggled to shed an image of representing sectarian Shi'a interests, while maintaining leadership that can implement a coherent health agenda. Perceived sectarianism has had a profound impact on access to health care. As one aid worker put it, "You want the doctor because he is a good doctor, you don't want him because he's Shi'a or Muslim or Sunni Muslim or Communist or Kurd." Turnover has been particularly high in administrative positions within the Ministry of Health and in hospitals in areas with high levels of armed conflict. Two informants noted that while in 2008 the upper leadership of the Ministry of Health has stabilized, prior to that high turnover of staff resulted in incoherent policy and allowed privatization of health to occur. UN and independent analysts are troubled by trends related to the deregulation of the health sector and the long-term consequences this poses for ordinary Iraqis:

> The unregulated health economy, the need to maximize professional income, and the individualistic, specialty-focused traditions of Iraqi medicine are creating a fragmented fee-for-service system mainly delivering curative care. This cannot meet basic health needs effectively, and is beyond the average citizen's pocket (Medact 2008:2).

"Disaster Capitalism": The Privatization of Health Reconstruction

The entangled relationship of war making and capitalism has recently come under scrutiny (Klein 2007; Mattei and Nader 2008). The assimilation of national and local economies within a global system has profound consequences for developing societies. When the imperative to "integrate" is mandated by external actors, neoliberal policies can become catalysts for the intensification of violence. The harmful consequences of structural adjustment programs on the public sector in developing countries have been well documented (Yong and Millen 2000). Badawi (2004:76) argues that globalization is most dangerous when developing countries are forced "to adopt certain structural and economic changes, which prematurely decrease expenditures on social services, including healthcare." This challenge is amplified in countries where the state is weak and challenged by internal conflict, occupation, or war, such as in contemporary Iraq (Docena 2007).

Given the sophisticated state of Iraq's health care into the 1980s, the decline of its health infrastructure and Iraqis' well-being is all the more dramatic. While some have blamed current health failures on the rule of Saddam Hussein, regime change and the introduction of neoliberal economic policies bear a special responsibility for the health crisis. Shortly after the United States invaded Iraq in 2003, Paul Bremer, administrator of the Coalition Provisional Authority, enacted several transitional laws that undermined the already weak health care sector. His first major reform, Order #1, was to fire some 500,000 state workers, including soldiers, professors, teachers, doctors, nurses, engineers, and judges (Klein 2007). This policy became known as "de-Baathification." Bremer's program to "de-Baathify" the government extended too deeply into the public sector to be considered merely an effort to purge Hussein loyalists. Instead, Bremer sought to radically "downsize" the public sector, adhering to neoliberal principles of privatizing government-run industries, eliminating subsidies, and firing state workers (Docena 2007).

The ideological fixation with privatizing the Iraqi state is apparent in numerous accounts of "postwar" U.S. policies. David L. Phillips (2005:146), a former senior advisor to the State Department, finds that de-Baathification "was about distributing power to Iraqis who subscribed to the vision of the new Iraq." The Bush administration, in part, framed the invasion of Iraq as an opportunity to spread democracy in the Middle East. In practice this vision meant implementing a neoliberal agenda by purging those who opposed economic liberalization.

The neoliberals "believed that privatization would open Iraq to foreign investment, bring in foreign companies, and create an Iraqi bourgeoisie whose prosperity would inspire Syrians, Iranians, and others to seek the same" (Phillips 2005:147). Indeed, through a series of orders issued by Bremer from May 2003 to June 2004, the United States instituted radical reforms to transform Iraq. Based on a plan written by the multinational corporation BearingPoint Inc. (formerly KPMG Consulting), these orders devolved public services and privatized key economic functions formerly performed by Iraq (Juhasz 2006).

Privatization and de-Baathification have entailed reconstruction contracting practices that enrich transnational corporations at the expense of Iraqis and U.S. taxpayers. While U.S.-funded programs have garnered attention, the limited spending on health care illustrates how public services fare poorly when militarism takes precedence. The Special Inspector General for Iraq Reconstruction (SIGIR) has provided insight into the challenges of reconstruction initiated during the Iraq War. Contracts to U.S. corporations working in Iraq have been characterized by systemic cost overruns, failure to complete projects, and corruption. SIGIR was highly critical of two contracts for health care infrastructure. An April 2006 audit of a $243 million contract with Parsons Delaware Inc. revealed that after almost $186 million had been spent over two years only six primary health care centers were completed and that 135 of 150 planned centers were partially constructed (SIGIR 2008). Of the latter, 121 centers were later "terminated for convenience." According to SIGIR, the contractor and United States Agency for International Development (USAID) were responsible for the failure to complete the health centers.

SIGIR's 2006 audit of Bechtel's contract to build the Basra Children's Hospital found that an original estimate of $50 million in construction costs ballooned to a projected $150 million. Again, the Inspector General cited USAID management failures, noting that only three USAID officers were overseeing $1.4 billion in contracts. Thus, while the United States has modestly invested in new health care facilities, such efforts have been marred by delays, cost-overruns, poor quality, a failure to address the long-term consequences of sanctions, and the impact of looting and deterioration since 2003.

Privatization also extends to humanitarian relief efforts. U.S.-funded NGO work in Iraq is concentrated among a few players, including International Medical Corps, CARE, and Mercy Corps, and a number of for-profits. Breaking from past practices of funding UN agencies, these health-related contracts were disproportionately awarded to the private sector. Yet several agencies and corporations engaged in technical assistance and development projects have been criticized for failing to work effectively with Iraqis in developing health policy and programs.

Conclusion: Challenges to Creating Health Policy and Reconstruction of the Health Sector

U.S. policies to invade Iraq, de-Baathify the government, and implement neoliberal economic policies represent one facet of the structural violence Iraqis have faced since 2003. Coupled with the long-term degradation of health infrastructure, the flight of health care professionals, and ongoing political conflict, Iraq requires full engagement of the international community to resolve its multiple and intertwined social, governance, and health crises.

Addressing the chronic material deprivation and multiple forms of mental health stress experienced by vulnerable Iraqis will require investment in health and educational policies that are comprehensive and sustained. Without a commitment to public health intervention, Iraq faces a future marred by the effects of declining health, pervasive trauma, and social exclusion. This latter condition is profound for youth and the elderly. Such problems will require substantial attention, yet adequate psychosocial supports are lacking in Iraq, within neighboring states hosting most Iraqi refugees, and to a lesser extent in Western states that have resettled Iraqi refugees. An added complication are the cultural barriers among Iraqis to seeking professional mental health services due to the stigma attached to psychosocial problems (ICMC 2008). These limitations are also pronounced for the sizeable community of Iraqis with physical disabilities. In an interview, a caseworker specializing in disabilities with experience in the Middle East noted that 30 years of conflict in Iraq has created a disability crisis. She described a situation where a large number of Iraqis with physical disabilities are confined to their homes and lack services and community support. The current war has amplified their social isolation.

Given the fractured state of the health sector, NGOs have played important roles in providing technical assistance and health care services to Iraqis in recent years. This reflects, in part, the UN's absence from Iraq due to security concerns and political instability. Yet international NGOs that operate alongside Iraqi counterparts are forced to maintain a low profile because of the targeting of humanitarian actors. Thus it remains difficult to comprehensively assess the impact of their efforts related to health and other unmet needs, while the effects of U.S. reconstruction on public health have been decidedly mixed.

Inhorn's (2008) admonishment of anthropologists to research the effects of war on health, particularly in Iraq and Afghanistan, demands a response. In Iraq, the work to uncover how U.S. military power and neoliberal reconstruction programs have contributed to the degradation of the public health system and health and well-being of Iraqis will require sustained and innovative research. It is vital that such analysis flourish in coming years in order to create momentum within the international community to address Iraq's public health crisis. Doing so will help ensure the rebuilding of Iraq's public health system and other key institutions and that those responsible for violations of human rights are held accountable.

Notes

1. The term "Iraqi" is a political construct that some communities in Iraq may not recognize, in particular, Kurds who seek an independent state. We use this term because it is the dominant frame of reference for most academic, official, and journalistic discourse.

2. Given the lack of reliable research that disaggregates health data on the basis of region, ethnic, or religious group affiliation, it is difficult to generalize about the well-being of Kurds versus Shi'a or Sunni Arabs in Iraq. Much data collection in Iraq on health and other social indicators over the past two decades has been rudimentary. In spite of these constraints there is a growing body of data gathered in surveys collected by UN agencies, the government of Iraq, and different nongovernmental organizations. Future research must better address differences in health infrastructure and outcomes by region, social class, ethnicity, and religious affiliation.

3. Our chapter is part of a larger study on NGO advocacy for displaced Iraqis that we began in late 2006. We conducted interviews and fieldwork in Jordan, Syria, Turkey, and the United States with more than 60 respondents working in humanitarian and human rights NGOs, the U.S. Congress, and UN agencies. We have not done interviews in Iraq, reflecting our reluctance to enter field sites in which both researchers and informants are vulnerable. In the United States, we interviewed NGO representatives engaged in advocacy and direct service to Iraqi refugees, and staff from Congress and the State Department. In the summers of 2007, 2008, and 2009 we spent a total of three months in Jordan, Syria, and Turkey interviewing informants from international and local NGOs, including a number of Iraqi refugees volunteering as outreach workers, who provided assistance to Iraqi refugees. We also interviewed several key respondents who played important roles in assessing and creating health policy in Iraq as well as UN officials. We did semi-structured interviews, with an emphasis on understanding the politics of NGO advocacy and the provision of humanitarian assistance. We asked informants about the social costs of endemic conflict in Iraq, the specific needs of Iraqi refugees, barriers to health care and service provision, the capacity of local and international NGOs to provide services, the role of key global actors like the US and UN, and the various strategy and tactics of advocacy on this issue by NGOs.

Works Cited

Al-Jadiry, A. M., and H. Rustam
2006 Mental health education and training in Iraq: An overview. *Journal of Muslim Mental Health* 1(2):117–122.

Amnesty International
2008 *Carnage and Despair in Iraq: Iraq Five Years On.* London: Amnesty International.

Ascherio, A., R. Chase, T. Cote, G. Dehaes, E. Hoskins, J. Laaouej, M. Passey, S. Qaderi, S. Shuqaidef, M. C. Smith, et al.
1992 Effect of the Gulf War on infant and child mortality in Iraq. *New England Journal of Medicine* 327(13):931–936.

Badawi, A. A.
2004 The social dimension of globalization and health. *Perspectives on Global Development and Technology* 3(1–2):73–90.

Brookings Institution
  2007, November 29   *The Iraq Index: Tracking Variables of Reconstruction and Security in Post-Saddam Iraq.* Washington, DC: Brookings Institution.
  2008, November 6   *The Iraq Index: Tracking Variables of Reconstruction and Security in Post-Saddam Iraq.* Washington, DC: Brookings Institution.

Buckley, C., and M. R. Gordon
  2007, November 19   U.S. says attacks in Iraq fell to the level of February 2006. *New York Times,* A1, A6.

Burnham, G., R. Lafta, S. Doocy, and L. Roberts
  2006   Mortality after the 2003 invasion of Iraq: A cross-sectional cluster sample survey. *Lancet* 368(9545):1421–1428.

Calhoun, C.
  2004   A world of emergencies: Fear, intervention, and the limits of cosmopolitan order. *Canadian Review of Sociology and Anthropology* 41(4):373–395.

Chikanda, A.
  2006   Skilled health professionals' migration and its impact on health delivery in Zimbabwe. *Journal of Ethnic and Migration Studies* 32(4):667–80.

Curie, C. G.
  2006   Health diplomacy in action: Helping Iraq rebuild its mental health system. *Journal of Muslim Mental Health* 1(2):109–116.

Daponte, B. O.
  2007   Wartime estimates of Iraqi civilian casualties. *International Review of the Red Cross* 89(868):943–957.

Docena, H.
  2007   Free market by force: The making and un-making of a neo-liberal Iraq. *International Journal of Contemporary Iraqi Studies* 1(2):123–142.

Dobson, R.
  2000   Sanctions against Iraq "double" child mortality. *British Medical Journal* 321(7275):1490.

Farrell, S., and R. A. Oppel Jr.
    2008, June 21   Big gains for Iraq security, but questions linger. *New York Times*, A1, A7.

Fund for Peace and Foreign Policy Magazine
    2008, July/August   *The Failed States Index*. Online: http://www.foreign policy.com/story/cms.php?story_id=4350. Accessed July 30, 2008.

Galbraith, P. W.
    2008   Is this a "victory"? *New York Review of Books* 55(16). Online: http://www.nybooks.com/articles/21935. Accessed October 15, 2008.

Garfield, R.
    1999   *The Impact of Economic Sanctions on Health and Well-Being*. London, UK: Relief and Rehabilitation Network, Overseas Development Institute.

Garfield, R., and C. S. Leu
    2000   A multivariate method for estimating mortality rates among children under 5 years from health and social indicators in Iraq. *International Journal of Epidemiology* 29:510–515.

Gupta, S., B. Clements, R. Bhattacharya, and S. Chakravarti
    2002   The elusive peace dividend. *Finance and Development* 39(4):49–51.

Hagopian, A., A. Ofosu, A. Fatusi, R. Biritwum, A. Essel, L. G. Hart, and C. Watts
    2005   The flight of physicians from West Africa: Views of African physicians and implications for policy. *Social Science and Medicine* 61:1750–1760.

Harding, S.
    2007   Man-made disaster and development: The case of Iraq. *International Social Work* 50(3):295–306.

Harper, A.
    2008   Iraq's refugees: Ignored and unwanted. *International Review of the Red Cross* 90(869):169–190.

Hicks, M. H.
    2006   *Mortality after the 2003 Invasion of Iraq: Were Valid and Ethical Field Methods Used in This Survey?* Households in Conflict Network Research Design Note 3. Essex: Institute of Development Studies, University of Essex.

Hiltermann, J. R.
    1991   Assessing the damage in Iraq. *Journal of Palestine Studies* 20(4):109–
            114.

Hosin, A. A., S. Moore, and C. Gaitanou
    2006   The relationship between psychological well-being and adjustment of
            both parents and children of exiled and traumatized Iraqi refugees.
            Journal of Muslim Mental Health 1(2):123–136.

Humaidi, N. S.
    2006   Resettlement prospects for inpatients at Al Rashad Mental Hospital.
            Journal of Muslim Mental Health 1(2):177–183.

Inhorn, M. C.
    2008   Medical anthropology against war. *Medical Anthropology Quarterly*
            22(4):416–424.

International Catholic Migration Commission
    2008   *Iraqi Refugees in Syria.* Washington, DC: International Catholic
            Migration Commission.

International Committee of the Red Cross.
    2007   *Iraq: Civilians without Protection. The Ever-Worsening Humanitarian
            Crisis in Iraq.* Geneva: International Committee of the Red Cross.
    2008   *Iraq: No Let Up in the Humanitarian Crisis.* Geneva: International
            Committee of the Red Cross.

International Crisis Group
    2008a   *Failed responsibility: Iraqi refugees in Syria, Jordan and Lebanon.* Brus-
            sels: International Crisis Group.
    2008b   *Oil for Soil: Toward a Grand Bargain on Iraq and the Kurds.* Kirkuk:
            International Crisis Group.

International Organization for Migration
    2008a   *Assessment on Psychosocial Needs of Iraqis Displaced in Jordan and Leba-
            non.* Amman: International Organization for Migration.
    2008b   *IDP Working Group: Internally Displaced Persons in Iraq—Update
            (June 2008).* New York: International Organization for Migration.

Iraq Body Count
    2009   Online: http://www.iraqbodycount.org/about. Accessed April 15,
            2009.

Iraq Family Health Survey Study Group
2008   Violence-related mortality in Iraq from 2002 to 2006. *New England Journal of Medicine* 358(5):484–493.

Juhasz, A.
2006   *The Bush Agenda: Invading the World, One Economy at a Time.* New York: ReganBooks.

Kami, A.
2008   Iraq tries to attract back doctors who fled violence. *Reuters News Service.* Online: http://www.reuters.com/article/featuredCrisis/idUSKAM 630998. Accessed June 30, 2008.

Keen, D.
2008   *Complex Emergencies.* Malden, MA: Polity Press.

Klein, N.
2007   *The Shock Doctrine: The Rise of Disaster Capitalism.* New York: Metropolitan Books.

Krause, K., and D. Mutimer
2005   Introduction. In *Small Arms Survey.* Geneva: Graduate Institute of International Studies.

Libal, K., and S. Harding
In press   Challenging U.S. silence: International NGOs and the Iraqi refugee crisis. In *International Migration and Human Rights: The Global Repercussions of U.S. Policy*, edited by S. Martinez. Berkeley: University of California Press.

Lubkemann, S. C.
2008   *Culture in Chaos: An Anthropology of the Social Condition of War.* Chicago: University of Chicago Press.

Marfleet, P.
2007   Iraqi refugees: "Exit" from the state. *International Journal of Contemporary Iraqi Studies* 1(3):397–419.

Mattei, U., and L. Nader
2008   *Plunder: When the Rule of Law Is Illegal.* Malden, MA: Blackwell.

Medact
2004   *Enduring Effects of War: Health in Iraq 2004.* London: Medact.
2008   *Rehabilitation under Fire: Health Care in Iraq, 2003–2007.* London: Medact.

NGO Coordination Committee in Iraq and Oxfam International
2007   *Rising to the Humanitarian Challenge in Iraq: Briefing Paper 105.* London: Oxfam International.

Nordstrom, C.
2004   *Shadows of War: Violence, Power, and International Profiteering in the Twenty-First Century.* Berkeley: University of California Press.

Opinion Research Business
2008   *Analysis "confirms" 1 million + Iraq casualties.* Online: http://www .opinion.co.uk/Documents/Revised%20Casulaty%20Data%20-% 20Press%20release.doc. Accessed February 15, 2008.

Oppel, R. A., Jr.
2006, November 11   Qaeda official is said to taunt U.S. on tape. *New York Times*, A8.

Pedersen, J.
2007   Three wars later: Iraqi living conditions. In *Iraq: Preventing a New Generation of Conflict*, edited by M. E. Bouillon, D. M. Malone, and B. Rowswell, 55–70. Boulder, CO: Lynne Rienner.

Phillips, D. L.
2005   *Losing Iraq: Inside the Postwar Reconstruction Fiasco.* Boulder, CO: Westview Press.

Popal, G. R.
2000   Impact of sanctions on the population of Iraq. *Eastern Mediterranean Health Journal* 6(4):791–795.

Rawaf, S.
2005   The health crisis in Iraq. *Critical Public Health* 15(2):181–188.

Roberts, L., R. Lafta, R. Garfield, J. Khudhairi, and G. Burnham
2004   Mortality before and after the 2003 invasion of Iraq: Cluster sample survey. *Lancet* 364(9448):1857–1864.

Sassoon, J.
2009   *The Iraqi Refugees: The New Crisis in the Middle East.* New York:
       I. B. Tauris.

Save the Children
2007   *State of the World's Mothers 2007: Saving the Lives of Children under 5.*
       Westport, CT: Save the Children.

Scheper-Hughes, N., and P. Bourgois
2004   *Violence in War and Peace: An Anthology.* Malden, MA: Wiley-Black-
       well.

Special Inspector General for Iraq Reconstruction
2008   *Quarterly Report to the United States Congress, April 30, 2008.* Wash-
       ington, DC: Special Inspector General for Iraq Reconstruction.

Steele, J., and S. Goldenberg
2008, March 19   What is the real death toll in Iraq? *The Guardian.* Online:
       http://www.guardian.co.uk/world/2008/mar/19/iraq. Accessed June
       30, 2008.

Susman, T.
2007, April 25   U.N. Report and Times data paint grim Iraq picture.
       Los Angeles Times. Online: http://fairuse.100webcustomers.com/fair
       enough/latimes965.html. Accessed April 27, 2007.

Susskind, Y.
2007   *Promising Democracy, Imposing Theocracy: Gender-Based Violence and
       the U.S. War on Iraq.* New York: MADRE.

Tirman, J.
2008, February 14   Counting Iraqi casualties—and a media controversy.
       Editor and Publisher. Online: http://www.nonviolentworm.org/
       FeaturedArticle/CountingIraqiCasualties. Accessed November 1,
       2008.

United Nations Assistance Mission for Iraq
2007a *Human Rights Report 1 November–31 December 2006.* New York:
       United Nations Assistance Mission for Iraq.
2007b *Humanitarian Briefing on the Crisis in Iraq.* New York: United Na-
       tions Assistance Mission for Iraq.

2007c *Humanitarian Crisis in Iraq: Facts and Figures.* New York: United
       Nations Assistance Mission for Iraq.

United Nations Children's Fund
1998   *Situation Analysis of Children and Women in Iraq.* New York: United
       Nations Children's Fund.
2007   *Immediate Needs for Iraqi Children in Iraq and Neighbouring Countries.*
       Geneva: United Nations Children's Fund.
2008a *Sanitation Becoming a Luxury in Iraq.* New York: United Na-
       tions Children's Fund. Online: http://www.unicef.org/media/media_
       43307.html. Accessed April 1, 2008.
2008b *Update for Partners on the Situation of Children in Iraq, First Quarter
       2008.* Geneva: United Nations Children's Fund.

United Nations Development Program
2002   *Living Conditions in Iraq.* New York: United Nations Development
       Program.
2008   *Human Development Report: Iraq 2007/2008.* New York: United Na-
       tions Development Program.

United Nations High Commissioner for Refugees
2008   *Assessment on Returns to Iraq amongst the Iraqi Refugee Population
       in Syria.* Geneva: United Nations High Commissioner for Refu-
       gees.

United Nations World Food Program
2003   *The Extent and Geographic Distribution of Chronic Poverty in Iraq's
       Center/South Region.* New York: United Nations World Food Pro-
       gram.
2004   *Baseline Food Security Analysis in Iraq.* New York: United Nations
       World Food Program.

United Nations World Food Program/Central Organization for Statistics and
Information Technology
2006   *Food Security and Vulnerability Analysis in Iraq.* Baghdad: United Na-
       tions World Food Program/Central Organization for Statistics and
       Information Technology.

World Health Organization
 2008   *Iraq.* Online: www.who.int/countries/irq/en. Accessed May 28, 2008.

Yong, J., and J. V. Millen, eds.
 2000   *Dying for Growth: Global Inequality and the Health of the Poor.* Monroe, ME: Common Courage Press.

CHAPTER THREE

CHILDREN AND REVOLUTION

Mental Health and Psychosocial Well-Being of Child Soldiers in Nepal

Brandon A. Kohrt, Wietse A. Tol,
Judith Pettigrew, and Rohit Karki

"I was thirteen years old when I joined the Party," Asha, a girl from a Dalit "untouchable" Hindu caste in southern Nepal, said describing how she became associated with the Maoist People's Liberation Army (PLA). "I was born into a poor family." She pointed to a few pounds of cornmeal and then the one buffalo outside her thatched hut. "We just have this much, nothing more." She continued, "I was a very good student [but] after I took my exams for fifth grade my parents told me: 'We are very poor, we have no money so you have to leave school and take care of your brothers and sister.'. . . Then, I left school." Asha's parents had forced her to leave school after fifth grade so that they could send her brothers to school.

Maoist women frequently visited Asha's home and told her to join them rather than stay at home doing nothing. They told her that Maoist woman and men were equal, and they promised her an opportunity to continue her studies if she joined the PLA. A few months later, Asha attended a Maoist cultural program and was impressed by the rhetoric. "Both sons and daughters should be treated equally, the Maoist leaders said. Husbands and wives should work together, too. . . . From that day, I didn't want to go back to my house." Believing that the Maoists were her only option for a future beyond domestic servitude, Asha, a slight girl of barely over four feet tall, left home to join the armed struggle.

During her time with the Maoists, Asha states that she was well treated, and the leaders encouraged her interest in art, enlisting her talents in painting propaganda signs. She encountered only one battle but also saw a number of comrades killed. After more than one year in the PLA, Asha returned home for a brief visit to see her family. On arrival, her mother immediately married her to a man from a distant community to prevent her from returning to the Maoists. She was 14, and he was 22 years old.

Asha describes her marriage as endless abuse and suffering. She was raped throughout the marriage by her husband and beaten by her in-laws. After two years of this abuse, Asha attempted suicide. Her father-in-law caught her hanging from the ceiling. He cut her down, handed her the rope, and said, "Go home and kill yourself." Then he kicked her out of the house. Asha now lives once again with her mother. She wept, concluding her life story, "Maybe if I hadn't joined the Maoists, my parents wouldn't have forced me to marry, and I wouldn't have had such a life of suffering. At 13 years old, what do you know? You just don't understand" (Koenig and Kohrt 2009; Koirala 2007).

The ethnographic analysis that follows analyzes the psychosocial well-being of child soldiers, their recruitment into armed groups, their types of participation and exposure within an armed group, and their experiences on returning home. We integrate the ecological-transactional model of child development and its attention to the microsocial-level ties with the critical medical anthropological attention to the macrosocial-level political economy. Although the ecological-transactional model suggests that children's participation in armed conflict grants them some agency on the micro-level, this agency is unbalanced and has serious long-term consequences for health and well-being. The data and our analysis indicate that since mental health is a social process, social scientific attention and political remedies should be sought on the level of its political-economic determinants, that is, on social rather than the individual level.

Background

One of the most pressing issues in global conflict is the exploitation of children by armed groups. An estimated 300,000 children across the globe are members of state militaries and other armed groups (United Nations Children's Fund [UNICEF] 2003:4). The 2007 Paris Principles refer to child soldiers as "children associated with armed forces or armed groups" meeting the following criteria:

Any person below 18 years of age who is or who has been recruited or used by an armed force or armed group in any capacity, including but not limited to . . . fighters, cooks, porters, messengers, spies or for sexual purposes. It does not only refer to a child who is taking or has taken a direct part in hostilities. (UNICEF 2007:7)

Following this characterization, we define "children" as individuals less than 18 years of age. However, we acknowledge that local definitions of "children" vary within and between cultural groups. Although armed groups used children throughout history, the widespread availability of small arms has made it physically possible for children to participate in a more lethal manner and thus be of greater value to armed groups (Wessells 2006).

The Hollywood image and those that some organizations employ to raise funds to support intervention programs for former child soldiers depict rogue armed groups violently tearing children away from idyllic family settings (Wessells 2006). The story continues that these haphazard militias shatter children's lives through the dehumanizing experiences of war, drugs, and crime, leading to severe psychological trauma and disability. Recovery and rehabilitation can be achieved through reunification with the children's families. Although such portrayals are accurate in some cases, the experience of child soldiers is a far more varied and complex picture (Betancourt et al. 2008; Wessells 2006).

Contexts that promote recruiting children into armed groups are the result of larger national and international processes that produce local vulnerability. Poverty, gender and ethnic discrimination, and legacies of state-sponsored violence create circumstances in which children voluntarily join armed groups. Asha, in contrast to the typical media representation of child soldiers, voluntarily joined a highly organized revolutionary force that claimed to practice gender equality (cf. Pettigrew and Shneiderman 2004; Yami 2007). Moreover, she considered the return home to be the most damaging part of her life, not her involvement in an armed group.

Research that pursues a more realistic and nuanced picture of child soldiers and the political, social, and economic processes that drive recruitment of minors is crucial for two reasons: first, to develop the most effective policy and advocacy to end the conscription of children into armed forces, and, second, to address the mental health and psychosocial needs of child soldiers. While it might be assumed that removing a child from an armed group is the best approach, it is not a panacea to ensure psychosocial well-being. The very focus of *reintegration* programs operates with an assumption that former child soldiers were previously *integrated* into their communities. In reality, some child soldiers join armed groups because they feel excluded from society. Moreover, the tremendous variation in exposure to traumatic events during involvement with armed groups and in resilience among child soldiers throws into question whether psychological trauma is a universal response (Wessells 2006).

Setting

Nepal is a landlocked country north of India and south of the Tibetan autonomous region of China, with a population of almost 28 million. Nepal's history represents a legacy of political, economic, and cultural processes that have marginalized large sectors of the population who recently have become the backbone of the Maoist revolution. Nepal ranks 142nd on the human development index—near the bottom of the medium human development category (United Nations Development Program 2007). This rank conceals strong inequalities by region (e.g., in agricultural production), gender (e.g., in literacy), and urban versus rural areas (e.g., in infant mortality) (Government of Nepal 2007). Thirty-one percent of the population lives below the poverty line. Moreover, Nepal has the highest income gap between rich and poor in Asia with the Gini coefficient having increased from 0.34 to 0.41 in the past decade (World Bank 2007). The population consists of more than 60 ethnic and caste groups, with a long history of hegemonic dominance by the Hindu high castes (Brahman and Chhetri) of minority ethnic groups (Janajati, who are predominantly Buddhist and shamanist) and also of those deemed to be low caste (Dalit). Although some of Nepal's ethnic groups have rejected caste ideology, no group has remained uninfluenced by it.

Nepal was unified as a Hindu monarchy in 1769. Against the backdrop of the autocratic Rana regime, the Communist Party of Nepal (CPN) was founded in Kolkata, India, in 1949. From the 1960s through 1980s, the CPN split into multiple factions that were involved in the fight for a multiparty democracy (Hachhethu 2002; Hoftun et al. 1999:238).

In 1990, Nepal became a multiparty democratic Hindu monarchy. The CPN, which formed in 1991 and included Prachanda and Babu Ram Bhattarai, rejected a November 1990 constitution promulgated by the king, referring to it as an inadequate basis for genuine democracy. The organization continued to demand a constituent assembly, the formation of a plan to draft a new democratic constitution, and eventually the formation of a People's Republic of Nepal (Karki and Seddon 2003). In 1994, the CPN divided into two parties: the CPN (Unity Center) and the Maoist Party (CPN [M]). The latter Maoist Party, headed by Prachanda, boycotted the elections.

In January 1996, Babu Ram Bhattarai presented a 40-point demand on behalf of CPN (M) to the Nepali government headed by the Nepali Congress party leader Sher Bahadur Deuba. The points dealt largely with rectifying economic and social injustice, abolishing monarchy, and establishing a constituent assembly and have been described by several non-partisan commentators in terms such as "reasonable and not dissimilar in spirit to the election manifestos of mainstream parties" (Thapa 2004:53). Bhattarai insisted that if no progress were made toward fulfillment of the demands by February 17, 1996, there would be no choice but to resort to armed struggle against the state. When these demands were not addressed, the CPN (M) went underground and began its agrarian revolution. On February 13, 1996 (four days before expiration of their deadline), the CPN (M) declared a People's War in Nepal, issuing a leaflet that called on the people of Nepal to "march along the path of the People's War to smash the reactionary state and establish a new democratic state." Violence commenced with the CPN (M) attacking police posts and a state-owned agricultural development bank.

Over 13,000 people were killed during the People's War, with the majority of deaths at the hands of the Royal Nepal Army and the government's police force (Mehta 2005). The war ended in November 2006, when the CPN (M) signed a peace treaty with the government, leading to the inclusion of the CPN (M) in the national government. During the April 2008 elections, the CPN (M) won a relative majority and now occupies the major posts in government.

During the war, children were recruited into the CPN (M)'s PLA and the Royal Nepal Army as soldiers, sentries, spies, cooks, and porters (Human Rights Watch 2007). Local groups estimate that at the conclusion of the war, approximately 9,000 members—one-third of the PLA—consisted of 14- to 18-year-olds with 40 percent being girls (Human Rights Watch 2007), and an even greater percentage of PLA soldiers now over the age of 18 years likely had joined before they were 18. Ten percent of the Royal Nepal Army during the conflict was under the age of 18 (Singh 2004).

Theoretical Approach

The social determinants of health model of critical medical anthropology (CMA) (Baer et al. 2003) and the ecological-transactional model of child development (Bronfenbrenner 1979) are complementary. Within the CMA theoretical model, the *macrosocial level* represents the institutions, structure of social relationships, and processes that drive socially patterned experience. This level, known as the macrosystem in the ecological-transactional model, includes economic, manufacturing, and corporate institutions that dictate employment availability and create niches of poverty (Cicchetti and Lynch 1993). In the work of Baer et al. (2003), elements of the macrosocial level include corporations and the medical-industrial complex.

The *intermediate social level* represents the institutions that translate global and national processes into regional variations in experience. The intermediate social level, also described as the exosystem, comprises the "formal and informal social structures that make up the immediate environment in which children and families function," such as neighborhoods, social support groups, and employers (Cicchetti et al. 2000:697). In the CMA model, this includes hospitals, pharmaceutical companies, and community clinics (Baer et al. 2003).

The *microsocial level* is the domain of immediate experience, which, in transaction with the individual, shapes experience through the amount of agency and/or resources an individual mobilizes. Belsky (1980) considers this level, named the microsystem in Bronfenbrenner's scheme, the family environment. Cicchetti et al. (2000) extend "the conceptualization of the microsystem to include any environmental setting that contains the developing person," including the home, school, and workplace. Baer et al. (2003) define the microsocial level as the interactions within the health care system between patients and physicians, medical translators, and nurses.

The *individual level* reflects children's different histories, personalities, and psychobiological states. This ontogenetic development examines how developmental history and genetic composition contribute to behavior and health through interactions with the social and physical environment (Cicchetti and Lynch 1993).

Many researchers have employed the ecological-transactional model to understand the well-being of children exposed to violence (cf. Belsky 1980; Cicchetti and Lynch 1993), including political violence (cf. Betancourt 2005; Tol et al. 2009). We propose that the synthesis of this ecological-transactional approach with the CMA social determinants model elucidates the multicausal reasons for why children are recruited into fighting forces as well as the psychosocial consequences of being a child soldier.

Methods

In our research, we employed a mixed-methods approach with qualitative and quantitative tools to understand the mental health and psychosocial consequences of children's participation in armed groups. Three of the authors (Kohrt, Karki, and Tol), working with a Nepali nongovernmental organization (NGO), Transcultural Psychosocial Organization (TPO) Nepal, conducted a study in 2007 of mental health and psychosocial needs among former child soldiers reintegrating into civilian communities. The qualitative component of the larger study included participatory approaches (with a technique known as Child Led Indicators, in which children developed their own psychosocial indicators of distress and well-being), narrative focus group discussions (*N* = 25 groups) with children and community members, key informant interviews (*N* = 152) with children and community members, and case studies (*N* = 8) of child soldiers. Study participants were identified through local NGOs involved in child protection (for a full description of the study selection process, see Kohrt et al. 2008). We highlight three of these case studies in our analysis (pseudonyms are used for all child case studies presented).

Data were gathered by a Nepali research team employed by TPO Nepal with a background in field research who received a monthlong training session on qualitative and quantitative data collection as well as on the ethics of research with vulnerable children. All interviews were translated into English and analyzed using Atlas.ti with a codebook developed by three independent coders (intercoder agreement: percent agreement = 0.90, Cohen's κ = 0.82). The qualitative data were further contextualized by drawing on Pettigrew's long-term ethnographic research in central Nepal, dating back to 1990 (Pettigrew 2003, 2004, 2007; Pettigrew and Shneiderman 2004). An additional source of information was interviews conducted for the ethnographic documentary film *Returned: Child Soldiers of Nepal's Maoist Army* (Koenig and Kohrt 2009) that were reviewed employing the codes developed for the primary study. The quantitative psychosocial epidemiological study was an assessment of 142 child soldiers and 142 matched children who were never conscripted by armed groups (Kohrt et al. 2008). We employed instruments developed in Nepal—some developed by former child soldiers—or adapted for use in Nepal using a standardized transcultural translation process (for a full description of instruments and psychometrics, see Kohrt et al. 2008).

Experiences of Child Soldiers

Joining the PLA

As described in the introduction to this chapter, Asha identified herself as voluntarily joining the Maoists at the age of 13 to pursue an education and also to escape poverty and gender discrimination in the home. The two cases presented here depict other motivations for children to become Maoists. Raj, also a Dalit, is a boy from the western hills of Nepal who was conscripted at 14 years of age. Shova, a Chhetri (high caste) girl from the southern plains of far-western Nepal, joined at 13 years old and spent three years with the PLA:

> In 2003. . . my father was plowing his field. Maoist boys and girls and their commander came and started beating my father so badly that he almost died. My father was innocent, but they said he had spoken against the Maoists. . . . I was so helpless. I could not do anything for my father because I was scared that the Maoists would kill me. My father lost consciousness. The Maoists came into our house and threatened to kill my father if I did not go with them. I told them that I wanted to continue my schooling, but they did not listen to me. I was forced to go with them. . . . I was only fourteen at that time. They took me . . . and I started training in their army. ("Raj" from Kohrt and Karki 2007)

I was thirteen years old. I was a very shy girl who wouldn't speak with people other than my mother. . . . In our village, people used to come to ask my hand in marriage even when I was very young. Even a mention of marriage gave me a headache. I hated it! I wanted to avoid marriage in any way possible. . . . I have a slightly older friend in the village. Against her will, her father married her off at a young age. She was miserable. She often said she would go to India or join the Maoists. She would die there, if need be. At least, she would be free from marriage. Like her, liberation was what I needed. At the time, many Maoist activities used to take place in our village. . . . I liked their cultural program. Very entertaining! What a wonderful life—I would often think—I would have if I became a Maoist. I would get to travel a lot and wouldn't have to be forced into marriage. Besides, I would also have a lot of friends! ("Shova" from Adhikari and Shrestha 2007)

Experiences during Participation in Armed Groups

The experiences of children during their association with the Maoist forces varied tremendously. While some children were in the military wing, children also were cooks, porters, spies, sentries, messengers, and performers in Maoist propaganda cultural programs. In our study, we found that children assumed multiple roles within the Maoist forces: 21 percent of the children conscripted by Maoists were part of the PLA, 47 percent were cooks, 35 percent were porters, 54 percent were sentries, 12 percent were spies, and 39 percent took part in cultural programs (total percentage is greater than 100 because of assuming multiple roles). However, as the following cases illustrate, the role alone did not determine a child's experience during association with the Maoists. Rather, each child was impacted differently based on the interaction of the personal life history, which they brought into their identity as a soldier, combined with variation in exposure and opportunity during participation.

Asha described her experience with the Maoists as generally positive. She especially enjoyed the opportunity to engage her artistic talents:

They taught me painting and writing. I distributed papers, printed pamphlets, and painted slogans throughout the villages. They liked me. They treated me well. . . . They taught me how to deliver speeches. They would encourage me to speak like them. . . . They didn't tell us anything about the Party's principles. They would tell me to speak with everyone the way they did. ("Asha" from Koenig and Kohrt 2009)

Raj reported a very different experience. During his involvement, a young comrade accidentally shot Raj in the leg. In another battle, Raj's friend was killed. The most painful memory from his war experience was his inability to give water to this dying friend:

> When I was with the Maoist armed forces, there were clashes from both sides and I feared all the time that I might get killed by the government army. . . . We had four young girls with us. When we were going to another village, the government army surprised us. They captured us and took two young girls from our group. They raped them, cut them with knives, poured chili powder in their wounds, and then killed them. We ran away, otherwise they would have killed us, too. . . . Many of my friends were dying, but I was so helpless that I could not do anything for them. . . . I still get scared and sweat when I think of that day. I cannot do any work if I think of that day. I get very disturbed and want to be just by myself in a quiet place. I need to keep myself busy to forget about that day. . . . When I think of those events, I still get very scared. I do not even want to think about those for a second. ("Raj" from Kohrt and Karki 2007)

Shova, in contrast to Raj, reports initial difficulties which were overcome through her perseverance. The experience allowed her to find an identity as an activist for women's rights:

> At first, I felt lonely because I didn't have friends. I couldn't mingle with people. Soon after, however, 15–16 other girls from my village also came to the Party. So eventually things were alright. At the beginning, I couldn't speak much, but slowly I improved. . . . Whenever there were at least two to four people, we used to practice our oratory skills. One person would play the chairperson, the other the guest, the third the audience, and the fourth, the speaker. . . . They got me involved in the women's organization. There, my job was to mobilize women. . . . Although I didn't miss home too much, I often regretted dropping out from school. . . . But as time passed, I adapted to the environment and gained a lot of political knowledge. Then I became actively involved in uniting women ("Shova" from Adhikari and Shrestha 2007)

Experiences of Return to and Reintegration
into the Civilian Community

As described in the introduction to this chapter, the abuse Asha suffered at the hands of her husband and in-laws after returning from the Maoists eventually led to a suicide attempt and being kicked out of her husband's house. Asha now lives in her parents' two-room hut but has little life beyond that. She describes that it is difficult to talk with or be with others. Asha says that these problems started after she was married and abused by her husband and his family. She wants to live alone:

> I didn't feel like coming home either. My mother told me that I made a mistake by leaving my husband. I always get nightmares. I feel as if somebody is threatening to kill me. I feel as if someone is yelling at me. I find myself terrified at times, but don't know why. Nowadays, I am passing time by doing household work, weeping, and thinking too much. I have no friends, and the friends I used to have do not talk with me. I think my life is worthless. Some people say that I am an unnecessary burden for my mother. Society does not try to understand my feelings. Why has god written such a fate on me? ("Asha" from Koirala 2007)

Raj, similarly, describes difficulties after returning home. He struggles with his inability to obtain employment, which he attributes to his caste status—a statement that echoes Maoist rhetoric about caste-based exclusion from economic opportunities. In addition, Raj, who is a traditional shamanic healer (*dhami-jhanki*), says that he is afflicted by uncontrollable possessions and can no longer heal people after his activities with the Maoists:

> Just yesterday, villagers were having a discussion about giving me a guard job in the community forest near my house, but they rejected my request for the position. I thought that if I would have that work, I would earn some money, and it would help me to run my family. They did not hire me because I am Dalit. . . . People do not give us an opportunity to participate in village activities because we are low caste. . . . When I was with the Maoists, I had to carry dead bodies and I started being possessed in a way I could not control. (Kohrt and Karki 2007)

Shova, in contrast, describes positively her life after returning despite some regrets. She reports how she uses her newfound talents for speech making and mobilization on behalf of the historically mainstream Communist Party, the Communist Party of Nepal (United Marxist Leninist Party) (CPN [UML]):

> First of all, I lost my education. I joined the Party when I was thirteen, at a time when I should have been going to school. . . . My friends who continued their studies have done well. But because I dropped out early, I feel I have lost an important part of my future. To do any job, one needs a good education or knowledge of English, both of which I lack. So when I think of my future, I feel sad. . . . [However,] the community here is very supportive. Although I had shocked them initially by joining the insurgency, they said I had done a good thing by returning home at last. They encouraged me to go back to school. They said I should do good things now that I was back. . . . Although they were not able to help me in material terms, they have given me their emotional support. . . . I have become capable of mobilizing women politically. For that reason, and also because I am able to speak up for women's rights, I have become a leader of the District Women's Organization of the UML ("Shova" from Adhikari and Shrestha 2007).

Child Soldiers' Experiences in a Broader Context

The case narratives of Asha, Raj, and Shova illustrate variation in experiences. The challenge is to place them within broader social, cultural, economic, and political context.

Push and Pull Factors

The social determinants that drive children to join armed groups are known as "push factors" (Somasundaram 2002). The macrosocial-level push factors involved in these cases include discrimination and marginalization resulting from a feudal legacy that concentrated wealth and political power among local elites based in Kathmandu, gender-based discrimination, and the marginalization of low castes and ethnic minorities (see figure 3.1). This has deprived many groups of education and full participation in the political process (Thapa 2005). At the intermediate social level, push factors include the failure to enforce child protection policies such as the ban on child marriages and the destabilization of communi-

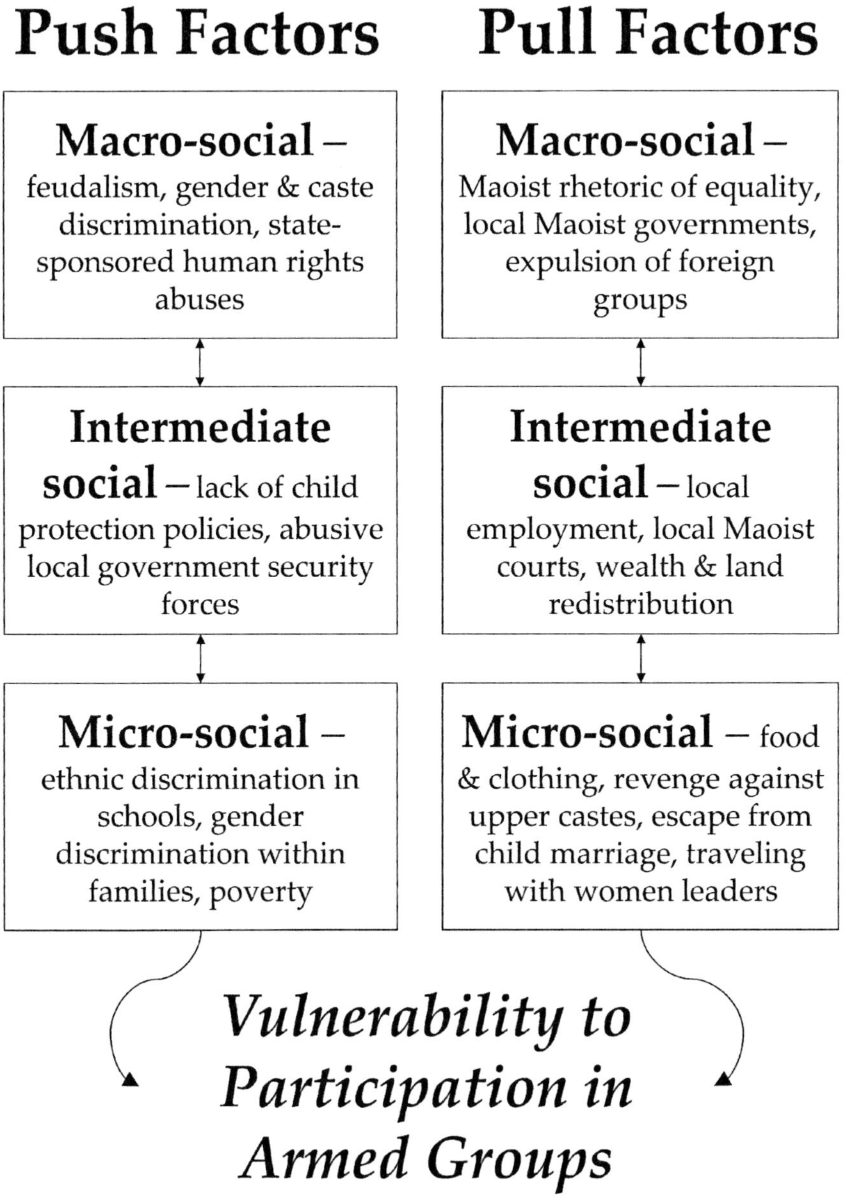

Push Factors   # Pull Factors

Macro-social – feudalism, gender & caste discrimination, state-sponsored human rights abuses	**Macro-social –** Maoist rhetoric of equality, local Maoist governments, expulsion of foreign groups
Intermediate social – lack of child protection policies, abusive local government security forces	**Intermediate social** – local employment, local Maoist courts, wealth & land redistribution
Micro-social – ethnic discrimination in schools, gender discrimination within families, poverty	**Micro-social** – food & clothing, revenge against upper castes, escape from child marriage, traveling with women leaders

Vulnerability to Participation in Armed Groups

Figure 3.1.   Social determinants of child conscription in armed groups.

ties by government security forces through widespread state-sanctioned human rights violations (Lykke and Timilsena 2002). Microsocial-level factors included local manifestations of the previously mentioned factors reflected in local historical, political, and ethnic tensions (cf. Shneiderman 2003) and other experiences of marginalization.

Maoist recruitment strategies, that is, "pull factors," draw on individual experiences that occur within a specific microsocial context. For example, the women's Maoist group that recruited Asha presented the macrosocial ideology of gender equality as an escape from her home situation. Shova also saw the Maoists as an escape from the ill fate of being forced into an arranged marriage as a teenager. In Shova's case, her friendship was probably an important microlevel factor. For children that were exposed to sexual violence at the hands of police or army, joining the Maoist army afforded an opportunity to take revenge on the perpetrators and to work toward a new country where there would be a Maoist-led security and justice system. For children who wanted to be part of the political process, joining the Maoists was a pathway that would result eventually in a government post in the "New Nepal" society. One of the more powerful elements of Maoist recruitment, however, was simply the promise of a good time in which children could travel the country singing and dancing or learning karate. The Maoists channeled these recreational tasks into cultural propaganda programs. Thus, Maoist recruitment met individual drives that reflected macrosocial forces within a microsocial context.

The positionality of a child in relation to these push and pull factors has important consequences for psychosocial well-being. For Asha and Shova, the push factors focused on escaping repressive environments for girls, and the pull factors were opportunities for women to assume roles of power and autonomy within the Maoists. In contrast, Raj did not describe push factors driving him away from his home and village. Instead, it was the acute and violent pull factor of the Maoists threatening to kill his father. Thus, mental health problems for Raj were personally attributed to the association with the Maoists, whereas for Asha, her mental health problems are not described in relation to time spent with the Maoists.

Furthermore, agency at the microsocial level of a family dictates susceptibility to Maoist pull factors. In our larger sample, we found that children who report being forcefully conscripted generally are those in the most vulnerable positions because of the marginalization of their families in the broader community context. Forcibly recruited children were distinguished from voluntary recruits by higher levels of family poverty. Among the poorest families, giving up a child was seen as the only option to meet Maoist demands. A resident of western Nepal explained, "Those who have money have to give them cash, those who have food have to give them rice, those who have clothes have to give them clothes, and those who have nothing have to give them one member of their family" (quoted in Ogura 2004:123–124).

These findings illustrate that participation, whether it be self-reported as voluntary or forced, of children within armed groups follows a predictable pattern based on the restriction of power and agency from the macrosocial all the way to the individual level in Nepali society. Understanding these power differentials is a first step to considering how to reduce the vulnerability of children to conscription in armed groups.

Unbalanced Agency

While push and pull factors interpreted in light of macrosocial through individual processes helps elucidate the process of recruitment, we propose the term "unbalanced agency" to understand the experience of child soldiers during association with armed groups and consequent impact on well-being. Unbalanced agency refers to the discrepancy between the benefits that children gain through participation in armed groups and the risks associated with this engagement. Many children we interviewed described some form of positive aspects about association with the Maoists. However, these came at the cost of loss of life or limb.

The benefits of participation described by Asha and Shova and echoed by other child soldiers highlighted "learning to speak better." Children also described the benefits of being able to travel around the country, to learn more about Nepal, its people, and its history. Both the rhetorical skills and travel throughout the country represented agency within the sociopolitical realm. For many, this was the first time they felt part of larger sociopolitical processes from which they had been excluded in their communities. Children could engage in political debates and display knowledge of the country outside their village; these were traits previously monopolized by elite males. It was a pathway of connecting with modernity, which had been previously the province of urban youth (Pettigrew 2003). The presence of these and other benefits may explain, in part, why child soldiers did not differ from never-conscripted children in our study on measures of positive psychosocial well-being. Child soldiers and never-conscripted children had the same levels of hope (a measure addressing children's ability to think of and exercise solutions to problems encountered) and prosocial behavior (a measure addressing children's positive social interaction with others).

Despite some degree of reported increased agency attributed to being a Maoist soldier, this autonomy was far from complete. Although there may have been fewer gender- and caste-based restrictions, overall daily actions were dictated by Maoist commanders, not by children's individual wishes. Whereas 54 percent of child soldiers said that they joined voluntarily, only 17 percent of the child soldiers said that they had control over their daily actions within the Maoists. Many children who joined voluntarily later felt disillusioned when the rhetoric of empowerment and freedom did not match the reality inside the PLA. And nearly all children forcibly conscripted did not report increased personal agency; they felt that they were used as "slave laborers."

The greatest imbalance in agency associated with joining the Maoists was the threat to life. Raj's account demonstrates the serious risks associated with being a child soldier. Moreover, although the majority of children—both civilians and soldiers—were exposed to life-threatening events during the war, the burden was considerably greater among child soldiers (Kohrt et al. 2008). Child soldiers on average were exposed to 2.54 life-threatening events compared with 1.44 events for civilian children. All children conscripted by the Maoists reported at least one traumatic event, 51 percent took part in combat, 56 percent experienced bombings, 29 percent witnessed or perpetrated violent deaths, and 29 percent witnessed, suffered, or perpetrated torture. This greater exposure to trauma played a major part in the mental health and psychosocial differences between child soldiers and never-conscripted children. Child soldiers had greater depression and posttraumatic stress symptoms, general psychological difficulties, and impaired daily functioning (Kohrt et al. 2008). As mentioned in the introduction to this chapter, before one interprets this as a general pathological effect for child soldiers as a group, it is important to stress that we found that the psychosocial difficulties were concentrated generally among those with a high trauma burden (i.e., those who experienced the most exposure to life-threatening events).

In sum, at best, children repositioned themselves outside the structure of their families and communities and replaced that social landscape with a highly regimented Maoist army structure. In other words, although engagement with the Maoists did provide a sense of agency with macrosocial, intermediate, and microsocial processes, these often minimal changes in agency came at the threat to personal functioning through increased exposure to traumatic events and greater postwar dysfunction. Importantly, as we describe next, it is not traumatic exposures alone but also the experience on return to the community that influences mental health.

(Re)integration

When children return to the community, they encounter a shift in interrelationships of agency and power. They came back from a Maoist revolutionary world with different conceptualizations of social hierarchy and power divisions to communities that adopted these conceptualizations in different degrees—some resisting changes, some adopting them. For girls, this was most profound at the family level. Some families were able to accommodate an increased sense of agency and gender equality among girls. We found that this was most acceptable among ethnic minority groups who had a greater sense of gender equity compared to Hindu caste groups. But families varied, even within Hindu castes; for example, different levels of education and access to political and economic power resulted in different beliefs. Some families, such as Shova's politically active family, were able to provide opportunities for Shova to move from the micro- to macrosocial level by engaging in women's mobilization. However, for girls in traditional families, there was significant conflict between the family's and the girls' models of gender equality and agency, which resulted, as with Asha, in high levels of psychosocial distress. School is also an area in which newfound child agency is contested. Many teachers actively forced returned child soldiers to sit on the floor rather than on benches with the other children. Teachers taunted former soldiers, "Hey little Maoist, where is your army?"

Involvement with the Maoists challenged prescribed intercaste social interactions. Community and family members often framed the difficulty to accept former child soldiers in their communities in terms of the Hindu concepts of pollution (*jutho*) and purity (*choko*). The concept of ritual purity dictates where a person resides in the caste—and thus social—hierarchy. Community members stated that child soldiers became ritually polluted through putative involvement in activities such as entering the house of a lower caste, eating with a different caste, interacting with menstruating women, eating beef, carrying dead bodies, and sexual activity. Raj considered himself polluted because he carried dead bodies. Asha, Shova, and many other girls, in contrast, saw the Maoist experience as challenging the traditional notions of purity-based discrimination. They rejected these modes of thinking and behaving when returning home.

The reception and experience in the community on return has dramatic psychosocial consequences. Former child soldiers who described their families, friends, teachers, and neighbors as supportive and caring had low levels of psychosocial distress. This was particularly evident in ethnic minority communities. In contrast, children returning to more conservative Hindu communities described high levels of discrimination and maltreatment. These difficulties produced high levels of psychosocial distress even among individuals with low levels of traumatic experience during participation with the Maoists. One of the surprising findings of this research was that the distinction of voluntarily versus forced association did not predict differences in mental health and psychosocial well-being (Kohrt et al. 2008).

The success of reintegration of former child soldiers depends partly on the compatibility of nontraditional, Maoist revolutionary attitudes toward gender and caste inequality of returning children with the varying attitudes of the families and communities to which they returned. In other words, what the revolution set out to do—to effect changes at the macrosocial level—actually resulted in children returning to contested power relations at the intermediate and microsocial levels with differing effects on their well-being.

Nepal's Maoist Conflict in the Context of the War on Terror

Before moving to the conclusions and recommendations, it is worthwhile to consider another macrosocial factor related to the People's War in

Nepal. While we have discussed macrosocial issues at the national level, it is also important to reflect on global macrosocial processes. The U.S. War on Terror has been associated with increased violence and human rights violations in conflicts throughout the world beginning in late 2001 (International Commission of Jurists 2009). Amnesty International (2005) suggested that the U.S. War on Terror provoked increased violence worldwide, particularly through the use and condoning of torture, which, for example, was employed readily by the Nepali government against Maoists or those accused of being Maoists (Lykke and Timilsena 2002). After 2001, both the United States and the United Kingdom gave U.S.$20 million each to the government of Nepal to combat the Maoist threat; the United Kingdom restricted the use of its funds to nonlethal activities, whereas the United States did not (Mehta 2005:67). Bhattarai et al. (2005:671) also associate the U.S. actions with increased malignancy of the Nepal conflict:

> Emboldened by the U.S. support, apparently provided within the framework of its global "war on terrorism," the [Nepali] State intensified its counterattacks against Maoist insurgents. . . . With its confidence greatly boosted by huge amounts of military aid and the U.S. commitment, the [Nepali] government hardened its position, intensifying its counteroffensive against the Maoists. [This led to the government's] ineffectual and violent response.

Mehta (2005:66–68) points out that the majority of casualties in the conflict were the result of Royal Nepal Army attacks from air. These were conducted with helicopters provided by India, the United States, Russia, and Poland with a technique adopted from U.S. military activities in Afghanistan known as *Tora Bora*, which is the free-fall delivery of mortar bombs from helicopters (Mehta 2005:17). Mehta suggest that this technique and the foreign-donated technology that made it possible drastically escalated the civilian causalities of the war. Bhattarai et al. (2005) also suggest that the War on Terror contributed to greater violence in the Nepal conflict. The recent report by Mary Robinson and the International Commission of Jurists, which investigated the transformation of the U.S. War on Terror into a global human rights crisis, also suggests that U.S. actions contributed to a climate wherein the monarchy of Nepal could grossly infringe on the civil liberties of its people:

> Maoist organizations were termed as terrorist organizations and the definition of terrorist acts was so ambiguous anything and everything was covered under the definition. . . . Civilians, lawyers who were working for the detainees and even judges were considered as terrorists and the military detained them. So society became silent. Human rights activists and lawyers providing legal aid to detainees were threatened by both the security forces and Maoists as well. (Mandira Sharma quoted in International Commission of Jurists 2009:134)

Although associations of the former Bush administration's War on Terror with the human rights violations committed by the Nepal monarchy and security forces against Maoists and innocent civilians increasingly have been demonstrated, further information is needed to identify if and how this contributed to widespread recruitment of children into armed groups.

Implications for Mental Health and Psychosocial Support of Former Child Soldiers

Employing the CMA framework to discuss the experience of child soldiers led to the elucidation of the factors that make children in Nepal vulnerable to recruitment. Moreover, the CMA framework helps to trace the origins of mental health and psychosocial problems among child soldiers, which, as it turns out, are not universal to all children and are as related to conditions before and after the war as they are to war-related trauma. In the more traditional psychiatric epidemiology of war, analyses tend to focus on specific traumas or the cumulative burden of trauma in predicting posttraumatic stress disorder (cf. Miller et al. 2006). Although such an approach may identify specific clinical treatments needed for individuals, that type of research does not illuminate how broader interventions could reduce vulnerability to traumatic events. In contrast, the CMA approach discussed here traces the pathway of vulnerability all from the individual experience up to larger political economic processes. Thus, this type of research sets the stage for recommendations and implications ranging from clinical care to national and international policy. In addition, such identification of contextual influences on mental health provides opportunities to conceptualize social interventions to improve health and well-being, a possibly cost-effective strategy in societies with very little mental health infrastructure.

To prevent recruitment of child soldiers, interventions at the national macrolevel are needed to promote the inclusion of children's issues and voices. These efforts would be helpful if they could contribute to narrowing the gap between returning child soldiers' and communities' differing conceptions of power distribution. In Nepal, the media organization Search for Common Ground is helping to facilitate children's voices being heard on radio and through other media. Other recent events have provided an opportunity for children's participation in the political process, such as the constitutional assembly and recent elections. Moreover, through dialogue with policymakers, advocacy is needed for increased child protection to tackle abuses such as forced child marriage and child conscription in armed groups, as well as further capacity building of local institutions concerned with human rights protection, which currently often take place in a culture of impunity (International Center for Transitional Justice and Advocacy Forum 2008). Further initiatives are required whereby children's voices could be incorporated in planning, designing, monitoring, and evaluating child protection programs.

At the macrosocial level, there also needs to be interventions to address the issues of poverty, ethnic discrimination, gender discrimination, protection of human rights, and decentralization of power. Caste discrimination specifically is an area that desperately requires attention. Caste discrimination played a major role in Maoist recruitment tactics and in determining which families were most vulnerable to exploitation by Maoists. Caste-based dependencies have also been reported to play a role in continued violence following the peace agreement in the south of Nepal (Hattlebak 2007) despite the fact that elimination of caste-based discrimination was high on the Maoist agenda. If there were more nonviolent alternatives to reducing caste disparities in well-being, low-caste children may not be as vulnerable to violence and exploitation in the future. In our work with adults in a rural community in western Nepal, we found that addressing caste-based differences in access to income-generating opportunities and reducing exposure to stressful life events could eliminate the caste disparities in rates of depression, which were two times greater in low-caste groups (Kohrt, Speckman, et al. 2009). At the intermediate social level, the main priorities should be locally enforcing child protection (such as enforcing the child marriage ban), promoting local safety and security, and distributing wealth between rich and poor to curb the ever-increasing income gap. With regard to the latter, Deraniyagala (2005) has shown that economic grievances were a driving factor in the Maoist rebellion and that economic imbalances (partly caused by uneven development efforts) intensified conditions for violence against the state.

Currently, macrosocial intervention at the international level is lacking for the case of child soldiers in Nepal. Policy and advocacy are needed to reduce small arms trade, which makes child soldiers more appealing, and to reduce the provision of large arms to militaries, such as the Royal Nepal Army, which, along with Maoists, was associated with torture, "disappearances," and other human rights violations, including torture of children. With recent efforts by the U.S. Obama administration to redress the human rights violations that characterized the Bush presidency, it will be important to observe how this impacts or fails to impact human rights protection in other regions, such as South Asia. With a Maoist-led government now in place, one should observe if they fulfill their promises to have more directly local benefits in areas that house these resources. Moreover, there should be continued international political pressure to encourage a more representative government inclusive of women, low castes, and ethnic minorities. Already, the Maoists have included more government officials from these groups than any other Nepali political party. Inclusion by itself, however, is not enough, and there is an urgent need to increase the active participation of these groups in government.

International political pressure is needed to ensure a transitional justice process that allows for the involvement and participation of children and youth. A clear mechanism for children to express their political rights, such as in the Truth and Reconciliation Bill, and citizenship is needed to supplant the system of child exploitation by political groups in Nepal and throughout South Asia. International pressure and monitoring bodies, such as the 1612 U.N. Task Force, can foster enactment of child-centered legislation and ensure that political and legal processes in Nepal meet international standards. As the new government moves forward, an important step will thus be ratification of the Mine Ban Treaty with full adherence to treaty provisions and further assurances to sign and ratify the Convention on Certain Conventional Weapons, Protocol V on Explosive Remnants of War. Children continue to suffer morbidity and mortality from unexploded devices, many of which have been found around schools.

Interventions at the microsocial level should promote local pathways to optimize the psychosocial well-being of children. One way to do this is through facilitating dialogues in which community members are encouraged to think about the processes by which children become child soldiers. In Nepal, there are numerous arenas to do this, be it through community-based organizations (mothers' groups, women's groups, youth clubs, child clubs, and so on), street drama programs, or dialogues ritualized in theatrical song and dance. Rather than focusing on blaming children, this approach should foster discussions in which individual instances of child conscription are tied to larger social processes in the community and country. This form of discussion may help to evoke possible micro- or macrosocial initiatives to improve the well-being of children. Ultimately, at the microsocial level, activities should promote empowerment of local groups rather than top-down approaches that embody the marginalization process that Maoists have been able to exploit.

At the individual level, one possible goal is to promote a sense of efficacy and empowerment of children in ways other than through participation with armed groups. Interventions that help children feel that they are influencing other aspects of the ecological system—in a non-violent manner—may contribute to building a society where children are less vulnerable to recruitment. This could be through the representation of individuals under 18 years of age in community activities such as in community forest management, microfinance initiatives, and adolescent health programs as well as local political representation and activities. Education is crucial to this, as it builds skills that contribute to community participation, health status, and employment opportunities. In addition, helping children develop vocations (such as tailoring, driving, electronic repair, and journalism) to be economically self-sufficient when they reach adulthood could reduce the lure of involvement in armed groups. Similarly, nonviolent forms of community and political engagement need to be fostered through peace committees, local peace initiatives, and child right's activism committees. In sum, children can be active agents for social changes, and for this, children's participation in reconciliation and peace-building initiatives should be prioritized.

Identifying contextual determinants of mental health, such as differences in (re)integration pathways, holds direct consequences for programs promoting the psychosocial well-being and mental health of former child soldiers. Currently, such programming has been divided by a nonproductive rift between an individually focused psychiatric paradigm versus a contextually focused psychosocial paradigm. Application of an ecological and CMA approach has the potential to integrate such efforts, by demonstrating the importance of considering former child soldiers' well-being within its larger social context. Identifying pathways through which individual health gets affected can aid in prioritizing target areas (e.g., areas where traditional notions and Maoist notions are likely to clash), target groups (e.g., girls in conservative Hindu areas), and types of interventions (e.g., attending to psychosocial distress for those exposed to traumatic events as well as facilitating integration efforts in families and schools).

Ultimately, researchers, interventionists, and policymakers need to address the broader political, economic, and cultural determinants of child conscription into armed groups both to improve former child soldiers' mental health and to work toward ending the recruitment of children into armed groups. CMA is one tool to help guide policy to guard the rights of children such as Asha, Raj, and Shova against exploitation by armed groups. Mental health is intrinsically a socially determined process and thus requires interventions that follow the pathway of vulnerability from individual cases through to broader macrosocial determinants of well-being.

Works Cited

Adhikari, Manju, and Renu Shrestha
 2007 Field notes for interview with "Shova." Farwestern Development Region, Nepal. Transcultural Psychosocial Organization Nepal. February 5.

Amnesty International
 2005 *Annual Report: USA's War on Terror* (Index AMR 51/072/2005).

Baer, Hans A., Merrill Singer, and Ida Susser
 2003 *Medical Anthropology and the World System*. Westport, CT: Praeger.

Belsky, J.
1980 Child maltreatment: An ecological integration. *America Journal of Psychology* 35:320–335.

Betancourt, Theresa S.
2005 Stressors, supports and the social ecology of displacement: Psychosocial dimensions of an emergency education program for Chechen adolescents displaced in Ingushetia, Russia. *Culture, Medicine and Psychiatry* 29(3):309–340.

Betancourt, Theresa Stichick, Ivelina Borisova, Julia Rubin-Smith, Tara Gingerich, Timothy Williams, and Jessica Agnew-Blais
2008 *Psychosocial Adjustment and Social Reintegration of Children Associated with Armed Forces and Armed Groups: The State of the Field and Future Directions.* Cambridge, MA: Psychology Beyond Borders.

Bhattarai, Keshav, Dennis Conway, and Nanda Shrestha
2005 Tourism, terrorism and turmoil in Nepal. *Annals of Tourism Research* 32(3):669–688.

Bronfenbrenner, Uri
1979 *The Ecology of Human Development: Experiments by Nature and Design.* Cambridge, MA: Harvard University Press.

Cicchetti, Dante, and Lynch, M.
1993 Toward an ecological/transactional model of community violence and child maltreatment: Consequences for children's development. *Psychiatry* 56:96–118.

Cicchetti, Dante, Sheree L. Toth, and Angeline Maughan
2000 An ecological-transactional model of child maltreatment. In *Handbook of Developmental Psychopathology*, edited by A. J. Sameroff, M. Lewis, and S. M. Miller, 689–722. New York: Kluwer Academic/ Plenum.

Deraniyagala, Sonali
2005 The political economy of civil conflict in Nepal. *Oxford Development Studies* 33(1):47–62.

Government of Nepal
2007 *Nepal Demographic and Health Survey, 2006.* Kathmandu: Ministry of Health and Population, New Era & Macro International, Inc.

Hachhethu, K.
2002   *Party Building in Nepal: Organization, Leadership and People.* Kathmandu: Mandala Book Point.

Hattlebak, Magnus
2007   *Economic and Social Structures That May Explain the Recent Conflicts in the Terai of Nepal.* Bergen: Chr. Michelsen Institute.

Hoftun, M., W. Raeper, and J. Whelpton
1999   *People, Politics and Ideology: Democracy and Social Change in Nepal.* Kathmandu: Mandala Book Point.

Human Rights Watch
2007   *Children in the Ranks: The Maoists' Use of Child Soldiers in Nepal.* Kathmandu: Human Rights Watch.

International Center for Transitional Justice and Advocacy Forum
2008   *Nepali Voices: Perceptions of Truth, Justice, Reconciliation, Reparations, and the Transition in Nepal.* Kathmandu: International Center for Transitional Justice and Advocacy Forum.

International Commission of Jurists
2009   *Assessing Damage, Urging Action: Report on the Eminent Jurists Panel on Terrorism, Counter-Terrorism, and Human Rights.* Edited by M. Robinson. Geneva: International Commission of Jurists.

Karki A., and D. Seddon
2003   *People's War in Nepal: Left Perspective.* Delhi: Adroit Publisher.

Koenig, Robert A., and Brandon A. Kohrt
2009   *Returned: Child Soldiers of Nepal's Maoist Army* (film, 30 minutes). Kathmandu: Adventure Pictures Productions. Distributed by Documentary Educational Resources.

Kohrt, Brandon A., Mark J. D. Jordans, Wietse A. Tol, Rebecca A. Speckman, Sujen M. Maharjan, Carol M. Worthman, and Ivan H. Komproe
2008   Comparison of mental health between former child soldiers and children never conscripted by armed groups in Nepal. *Journal of the American Medical Association* 300(6):691–702.

Kohrt, Brandon A., and Ramesh Karki
2007   Field notes for interview with "Raj." Midwestern Development Region, Nepal. February 7.

Kohrt, Brandon A., Rebecca A. Speckman, Richard D. Kunz, Jennifer L. Baldwin, Nawaraj Upadhaya, Nanda Raj Acharya, Vidya Dev Sharma, Mahendra K. Nepal, and Carol M. Worthman

2009   Culture in psychiatric epidemiology: Using ethnography and multiple mediator models to assess the relationship of caste with depression and anxiety in Nepal. *Annals of Human Biology* 36(3):261–280.

Koirala, Pitambar

2007   Field notes for interview with "Asha." Central Development Region, Nepal. Transcultural Psychosocial Organization Nepal. August 7.

Lykke, Jakob, and Mukti Nath Timilsena

2002   Evidence of torture in the mid west region of Nepal. *Danish Medical Bulletin* 49(2):159–162.

Mehta, Ashok K.

2005   *The Royal Nepal Army: Meeting the Maoist Challenge.* New Delhi: Rupa and Co.

Miller, Kenneth E., Madhur Kulkarni, and Hallie Kushner

2006   Beyond trauma-focused psychiatric epidemiology: Bridging research and practice with war-affected populations. *American Journal of Orthopsychiatry* 76(4):409–422.

Ogura, Kiyoko

2004   Realities and images of Nepal's Maoists after the attack on Beni. *European Bulletin of Himalayan Research* 27:67–125.

Pettigrew, Judith

2003   Guns, kinship and fear: Maoists among the Tamu-mai (Gurungs). In *Resistance and the State: Nepalese Experiences*, edited by D. N. Gellner, 305–325. Delhi: Social Science Press.

2004   Living between the Maoists and the army in rural Nepal. In *Himalayan People's War: Nepal's Maoist Rebellion*, edited by M. Hutt, 261–285. Bloomington: Indiana University Press.

2007   Learning to be silent: Change, childhood and mental health in the Maoist insurgency in Nepal. In *Nepalis inside and outside Nepal: Political and Social Transformations*, edited by H. Ishi, D. N. Gellner, and K. Nawa, 307–384. Delhi: Manohar.

Pettigrew, Judith, and Sara Shneiderman

2004   Women and the Maobaadi: Ideology and agency in Nepal's Maoist movement. *Himal Southasian* 17(1):19–29.

Shneiderman, Sara
2003 Violent histories and political consciousness: Reflecting on Nepal's Maoist movement from Piskar village. *Himalaya: The Journal of the Association for Nepal and Himalayan Studies* 23(1):39–48.

Singh, Sonal
2004 Post-traumatic stress in former Ugandan child soldiers. *Lancet* 363(9421):1648.

Somasundaram, Daya
2002 Child soldiers: understanding the context. *British Medical Journal* 324(7348):1268–1271.

Thapa, Deepak, with Bandita Sijapati
2005 *A Kingdom under Siege: Nepal's Maoist Insurgency, 1996 to 2004.* London: Zed Books.

Tol, Wietse A., Mark J. D. Jordans, Ria Reis, and Joop T. V. M. De Jong
2009 Ecological resilience: Working with child-related psychosocial resources in war-affected communities. In *Treating Traumatized Children: Risk, Resilience, and Recovery,* edited by D. Brom, R. Pat-Horenczyk, and J. D. Ford, 164–182. London: Routledge.

United Nations Development Program
2007 *Human Development Report 2007/2008.* New York: Palgrave Macmillan.

United Nations Children's Fund
2003 *Fact Sheet: Child Soldiers.* New York: United Nations Children's Fund.
2007 *Paris Principles: Principles and Guidelines on Children Associated with Armed Forces or Armed Conflict.* New York: United Nations Children's Fund.

Wessells, Michael G.
2006 *Child Soldiers: From Violence to Protection.* Cambridge, MA: Harvard University Press.

World Bank
2007 *Nepal at a Glance.* Washington, DC: World Bank.

Yami, Hisila
2007 *People's War and Women's Liberation in Nepal.* Kathmandu: Janadhwani Publications.

PART TWO

THE ENVIRONMENT OF WAR AND ITS IMPACT ON THE HUMAN ENVIRONMENT

CHAPTER FOUR

THE CAUSES AND HUMAN COSTS OF TARGETING IRAQ

Elaine A. Hills and Dahlia S. Wasfi

This chapter assesses the public health costs of Iraq's prominent position in the global imperialist struggle for oil, from the mid-twentieth century through the U.S.-led 2003 invasion and resulting occupation of Iraq. We employ a political economic perspective (Roseberry 1988) to examine the changing structural factors that determine Iraq's role in the capitalist world system, resulting from increased attempts made by the United States to dominate global capitalism (Knauft 2007) through attempts to control Iraq's abundant oil resources.

Our analysis of the effects of the struggle for the control of oil on the Iraqi people is based on a range of population-level data including medical, demographic, and economic findings as well as ethnographic research we conducted in 2006 in Baghdad and Basra, two of the largest cities of Iraq, and also among resettled Iraqi refugees living in the northeastern United States in 2008. Interviews with Iraqis (both in and out of Iraq), U.S. soldiers, nonviolence workers, representatives of refugee resettlement agencies, and journalists who have spent time in Iraq and/or surrounding nations since the 2003 invasion inform our perspective. From these sources, we trace war-induced changes in the Iraqi public health infrastructure and the direct effects that this and other aspects of imperialist aggression have had on Iraqis' personal and population health. American military aggressions and economic sanctions waged against Iraq since 1991 have increased disease transmission by repeatedly decimating public health infrastructure, depriving Iraqis of necessities for day-to-day living, and causing widespread environmental contamination from repeated use of toxic war munitions. For Iraqis struggling to survive amidst this routine deadly violence as well as for those Iraqis who have resettled in other countries, the personal psychological costs and costs from collective social suffering have been enormous. Imperialist aggression against Iraq has resulted in very real, daily human costs. Apparent disregard for human well-being has been an inherent part of the global war machine that aims to protect capitalist interests through violent assault.

Iraq: Before the 2003 U.S. Invasion

Political-Economic History

The Pre-Oil Era

The country that is today known as Iraq is situated in the land of ancient Mesopotamia and the "cradle of civilization." For centuries, Iraq was at the center of religious, political, and economic exploits. This deep history has been documented in thousands of sites of cultural, historical, and archaeological significance, many of which place Iraq at the center of Islam and other major world religions. For thousands of years, foreign invaders have sought to conquer the region to control its wealth and rich resources. From the sixteenth century to the early twentieth century, Iraq was under Ottoman rule.

The Oil Era

With the discovery of oil in the region in 1871, the modern geopolitical importance of Iraq took on new meaning (Munier 2004). Since then, violent exploits have aimed to secure the region's oil resources, with Iraq sometimes positioned as an ally to Western powers and other times the enemy. The struggle for control of Iraq's oil has proven pivotal in the fight for global domination by Western powers because oil has become the primary currency of capitalist empire building. Waging World War I required oil, and this accelerated the contest for Iraq's resources among the great powers. Britain invaded Iraq (with a force of Indian soldiers) in 1914 as the war began. Although initially defeated by the Turks, British forces took Baghdad from the Ottoman Empire in 1917 and Mosul in 1918 but met local resistance from the outset. Since then, the increasing reliance on oil for virtually every facet of capitalist productivity has made oil-rich Iraq a centerpiece of military interventions in and around the region.

By the 1950s, the industrialization of oil dominated Iraqi economic and political development and led to the formation of alliances between Iraq and major Western powers, particularly the United States and Great Britain. In 1955, Iraq signed the Baghdad Pact with Iran, Turkey, Pakistan, and Great Britain, and in 1956 the United States joined as an associate member (Ali 2003). This treaty was ostensibly intended to affirm friendly relations among signatories as well as help to isolate the Soviet Union and communist influences that were a threat to capitalist developments to militarily protect Middle East oil resources. The involvement of Western powers in the Baghdad Pact widened foreign access to Middle Eastern oil, providing a critical inroad for U.S. and British companies that were among the major catalysts of the global capitalist acceleration that characterized the late twentieth century. At the same time, U.S. intelligence agencies aimed to strengthen and defend Western access to Iraqi oil resources. In 1963, seeking to defeat the Iraqi Communist Party during the Cold War, the U.S. government supported the rise of the rival Ba'ath Socialist Party to power (Ali 2003), ultimately leading to the ascendancy of Saddam Hussein as Iraq's political leader.

Western oil companies reaped profits from eased access to Iraq's oil through the 1950s and 1960s, but that colonialist arrangement changed with the Ba'ath Party's nationalization of Iraqi oil in 1972 (Global Policy Forum 2008). Iraqi nationalization of oil profits led to an increase in the Iraqi standard of living, positioning Iraq as one of the "most developed" Arab countries (Global Policy Forum 2008). By the mid-1970s, the strength of the Iraqi economy was reflected in the fact that one Iraqi dinar was the equivalent of over three U.S. dollars (eDinar Financial 2009).

The War Era: The Iran-Iraq War and Its Aftermath

In 1980, the Iraqi economy was transformed from a predominantly oil-based economy to a war-based economy. Because of long-standing border disputes and ideological disagreements between the secular Iraqi government and neighboring Iranian theocracy, Iraq launched the Iran-Iraq War in 1980 with the backing of the United States, Saudi Arabia, and other Gulf states. Lasting from 1980 to 1988, the war afforded the

U.S. Reagan administration a renewed political alliance with Iraq through military support and satellite intelligence to aid the war effort. In secret, however, U.S. arms sales were simultaneously conducted with Iran via the infamous Iran-Contra affair.

In 1988, at the end of the eight-year war with Iran, Iraq needed oil-sale profits to fund vital infrastructure reconstruction projects, but neighboring Kuwaiti rulers interfered on three economic fronts (Clark 1992). First, Kuwait flooded the oil market above OPEC limits set by the Organization of the Petroleum Exporting Countries, causing crude prices to fall. Second, Kuwait was slant drilling from its side of the border with Iraq into the Iraqi oil fields in Rumaila, effectively stealing Iraqi oil. Third, after financially supporting Iraq's war effort against Iran, Kuwait demanded repayment of $30 billion. However Iraq's previously reliable oil income was severely hampered by Kuwait's actions, which meant that Iraq was unable to repay its war debt to Kuwait. From 1988 to 1990, Iraq tried to resolve these oil-based economic issues using diplomacy; however, Kuwait rejected all negotiations (Clark 1992).

The War Era: Gulf War I and Its Aftermath

In the summer of 1990, Iraqi president Saddam Hussein ceased attempts at diplomatic negotiations with Kuwait and resorted to military force to protect Iraq's oil and economic interests. On August 2, 1990, Iraqi troops crossed their southern border into Kuwaiti territory. Just days before, Hussein had consulted the U.S. ambassador to Iraq, April Glaspie, about the decision to invade Kuwait. She assured him that "we have no opinion on Arab-Arab conflicts, like your border disagreement with Kuwait" (Clark 1992:23). Despite this assurance from the U.S. ambassador, four days after Iraq invaded Kuwait, the United States wielded its power on the UN Security Council (UNSC) to pass a resolution instituting economic sanctions against Iraq. The sanctions were touted as punishment for Iraq's invasion of Kuwait but were also intended as retaliation for the invasion's destabilization of outside access to the region's rich oil resources—what U.S. General Norman Schwarzkopf called "the West's lifeblood" in testimony before the Senate Armed Services Committee in 1990 (Blum 2004). Seemingly overnight, U.S. relations with Iraq changed from friendly to hostile. When the UN embargo took effect in late 1990,

Iraq's oil sector economy and accompanying standard of living were virtually destroyed.

Following the institution of sanctions against Iraq, the United States and Britain built a coalition of international forces that worked not only to debilitate Iraq from within but also to attack Iraq using the military force of allied forces during the 1991 Gulf War. China, as a member of the UNSC, threatened to veto the UN resolution permitting the 1991 invasion of Iraq. While China argued that such an attack would be a violation of Iraqi sovereignty, the United States threatened to remove China from most-favored-nation economic status with the United States if China attempted to veto the resolution (Dreyer 2007). This threat prompted China's representatives on the UNSC to abstain from voting on the resolution and thus aided its passage (Bennis and Halliday 2000). The ensuing 1991 Gulf War became an international measure to destroy Iraq as the region's emerging power and therefore protect Western hegemony over Iraqi oil resources.

The Gulf War included a range of sea, air, and ground armaments aimed not only at the Iraqi military but also at the destruction of the infrastructure used to support day-to-day life in Iraq. Power stations and substations, water and sewage treatment plants, factories, dams, pumping stations, telecommunications equipment, oil refineries, railroads, bridges, and highways were among targets systematically destroyed or damaged by the United States and Gulf War coalition forces. The 42-day assault was a calculated effort to devastate Iraqi society by targeting the facilities critical to survival (Clark 1992). After the war, the Pentagon admitted that the attacks were intended to demoralize the civilian population into surrender (Blum 2004). This was the Pentagon's strategy despite the fact that the attacks violated the Geneva Convention rules for the protection of civilians in wartime adopted by the international community in 1949 (United Nations High Commissioner for Human Rights 1949).

The economic embargo that had been imposed on Iraq prior to the 1991 Gulf War was sustained until the 2003 U.S. invasion. Therefore, in the lead-up to the 2003 invasion, Iraqi society reeled from the calamitous state of affairs left by decades of war and more than a decade of debilitating sanctions. By 1999, the International Red Cross declared that "the Iraqi economy lies in tatters" (quoted in Chomsky 2003:128). By 2003, the value of the Iraqi dinar had plummeted, with one American dollar then equivalent to approximately 3,700 Iraqi dinars (eDinar Financial 2009).

Modern Iraqi Public Health: 1970s–2002

The portrait of modern Iraqi public health can be said to have closely followed the evolution of Iraq's oil- and war-based economy. With the nationalization of oil profits under Ba'ath Party rule in the 1970s, public health infrastructure grids such as electricity, water, and sewerage systems were significantly improved. These infrastructural advancements translated into improvements in basic health measures. The infant mortality rate (IMR) declined from about 120 per 1,000 live births in 1960 to approximately 45 per 1,000 by the late 1980s (Pellett 2000), while life expectancy rose from 49 to 67 years (Hoskins 2000).

Despite the strain put on the Iraqi economy and the hundreds of thousands of dead and injured as a result of the eight-year-long war with Iran in the 1980s (Ali 2003), the improvements in basic health measures sustained from the previous years of economic prosperity continued virtually unharmed. The Iran-Iraq War left electricity and water treatment infrastructure intact. In addition, Iraq's IMR was actually reduced by nearly 50 percent during the Iran-Iraq War (Hoskins 2000). By the late 1980s, Iraq boasted a first-class range of medical facilities known as the "jewel of the Arab World" and held one of the region's highest per capita food availability ratings (Hoskins 2000).

The rich oil economy of Iraq that had previously provided some of the best social and health services in the region was devastated by the 1991 Gulf War. The intentional targeting of civilian infrastructure crippled key components of Iraq's medical and public health systems. When the Gulf War cease-fire was agreed to on February 28, 1991, the destruction of Iraq persisted through UN sanctions and U.S. and British no-fly-zone bombing campaigns. Between March 1991 and the March 19, 2003, U.S.-led invasion, more armaments were dropped on Iraq than during the Gulf War. Meanwhile, economic sanctions caused critical shortages of food, lifesaving pharmaceutical drugs, medical equipment, and supplies necessary for routine repair and updating of electrical and water grids (Garfield 1995; Hoskins 2000). As a result, several sectors of public health were detrimentally affected, and by the start of the twenty-first century,

Iraq had the lowest well-being index of any country in the world, based on combined measures of human and environmental well-being (Prescott-Allen 2001). Next we review the post–Gulf War increases in mortality, the spread of communicable diseases, and malnutrition. In addition, we examine the rising incidence of cancers and congenital anomalies believed to be associated with the repeated use of toxic munitions.

Mortality Measures

The United Nations Children's Fund (UNICEF) estimated that as many as 500,000 excess deaths of children under age five occurred because of the Gulf War and the enduring effects of postwar sanctions (Levy and Sidel 2008). In total, through the structural violence of sanctions and continued exposure to toxic armaments, more Iraqi deaths are believed to have occurred after than during the Gulf War (Medact 2004). By 1998, Iraq's IMR rose to more than 100 per 1,000 live births (Pellett 2000), while maternal mortality had doubled since the preceding decade (Medact 2004). The under-five mortality rate, which had declined considerably between 1960 and 1990, rose precipitously by 2002 (see figure 4.1). As shown in figure 4.1, no other country in the region demonstrated this staggering increase in under-five mortality. In fact, UNICEF's 2007 "State of the World's Children" report stated that the increase in Iraq's

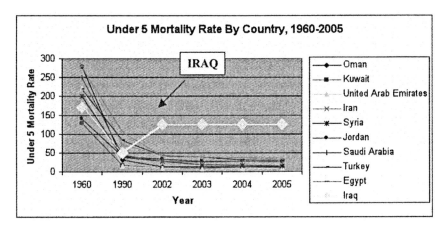

Figure 4.1. Under-five mortality rate by country, 1960–2005. Adapted from UNICEF State of the World's Children Data, 2004-2007.

under-five mortality between 1991 and 2002 was the worst regression in a child welfare measure of all 193 countries surveyed (Chomsky 2003).

Communicable Disease Control
Destruction of the electrical grids alone incapacitated the medical system. In January 1991 (the month the Gulf War began), Iraq's primary health care and preventive health services ceased to exist (CARE International in Iraq 2003). Basic preventive services for communicable disease were debilitated because of the collapse of water and sanitation services, coupled with a U.S. blockade of potable water and childhood vaccine imports[1] (Chomsky 2003; UNICEF 1995). There were critical shortages of lifesaving drugs and equipment (UNICEF 1995), including materials needed to repair damaged infrastructure, such as water treatment facilities and laboratories that are critical to the prevention and diagnosis of communicable diseases (Hoskins 2000). As a result, cholera, which had been virtually eradicated in Iraq before the Gulf War, became endemic in the 1990s (Hoskins 2000). Typhoid spread rapidly, and outbreaks of polio, measles, and hepatitis were common (Hoskins 2000). Easily treatable diseases, such as respiratory infections and diarrhea, accounted for 70 percent of child deaths under the age of five (World Health Organization [WHO] 2003).

Malnutrition
Although Iraq was dependent on imports for 70 percent of its food supply prior to the Gulf War, food imports were blocked during the economic embargo (Blum 2004). This resulted in widespread malnutrition and starvation. In response, the Iraqi government instated a food-rationing system to support the population. However, by 1995, UNICEF reported that the food-rationing system was inadequate because it provided recipients with less than 60 percent of their required daily caloric intake (UNICEF 1995). UNICEF therefore concluded that economic sanctions were yielding "a minimum of political dividends . . . against a high human price paid primarily by women and children" (UNICEF 1995).
Concerns over the "serious nutritional and health situation of the Iraqi population" (UNSC 1995:1) prompted implementation of the UN Oil-for-Food program, which was outlined in UN Security Council Resolution

986 in April 1995 (UNSC 1995). While it alleviated critical food short-ages for some, the program could not reverse the harm already done by five years of bombing and sanctions. By 1997, nearly 1 million Iraqi chil-dren (in a total population of 26 million) were malnourished—an increase of 72 percent since 1991 (UNICEF 1997).

Cancer and Toxic Munitions

In 1998, Iraqi Cancer Registry data revealed a fivefold increase in can-cer incidence since the Gulf War (Ammash 2000). In addition, new types of cancers were identified that had never before been seen in Iraq, and cancers appeared in younger individuals than had previously been the case. Among Iraqi veterans, from 1991 to 1997, 1,425 incident cancer cases were recorded, including lymphoma, leukemia, and lung, brain, bone, liver, gas-trointestinal, and pancreatic cancers (Ammash 2000). A rapid increase in congenital abnormalities in Iraqi children born after the Gulf War, such as children born with missing limbs, ears, and eyes, was also found (Ammash 2000). Iraqi physicians believe precipitous increases in these conditions to be associated with exposure to depleted uranium (DU) shells dropped by the U.S. and other Gulf War forces (Al-Azzawi 2006).

The 2003 U.S.-Led Invasion and Occupation of Iraq

Political-Economic Thirst for War

The U.S. military-industrial complex did not stop targeting Iraq after the 1991 Gulf War. In 1997, the conservative think tank Project for the New American Century (PNAC) was formed largely as a means of pres-suring the U.S. government to again wage war on Iraq (PNAC 2000). PNAC urged the Clinton administration in 1998 (PNAC 1998) and, later, President George W. Bush to engage in direct military conflict with Iraq prior to the 2003 invasion. PNAC and its members openly advocated increasing U.S. defense spending by $15 billion to $20 billion annually to attain their core mission to "fight and decisively win multiple, simultane-ous major theater wars" and thus demonstrate U.S. military superiority in the world (PNAC 2000). For PNAC, the Gulf War conflict with Iraq allegedly remained "unresolved," and Iraq was viewed as a pivotal nation that threatened U.S. access to Middle East oil resources (PNAC 2000).

Leading up to the 2003 U.S.-led invasion, the PNAC agenda was easily translated into Bush administration policy. Many top Bush administration officials, including Vice President Dick Cheney, Secretary of Defense Donald Rumsfeld, and Deputy Secretary of Defense Paul Wolfowitz, were members of PNAC and signatories to the organization's Statement of Principles before their tenure in the administration (PNAC 1997). The Bush administration thus seized the opportunity to rally the American public for a new war against Iraq beginning just hours after the September 11, 2001, attacks on the United States (Leopold 2003) despite the total lack of evidence for any connection between Iraq and the September 11 attacks.

As evidenced in the now famous British Downing Street Memo, information then publicly presented as intelligence and facts to justify an invasion of Iraq were fabricated to support the U.S. administration's policy wishes (Sunday Times 2005). By March 2003, the administration had spent months building a false case for war against Iraq by fabricating elaborate stories about alleged attempts by Iraq to secure weapons-grade uranium and repeatedly suggesting untrue associations between Iraq and the September 11 attacks. In February 2003 testimony before the United Nations, the Bush administration made a final attempt to rally international support for going to war with Iraq by poising historical documents about Iraqi possession of weapons of mass destruction as contemporary evidence of a global threat warranting military attack (Chomsky 2003). This sequence of events marked a significant turning point in the political-economic history of Iraq and would also usher in a new phase in Iraq's public health history.

Despite the lack of UN support or approval, the Bush administration fulfilled a core PNAC principle in March 2003 by invading Iraq in an illegal military campaign dubbed "Shock and Awe." In conjunction with the U.S. assault on Afghanistan, the Iraq War offered the Bush administration a means of engaging simultaneous wars of large proportions. The Shock and Awe military strategy mapped out in advance of the invasion called for the United States to launch 800 cruise missiles—more than double the number of missiles launched in the entire Gulf War—in the first two days of the invasion (West 2003). One Pentagon official told CBS News that a key purpose of the campaign was to hit Baghdad with a force never before contemplated, while the National Defense University's chief Shock and Awe architect explained that the strategy was to target power and water supply sources and to physically, emotionally, and psychologically exhaust the Iraqi people (West 2003). By September 2004, then Secretary-General of the United Nations Kofi Annan proclaimed the invasion illegal because it breached the UN Charter (MacAskill and Borger 2004).

The PNAC mission of increasing defense spending by $15 billion to $20 billion annually was met and exceeded by 2003, with numerous contracts geared around the Iraq invasion. In fiscal year 2003, defense spending increased by $28.2 billion over the previous year (U.S. Department of Defense 2004); in fiscal year 2004, spending increased by $21.7 billion (U.S. Department of Defense 2005); and in fiscal year 2005, spending rose by $38.5 billion (U.S. Department of Defense 2006). Vice President Cheney's corporate ties to the defense industry offered perhaps the most direct link between profit making from the 2003 invasion and ensuing occupation of Iraq (Drutman and Cray 2003). Since 2003, Halliburton, a private company and Cheney's former employer immediately prior to his tenure as vice president, has consistently ranked among the top 10 defense contractors by securing multi-billion-dollar contracts for its support services for U.S. military personnel in Iraq (U.S. Department of Defense 2004, 2005, 2006).

Increasing privatization of U.S. military efforts has bolstered profits for Halliburton and many others since the first Gulf War (Drutman and Cray 2003). This is evidenced by the ratio of private contractors to military personnel deployed in recent conflicts with Iraq. In the 1991 conflict, one of every 60 people deployed for the U.S.-led war was a high-priced private contractor; by 2003, that ratio had increased to one in three (Scahill 2008). While the Uniform Code of Military Justice governs all uniformed members of the U.S. armed services, there is virtually no accountability for the actions of private military contractors, many of whom are heavily armed and unsupervised (Scahill 2008). In the case of at least one private contractor, Blackwater, accountability was situated directly in the hands of the Bush White House, to whom they reported (Scahill 2008).

The dissolution of law and order that has resulted from the invasion and occupation has been exacerbated by the continuing presence of private military contractors among Iraq's occupying forces. The March 2003 invasion included the largest number of private contractors ever deployed in a war, and the size of their force eventually increased to nearly a one-to-one ratio with U.S. soldiers (Scahill 2008). Private contractors' actions were emboldened by Order 17, a U.S.-imposed decree issued in 2004 that immunized them from prosecution for crimes they commit in Iraq (Scahill 2008). Such immunity has resulted in brazen disregard for Iraqis. In a U.S. House of Representatives Committee on Oversight and Government Reform study conducted between 2005 and 2007, one single military contractor, Blackwater, was reported to have opened fire on Iraqis on at least 195 occasions, and in more than 80 percent of those, Blackwater fired first (Scahill 2008). In September 2007, Blackwater contractors earned international fame for committing the Nisour Square massacre of 17 civilians. As of the spring of 2008, private military contractors had not been prosecuted for their crimes against the Iraqi people (Scahill 2008).

Costs of the Invasion and Occupation

Dissolution of Law and Order

The Iraqi way of life—already harmed by 13 years of draconian sanctions—was further devastated by the dissolution of law and order that followed the illegal March 2003 invasion. All social systems were impacted not only by bombing campaigns and other forms of violence but also through rampant looting and general lack of security. Humanitarian workers report that homes in Baghdad and other cities now receive just two hours of electricity per day (Oxfam International 2007). In 2007, nearly half the population (43 percent) suffered from absolute poverty, while over half was without work (Oxfam International 2007).

Perhaps no other region of Iraq exemplifies the brutal devastation brought by the war and occupation better than Fallujah, the once-bustling city of 300,000 residents. During the April 2004 siege of Fallujah, U.S. Marines closed the bridge to the city and the hospital road. The U.S. military and its vehicles stood at the hospital entrance, and snipers were positioned on rooftops, targeting ambulances and the clinic doors (Jamail 2004a). Fallujah residents told the *Washington Post* that U.S. forces patrolled neighborhoods and fired on civilians almost randomly, with little regard for human life (Scahill 2008). Every one of these "tactics" is a war crime according to the Geneva Convention (Medact 2008). The end result: between 600 and 800 civilians were killed in the April 2004 siege.

In November 2004, the second major siege of Fallujah began (Lorimer 2004). On November 6, Fallujah's Nazzal Emergency Hospital was leveled to the ground, and on November 8, the U.S. military seized the Fallujah General Hospital. Doctors described the horrific events: "We were tied up and beaten despite being unarmed and having only our medical instruments" (quoted in Jamail 2004b). Burhan Fasa'a, a cameraman with the Lebanese Broadcasting Company, reported, "There were American snipers on top of the hospital . . . shooting everyone in sight" (Jamail 2004b). In addition, the U.S. military blocked the Iraqi Red Crescent from entering the city for seven days (Jamail 2004c). In total, 70 percent of the buildings in Fallujah were leveled by the U.S. military, and virtually none of the remaining 30 percent escaped damage. The end result of this cascade of Geneva Convention violations (Medact 2008) was a death toll of between 6,000 and 8,000 civilians. This means that the Iraqi death toll in November 2004, in Fallujah alone, surpassed the death toll for all the countries that participated in the first five years of the invasion and occupation of Iraq.

Public Health
The violent invasion and continued occupation of Iraq has exacted lasting consequences on every imaginable facet of Iraqi public health and well-being. American and British forces have attacked key elements of public health infrastructure, including hospitals, ambulances, bridges, and homes (Medact 2008). Security risks delay the delivery of supplies of all types and further hamper the ability of hospitals and other agencies to provide relief to the Iraqi people. As a result, sanitation facilities, power-generating stations, hospitals, and other essential services for preserving public well-being, already debilitated before the 2003 invasion, are now devastated. Substantial increases in physical trauma, the incidence of diseases, deaths from violence and other causes, rare cancers and birth defects, psychological and emotional trauma, and nutritional deficiencies have resulted. These and other war-induced changes to Iraq's public health system since the 2003 invasion are reviewed next.

Mortality Risk and Life Expectancy. Previously stable life expectancy and mortality measures that changed little from 1990 to 2000 were dramatically affected by 2006 (see table 4.1). This was particularly true for

Table 4.1. Changes in Select Public Health Measures in Iraq, 1990–2006

	1990	*2000*	*2006*
Life expectancy at birth (years)			
Male	64	65	48
Female	69	70	67
Adult mortality rate (probability of dying between 15 and 60 years of age per 1,000 population)			
Male	233	234	607
Female	160	153	187
Immunization coverage among one-year-olds (%)			
MCV	75	85	60
DTP3	83	78	60

Source: Adapted from (WHO 2008b).

males, among whom life expectancy at birth decreased by 17 years, while the male adult mortality rate nearly tripled by 2006.

From afar, the death toll from violence is monitored in statistical compilations showing that, on average, hundreds of Iraqi civilians and security forces die weekly from the violence (cf. http://icasualties.org). Epidemiologic research employing a cluster sample design estimated the excess mortality from the 2003 invasion and occupation of Iraq at nearly 100,000 deaths by September 2004 (Roberts et al. 2004). An updated survey conducted in mid-2006 estimated more than 650,000 excess deaths, with a confidence interval ranging from 392,979 to 942,636 deaths (Burnham et al. 2006). More recently, the estimated death toll from violent conflict alone was estimated at over 1.2 million (Opinion Research Business 2007). We interviewed one extended Iraqi family who had immigrated from Baghdad to the United States in two waves, first after concerns over Saddam Hussein's brutal rule following the Gulf War and then after the kidnapping of one of their sons after the 2003 U.S. invasion. They told us that the day-to-day violence resulting from complete lack of U.S. respect for their humanity after the 2003 invasion makes the Saddam Hussein regime look like "the good old days."

Child Health Measures. Essential immunization provisions reached a smaller proportion of the population in 2006 than in previous decades (see table 4.1). It is estimated that 270,000 children born between March 2003 and July 2006 have had no immunizations (Laurance 2006). Household survey data from late 2003 showed that 17 percent of children were underweight and that 32 percent were chronically malnourished (Medact 2004). Others have offered similar estimates and suggested that malnutrition has continued to rise since the 2003 invasion (Oxfam International 2007). In 2008, UNICEF reported that only 40 percent of Iraqi children have routine access to safe drinking water (Hajaj 2008). Five years after the initial invasion, at least one in five Iraqi children have been unable to attend school (Hajaj 2008) because of daily chaos, lack of security, severe poverty, and fears of children being kidnapped for ransom (Ismael 2007). The chance that a child will live beyond age five has plummeted faster than anywhere else in the world since 1990 (Save the Children 2007). In 2005, one in eight Iraqi children died of disease or violence in the first five years of life. This is the dire picture of reality for Iraqi children after the 2003 invasion and occupation despite the fact that the United Nations declared the first decade of the twenty-first century the "International Decade for a Culture of Peace and Non-Violence for the Children of the World."

Communicable Disease Control. After the 2003 invasion, despite extensive looting, Iraqis have persisted in efforts to operate drinking water facilities, sewage treatment plants, and other infrastructure critical to preventing disease transmission. However, by 2004, nearly 500,000 tons of raw and partially treated sewage continued to discharge into rivers each day (Medact 2004), fueling waterborne spread of communicable diseases. In 2003, it was estimated that 50 percent of Iraqis lacked access to clean drinking water; by 2007, this figure rose to 70 percent (Oxfam International 2007). Eighty percent of Iraqis also lacked effective sewerage in 2007 (Oxfam International 2007).

Malnutrition. Limited access to food after the 2003 invasion has resulted in widespread nutritional deficiencies. The public food-rationing systems originally installed by the Ba'athist regime in response to economic sanctions were already known to be micronutrient deficient (Hoskins 2000) but continued operating in order to prevent starvation. By late 2003, these systems became the primary food source for 25 percent of the population (Medact 2004) but still failed to adequately meet nutritional needs. As a result, Iraq's poorest households were left with chronic nutritional deficiencies and no financial means to secure additional food resources. In 2007, an estimated 4 million people (14 percent of the population) were deemed food insecure and in dire need of assistance (Oxfam

International 2007). While 96 percent of those in need of food assistance received food rations in 2004, only 60 percent did by 2007.

Middle-class urban Iraqi men whom we interviewed after their resettlement in the northeastern United States explained that difficulty accessing food and other crucial resources in postoccupation Iraq leads families to join the resistance to the occupation since the resistance offers these supplies in exchange for their participation. Nongovernmental organizations (NGOs) are hard pressed to fill this gap. Oxfam International (2007), for instance, reports the security situation in Iraq since 2003 has been too dangerous to keep a staff in country. Medact (2008:3) reports that "Iraq has . . . become the world's deadliest country for aid workers." As a result, smaller NGOs attempting to meet food and other basic needs in select cities have provided larger NGOs in-country support, but, because of security risks, the smaller NGOs have remained anonymous in all reporting.

Chemical Weaponry, Environmental Contamination, and Health. Chemical and conventional weapons used since the 2003 invasion and occupation have left behind a toxic mess of pollution (Al-Azzawi 2006; Information Clearing House 2005). Toxic residues uncovered to date have included napalm, a mixture of benzene, gasoline, or jet fuel with polystyrene (Iraq Analysis Group 2005); white phosphorus, a hazardous air pollutant manufactured from phosphate rocks (ATSDR 1997) that the U.S. Army reported using in Fallujah in November 2004 (Cobb et al. 2005); and DU, a radioactive waste product that is widely used as an alloy in modern armor and weaponry and whose chemical toxicity resembles lead (Harper 2007). In addition, nitrogen, sulfur, and carbon oxides are released from the detonation of conventional weapons, while soot and carcinogenic hydrocarbons contaminate the air where oil wells have burned (Al-Azzawi 2006). Extensive ground and water pollution has resulted from damaged sewage treatment plants and the destruction and looting of industrial buildings. Laser-guided missiles and radar equipment pollute the environment with pathogenic free radicals (Al-Azzawi 2006). Land erosion and flooding have resulted from the traffic of military equipment and bomb craters, which have also contributed to the increased incidence of sandstorms. And when these sandstorms arrive, they agitate the tons of microscopic radioactive contamination from DU and other chemical residues (Al-Azzawi 2006).

Several of the residues from chemical weapons used since the invasion—particularly white phosphorus, napalm derivatives, and DU—have been widely speculated to have carcinogenic and genotoxic health effects (Ammash 2000; Harper 2007; Iraq Analysis Group 2005). As with the Gulf War, use of DU in particular has led to concerns of increased cancer incidence in the Iraqi civilian population as well as occupying soldiers. The Scottish *Sunday Herald* in 2004 reported that WHO studies of the health effects of DU in Iraq were suppressed (Edwards 2004). Some of the world's most renowned scientific bodies, including the WHO, the United Nations Environment Program, the British Royal Society, and the U.S. National Academy of Sciences, have published some general studies on the health effects of DU that suggested that the greatest health risks are found among children in postconflict zones (Harper 2007), such as Iraq. As was the case following the 1991 Gulf War, Iraqi doctors have been documenting evidence of increased incidence of morbidity and mortality in their patient populations since the U.S. occupation began. Their descriptive, small-scale evidence shows an increased incidence of rare cancers (Al-Darraji 2008). Yet, because of the continued occupation and lack of security, the population-wide impacts of these exposures on the Iraqi people have been incredibly difficult to assess and document. Foreign staff of the WHO, for instance, were withdrawn in August 2003 and not reinstated until five years later in July 2008 (WHO 2008a). Therefore, health officials have been unable to conduct definitive epidemiologic studies of these exposure–disease relationships in Iraq.

In Fallujah, as in other cities in Iraq, there have been no efforts to clean up contaminants from the extensive U.S. military assaults that left behind napalm, white phosphorus, and other residues (Al-Azzawi 2008). One physician from Fallujah whom we spoke with said he and other Fallujah physicians believe that the increase in disease and the appearance of new pathologies is related to this pollution as well as widespread starvation and a devastated health system (Al-Darraji, personal communication). They have compared personal documentation of disease incidence from February 2004 with that of February 2006—two time periods that straddle the April 2004 and November 2004 sieges conducted by U.S. forces, both of which left extensive weapons contamination in the local environment. Their data demonstrate a dramatic shift in the types of pathology seen (see tables 4.2 and 4.3), including a marked increase in

Table 4.2. Fallujah Illnesses Diagnosed in February 2003

February 2003	Diagnosis	Number of Cases
I	Epidemic diarrhea	200
2	Low growth hormone	47
3	Acute renal failure	42
4	Brain hydatid cyst	20
5	Breast cancer	10
6	Diabetes mellitus	10
7	Leukemia	10
8	Congenital heart disease	5
Total		344

child morbidity and mortality. For the first time ever, in 2006, doctors in Fallujah began seeing cases of meningitis, thalassemias, septicemia from rare pathogens, congenital spinal and renal abnormalities, and diseases of unknown etiology (Al-Darraji 2008). More formal studies are necessary to evaluate the specific causes underlying these new disease patterns and the changing demographics in which these disease patterns are seen.

Insecurity. Many Iraqis we spoke with reported that assassinations and kidnappings have become routine in all sectors of society—no ethnic group is immune, nor is any social class. As one man put it, "We all now fear each other." Prior to fleeing Iraq, he had lived his entire life in Baghdad working as a gainfully employed engineer until shortly after his elder son was kidnapped in 2007, and he and his family fled the country out of fear for the lives of their remaining children.

Table 4.3. Fallujah Illnesses Diagnosed in February 2006

February 2006	Diagnosis	Number of Cases
I	Septicemia*	135
2	Congenital spinal cord abnormalities	114
3	Undiagnosed	97
4	Congenital renal abnormalities	87
5	Meningitis	80
6	Thalassemia	17
7	Leukemia	7
8	Brain tumor	5
Total		542

*Septicemia is believed to be arising from pollution following military assaults. Studies have not yet been done to identify definitive cause(s).

Iraqi women have all but disappeared from their roles in the work-force because of insecurity. Once substantial contributors to Iraqi society as teachers, judges, lawyers, doctors, engineers, traffic police, and more, the threat of violence and kidnapping now imprisons many women in their homes (Jamail 2008). This was reported to us repeatedly during our 2006 fieldwork in Basra. In addition, during our fieldwork among re-settled Iraqis in the northeastern United States, Mohammed and Zaineb (pseudonyms) explained that they felt forced to flee their town because of threats against women since the occupation began. Mohammed and Zaineb are a couple in their mid-forties who owned a thriving jewelry store and beauty salon in the Al-Anbar region of Iraq. When assassination threats specifically targeting women who did not cover themselves became regular postings on fliers in their town, they moved the women and girls of the family to Damascus and closed down their beauty salon in the interest of the family's safety. They chose to flee despite the fact that the women of this family had never before covered their hair with "hijab" and had never felt threatened prior to the insecurity wrought by the occupa-tion. Although the men stayed in Iraq to work, they reduced the length of their business hours because of the security threats posed by keeping their once-thriving business open at night. Ultimately, the security situation grew too dangerous to keep running the capital-intensive jewelry store, which became the victim of theft from local police authorities. Approxi-mately one year after relocating the women to Damascus, the men of the family became refugees as well. Mohammed and Zaineb's once-thriving and secure livelihood is evidenced by the two houses they own in separate regions of Iraq. But neither home felt safe enough to reside in given the postoccupation living conditions.

People often flee Iraq as refugees because of direct threats by un-known groups. Targeted sectarian violence against women prompts many families to flee, as was the case for Mohammed, Zaineb, and their family. The risks of kidnapping and of general insecurity are also real, as de-scribed through the stories of Mustafa and of Abu Ahmed and his family. Kidnapping risks are perhaps greatest for those who may be able to offer a ransom in return for their loved ones' safe return. Among the refugees we studied in the northeastern United States, approximately one-quarter of them had fled Iraq because one of their immediate family members had been kidnapped. In some instances the ransom was paid, and their family member was returned safely. In other instances, the family member's whereabouts remain unknown. For all, the experience was traumatic and left lasting mental scars that may never heal.

Those who have collaborated with the U.S. military—or are in any way affiliated with the occupation—are often perceived as traitors to the Iraqi people and are marked for death. One former Red Crescent worker now resettled as a U.S. refugee described receiving a phone call in which he was told, "You'll find your head separated from your body." Others who have worked with occupation forces have lived through the horror of their children being kidnapped and disappeared, while others have seen their relatives murdered. American news reports of resettled refugees almost invariably reference resettled individuals by initials only or by false names because those being interviewed fear for their relatives still in Iraq. Similar measures of protection are instituted for refugees resettled in other countries who assisted coalition forces but fear reprisals from their fellow resettled refugees (cf. Obaid-Chinoy 2008).

The health workforce has not been impervious to this targeted brutality. One medical resident working in Baghdad in 2004 told us that doctors were subject to abuse by patients if they did not provide the prognoses or medication that some patients demanded of them. As of October 2006, because of targeted assassinations throughout Iraq (Brussels Tribunal 2006), it is estimated that 2,000 doctors and 164 nurses were murdered and another 250 kidnapped for high-price ransoms (Laurance 2006). Yarmouk Hospital reports that patient care is regularly hampered by intrusion from occupation forces, policemen, and militiamen in desperate search of treatment for their comrades (Oxfam International 2007). These disruptions include storming of emergency rooms, with threats made against doctors and medical staff and shots fired inside the hospital to intimidate patients (Jamail 2005; Oxfam International 2007).

On top of the medical infrastructure's pressures to support an increased caseload in the face of dangerous working conditions, hospitals are additionally hampered by reduced staff due to medical personnel fleeing out of fear for their lives. The Iraqi Medical Association reported in 2006 that half of Iraq's 34,000 doctors had left the country since the 2003 invasion (Oxfam International 2007). By 2008, it was estimated that only 9,000 doctors remained in Iraq, virtually none of them with access to rural areas of the country (Medact 2008). Some Baghdad hospitals state that they have lost as many as 80 percent of their professional staff.

Many of Iraq's hospitals were looted following the 2003 invasion, and the general lack of security continues to delay or prevent delivery of life-saving supplies. KEMADIA, the state-owned medical supply company, is no longer able to support hospitals and primary health care centers (Oxfam International 2007). As a result, 90 percent of Iraq's hospitals lack basic medical and surgical supplies, such as epidural anesthesia for child labor or other indications. Some of the Iraqis we spoke with in Basra in 2006 said that the hospitals were in such disrepair that they were afraid to go to them for care when it was needed, even for childbirth. The situation was so dire that, during part of 2006, a worker at one of the main hospitals in Basra explained to us that they could not perform operations for a week because they had no gauze. Iraqi doctors have also stated that little money is being distributed from the U.S.-operated Ministry of Health to help the supply situation. As one doctor described, "Before the invasion, we had a much better supply situation, 80 percent better than now" (Jamail 2005). That is, the situation was 80 percent better under a brutal dictator and deadly economic sanctions than in "liberated" Iraq.

Trauma, Mental Health, and Social Suffering. The plight of the Iraqi people proves the adage that the experience of suffering cannot be effectively conveyed by quantitative analyses alone. As the occupation continues, millions of Iraqis suffer every day, watching the death tolls increase around them. Daily exposure to graphic violence weighs heavily on the hearts of those who remain in Iraq, amidst the carnage, fear, and uncertainty over what lies ahead. Those who have emigrated look back on their loved ones with fear, knowing full well how fragile life in Iraq is today.

During our 2006 fieldwork in Basra, we observed and heard stories of life as a constant struggle. As one Iraqi man expressed to us, "From what I witness every day in my country, I see traumatization is going on and ordinary people [whose] main goal is to survive their day." An Iraqi mental health professional we spoke with during our interviews compared Iraq to hell, exclaiming that any Iraqi family in Baghdad or any other major city will tell you the magnitude of pain and agony felt, "walk[ing] along the streets in their daily activities where dead bodies [are] scattered here and there, and homeless pets find these bodies a good source to satisfy their hunger."

Mustafa (pseudonym), who lived in Baghdad when he wrote to us in January 2007, described his version of hell. In the month since his father had been kidnapped by men with Glock pistols, each week he risked his life by traveling to the morgue to search for answers about his father's whereabouts. To facilitate the searching process for its visitors, the morgue used a wide screen to display the bodies of the dead. To no avail, Mustafa searched for his father week after week. His hopelessness—for his family and the plight of his countrymen—was utterly palpable when he exclaimed, "We Iraqis are all registered on the very long list of death, and nobody is exempted!"

Communities previously connected by family ties and relationships long developed through school and other community venues now struggle to survive. Displaced families and friends who have managed to escape and find refuge are spread across countries and continents. Those who remain in Iraq stand in fear of the gangs who prowl the streets and roadways, regularly executing drivers in cars to make the job of stealing their few assets that much easier. These frightful scenarios were described to us by Iraqi refugees who resettled to the United States in 2008, looking back on their homeland with fear but still connected to their loved ones who remain there. Others who remain in Iraq shared similar stories with us about the great risk of staying in their homeland. Mustafa, for instance, stayed in his hometown of Baghdad following his father's kidnapping. After moving his mother and brothers to another city in hopes that it would offer greater safety than Baghdad, Mustafa could no longer bear to visit his childhood home for fear that it had been taken over by gangs or militia, which he and others told us is common.

Visits to friends, trips to work, market outings, travel to schools, and all other aspects of normal daily life that used to be routine are now dangerous missions. Families, friends, and community networks who remain in Iraq are disconnected, detoured by roadblocks and walls erected by the U.S. Army Corps of Engineers to barricade neighborhoods. For many, social outings bear too heavy a price to be maintained. One of our informants explained that for the elderly ladies who continue to meet for morning coffee in their Baghdad neighborhood, as they have for years, the risk is worth the simple joy of a routine pleasure with the familiar faces that remain amidst the chaos. Perhaps the ladies possess an intuition about what the medical literature tells us: the refusal to abandon social networks may help prevent development and progression of posttraumatic stress disorder (PTSD) (Klein and Alexander 2006). For others, the joys of celebratory gatherings that used to be routine and harmless have often ended tragically. Gunshots and fireworks, traditionally used to mark Iraqi weddings and celebrations, have too often been mistaken as assaults by nearby U.S. military personnel who then attack the revelers. For the survivors of such attacks, the freedom to enjoy and celebrate life may never be regained.

Iraqis cannot help but be keenly aware of their suffering, for the trauma they endure is too real and too deep to allow any escape. Abu Ahmed (pseudonym) cannot sleep at night. He displays personality traits that his family told us they have never seen in him before, including feelings of helplessness and fear in the most normal of life situations. His eldest son was kidnapped years ago, and now Abu Ahmed is left with no indication of whether his son is alive, dead, or ever to be seen again. His home was nearly destroyed when a bomb fell just meters away, shattering every piece of glass in and around the house, including on the car outside. He shows many signs of PTSD and is struggling to start a new life as a refugee. Despite Abu Ahmed's scarring experiences that portend difficulties unimaginable to some, he sees his plight as normal for the Iraqi people today. "We [Iraqis] are all in trauma," he says. Despite this, he remains one of the rapidly shrinking number of Iraqis who have voiced optimism about the future since the 2003 invasion (Levy and Sidel 2008) and about the prospect of one day returning to Iraq. Through eyes welled with tears, Abu Ahmed explains that going home is a necessity because he must find his disappeared son.

Systematic mental health research in Iraq is limited by the same dangers that threaten daily life. No epidemiologic studies of adult mental health among people currently living in Iraq have been published. However, with support from the WHO, a number of Iraqi mental health professionals investigated the mental health of Iraqi children in three cities in early 2006 (Razokhi et al. 2006). In the city of Dohuk in northern Iraq, 120 working street children were compared to an equal number of children in school. The prevalence of mental disorders among the working children was nearly three times as high as among those attending school. In Mosul, nearly a third of adolescents screened from eight secondary schools had symptoms of PTSD, and the overwhelming majority (92 percent) had not received any form of treatment. Nearly half of 600 primary school children from 16 schools in Baghdad reported exposure to a major traumatic event, and nearly twice as many girls (17 percent) had PTSD than boys. This striking gender difference may reflect the embodiment of greater security risks for women and girls in postoccupation Iraq that were described to us by Mohammed and Zaineb but also by others who have commented that never before have they seen such repression of women in Iraq.

Given the regularity of torture and violence in the past three decades in Iraq, trauma-related disorders are estimated to be the largest public health problem (Al-Saffar 2007). Yet surveys conducted in Iraq in 2003 and 2006 found no community mental health day-treatment services or any community mental health residential facilities (Medact 2004; WHO 2006). As of 2004, just two mental hospitals and 25 outpatient mental facilities served a population of 28.5 million. In 2004, Iraq had a total of 91 psychiatrists, 7 assistant psychiatrists, 16 psychologists, and 25 social workers. Just 8 percent of primary and secondary schools had a mental health social adviser, while less than one-fifth had school-based activities geared toward mental health promotion. As of 2006, psychosocial support for traumatized populations was a top area identified for future mental health work but remained unfunded.

A growing number of researchers have been documenting PTSD and other reactions to traumatic events among Iraqis following the first Gulf War. Among child survivors of the Gulf War, the effects have been most startling. Nearly two-thirds of primary school–age children interviewed by one group of psychologists did not believe that they would survive to adulthood (Ismael 2007). Despite their 15 years of fieldwork in war-torn countries, the psychologists reported seeing higher levels of anxiety, stress, and pathological behavior in Iraqi children than they had previously seen among children who survived war. Other studies of Gulf War refugees have reported that more cases of PTSD and other health problems were documented in Gulf War refugees compared to other populations (Jamil et al. 2002). No estimates have been offered regarding what effect this preexisting trauma might have on the ability of Iraqis to cope with traumatic events from the 2003 invasion and subsequent occupation. However, comparisons of mental health among Iraqi refugees following the 2003 invasion compared to those who survived other conflicts in Kosovo, Somalia, Iran, and Afghanistan suggest that Iraqis have a significantly higher prevalence of depression, anxiety, PTSD, and more widespread exposure to traumatic events than others (IPSOS 2007).

Wars are routinely cited for breaking down the social fabric of life, causing great suffering and distress in individuals, with long-term mental health effects that can persist for as long as 50 years (Pedersen 2002). But the mental health effects of back-to-back wars, coupled with severely restricted access to the basic resources necessary for social and physical mending in between conflicts, as has occurred in Iraq, are unknown. Given the regularity with which wars are waged (cf. Blum 2004), relatively little is known about the population-level mental health effects of war-torn countries like Iraq, particularly when compared to the growing literature on the mental health effects of war on soldiers (Pedersen 2002). This startling gap in the medical and public health literature is a testament to the larger problem of analyses of responses to trauma being compartmentalized into individually experienced, discrete clinical disorders with little understanding of the contextual circumstances that give rise to the condition at hand. Moreover, no mechanism exists for moving beyond individual-level analyses to diagnose the mental health of communities (Kienzler 2008). Thus, for instance, characterizing PTSD among individual Iraqis today does little to enrich our understanding of the shared conditions that give rise to and that can also mitigate the experience of suffering, nor does it fully inform our ability to diagnose communities rattled by the trauma of war.

Refugees: A Second Dimension of Iraqi Social Suffering. Ethnic cleansing by occupation militias has displaced millions of Iraqis and added to the mental distress of daily life in Iraq. An estimated 60,000 Iraqis are forced to leave their homes each month (UNHCR 2007). Approximately 2.2 million Iraqis have been internally displaced, at least a third of whom are extremely vulnerable and in need of emergency assistance. Another 2.5 million are legal refugees who have fled Iraq and resettled (at least temporarily) primarily in Syria, Jordan, and other countries in the region. Through 2007, Syria was widely sought for asylum because the Syrian government offered Iraqi families the opportunity of asylum without visas. However, the Syrian government has since instituted a visa requirement as a means of reducing its post-2003 influx of refugees.

Following Syria's 2007 institution of a visa requirement for Iraqi refugees, resource-poor Iraqis have had almost no option for legal relocation out of Iraq. Unknown numbers of people have managed to resettle illegally outside Iraq. The Danish Refugee Council (2007) recently surveyed over 1,000 Iraqi refugees in Lebanon and discovered that most were there illegally. Such displaced persons quickly encounter difficulties from a lack of access to health insurance and social assistance. Many are also subject to detention by authorities.

The dwindling numbers of Iraqi refugees who do have the resources and ability to resettle legally often report inadequate support from resettlement organizations such as the UNHCR and other organizations and countries that offer resettlement assistance. A large proportion of resettled Iraqis require medical assistance, and they often are solely responsible for these costs. In Syria, Jordan, and Lebanon, where most Iraqi refugees flee (UNHCR 2007), a substantial proportion deplete their savings or rely on direct transfers from family members in Iraq and elsewhere to cover the costs of medical payments, food, and other basic necessities (Danish Refugee Council 2007; IPSOS 2007). These financial obstacles have prompted some refugees to engage in prostitution and other risky and illegal activities when opportunities for legal sources of income are unavailable or depleted (Obaid-Chinoy 2008). International organizations (e.g., Danish Refugee Council 2007) and individuals alike report that the sheer difficulty of physical survival among refugees threatens Iraqi human dignity. One Iraqi man we interviewed was pained to think of how Iraqis have lost both their state and their dignity. Such realizations clearly compound the mental anguish felt by Iraqis already struggling to pick up the pieces of their life and face each new day.

In the United States, refugee benefits from the U.S. State Department are sent to local resettlement agencies that then allocate the monies to refugees. The benefits last for a period of four to eight months[2] before the displaced are required to either survive on their own or secure public assistance. Although benefits are provided to resettled families almost immediately on their arrival, many resettlement workers we spoke with noted that the level of benefits provided amounts to resettling refugees into poverty. In some cities, if volunteers do not identify and prepare apartments for newly arriving individuals and families, refugees may arrive to apartments in squalid condition (e.g., filthy, mouse infested, and no heat in winter). Refugees then work with resettlement agencies to apply for food stamps, Medicaid, and in some cases additional cash assistance. Those who do not find at least minimum-wage employment must apply for further public assistance, again maintaining a standard of living in poverty. After their initial Medicaid benefits expire, access to medical care is no more guaranteed for Iraqi refugees than for the general U.S. population. Many Iraqis we spoke with who have family members who resettled in European nations said that their family members elsewhere receive far better resettlement assistance than what is provided in the United States, particularly in the realm of medical care.

Depending on financial limitations, families have been divided between multiple cities, countries, and continents, thereby intensifying the challenges of resettlement. Previously accustomed to strong, locally accessible social and familial support networks, Iraqis are now often forced to face financial, health, and other daily challenges in virtual isolation. This is a common pattern amongst war-displaced peoples. As noted by Pedersen (2002:182), "The displaced are usually deprived from social, material, and emotional support systems, which may make them more fragile and vulnerable to environmental adversities and social distress." Two refugee women from Baghdad with whom we spoke in 2008, a mother and her young adult daughter, exemplified this struggle. The family's father had been killed in Iraq and the mother wounded. The daughter spoke no English on arrival in the United States, had never worked outside the home, and could not imagine life without direct contact and support from her siblings, who are now split between Sweden, Germany, and Iraq. While thankful for a new life free of the daily threat of physical violence, they questioned how they would survive emotionally and financially at the end of their four-month term of resettlement benefits.

Refugee life can be fraught not only with the trauma of resettling in the aftermath of war but also with the difficulties of cultural assimilation. For Iraqis, this is perhaps uniquely evident in the United States—the aggressor nation whose violence many Iraqis seek to escape—than in any other country accepting Iraqi refugees from the current conflict. Some resettled Iraqis and the agencies they work with have told us of targeted discrimination by Americans against Iraqis. At the same time, among Iraqi refugees, we have witnessed a range of tolerance for U.S. culture and also for the actions of their fellow resettled Iraqis. This has had direct bearing on the ability of individuals to assimilate and start a new life. In addition, these differences have sometimes fostered divisions within resettlement communities that can hamper the ability of refugees to create new, local emotional support systems with one another.

The difficulties of cultural assimilation often stem from the daily practicality of starting over in a new country and a new bureaucracy without a reliable income. This frequently leaves refugees feeling helpless and demoralized. As one refugee exclaimed, "I feel like I am in kindergarten." Another family frequently expressed their confusion over the many different bills they must pay to maintain a U.S. household (e.g., rent, water, electric, phone, and so on) since they were accustomed to a more socialized system with little paperwork in Iraq. This cultural disparity between old and new service systems was perhaps most evident in regard to health care. Several Iraqis we observed and interviewed in the United States needed frequent medical attention. Resettlement agency officials whom we spoke with also reported that the Iraqi population in the United States has many medical needs. A UNHCR representative in Damascus reported that one in five refugees who register with UNHCR before their official resettlement elsewhere are victims of violence or torture in Iraq. However, it is not clear that U.S. resettlement agencies are prepared to address this in the Iraqi population. Anecdotal evidence suggests that Iraqi refugees have unmet mental health needs that resettlement agencies are unprepared to address. For instance, some resettlement agency volunteers expressed concern over depression and other psychological disorders among Iraqis but knew of no ways to advise Iraqis on how to address these issues using their very basic medical coverage—on top of the difficulty of securing translation services for specialized needs such as psychiatric visits. At the same time, we observed some Iraqis who, in addition to their genuine need for medical services, appeared to frequently consult medical services even in times of good health. Resettlement agency volunteers explained that part of the education process in their work with Iraqis has come to include explanation of the costs of medical visits in the U.S. private-payer system as compared to the more socialized medical system to which they were accustomed.

The United States is not only culturally disparate for Iraqis but also fraught with structural inadequacies for handling refugees. These systematic deficiencies compound the distress of resettlement. For instance, classes in English as a second language are often offered on resettlement, but basic language-learning tools, such as dictionaries, are not always provisioned. This lack of support exacerbates the inherent difficulty of adjusting to life in a new place and a new culture. This is but one example of how resettlement agencies are not able to adequately address the basic needs for refugees.

Several resettlement agencies either directly reported to us or demonstrated through their actions that they are always operating in "crisis mode" when welcoming and resettling refugees. One resettlement agency noted that the distribution of funds and the chain of communication is so poorly administered from the U.S. State Department to the local level that the system is simply inadequate by design. This has clearly added to the distress felt by refugees in such a culturally disparate nation. Some we spoke with have gone so far as to say that they wish they could return to Syria instead of attempting to cope with the U.S. system; others have felt so distraught that they said they would rather return to Iraq.

Conclusion

In the twentieth and twenty-first centuries, oil has become the primary currency for building capitalist empires. Iraq sits on oceans of oil in a region whose vast resources have made it the centerpiece of repeated imperialist aggressions. Specifically, since 1990, there has been no respite for Iraqis from the suffering inflicted by U.S. foreign policy aims. Water, sanitation, and electricity grids, once bolstered by nationalized oil profits, were targeted repeatedly from 1991 through the 2003 U.S.-led attacks that aimed to weaken Iraq's oil sovereignty. Coupled with more than a decade of economic embargo and no-fly-zone bombing campaigns, imperialist-motivated attacks on Iraq have debilitated the Iraqi infrastructure—and the health of the Iraqi people has followed suit.

Rather than liberation, the 2003 invasion and ensuing illegal occupation of Iraq have defined Iraqi society by death squads, checkpoints, detentions, kidnappings, blood in the streets, and constant violence. Occupied Iraq is a sea of war crimes committed in violation of the UN Charter, the Geneva Convention, and the Universal Declaration of Human Rights. The very real, daily suffering felt today by the Iraqi people is the direct result of the modern political-economic world system.

Iraqi health is worse today than at any other time in history. Life expectancy has decreased, child health measures have plummeted, malnutrition is on the rise, and rare new cancers define Iraq's chronic disease experience. The Iraqi people have been devastated by traumatic bombings with unconventional weapons and years of insecurity. This has caused an alarming decline in mental health—so much so that the mental health community has been hard pressed to characterize or treat it. At the same time, millions of refugees have rapidly fled Iraq, exacerbating the collective social suffering experienced by the Iraqi people. When asked to comment on this, one emigrated Iraqi woman whom we interviewed in the United States proclaimed, "Damn the oil that was never a gift to us but a curse. A country like Iraq that floats on oil and its people are refugees living way below poverty standards in neighboring poor countries with no resources. It is utterly heartbreaking to see my Iraqi people live through this horrible time of history." For those who choose to monitor the effects of the global war machine, what has become obvious in Iraq is that societal destruction is not collateral damage; it is the nature of modern warfare, with the U.S. capitalist interests at the helm.

Acknowledgments

We would like to thank the many Iraqis with whom we had the honor of interviewing, observing, and working. You have touched our lives, and for this we are forever indebted. We would also like to thank the many journalists, aid workers, activists, and researchers whose tireless efforts helped inform this chapter. For very helpful editorial assistance, we thank Dr. Andrew Coates, Dr. Merrill Singer, and Dr. G. Derrick Hodge. Any errors or omissions are, of course, our own.

Notes

1. The U.S. attempt to prevent deliveries of vaccines to Iraq was reversed after vehement protests from UNICEF and the World Health Organization (Chomsky 2003).

2. The duration of benefits allotted depends on eligibility and available funds. Former interpreters for U.S. forces receive the longest duration of benefits. All

others receive either a four- or a six-month allotment, depending on the grant funds available to resettlement agencies.

Works Cited

Al-Azzawi, Dr. Souad N.

2006   *Depleted uranium radioactive contamination in Iraq: An overview.* On-line: http://www.brusselstribunal.org/pdf/DU-Azzawi.pdf. Accessed May 3, 2008.

2008   *Crimes of the century: Occupation and contaminating Iraq with deplete uranium.* Online: http://www.brusselstribunal.org/pdf/DU-Azzawi2 .pdf. Accessed April 1, 2009.

Al-Darraji, Dr. Muhamad T. A.

2008   Prohibited Weapons Crisis: The effects of pollution on the public health in Fallujah. Paper presented at the seventh session of the United Nations Human Rights Council, Geneva, March 3–28.

Al-Saffar, S.

2007   Integrating rehabilitation of torture victims into the public health of Iraq. *Torture* 17(2):156–168.

Ali, Tariq

2003   *Bush in Babylon: The Recolonisation of Iraq.* New York: R. R. Don-nelley & Sons.

Ammash, Huda S.

2000   Toxic pollution, the Gulf War, and sanctions. In *Iraq under Siege: The Deadly Impact of Sanctions and War*, ed. Anthony Arnove, 169–78. Cambridge, MA: South End Press.

ATSDR

1997   *Toxicological Profile for White Phosphorous.* Atlanta: U.S. Department of Health and Human Services, Public Health Service.

Bennis, Phyllis, and Denis J. Halliday (Interviewed by David Barsamian)

2000   Iraq: The impact of sanctions and US policy. In *Iraq under Siege: The Deadly Impact of Sanctions and War*, ed. Anthony Arnove, 35–46. Cambridge, MA: South End Press.

Blum, William

2004   *Killing Hope: U.S. Military and C.I.A. Interventions Since World War II.* Monroe, ME: Common Courage Press.

Brussels Tribunal
2006   *Madrid International Seminar on the Assassination of Iraqi Academics and Health Professionals.* Online: http://www.brusselstribunal.org/SeminarMadrid.htm. Accessed May 3, 2008.

Burnham, Gilbert, Riyadh Lafta, Shannon Doocy, and Les Roberts
2006   Mortality after the 2003 invasion of Iraq: A cross-sectional cluster sample survey. *Lancet* 368:1421–1428.

CARE International in Iraq
2003   *Humanitarian assistance capacity in Iraq, January 2003.* Published by Johns Hopkins University Center for International Emergency, Disaster and Refugee Studies. Online: http://www.who.int/disasters/repo/9353.pdf. Accessed June 5, 2008.

Chomsky, Noam
2003   *Hegemony or Survival: America's Quest for Global Dominance.* New York: Metropolitan Books.

Clark, Ramsey
1992   *The Fire This Time: U.S. War Crimes in the Gulf.* New York: Thunder's Mouth Press.

Cobb, Captain James T., First Lieutenant Christopher A. LaCour, and Sergeant First Class William H. Hight
2005   The fight for Fallujah. *Field Artillery*, March–April 2005, 22–28. Online: http://sill-ww.army.mil/FAMAG/2005/MAR_APR_2005 MAR_APR_2005_FULL_EDITION.pdf. Accessed March 24, 2009.

Danish Refugee Council
2007   *Iraqi population survey in Lebanon.* Stockholm: Danish Refugee Council.

Dreyer, Jane Teufel
2007   *Chinese foreign policy.* Online: http://www.fpri.org/footnotes/125.200702.dreyer.chineseforeignpolicy.html. Accessed April 5, 2009.

Drutman, Lee, and Charlie Cray
2003   *Halliburton, Dick Cheney, and wartime spoils.* Online: http://www.commondreams.org/views03/0403-10.htm. Accessed: March 31, 2009.

eDinar Financial
2009   *History of Iraqi dinar and Iraq dinar stock exchange.* Online: http://
www.edinarfinancial.net/history.php. Accessed April 4, 2009.

Edwards, Rob
2004   *WHO "suppressed" scientific study into depleted uranium cancer fears in
Iraq.* Online: http://www.commondreams.org/headlines04/0222-
08.htm. Accessed August 11, 2008.

Garfield, Richard
1995   Health and well-being in Iraq: Sanctions and the impact of the Oil
for Food Program. In United Nations Children Fund, *Iraq Emergency Country Profile.* New York: United Nations Children Fund.

Global Policy Forum
2008   *History of oil in Iraq.* Online: http://www.globalpolicy.org/security/
issues/iraq/history/oilhistindex.htm. Accessed August 1, 2008.

Hajaj, Claire
2008   *UNICEF appeals for $37 million to save vulnerable Iraqi children.*
Online: http://www.unicef.org/infobycountry/iraq_42810.html Accessed February 19, 2008.

Harper, Janice
2007   Depleted Uranium and the Scientific Battlefields behind the Front-
lines. Paper presented at the Society for Applied Anthropology Annual Meetings, March 29, 2007, Tampa, Florida, U.S.A.

Hoskins, Eric
2000   Public health and the Persian Gulf War. In *War and Public Health,*
ed. Barry S. Levy and Victor W. Sidel, 254–278. Washington, DC:
American Public Health Association.

Information Clearing House
2005   *Fallujah—The hidden massacre.* Online: http://www.information-
clearinghouse.info/article10907.htm. Accessed August 1, 2008.

IPSOS
2007   *Second IPSOS Survey on Iraqi Refugees (31 October–25 November
2007): Final Results.*

Iraq Analysis Group
2005   *Fire bombs in Iraq: Napalm by any other name.* Online: http://www
.iraqanalysis.org/local/459_20050330IAGFirebombs.pdf. Accessed
April 1, 2009.

Ismael, Shereen T.
2007   The cost of war: The children of Iraq. *Journal of Comparative Family Studies* 38(spring 2007):337–357.

Jamail, Dahr
2004a   *Americans slaughtering civilians in Fallujah.* Online: http://www.antiwar.com/orig/jamail.php?articleid=2303. Accessed February 18, 2009.
2004b   *Fallujah refugees tell of life and death in the kill zone.* Online: http://dahrjamailiraq.com/fallujah-refugees-tell-of-life-and-death-in-the-kill-zone. Accessed February 9, 2008.
2004c   *US military obstructing medical care in Iraq.* Online: http://www.dahrjamailiraq.com. Accessed June 4, 2008.
2005   *Iraqi hospitals ailing under occupation.* Online: http://www.dahrjamailiraq.com. Accessed June 5, 2008.
2008   *Women's Day Iraq—Surviving somehow behind a concrete purdah.* Online: http://dahrjamailiraq.com/womens-day-iraq-surviving-somehow-behind-a-concrete-purdah. Accessed February 17, 2009.

Jamil, Hikmet, Julie Hakim-Larson, Mohamed Farrag, Talib Kafaji, Issa Duqum, and Laith H. Jamil
2002   A retrospective study of Arab American mental health clients: Trauma and the Iraqi refugees. *American Journal of Orthopsychiatry* 72:355-361.

Kienzler, Hanna
2008   Debating war-trauma and post-traumatic stress disorder (PTSD) in an interdisciplinary arena. *Social Science and Medicine* 67:218–227.

Klein, Susan, and David A. Alexander
2006   Epidemiology and presentation of post-traumatic disorders. *Psychiatry* 5(7):225–227.

Knauft, Bruce M.
2007   Provincializing America: Imperialism, capitalism, and counterhegemony in the twenty-first century. *Current Anthropology* 48(6):781–805.

Laurance, Jeremy
2006, October 20   Medics beg for help as Iraqis die needlessly. *The Independent.* Online: http://news.independent.co.uk/world/middle_east/article1904962.ece. Accessed February 22, 2008.

Leopold, Jason
2003, August   Wolfowitz admits Iraq War planned two days after 9-11.
Utne Reader. Online: http://www.utne.com/2003-08-01/Wolfowitz-
Admits-Iraq-War-Planned-Two-Days-After-9-11.aspx. Accessed
March 25, 2009.

Levy, Barry S., and Victor W. Sidel
2008   The Iraq War. In *War and Public Health*, 2nd ed., ed. Barry S. Levy
and Victor W. Sidel, 243–263. New York: Oxford University Press.

Lorimer, Doug
2004   U.S. launches mass slaughter in Fallujah. *Green Left Online.* Online: http://www.greenleft.org.au/2004/606/31395. Accessed July 8,
2008.

MacAskill, Ewan, and Julian Borger
2004   Iraq War was illegal and breached UN charter, says Annan. *The
Guardian.* Online: http://www.guardian.co.uk/world/2004/sep/16/
iraq.iraq. Accessed March 25, 2009.

Medact
2004   *Enduring Effects of War: Health in Iraq 2004.* London: Medact.
2008   *Rehabilitation under Fire: Health Care in Iraq 2003–7.* London: Medact.

Munier, Gilles
2004   *Iraq: An Illustrated History and Guide.* Northampton: Interlink Publishing Group.

Obaid-Chinoy, Sharmeen
2008   *The lost generation: A film.* Available at http://sharmeenobaidfilms
.com.

Opinion Research Business
2007   *More than 1,000,000 Iraqis murdered.* Online: http://www.opinion
.co.uk/Newsroom_details.aspx?NewsId=78. Accessed July 29, 2008.

Oxfam International
2007   *Rising to the Humanitarian Challenge in Iraq.* New York: Oxfam
International.

Pedersen, Duncan
2002   Political violence, ethnic conflict, and contemporary wars: Broad
implications for health and well-being. *Social Science and Medicine*
55:175–190.

Pellett, Peter L.
2000   Sanctions, food, nutrition, and health in Iraq. In *Iraq under Siege: The Deadly Impact of Sanctions and War*, ed. Anthony Arnove, 151–168. Cambridge, MA: South End Press.

Prescott-Allen, Robert
2001   *The Wellbeing of Nations*. Washington, DC: Island Press.

Project for the New American Century
1997   *Statement of principles*. Online: http://www.newamericancentury.org/ statementofprinciples.htm. Accessed March 21, 2009.
1998, January 27   Speaking of Iraq. Letter to President Clinton. *Washington Times*, A21.
2000   *Rebuilding America's Defenses: Strategies, Forces, and Resources for a New Century*.

Razokhi, Ali H., Issam K. Taha, Nezar Ismat Taib, Sabah Sadik, and Naeema Al Gasseer
2006   Mental health of Iraqi children. *Lancet* 368:838–839.

Roberts, Les, Riyadh Lafta, Richard Garfield, J. Khudhairi, and Gilbert Burnham
2004   Mortality before and after the 2003 invasion of Iraq: Cluster sample survey. *Lancet* 364:1857–1864.

Roseberry, William
1988   Political economy. *Annual Review of Anthropology* 17:161–185.

Save the Children
2007   *State of the world's mothers 2007: Saving the lives of children under 5*. Online: http://www.savethechildren.org/campaigns/state-of-theworlds-mothers-report/2007. Accessed June 23, 2008.

Scahill, Jeremy
2008   *Blackwater: The Rise of the World's Most Powerful Mercenary Army*. New York: Nation Books.

Sunday Times
2005   The Secret Downing Street memo. Online: http://www.timesonline .co.uk/tol/news/uk/article387374.ece. Accessed March 24, 2009.

United Nations Children's Fund
1995   *Iraq Emergency Country Profile*. Geneva: United Nations Children's Fund.

1997   *Nearly one million children malnourished in Iraq.* Online: http://www
        .unicef.org/newsline/97pr60.htm. Accessed June 6, 2007.

2007   *The state of the world's children.* Online: http://www.unicef.org/sowc/
        index_38236.html. Accessed March 21, 2009.

United Nations High Commissioner for Human Rights
    1949   Geneva Convention relative to the protection of civilian persons in
            time of war. Online: http://www.unhchr.ch/html/menu3/b/92.htm.
            Accessed April 5, 2009.

United Nations High Commissioner for Refugees
    2007   *Statistics on Displaced Iraqis around the World, September 2007.* Ge-
            neva: United Nations High Commissioner for Refugees.

United Nations Security Council
    1995   *United Nations Security Council Resolution 986 (1995).* Online:
            http://daccessdds.un.org/doc/UNDOC/GEN/N95/109/88/PDF/
            N9510988.pdf?OpenElement. Accessed April 5, 2009.

U.S. Department of Defense
    2004, February 11   DoD announces top contractors for fiscal year 2003.
            Office of the Assistant Secretary of Defense (Public Affairs) News
            Release No. 098-04.

    2005, January 27   DoD announces fiscal 2004 report. Office of the Assistant
            Secretary of Defense (Public Affairs) News Release No. 012-05.

    2006, January 26   DOD releases fiscal 2005 top contractors report. Office
            of the Assistant Secretary of Defense (Public Affairs) News Release
            No. 006-06.

West, Andrew
    2003, January 26   800 missiles to hit Iraq in first 48 hours. *Sydney Morning
            Herald.*

World Health Organization
    2003, March 19   *Humanitarian situation report number 1.* Published by the
            Office of the Humanitarian Coordinator for Iraq. Online: http://
            www.who.int/disasters/repo/9469.pdf. Accessed March 4, 2008.

    2006   *WHO-AIMS report on mental health system in Iraq.* Online: http://
            www.who.int/mental_health/evidence/iraq_who_aims_report.pdf.
            Accessed June 6, 2008.

2008a *WHO restores permanent international presence in Iraq.* Online: http://www.who.int/hac/crises/irq/sitreps/who_presence_in_iraq/en. Accessed July 20, 2008.

2008b *World health statistics 2008.* Online: http://www.who.int/whosis/whostat/EN_WHS08_Full.pdf. Accessed July 23, 2008.

CHAPTER FIVE

THE IMPACT OF THE WAR MACHINE ON GLOBAL WARMING AND HEALTH
A Political-Ecological Perspective
Hans Baer

Various forces—the production and transport of commodities to solve crises of overaccumulation, the increasing proliferation of motor vehicles, an expanding number of airplane flights worldwide, the overheating and overcooling of commercial operations, deforestation, animal production for food, and industrial agriculture—are often cited as sources of global warming. War and war machines, as defined in this volume, are not usually included on this list. As the simple scheme illustrated here indicates, in addition to its direct effects on human health and well-being, the war machine generates a considerable level of greenhouse gas emission, which, in turn, contributes to global warming and negative impacts on health. At the same time, global warming contributes to armed conflict, creating a vicious cycle for the planet and its inhabitants.

War and the Motor Vehicle–Oil Complex

In their monumental book *Monopoly Capital*, Paul Baran and Paul Sweezy (1996) identified the steam engine, the railroad, and the automobile as having had "epoch-making" impacts on capitalist development in their respective eras of technological dominance. They argued that the petroleum industry in large part has been a creation of the automobile. While states and empires have long engaged in "resource wars," as Michael Klare (2001) so aptly observes, the discovery of oil in the late

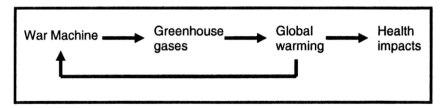

Figure 5.1   The impact of the war machine on global warming and health.

nineteenth century added a new dimension to warfare. According to Kolko (2006:177),

> The destructive potential of weaponry has increased exponentially, and many more people and nations have access to it. . . . The world has reached the most dangerous point in recent, or perhaps all of, history. There are threats of war and instability unlike anything that prevailed when a Soviet-led bloc existed. Since the beginning of the twentieth century, oil has played a significant part in both world and regional wars.

Moreover, as McQuaig (2004:3) usefully observes, "Even as the competition over dwindling reserves heats up and threatens to cause international conflict, we are faced with a still more devastating consequence of our addiction to oil—global warming."

While war contributes to global warming in terms of greenhouse gas emission, as indicated in figure 5.1, the converse is also true. One of the consequences of global warming is increased dispute and armed conflict. This pattern already can be seen in sub-Saharan Africa through the increase in warfare in drought-stricken regions, with each conflict involving even larger-scale fighting as the ever-worsening twenty-first-century effects of global warming unfold. Bearing in mind the integral connections between fossil fuel–powered motor vehicles, oil, and war, one may pinpoint the motor vehicle/oil/military complex as a principal engine of production within the capitalist world economy and hence a central component of the war machine.

As figure 5.2 illustrates, the unrelenting capitalist drive for profits, as it is played out somewhat differently within individual nations (e.g., the United States, England, Japan, Germany, Russia, and China), leads to an ever-expanding need to extract oil from the environment in order to provide fuel for motor vehicles and other forms of transportation, including those used for military purposes. Motor vehicles, of course, impact human health as a result of accidents, but in addition they impact human health because the by-products of fossil fuel combustion are various highly toxic environmental pollutants (e.g., carbon monoxide, benzene, and nitric oxide) and carbon dioxide (CO_2), a greenhouse gas.

Global warming and other environmental degradations pose serious problems not only for human settlement and subsistence patterns but also for human health in the form of increased heat stress and exhaustion, flooding, and infectious diseases that have spread because of the warming of environments at greater distances from the equator and at higher elevations. The systemic drive for ever-increasing profit pushes for expanded power to ensure the ability to gain control of energy and other resources, driving up the war machine's need for fuel and consequent environmental damage, in turn creating new conflict over dwindling usable resources. Eventually, resource wars erupt in various regions, thereby creating scenarios in which the carbon-based military machine pollutes the environment, causes global warming, creates diseases and other health problems, and kills and maims people. The end result is an ever more impactful—in terms of fiscal, human, and ecological costs—upward spiral of adverse interactions between the war machine, the environment, and human health.

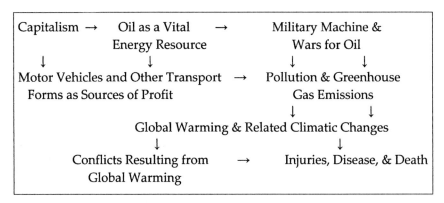

Figure 5.2. Model of the relationships between the oil/motor vehicle/military complex, war, global warming, and health.

Oil for Military Operations and Wars

Although the discovery of oil preceded the advent of the automobile era by about five years, the rise of the petroleum and the automobile industries were intricately interwoven. Oil was the principal source of economic growth during most of the twentieth century and continues to be so in the twenty-first (Heinberg 2006:1). It is estimated that nearly half of worldwide oil consumption is devoted to the global auto and aircraft industries. While most motor vehicles and airplanes are used by civilians, a notable number of them are owned by the military and are used in military operations and in wars.

Militaries, with their heavy reliance on airplanes (ranging from jet fighters to planes carrying troops and cargo to Air Force One), battleships, aircraft carriers, tanks, and other military equipment, rely heavily on oil. Indeed, the Post Carbon Institute (2007) reports that the Pentagon is the single largest consumer of oil in the world, using 320,000 barrels of oil per day for vehicle transport and facility maintenance. The official figure does not include "energy for the manufacture of vehicles, energy for building and dismantling of military facilities, energy for construction of roads, and energy consumed while rebuilding whatever the military blows up" (Fitz 2007:1). Klare (2003:11) maintains that the Pentagon consumed 134 million barrels of oil in 2005, as much as the entire country of Sweden. He also reports that during the Second World War the American military burned approximately one gallon of oil per soldier per day. This increased to four gallons per soldier per day during the first Gulf War of 1990-91, and during the Bush wars in Iraq and Afghanistan consumption jumped to 16 gallons per soldier per day. One-third or more of U.S. military oil consumption reportedly occurs outside the United States. Two decades ago, Smith (1990–1991:1) reported,

> The biggest gas-hogs in the Pentagon's arsenal are the Navy's non-nuclear aircraft carriers that burn 134 barrels per hour and battleships which consume 68 barrels per hour. At a speed of 25 knots, the USS *Independence* (a 1,070-foot-long aircraft carrier with . . . a flight deck and a crew of 2,300) consumes 150,000 gallons of fuel a day.

Consumption levels have continued to rise along with the constant development of new and more powerful war vehicles. An armored division of 348 tanks requires nearly half a billion gallons of fuel per day. A B-52 bomber requires 86 barrels per hour, and F-4 Phantom fighter/bombers consume 25 gallons of fuel per minute. Ironically, the U.S. Army is redesigning the Humvee, a battlefield vehicle that has been modified for the civilian market, because it travels as little as four miles per gallon in city traffic and only eight miles per gallon on the open road (Peak-Oil News and Message Boards 2009). More so than all the other countries in the world, as George W. Bush noted in his State of the Union Address on January 31, 2006, "America is addicted to oil." Klare (2003:16) adds that oil is "absolutely essential to U.S. national security, in that it powers the vast array of tanks, planes, helicopters, and ships that constitute the backbone of the American war machine."

Gwynne Dyer (2008), an international affairs journalist, posits diminishing natural resources, massive population shifts, "natural disasters," spreading epidemics, droughts in some regions, rising sea levels, declining agricultural productivity, economic crises, and political upheaval as some of the possible consequences of global warming and associated climatic changes that may come to drive international conflicts as the twenty-first century unfolds. His futuristic book foresees potential security crises in the United States in 2029, northern India in 2036, and China in 2042. It is evident in various studies and committees commissioned by the Pentagon (Walsh 2009) that there is growing awareness within the war machine that global warming is likely to be a primary source of future conflict.

Hot and Cold Wars for Oil

Oil has long been a factor in international power initiatives and conflict. The Japanese attack on Pearl Harbor on December 7, 1941, for example, was in part prompted by the American decision to cut off oil exports to Japan earlier that year (Heinberg 2006). Prior to this event, Japan had relied very heavily on imported oil from the United States and invaded the Dutch East Indies in part to access its rich oil fields.

Since World War II, Western powers have continued to employ military might to ensure access to oil. In his discussion of "petro-imperialism," Altvater (2006:51) argues that "oil security" constitutes one of the priorities of the United States and other powerful oil-consuming countries and blocs, such as the European Union. He delineates three strategies that these countries and blocs have utilized in their efforts to gain strategic control over oil: "diplomacy, and the establishment of friendly inter-state relations, as in the Gulf region; or by means of subversion, as in some Latin American and African countries; or by using massive military power, such as in Iraq, and to a lesser extent also in Central America—and perhaps in the future against Iran and Venezuela" (Altvater 2006:51). The 1953 coup in Iran orchestrated by the United States and the United Kingdom that resulted in the overthrow of Prime Minister Mossadegh was in large part prompted by his call to nationalize his country's oil fields (Wheelwright 1991).

During the Cold War, Baran and Sweezy (1966:183) argue, the United States employed its military and economic power to "attract large segments of old colonial empires into its own neo-colonial empire." In its assertion that it constituted the principal bulwark against the spread of communism, the United States in the wake of World War II: 1) provided economic support to various capitalist powers, particularly the United Kingdom, West Germany, and Japan; 2) created an elaborate system of military alliances and bases around the massive perimeter of the Soviet bloc and elsewhere; and 3) developed a massive military force that essentially functioned as a form of state capitalism under the guise of what Eisenhower aptly termed the "military-industrial complex," of which the motor vehicle–military complex constitutes a major component (Baran and Sweezy 1966:191). In contrast, while the Soviet Union developed its own military-industrial complex, its stance toward foreign relations was largely defensive, including using its military muscle to create a subordinated buffer zone between itself and the West by establishing and maintaining satellites in Eastern Europe.

The rich oil reserves of the Persian Gulf region have long served as a locus of the resource wars. Following colonial and neocolonial interventions in the area by Britain, Russia, France, and Germany, the United States has established itself the major world power in the region. According to Klare (2002:x), "By the end of the twentieth century, safeguarding the flow of oil from the Persian Gulf had become one of the most important functions of the U.S. military establishment."

Indeed, tensions in the Middle East are one of the factors that have affected the price of oil over the course of the past three decades or so. As the editors of *Monthly Review* reported a few months before the U.S. invasion of Iraq in 2003,

Military, political, and economic aspects are intertwined in all stages of imperialism, as well as capitalism in general. However, oil is the single most important strategic factor governing U.S. ambitions in the Middle East. (Editors 2002:9)

Middle Eastern governments, such as Saudi Arabia, Iran, and Iraq, have used their oil earnings to purchase more weapons and have assisted arms manufacturers in capitalist economies to earn tremendous profits. What Nitzan and Bichler (2004:310) term the "Weapondollar-Petrodollar Coalition" requires an "atmosphere of permanent threat," a role played for the United States by the Soviet Union during the Cold War. At the same time, while the United States has acted in an increasingly imperialist manner in the Middle East, the war in Iraq has split the countries of the European Union in various ways and has revealed internal tensions within the core countries of the capitalist world system (Boswell 2004).

Many countries, in both the developed and the developing worlds, have a strategic interest in securing access to petroleum and other energy supplies. The United States, far more than any other country, has employed its military for this purpose. According to Dancs et al. (2008:35),

Without including costs of war, we estimate that approximately $100 billion out of the military budget is spent to fulfil the mission of securing access to energy in fiscal year 2009. If we include three-fourths of the spending on the Iraq War, the figure doubles. Without war, securing energy access accounts for about 20 percent of the Department of Defense budget. With the majority of the Iraq War spending included, the proportion rises to nearly one-third of the budget.

Darfur in southern Sudan and other parts of sub-Saharan Africa constitute the loci for a new Cold War, one focusing on competition for oil between Western powers and China. Increasingly, China requires massive amounts of this commodity in order to support its monumental economic growth (Engdahl 2007). China now extracts an estimated 30 percent of the oil it needs from Africa with about 8 percent coming from southern Sudan alone. The China National Petroleum Corporation (CNPC) owns 40 percent of the Greater Nile Petroleum Operating Company, with the Sudanese National Energy Company owning 60 percent of the consortium. CNPC has constructed a pipeline to connect its concession blocs 1,

2, and 4 in southern Sudan to a new terminal at Port Sudan in the Red Sea. It also holds concession rights to bloc 6, which straddles Darfur, near the borders with Chad and the Central African Republic. Sudan was China's fourth-largest foreign oil source in 2006 (ibid.).

The United States is also active in sub-Saharan Africa. It now obtains more than 15 percent of its oil from various West African countries, almost as much as it acquires from Saudi Arabia. The United States has carefully courted the oil-producing countries Angola, Nigeria, Chad, and Equatorial Guinea. All of these nations have despotic regimes to varying degrees. In Angola, Jose Eduardo dos Santos has used oil revenues to build both a massive army and secret police force. While U.S. oil companies were signing contracts with Gabon, Nigeria, Equatorial Guinea, Angola, and Algeria, the Bush administration increased aid to and stationed military advisers in various African countries (Turshen 2004:2). Furthermore, in their efforts to grab oil,

> The leading energy-consuming nations have tried to protect access to vital materials by providing arms and military training to the armed forces of their primary suppliers, thereby encouraging the rulers of these countries to rely on brute force rather than compromise and inclusion when dealing with any group that seeks a greater share of oil or mineral revenues. More often than not, this guarantees an endless succession of coups at the top and revolts, ethnic upheavals, and gang wars below. (Klare 2008:176)

Indeed, one reading of the initiation by the Bush administration of the $50 billion President's Emergency Plan for AIDS Relief, most of which goes to 21 African nations, is that it is part of an effort to court relations and goodwill in Africa in light of the growing importance of African oil to the U.S. economy.

Another cold war of sorts has developed between the United States and various South American countries, particularly Venezuela, over the past several years. As part of his anti-imperialist policies, Venezuelan President and populist Hugo Chavez has used the oil income of his country's nationalized oil industry to finance ambitious social programs, especially in education and health care. He also provides Cuba with 53,000 barrels of oil a day (Jones 2007:288). In turn, financially strapped Cuba is allowed to pay with a combination of money, goods, and services. This has been termed the "Bolivarian matrix" (see Monreal 2006). This arrangement is estimated to be worth $550 million a year and is intended to provide Cuba with one-third of its needed oil supply. Venezuela has also struck an agreement to sell oil to China and will obtain 18 ships in return (Jones 2007:443). Under Chavez's presidency, Venezuela has encouraged its hemispheric neighbors to create regional oil consortia for the Caribbean (Petrocaribe), the Andean region (Petroandino), South America (Petrosur), and Latin America (Petroamerica). Chavez also assisted Argentina in paying its debt to the International Monetary Fund, assisted Bolivia in paying off some of its debts, and "pledged $1 billion in credit assistance to Ecuador" (Rothkoff 2008:186). He has visited numerous countries, including Russia, China, Belarus, Iran, Indonesia, Vietnam, Malaysia, Portugal, Qatar, Syria, Mali, Benin, and Angola, and there is little doubt that oil was a key item of discussion with other heads of state. While undoubtedly Chavez's extensive exercises in foreign diplomacy have cut into monies that could be spent for domestic programs, he has quickly evolved into a major player among a network of countries that are seeking in a variety of ways to challenge U.S. economic and military hegemony. The Bush administration sought as much as possible to undermine his influence both on the global scene and within his own country by backing ventures to depose him (Lebowitz 2006:95). In contrast, President Barack Obama, as was manifested in his cordial demeanor toward Chavez at the Fifth Summit of the Americas in Port du Spain, Trinidad, in April 2009 and his promise of reestablishing diplomatic ties with Venezuela, has adopted a "doctrine of engagement" toward the populist (if demagogic) president who embraces socialist values.

Oil and War as Generators of Greenhouse Gas Emissions

McQuaig (2004:3) succinctly captures the linkage between the demand for oil and the environmental consequences of its use, arguing that we are "in a strangely paradoxical situation: there's not enough oil to meet the world's growing consumption, but that growing consumption is itself threatening to ruin the world." Caught now between "the frying pan and the fire, we seem to be squeezed into a space without a lot of wiggle space" (McQuaig 2004:3). The exact level of contribution of military operations to global warming remains an underresearched topic. Biswas (2000) assesses the long-term consequences of specific wars on the environment, discusses impacts on land, water, and air quality as well as on noise pollution, resource depletion, and the generation of hazardous wastes, but he downplays the impact of war on global warming. In commenting on greenhouse gas emissions resulting from the first Gulf War, he observes that "carbon dioxide emissions from the war are now estimated at 300 million metric tons, only about 1.5 percent of the current global emissions from the burning of fossil fuels and biomass . . . the impact on global warming is likely to be so small that [it is] immeasurable because the extent, intensity, and duration of the fires were not significant on a global scale" (Biswas 2000:313). In fact, however, it appears that Biswas grossly understates the contribution of war to global warming. The Pentagon's activities in 1988, for example, reportedly resulted in about 46 million tons, or 3.5 percent of U.S. carbon dioxide emissions, that year.

> Estimating a global figure for carbon emissions from the military is fraught with uncertainty. A back-of-the-envelope calculation for the late 1980s yields an estimate of about 150 million tons: almost three percent of the global total, or nearly equal to the annual carbon emissions of the United Kingdom. If the energy consumption of arms-producing industries were included, these numbers could well double. (Renner 1997:121)

More recent figures indicate that CO_2 emissions came to 60 million tons from U.S. military operations in 2005 and 5 million tons from U.K. military operations in the same year (Parkinson 2007:4). In 2005, in its Emissions of Greenhouse Gases Report, the Energy Information Administration (2008) indicates that the United States produced 6,023 million metric tons of CO_2. Since a metric ton equals 2,204.6 pounds, this means that the United States produced 6,630 million tons of CO_2 in 2005, about 1 percent of which was produced by military activities. However, this figure refers only to active military engagements. Fixed military installations significantly increase this amount. For example, in Alaska, which is expected to be especially hard hit by the effects of global warming, there are 241 power plants emitting CO_2. Two of these, the Eielson Air Force Base Plant and the Fort Wainwright Central Heating and Power Plant, rank among the "dirtiest" energy production facilities in the United States, based on their total carbon emissions per megawatt of electricity produced (O'Hara 2007). These two military facilities produce about 6,000 pounds of CO_2 per megawatt of electricity, or more than five times the CO_2 emission level per megawatt of energy produced by the gas turbine plant at Beluga, Alaska, the state's largest electrical producer.

While it remains difficult to determine the precise level of greenhouse gas emissions during actual fighting, according to Martinot (2007:2) the U.S. Army in 2004 alone "burned 40 million gallons of fuel in three weeks of combat in Iraq, or almost 2 million gallons per day, an amount equivalent to the gasoline consumed by all Allied armies combined during the four years of World War I." During the first Gulf War, Iraq allowed over 600 oil wells to burn for a period of time, thus emitting an undetermined amount of CO_2 into the atmosphere among other substances that impact human health. According to one source, "An estimated three to six million barrels of oil per day were burnt (compared with an average daily consumption of oil in all Western Europe of 12 million barrels)" (Castells 2000:214).

The Impact of Global Warming on Security

Numerous reports have been issued by the Pentagon or other entities that express growing concern about the impact of global warming on U.S. national security. In one of the earliest of these documents, Homer-Dixon (1990) delineated the following clusters of environmental problems that potentially contribute to armed conflict: greenhouse warming, ozone depletion, deforestation, acid rain, land degradation, overutilization of water supplies, and fish stock depletion. In 2007, recognizing that global warming or climate change may pose a "security threat" to the United States, the Pentagon commissioned the CNA Corporation, a nonprofit national security organization, to write a report on this issue. CNA convened a panel of retired military officers and national security experts as part of its effort to assess the security implications of global warming. In its report, CNA (2007:6) asserts that global warming "acts as a threat multiplier for instability in some of the most volatile regions of the world" and "will seriously exacerbate already marginal living standards in many Asian, African, and Middle Eastern nations, causing widespread political instability and the likelihood of failed states." CNA stresses that global warming poses the possibility of an even greater number of people attempting to emigrate, either legally or illegally, from Mexico to the United States and more turbulent seas, which could adversely affect U.S. naval operations in the North Atlantic.

In 2003 Peter Schwartz and Doug Randall authored another Pentagon-commissioned report titled "An Abrupt Climate Change Scenario and Its Implications for United States National Security," in which they lay out worst-case scenarios that, while not likely, are "plausible" and thus would "challenge United States security in ways that should be considered immediately." Schwartz and Randall foresee the possibility of food shortages caused by diminished "net global agricultural production," "decreased availability and quality of fresh water in key regions," and "disrupted access to energy supplies due to extensive sea ice and storminess" (2002:1).

More recently the German Advisory Council on Global Change (2007:1) released a report in which it states,

> Climate change will draw ever-deeper lines of division and conflict in international relations, triggering numerous conflicts between and within countries over distribution of resources, especially water and land, over management of migration, or over compensation payments between countries mainly responsible for climate change and those countries most affected by its more destructive effects.

Dan Smith and Janani Vivekananda (2007:3), two policy analysts associated with International Alert (an international organization that focuses on building peace and security in countries that have endured armed conflict) authored a report that asserts that many of the world's poorest countries and communities face a "double-headed" dilemma: global warming and the potential for violent conflict. Like others, they maintain that global warming "could compound propensity for violent conflict, which in turn will leave communities poorer, less resilient and less able to cope with consequences of climate change" (Smith and Vivekananda 2007:46). They further argue that the 46 countries in which the "effects of global warming interacting with economic, social and political problems could create a high risk of violent conflict" are home to some 2.7 billion people and that the 56 countries "where governments will have great difficulty taking the strain of climate change on top of all their other current challenges" are home to some 1.2 billion people. Indeed, a growing number of analysts have referred to the conflict in Darfur as the first climate war. For Faris (2009:16), "Darfur may be a canary in the coal mine, a foretaste of climatically driven political chaos."

In another effort to assess the impact of climate change on security, Kurt Campbell and colleagues (2007) gathered a group of U.S. nationally recognized experts in climate science, foreign policy, political science, oceanography, history, and national security under the auspices of the Center for Strategic and International Studies and the Center for a New American Security. This team, recognizing that there remain many uncertainties about the pace at which global warming is occurring, examined the effects of three different possible climate change scenarios. The first, an expected scenario in which the average global temperature increases 1.3°C by 2040, predicts "heightened internal and cross-border tensions caused by large-scale migrations; conflict sparked by resource scarcity, particularly in the weak and failing states in Africa; increased disease proliferation . . . ; and some geopolitical reordering as nations adjust to shifts in resources and prevalence of disease" (Campbell et al. 2007:6). The second, a more severe scenario, assumes an average global temperature increase of 2.6°C by 2040 and predicts the likelihood of "armed conflict between nations over resources, such as the Nile and its tributaries," and the possibility of nuclear war (Campbell et al. 2007:7). Finally, the catastrophic scenario of an average global temperature increase of 5.6°C by 2100 predicts the possibility of the rapid decline of the global economy and the collapse of alliance systems and multilateral institutions, such as the United Nations and its Security Council. There would follow a substantial reduction of "U.S. military's worldwide reach" due to the "demand of missions near [U.S.] shores" resulting from "migration toward U.S. borders by millions of hungry and thirsty southern neighbors" (Campbell et al. 2007:104). Given the ever-faster pace at which climate scientists have observed global warming processes and changes, the potential for a worst-case scenario has been building in recent years.

In that global warming will contribute to a shortage of water in some areas as well as adverse affects on agriculture production in much of the world, conflicts over basic resources are likely to emerge in various regions as global warming progresses. McGuire (2008:130) posits the possibility of water wars erupting in places such as East Africa, where Uganda has been draining water from Lake Victoria, and between Bangladesh and India, given that India plans to "divert up to one third of the flow of Brahmaputra, Ganges and other rivers to drought-prone waters in the south of the country." Similar patterns are likely to develop at other hot spots around the world as the rising temperature shrinks or dries up potable water sources and diminishes agricultural production.

The Impact of Global Warming on Health

The war machine's contributions to global warming have clear and significant health implications for diverse populations. Various scholars have recognized the impact of global warming on health. In his now-classic *Planetary Overload*, Anthony McMichael (1993), an epidemiologist at the Australian National University, discussed the direct health effects of global warming in the form of heat stress and respiratory ailments, and indirect effects in terms of an increase in vector-borne and waterborne diseases. More frequent heat waves, particularly in urban areas, threaten the health and lives of vulnerable populations, such as the elderly, the sick, and infants. The mortality of some 35,000 people during the heat wave of the summer of 2003 in Europe, particularly France and Spain, was associated not only with high temperatures but also with the fact that the nighttime low temperatures have been rising nearly twice as fast as daytime temperatures. The lingering nighttime heat deprived people of normal relief from blistering daytime temperatures and from the opportunity to recuperate from heat stress. Temperature increases also contribute to an increase of ozone in the atmosphere. Air pollution linked to longer, warmer summers particularly affects those suffering from respiratory ailments, such as asthma. According to Epstein and Rogers (2004:6),

> Heat waves take a disproportionate toll on those living in poor housing lacking air conditioning, and those with inadequate social supports. The

majority of those affected during the 1995 heat wave in Chicago, for example, were African-Americans living in substandard housing.

Notably, global warming appears to be the primary impetus behind the spread of infectious disease north and south of the equator and to higher elevations. While global warming is not the only factor involved—globalization and the rapid flow of people, commodities, and pathogens in conjunction with increased technological and economic developments are also critical—it is a primary force contributing to the capacity for the spread of various diseases, as seen in the increasing rise of malaria in sub-Saharan Africa. In that malaria is worsened by inadequate diet, global warming may have a doubling impact on the health burden of malaria in Africa in coming years. Global warming appears also to have contributed to the resurgence of various other epidemics, including cholera in Latin America in 1991, pneumonia plague in India in 1994, and the outbreak of the hantavirus epidemic in the U.S. Southwest in 1994. In this regard, McMichael (2001:302) makes the following observations:

> The main anticipated impact of climate change on the potential transmission of vector-borne diseases would be in tropical areas. In general, populations on the margins of endemic areas in the tropical and subtropical countries would be most likely to experience an increase in transmission. . . .This appears to reflect a combination of increasing population mobility, urbanization, poverty and regional warming, along with a slackening of mosquito control programmes. Meanwhile, in temperate zones, climate change may also affect diseases such as tick-borne encephalitis (which occurs in parts of Western Europe, Russia, and Scandinavia) and Lyme disease.

As a result of these factors, it is appropriate to speak of the "diseases of global warming" (Baer and Singer 2009). This includes "tropical disease" that spreads to new places and peoples, but also failing nutrition and freshwater supplies because of desertification of pastoral areas or flooding of agricultural areas, and other diseases such as heat stroke. The UN Food and Agriculture Organization has warned that in some 40 percent of the poorest-developing societies in which 2 billion people live, global warming may drastically increase the numbers of malnourished peoples. In this, it is evident that the war machine plays an important part in reshaping the environment in ways that enhance both global warming and the array of diseases and health problems associated with it. These consequences expand the steep human toll of armed conflict specifically and of the war machine generally.

Conclusion

I have demonstrated in this chapter that the motor vehicle/oil/military complex as an integral component of the capitalist world system is a significant contributor to global warming. While the contribution of fossil fuels—oil, coal, and natural gas—and the heavy global reliance on motor vehicles and other modes of fossil fuel–based transportation to global warming have received considerable attention, the specific role of the war machine in growing environment and health crises has not. In this chapter, I have attempted to begin the process of unraveling the complex dynamic involving the petroleum and motor vehicle industries and the war machine as well as the impact of the motor vehicle/oil/military complex on global warming and ultimately on health. As Singer and I argue in *Global Warming and the Political Ecology of Health* (Baer and Singer 2009), mitigation of global warming will require transcending global capitalism and replacing it with an alternative global economic system committed to meeting the basic social needs of all peoples and achieving social parity, democratic processes, and environmental sustainability—what Singer, Susser, and I have termed "democratic eco-socialism" (Baer et al. 2003).

No doubt, global capitalism is a well-entrenched system with an arsenal of violence to sustain it. Still, the impact of global warming and other ecocrises ultimately may destabilize capitalist institutions internationally. John Urry (2008) cautions that a dystopian world may be produced by the ongoing and ever-increasing effects of global warming. He argues that as global and national governance systems deteriorate, local warlords will control access to water, oil, and gas. "With extensive flooding, extreme weather events, and the break-up of long distance oil and gas pipelines, these resources [will] become exceptionally contested and protected by armed gangs" (Urry 2008:348).

In order to ward off such calamitous scenarios, various voices are challenging global capitalism from many quarters, including the global justice or anti–corporate globalization, environmental, labor, indigenous and ethnic rights, and peace movements as well as socialists, anarchists, and even left-liberals and Social Democrats. Indeed, a distinct climate justice movement has emerged over the past few years, built on warnings about the dangers of global warming emanating over the past two decades from climate scientists, environmental groups, and indigenous groups in the Arctic and South Pacific. This movement remains very disparate and is presently struggling to develop meaningful strategies that will effectively challenge global capitalism and its political allies in world governments. Opposition to the motor vehicle–oil–military complex in one form or other is particularly embodied in the environmental, pro–public transportation and cycling, and peace movements, although these movements often tend to adopt a single-issue perspective. To date, most analyses of global warming have not factored in the contribution that the war machine makes to this phenomenon. It is evident, however, that any proposal for mitigating global warming needs to come to terms with the role of the war machine, in all its varied expressions and components, to both global warming and health problems. As Martinot (2007) argues, the environmentalist, anticonsumption, alternative energy will also need to be "antimilitarist."

Works Cited

Altvater, Elmar
  2006   The social and natural environment of fossil capitalism. In *Socialist Register 2007—Coming to Terms with Nature*, edited by Leo Panitch and Colin Leys, 37–59. London: Merlin Press.

Baer, Hans A., and Merrill Singer
  2009   *Global Warming and the Political Ecology of Health*. Walnut Creek, CA: Left Coast Press.

Baer, Hans A., Merrill Singer, and Ida Susser
  2003   *Medical Anthropology and the World System: A Critical Perspective*. Westport, CT: Praeger.

Baran, Paul A., and Paul M. Sweezy
  1966   *Monopoly Capital: An Essay on the American Economic Order*. New York: Monthly Review Press.

Biswas, Asit K.

2000 Scientific assessment of the long-term environmental consequences of war. In *The Environmental Consequences of War: Legal, Economic, and Scientific Perspectives*, edited by Jay E. Austin and Carl E. Bruch, 303–315. Cambridge: Cambridge University Press.

Boswell, Terry

2004 American world empire or declined hegemony. *Journal of World Systems Research* 10:516–524.

Campbell, Kurt M., Jay Gulledge, J. R. McNeill, John Podesta, Peter Ogden, Leon Fuerth, R. James Woolsey, Alexander T. J. Lennon, Julianne Smith, Richard Weitz, and Derek Mix

2007 *The Age of Consequences: The Foreign Policy and National Security Implications of Global Climate Change.* Washington, DC: Center for Strategic and International Studies and Center for a New American Security.

Castells, Manuel

2000 *End of Millennium.* 2nd ed. Malden, MA: Blackwell.

CNA Corporation.

2007 *National Security and the Threat of Climate Change.* Alexandria: VA. CNA Corporation.

Dancs, Anita, Mary Orisich, and Suzanne Smith

2007 The military cost of securing energy. Online: http://www.national priorities.org. Accessed May 1, 2009.

Dyer, Gwynne

2008 *Climate Wars.* Melbourne: Scribe.

Editors

2002 U.S. imperial ambitions and Iraq. *Monthly Review* 57(7):1–14.

Energy Information Administration

2008 Emissions of Greenhouse Gases Report. Report No. DOE/EIA-057. Online: http://www.eia.doe.gov/oiaf/1605/ggrpt/carbon.html. Accessed June 2, 2009.

Engdahl, F. William

2007 China and USA in new Cold War over Africa's oil riches: Darfur? It's the oil, stupid. Online: http://globalresearch.ca. Accessed October 17, 2008.

Epstein, Paul R., and C. Rogers
2004   *Inside the Greenhouse: The Impacts of CO_2 and Climate Change on Public Health in the Inner City.* Report from the Center for Health and Global Environment. Cambridge, MA: Harvard Medical School.

Faris, Stephan
2009   *Forecast: The Consequences of Climate Change, from the Amazon to the Arctic.* Melbourne: Scribe.

Fitz, Don
2007   What's possible in the military sector? Greater than 100% reduction in greenhouse gases. Online: http://www.zmag.org. Accessed September 22, 2008.

German Advisory Council on Global Change
2007   *Climate Change as a Security Risk.* London: Earthscan.

Heinberg, Richard
2006   *The Oil Depletion Protocol: A Plan to Avert Oil, Wars, Terrorism and Economic Collapse.* Gabriola Island: New Society Publisher.

Homer-Dixon, Thomas F.
1990   Environmental Change and Violent Conflict. Occasional Paper No. 4. Cambridge, MA: International Security Studies Program, American Academy of Arts and Sciences.

Jones, Bart
2007   *!Hugo! The Hugo Chavez Story from Mud Hut to Perpetual Revolution.* Hanover, NH: Steerforth Press.

Klare, Michael T.
2002   *Resource Wars: The New Landscape of Global Conflict.* New York: Henry Holt.
2003   Blood for oil: The Bush-Cheney energy strategy. In *Socialist Register 2004—The New Imperial Challenge*, edited by Leo Panith and Colin Leys, 166–183. London: Merlin Press.
2007   Iraq and climate change. Online: http://www.fpif.org. Accessed September 22,
2008   *Rising Powers, Shrinking Planet: The New Geopolitics of Energy.* New York: Metroplitan Books.

Kolko, Gabriel
2006   *The Age of Wars: The United States Confronts the World.* Boulder, CO: Lynne Rienner.

Lebowitz, Michael A.
2006   *Build It Now: Socialism for the Twentieth-First Century.* New York: Monthly Review Press.

Martinot, Steve
2007   Militarism and global warming. *Synthesis/Regeneration* 42(winter): 1–5. Online: http://www.greens.org. Accessed February 17, 2009.

McGuire, Bill
2008   *Seven Years to Save the Planet: The Questions . . . and Answers.* London: Weidenfeld & Nicholson.

McMichael, A. J.
1993   *Planetary Overload: Global Environmental Change and the Health of Human Species.* Cambridge: Cambridge University Press.
2001   *Human Frontiers, Environments and Disease: Past Patterns, Uncertain Futures.* Cambridge: Cambridge University Press.

McQuaig, Linda
2004   *Crude, Dude: War, Big Oil and the Fight for the Planet.* Scarborough: Doubleday Canada.

Monreal, Pedro
2006   Cuban development in the Bolivarian matrix. *Report on the Americas* 39 (4): 22–26.

Nitzan, Jonathan, and Bichler, Shimshon
2004   Dominant capital and the new wars. *Journal of World Systems Research* 10(2):255-327.

O'Hara, Doug
2007   Alaska's top CO_2 producers. Online: http://www.farnorthscience .com/2007/11/20/climate-news/alaskas-top-co2-producers. Retrieved June 2, 2009.

Parkinson, Stuart
2007, February   Guns and global warming: War, peace and the environment. Web version of presentation given at the Network for Peace AGM, London, Scientists for Global Responsibility. Online: http://www.sgr.org.uk/ArmsControl/NfPAGMnotes_feb07.html. Accessed June 2, 2009.

Peak-Oil News and Message Boards
2009   http://www.peak-oil-news. Accessed May 1, 2009.

Post Carbon Institute
2007, February   Energy bulletin. Online: http://www.energy.bulletin. Accessed August 27, 2008.

Renner, Michael
1997   Environmental and health effects of weapons production, testing, and maintenance. In *War and Public Health*, edited by Barry Levy and Victor Sidel, 117–136. Washington, D.C.: American Public Health Association.

Rothkoff, David
2008   *Superclass: The Global Power Elite and the World They Are Making.* London: Little, Brown.

Schwartz, Peter, and Doug Randall
2003   An abrupt climate change scenario and its implications for United States national security. Online: http://www.gbn.com. Accessed October 21, 2008.

Smith, Dan, and Janani Vivekananda
2007, November   A climate of conflict: The links between climate change, peace and war. International Alert.

Smith, Gar
1990-1991   How fuel-efficient is the Pentagon? Military's oil addiction. *Earth Island Journal* (Winter). Online at http://www.envirosagainst war.org/know/read.php?itemid=593 Accessed June 12, 2008.

Turshen, Meredith
2004   The politics of oil in Africa. Online: http://www.barnard.edu/sfon line. Accessed November 7, 2008.

Urry, John
2007   Governance, flows, and the end of the car system? *Global Environmental Change* 18:343–349.

Walsh, Byran
2009   Does global warming compromise national security? Online: http://www.time.com/time/specials/2007/article/0,28804,1730759_ 1731383_1731632,00.html. Accessed June 2, 2009.

Wheelwright, Ted
1991   *Oil and World Politics: From Rockefeller to the Gulf War.* Sydney: Left Book Club.

CHAPTER SIX

DYING OF SORROW
Expulsion, Empire, and the People of Diego Garcia
David Vine

"Welcome to the Footprint of Freedom," says the sign at the U.S. military base on the Indian Ocean island Diego Garcia. Although few know that it exists, Diego Garcia is one of the most strategically important and secretive U.S. military installations in the world: the island was a major launch pad for the invasions of Iraq and Afghanistan, served as a top-secret Central Intelligence Agency detention center for terrorism suspects, and has been a centerpiece of U.S. control of Middle East oil shipping routes for three decades. Even less widely known, during creation of the base, the U.S. government expelled the entire indigenous population of Diego Garcia and the surrounding Chagos Archipelago. Between 1968 and 1973, with the help of Great Britain, the United States planned, ordered, and financed the removal of 1,500 to 2,000 Chagossians 1,200 miles away to Mauritius and the Seychelles Islands. The Chagossians effectively received no resettlement assistance and quickly became impoverished in exile. Numbering more than 5,000 today, most remain deeply impoverished and in poor health.

The Chagossians' ancestors began arriving in the previously uninhabited Chagos Archipelago in the late eighteenth century. Most were from Madagascar and southwestern Africa, later to be joined by others from India. All were brought as enslaved or indentured laborers to work on coconut plantations established by Franco-Mauritians. Over two centuries, this diverse workforce developed into a distinct, emancipated society and a people with its own Chagos Kreol language, known initially as the *Ilois* (the Islanders). According to contemporary definitions of "indigenous peoples" employed by the United Nations, anthropology, and international law, the Chagossians are the indigenous people of the Chagos Archipelago (Vine 2003).

By the 1960s, Chagossians lived in what remained a plantation society that, while far from luxurious, provided a secure life, generally free of want. Having won relatively good labor conditions from the plantation owners, Chagossians enjoyed near universal employment and numerous social benefits, including regular if small salaries, plots of land, free housing, education, child care, pensions, burial services, and basic health care on islands described by many as "idyllic" (see Vine 2009).

In 1965, this life began to collapse. After several years of negotiations, the U.S. government convinced the British government to give it permission to build a military base on Diego Garcia. Britain would do so by separating the entire Chagos Archipelago from colonial Mauritius (contrary to UN rules on decolonization) to create what was called the British Indian Ocean Territory as a dedicated military colony. As part of the agreement, U.S. officials insisted on receiving Diego Garcia and, as the bureaucratically worded expulsion order put it, "exclusive control (without local inhabitants)" (U.S. Embassy London 1964).

The two governments confirmed the deal with a 1966 "exchange of notes" that effectively created a treaty but circumvented the need for congressional or parliamentary notification or authorization. In addition to the notes, U.S. and U.K. officials signed a secret agreement that made provision for those "administrative measures" necessary to remove the Chagossians, including a U.S. payment of $14 million to carry out the plan (Bandjunis 2001; Chalfont 1966). Those administrative measures meant that beginning in 1968, any Chagossians who left Chagos for medical treatment or for regular vacations in Mauritius were barred from returning to Chagos. Often they were marooned without family members and almost all their possessions.

British officials soon began restricting food and medical supplies to Chagos, effectively expelling the Chagossians by starving them out. In cooperation with U.S. officials, the British meanwhile designed a public relations plan aimed at, as one official put it, "maintaining the fiction" that the Chagossians were transient contract workers rather than people with roots in Chagos for five generations or more (Aust 1970).

In 1971, the U.S. Navy began construction of a base on Diego Garcia and ordered the British to complete the removals. When a few naval officers expressed concern about the deportations, the navy's highest-ranking officer, Admiral Elmo Zumwalt, responded with three words: "Absolutely must go" (Cochrane 1971). And so, British agents and U.S. soldiers began herding the Chagossians' pet dogs into sealed sheds. There they gassed the howling dogs with the exhaust from U.S. military vehicles and burned them in front of their traumatized owners (Moulinie 1999; Vine 2009). Between 1971 and 1973, British agents forced the islanders to board overcrowded cargo ships and left them on the docks in Mauritius and the Seychelles.

The Chagossians arrived in Mauritius and the Seychelles unemployed, homeless, and with little money. They received little or no resettlement assistance. Most had only a small box of belongings and the sleeping mat they were allowed to take with them during the deportations. When a *Washington Post* reporter broke the story of the expulsion in the Western press in 1975, he found the people living in "abject poverty" (Ottaway 1975). A year later, a British official described the Chagossians as "living in deplorable conditions" (Prosser 1976:6).

In 1978 and between 1982 and 1985, some Chagossians in Mauritius received from the British government small amounts of compensation in the form of land, housing, and cash totaling approximately $6,000. The smaller group of Chagossians in the Seychelles (today numbering around 600) received nothing. Despite the compensation, conditions appear to have improved only marginally for most. Some sold their compensation land and houses for cash to pay off large debts accrued since the expulsion. In 1997, a World Health Organization (WHO)–funded report found that the Chagossians were "still housed in tin shacks in the disadvantaged slums of Port Louis, without fixed incomes and without *de facto* access to education or health care" (Draebel 1997:4).

In 2001, lawyers representing the Chagossians in lawsuits against the U.S. and U.K. governments asked Philip Harvey, S. Wojciech Sokolowski, and me to serve as expert witnesses by documenting the effects of the expulsion on the Chagossians' lives.[1] Our resulting research (Vine 2003; Vine et al. 2005, 2008) and eight years of subsequent individual research (Vine 2004, 2006, 2009) detailed how the displacement has transformed the lives of the people. This collaborative research has shown that as a result of their expulsion the Chagossians have collectively experienced severe, chronic impoverishment, resulting in particularly poor health outcomes (Vine et al. 2005).

This chapter reports the health effects of the expulsion, exploring the islanders' frequent reports of death from sadness, heartbreak, or—as they say in their French-laden and Bantu-structured Kreol—*sagren* (profound sorrow). According to mortality statistics produced by the Chagos Refugees Group (2001),[2] 60 of 396 individuals who have died in exile (for whom a cause of death was indicated) died in part or wholly due to "sadness" or "homesickness." One of the islanders, 80-year-old Marie Rita Elysée Bancoult,[3] explained to me from her small sitting room in Mauritius, "many people have died like that. . . . *Sagren!* Yes! When one has *sagren* in your heart, it eats at you. No doctor, no one will be able to heal you! . . . There are many people that can't bear it."[4]

This chapter asks what dying of *sagren* tells us about the expulsion, about the Chagossians' experience in exile, and, ultimately, about the health effects of military bases and militarization.[5] I draw on Paul Farmer's (1997) model for understanding extreme suffering and a critical medical anthropological approach pairing interpretive anthropology and political-economic investigation (see Baer et al., 1986, 2003; Singer 1986; Singer and Baer 1995). Following Farmer (1997), I use the explanatory power of representative biography—focusing on the experiences of Rita Bancoult and her family to illustrate broader patterns found among exiled Chagossians.[6] Analyzing Rita and other Chagossians' experience in tandem with findings about illness and impoverishment among displaced peoples and others, the data indicates that the illnesses suffered by Chagossians represent for them all the material difficulties of life in exile combined with the emotional and psychological pain of being separated from their homeland. Illnesses like *sagren* have become not only an unsurprising consequence of forced displacement but also metaphors for all the suffering of expulsion and exile.

"You Will Never Go There Again"

Marie Rita Elysée Bancoult and her family were some of the Chagossians who in 1968 were visiting Mauritius for vacations or for medical care unavailable in Chagos's small hospitals. Rita, or Aunt Rita as she is known, was in Mauritius seeking an operation for her youngest daughter, Noellie, whose foot had been crushed in an accident. Doctors operated but were unable to save Noellie, and she died within a month of arriving in Mauritius.

Mourning her daughter's death, Rita went to the steamship company to arrange for her family's return to Chagos. When she came back to her family, she was unable to speak. Rita said she felt like the "blood had been drained out of her." "What happened?" her husband asked. "Did someone attack you?" her children demanded. For an hour she said nothing, her heart "swollen" with emotion. "I heard everything they said," Rita explained, "but my voice couldn't open my mouth to say what had happened."

Finally she blurted out, "We will never again return to our home! Our home has been closed!" As she recounted for me almost 40 years later, the man at the steamship company told her, "Your island has been sold. You will never go there again." When Rita's husband, Julien Bancoult, heard his wife's news, he collapsed backward, his arms splayed wide. Now he was speechless. Prevented from returning home, the family found themselves in a foreign land, separated from their homes, their land, their animals, their jobs, their community, and most of their possessions. The Bancoults had been, as Chagossians came to say, *derasine* (deracinated, uprooted, and torn from their homeland). "His sickness started to take hold of him," Rita explained. "He didn't understand anything" she said. Soon Julien suffered a stroke, his body growing rigid and increasingly paralyzed. Before the year was out, Rita would spend several weeks in a psychiatric hospital.

Left on the Docks

Like Rita and Julien's family, exiled Chagossians found themselves homeless and jobless in a foreign land, separated from their islands, their communities (both those living and those buried on the islands), and their entire way of life. After the deportations began in 1971, Chagossians were literally left on the docks of the Mauritian capital, Port Louis. "The Ilois walked bewildered off their ships and tramped through the slums of the capital," investigative journalist John Madeley recounts, "to try to find a relative or friend who would offer accommodation" (Madeley 1985:5).

Another reporter saw how many had "to go begging to survive, and live in shacks which are little more than chicken coops" (Sunday Times

[London] 1975:10). More than half lived in single-room houses with as many as nine people in a room. In one case in Cassis, seven Chagossian families moved into a single courtyard that already housed 10 other families. They shared one water tap, one toilet, and one shower among them (U.S. Congress, House of Representatives, 1975:114–121).

Already scattered over 1,200 miles between Mauritius and the Seychelles, Chagossians dispersed further around Port Louis and the main island in the Seychelles, Mahé. Although many in Mauritius settled around other Chagossians, most of the social networks and village ties that had previously connected people were severely ruptured. Chagossians deported to the Seychelles were even more isolated, crowding into the homes of relatives or squatting on the land of others. Some families lived "*anba lakaz*," or underneath another family's stilt-elevated house. One family lived in a vacant cowshed, slowly transforming it into a formal house over many years.

In Mauritius, Chagossians found themselves on an overcrowded island that population experts had warned might soon become a "catastrophe" given that it had one of the fastest-growing populations in the world (Titmuss and Abel-Smith 1968). Novelist V. S. Naipaul (1984) called the island an "overcrowded barracoon." Conditions in Port Louis were particularly bad, according to British experts:

> The housing conditions in parts of Port Louis are worse than anything we saw in the villages [in rural Mauritius]. Hundreds of people are crowded into tin shacks hardly fit for animals. Not surprisingly, tuberculosis and other diseases are very common in these slums, and a large proportion of the families depend on the help, regular and irregular, of the Public Assistance Department. Urban rents are relatively high and there is a serious shortage of housing in the towns; a situation made worse by the cyclone damage in 1960. (Titmuss and Abel-Smith 1968:7)

Amid their other problems, Chagossians faced systemic unemployment and interethnic tensions and violence between Indo-Mauritian Muslims and Afro-Mauritians (see, e.g., Selvon 2001:394). With high rates of unemployment, almost half of the islanders depended after their arrival, in whole or in part, on nonwork income, including public welfare, the help of family and friends, charity, loans from moneylenders, and other informal sources (Vine et al. 2005). By 1975, only around one-quarter of heads of households in Mauritius had full-time work. Most of those who were employed at all were working in the lowest-paid jobs: dockers and stevedores, domestic workers, fisherfolk, and truck loaders (Ottaway 1975; U.S. House of Representatives 1975:112–121).

Declining Health

By most accounts health in Chagos was "if anything somewhat better than in Mauritius" (African Research Group 2000:3, 5), soon after their arrival, many Chagossians began to fall ill and die. A survey conducted by a small Mauritian support group, the Ilois Committee Fraternal Organization (ICFO),[7] documented "an impressive number of cases where Ilois have found death after having landed in Mauritius, i.e. from one to 12 months' stay." The dead totaled at least 44 by 1975 "because of unhappiness, poverty and lack of medical care" (Comité Ilois Organisation Fraternelle n.d.:2–5).

At least 11 others were reported to have died by suicide. "According to an enquiry made with their parents and friends," the ICFO found, "the reasons behind these suicides are disgust of the life they have been living in Mauritius and of poverty: no roof, no job and uncared. They were demoralized, and instead of living a depraved life, they found in death a remedy." Among the suicides were Joseph France Veerapen Kistnasamy, who "burnt himself" two days before Christmas 1972; Syde Laurique, who had "no job, no roof, drowned herself"; Elaine and Michele Mouza, who as "mother and child committed suicide"; and Leone Rangasamy, born in Peros Banhos, who "drowned herself because she was prevented from going back" (Comité Ilois Organisation Fraternelle n.d.:2–3).

Other deaths seem to have been the result of Chagossians' vulnerability to illnesses that were rare or unknown in Chagos (I. Walker 1986:14). By 1975, 28 children had died of influenza: "Adults and children died of the diphtheria against which Mauritians are automatically vaccinated," the *Manchester Guardian* wrote. "And the cultural shock of arriving in the teeming, humid, poorer quarters of Port Louis still takes its toll" (M. Walker 1975).

At least 16 were admitted for psychiatric treatment. They included one islander who "on the death of his child due to lack of food . . . burnt his wife and wanted to commit suicide." Another "was mentally affected" after having to admit his children to a convent when he was unable to support them. Another "lost his head" on the ship and "was admitted as soon as he landed" (Comité Ilois Organisation Fraternelle n.d.:2).

According to Madeley (1985:5), by mid-1975 "at least 1 in 40 [Chagossians in Mauritius] had died of starvation and disease." These reports indicate increased mortality compared with life in Chagos. Yearly average death figures during the last years in Chagos for individuals born there are 0.75 per year in Diego Garcia, 4.75 in Peros Banhos, and 2.33 in Salomon (B.I.O.T. Death Peros-Banhos n.d.).

The ICFO's report describes how "the causes mostly are: unhappiness, non-adaptation of Ilois within the social framework of Mauritius, extreme poverty, particularly lack of food, house, job. Another cause of this mortality was family dispersion." The report concludes that "the main cause of the sufferings of the Ilois was the lack of proper plan to welcome them in Mauritius. There was also no rehabilitation programme for them" (Comité Ilois Organisation Fraternelle n.d.:3).

This is hardly surprising, since the population was displaced against its will and abandoned with no resettlement assistance. Research aggregating findings from hundreds of forcibly displaced groups around the globe—pushed off their lands by dam construction, warfare, environmental disasters, and other causes—has come to an unambiguous conclusion: absent proper resettlement programs and other preventive measures, involuntary displacement generally causes "the impoverishment of considerable numbers of people" (Cernea 1993).

Often, one of the major risks and dynamics of this overall impoverishment is increased morbidity and mortality. Michael Cernea (1997) explains that "expulsion threatens to cause serious declines in health levels," and "empirical research show[s] that displaced people experience higher levels of exposure and vulnerability to illness and severe disease than they did prior to expulsion." In addition to a general deterioration of health, displaced people are likely to suffer from "expulsion-induced social stress and psychological trauma" (Cernea 1997:27–29).

"*Sagren* in Your Heart"

One night, five years after they were marooned in Mauritius, Julien Bancoult nudged Rita abruptly as they slept. Rita awoke and began speaking to Julien. He did not respond. Rita yelled for her uncle, who, with his wife, was living in the other room. When he came and looked at Julien, he knew right away that he was sick. "His arm, his hand, his foot, it was all dead," paralyzed, Rita recounted. They rushed him to the hospital. "He stayed a month, a month and 15 days in the hospital," she said. "It went on, and on, and on, until he died. He had *sagren*, David. *Sagren* is what he had. . . . You know, he saw his children, every day they went without food. He didn't have a job that he could work to be able to give them food. That's what made him sick. He wasn't used to life like that, you understand?"

Although Rita spoke about her own family's experience of illness and death, her words illustrate patterns found across the exiled community. Pointing to the gendered impact of forced displacement, Rita added: "What happened to me—how can I say it—I wasn't able to bear it. But my husband, he was able to bear it even less than I was, because a man— the load is supposed to be on him. He had six children to feed. How was he going to do it? He suffered a stroke."

I asked Rita to explain what she meant that Julien had died of *sagren*. "*Sagren*, that's to say, it's *sagren* for his country. Where he came from, he didn't experience *mizer* [miserable, abject poverty] like we were experiencing here. He was seeing it in his eyes—Chagos. His children were going without, were going without food. They didn't have anything," Rita said. "And so he got so, so many worries, do you understand? That's *sagren*. Many people have died like that. You know, David? . . . When one has *sagren* in your heart, it eats at you. No doctor, no one will be able to heal you! If you have a *sagren*, if you, even—you can't get it out. That's to say, David—*Ayo*! What can you do? Let it go—something that came on like that. There are many people that can't bear it. . . . Do you understand? Then, it goes, it goes, until at the end, you don't want to eat, you don't want anything. Nothing. You don't want it. . . . There's nothing that you do, that you have that's good. You've withdrawn from the world completely and entered into a state of *sagren*."

"Have you experienced *sagren*?" I asked.

"Yes. *Sagren*. Yes. Do you understand? You have *sagren* when in your country you haven't experienced things like this. Here you're finding food in the trash can. . . . There *wasn't* sickness" like strokes or *sagren* in Chagos. "There wasn't that sickness. Nor diabetes, nor any such illness. What drugs?" she asked rhetorically. "This is what my husband remembered and pictured in his mind. Me too, I remember these things that I've said about us, David. My heart grows heavy when I say these things, understand?"

After Julien's death, the Bancoults' son Alex lost his job as a dockworker. He later died at 38, addicted to drugs and alcohol. Their son Eddy died at 36 of a heroin overdose. Another son, Rénault, died suddenly at age 11, having suffered from flu-like symptoms one night after selling water and begging for money at a local cemetery.

"My life has been buried," Rita told me. "What do I think about it? . . . It's as if I had been pulled from my paradise to put me in hell. Everything here you need to buy. I don't have the means to buy them. My children go without eating. How am I supposed to bear this life?"

Severe and Chronic Impoverishment

Although some Chagossians did finally receive small amounts of compensation 5 and 10 years after the last deportations, most still live in conditions that are among the worst in Mauritius and the Seychelles. They are still concentrated in the poorest, least desirable, least healthy, and most disadvantaged neighborhoods. Many live in homes cobbled together out of wood and corrugated iron. Large numbers have limited access to basic water and sanitation; according to our 2002–2003 survey (Vine et al. 2005), 40 percent were without indoor plumbing, and more than one-quarter lacked running potable water. In Mauritius, the islanders' housing conditions were broadly comparable to those found in the poor townships of South Africa. (Generally, housing problems have been more critical for those in Mauritius than for those in the Seychelles, in line with wider national differences.)

Robbed of their right to work and torn from the universal employment of Chagos, the exiles have never recovered their economic stability. At the time of our survey, just over a third (39 percent) of the first generation and less than two-thirds (61 percent) of the second generation were working (among those of working age), the majority being employed in manual labor jobs. Median income was around $2 a day (see Vine 2009), far below that of their Mauritian and Seychellois neighbors. Of those who are employed, many have jobs at the bottom of the Mauritian pay scale, characterized by high job insecurity, temporary duration, and informal employment commitments. Chagossians are still employed primarily in manual labor: as dockers and stevedores in the shipping industry; as janitorial, domestic, and child care workers; as informal construction workers and bricklayers; and as factory workers. Some find various piecework employment, often to supplement other jobs, including stitching shoes, assembling decorative furnishings, and weaving brooms from coconut palms (Vine et al. 2005). Now in nations with relatively high levels of literacy and educational attainment that has become increasingly important to securing employment, Chagossians have been (like others among the Mauritian poor) systematically disadvantaged in their schooling; their literacy rate is only 46 percent (Vine et al. 2005).

Among many in both countries, there remains deep pessimism about their economic and employment prospects. The French aphorism "Ceux qui sont riches seront toujours riches, ceux qui sont pauvres restent toujours pauvres" (the rich will always be rich; the poor will always be poor) is a kind of chorus in Mauritius among some young-adult Chagossians.

I asked Jacques Victor, who was then working weekends as an informal clothing vendor, if he thought it would be possible to find a better-paying job. "In Mauritius, no. In Mauritius, no," Mr. Victor responded in English; he is one of a very few islanders able to speak at least some of the official national language, which is generally a marker of middle- or upper-class status. "Ilois have the qualifications," he explained, but Mauritian employers say, "How can they have this kind of qualification?' They much prefer [us] lower than low. It's like that."

As we ended our conversation, I asked Mr. Victor if there were anything else he wanted to tell me. "I want to return to our land. Be there now—get our lives that we were living, yesterday," he said. "Maybe my children will get jobs."

Sagren as Synecdoche

"It gave me such suffering, David, and to this day, I still have this suffering. In my heart, it's not at all gone. Not at all gone," Rita told me from her home in Mauritius. "Look at how many of my children have died. How can I explain it to you? If we were *there* [in Chagos], Alex would be here, Eddy would be here, Rénault would be here. . . . Eddy died from drugs but *there*, we didn't have them."

Rita continued, "They pulled us from there to come take us to hell. Drugs are ravaging people. The children aren't working, they're following friends to the side of having problems, understand? It's always the same, it's not easy. . . . There, in St. George's cemetery, I have three boys—three boys, two girls," she said. To the deaths of her own four children, Rita added the death of Alex's wife, who committed suicide in 2001, dousing herself with gasoline and setting herself afire. Their five boys—five of Rita's grandchildren—were left orphaned.

We return to the deaths of Julien and others from *sagren* and the comparison of a disease-free, healthy life in Chagos to one of illness, drugs, and death in exile. Examining first the contrast between lives of health and lives of illness, the islanders' diagnosis is an accurate one: the contrast they describe represents an accurate portrayal of changing health conditions before and after the expulsion. While Chagossian health was once better than that in Mauritius, it is now comparable to the low levels of health characterizing the poorest sectors of Mauritian society, a state with one of the highest incidences of chronic disease in the world (Draebel 1997).

A WHO-funded study found that Chagossians suffer from high levels of chronic colds, fevers, respiratory diseases, anemia, and transmissible diseases like tuberculosis as well as problems with cardiovascular diseases, diabetes, hypertension, work accidents, and youth alcohol and tobacco abuse. The report found children and the elderly particularly vulnerable to disease, including waterborne diseases tied to contaminated water supplies, like infant diarrhea, hepatitis A, and intestinal parasites. The people also exhibited a large number of work accidents, most likely related to physical labor and limited work protections (Draebel 1997:18–25, 34).

At the same time, Chagossians do not enjoy the same access to health care services as others in Mauritius because of their poverty, their limited knowledge of the health care system, and their limited confidence in both health care providers and the efficacy and quality of treatment (Draebel 1997:26–35). Around 85 percent of the Chagossians that I surveyed reported needing more health care—more than any other reported social service need (Vine et al. 2005:213).

In 2002 and 2003, we asked survey respondents if they needed help or treatment for an alcohol or drug problem, well aware that survey questions asking about substance abuse are renowned for underreporting actual use. The response was striking: 20 percent admitted to a problem, and less than 2 percent said they were receiving treatment (Vine et al. 2005:229). "There wasn't sickness" like strokes or *sagren*, we remember Rita saying. "There wasn't that sickness. Nor diabetes, nor any such illness. What drugs?" she said rhetorically, having lost Alex and Eddy to drug and alcohol abuse.

As Rita's words and the prevalence of addiction suggest, when people contrast a life filled with illnesses and drugs with a nearly disease-free life in Chagos, the comparison represents more than a depiction of rising morbidity and declining health. The contrast also represents a commentary on and implicit critique of the expulsion. It represents a sign and recognition of the emotional and psychological damage the expulsion has caused.

"What must be heard" at the "emotional core" of stories of displacement, says psychiatrist Mindy Fullilove in the context of displacement caused by urban renewal in the United States, "is the howl of amputations, the anguish at calamity unassuaged, the fear of spiraling downward without cessation, and the rage at poverty imposed through repeated dispossession" (Fullilove 2004:224).

For many Chagossians, the illnesses that they and their relatives and friends have experienced have come to represent all the difficulties of life in exile and the pain of being separated from their homeland. Illness, disease, and addiction have become metaphors, synecdoches—one part representing the whole—for all the suffering of the expulsion.

Embodied Illness

"So many troubles. My head went to a mental hospital. I already went before to a mental hospital, where I had shocks."

"Shocks?" I asked, fearing that Rita meant electroshock therapy.

"I had too many troubles."

"What happened?"

"The same, the same deal like before. I got the treatment. My children didn't have food in the house, and one by one they were dying like dead coconuts falling from the tree. So they gave me shocks."

When Chagossians describe people dying of *sagren*, they are not just speaking metaphorically. As noted earlier, the Chagos Refugees Group counts at least 60 community members who have died in exile of sadness or homesickness. *Sagren* "explains illness and even the deaths of members of the community," explains the WHO-funded study. "The notion of *sagren* has an important place in the explanative system for illness." *Sagren* is "nostalgia for the Chagos islands. It is the profound sadness of facing the impossibility of being able to return to one's home in the archipelago." *Sagren* is then an example of an "idiom of distress" embodying "somatic, emotional, and social meaning" and explaining in socially and historically specific ways the totality of Chagossians' suffering (Kirmayer and Young 1998:424).

The WHO report cites the case of one elderly man who died after suffering from diabetes, hypertension, and paralysis for many years. Before his death, he left his home only once every three months when an ambulance drove him to get treatment. After his death, one of his friends said he had died of *sagren*: "Knowing that he would never again return to the island of his birth, he had preferred to let himself die" (Draebel 1997:25).

Sagren is an example of what Fullilove (2004) has called the "root shock" of forced displacement. Root shock is the traumatic stress reaction to the destruction of all or part of one's emotional ecosystem. It has important parallels to the physiological shock experienced by a person who, as a result of injury, suddenly loses massive amounts of fluids. Such a blow threatens the whole body's ability to function. The nervous system attempts to compensate for the imbalance by cutting off circulation to the arms and legs. Suddenly the hands and feet will seem cold and damp, the face pale, and the brow sweaty. This is an emergency state that can preserve the brain, the heart, and the other essential organs for only a brief period of time. If the fluids are not restored, the person will die. Shock is the fight for survival after a life-threatening blow to the body's internal balance (Fullilove 2004:11).

With other symptoms that include wasting and weakness, confusion and disorientation, sadness and depression, shaking, and paralysis that might ultimately result in death, *sagren* also resembles the affliction of *nervos* found among many in the world but especially among the poor and marginalized in the Mediterranean and Latin America. Medical anthropologist Nancy Scheper-Hughes has shown through work with the poor in northeastern Brazil how *nervos* is far from a matter of somatization or malingering, at least as they are typically understood by medical professionals. *Nervos* is instead "a collective and embodied response" to poverty and hunger and to a corrupt, violent political system that colludes to entrap the poor in these conditions—what she calls everyday forms of violence (Scheper-Hughes 1992:173–187). The roots of such afflictions are not psychological, as those who administered Rita's electroshock therapy likely thought. The roots of such afflictions are social, political, and economic. The violence of displacement becomes embodied in the sick and dead bodies of its victims.

Dying of *Sagren*

As the sometimes fatal illnesses of root shock and *nervos* indicate, Chagossians are not alone in finding that forms of grief and sadness can cause death.[8] "There is little doubt," Theodore Scudder and Elizabeth Colson explain, "that relocatees often believe that the elderly in particular are apt to die 'of a broken heart' following removal." Importantly, this belief appears to have medical support: "The evidence is highly suggestive" that sadness can cause death "for Egyptian and Sudanese Nubians . . . and the Yavapai. . . . Elderly persons forced into nursing homes or forcibly removed from one nursing home to another are reported to have high mortality rates in the period immediately succeeding the move" (Scudder and Colson 1982:269).

Other research has shown that acute stress can bring on fatal heart spasms in people with otherwise healthy cardiac systems (Sharsky et al. 2005:472–479; Wittstein et al. 2005:539–548). Among Hmong refugees in the United States who fled Laos in the 1970s, sudden unexpected death syndrome was the leading cause of death for years after their arrival. The syndrome is "triggered by cardiac failure, often during or after a bad dream. No one has been able to explain what produces the cardiac irregularity, although theories over the years have included potassium deficiency, thiamine deficiency, sleep apnea, depression, culture shock, and survivor guilt" (Fadiman 1997:188).

Ranjit Nayak's work with the Kisan of eastern India provides still more evidence of the connections between the grief of exile and health outcomes and between mental and physical health. "The severance of the Kisan bonds from their traditional lands and environment is a fundamental factor in their acute depression and possibly in increased mortality rates, including infant mortality," Nayak writes. Like Chagossians grieving for their lost origins in Chagos, for the Kisan, "a continuous pining for lost land characterizes the elderly. Anxiety, grieving, various neuropsychiatric illness and post-traumatic stress disorders feature among the Kisan. In essence, they suffer from profound cultural and landscape bereavement for their lost origins" (Nayak 2000:95–96). This is what Scudder (1973) refers to among displacees as the "grieving for a lost home" syndrome.

For many, the intimacy of their connection to Chagos is closely related to the fact that their ancestors are buried on the islands. Since the expulsion, Chagossians have repeatedly requested permission to visit the islands to clean and tend to the graves of their ancestors. In 1975, hundreds petitioned the British and U.S. governments for aid and the right to go back to their islands. If they were to be barred from returning, they asked the governments to at least "allow two or three persons from among us to go clean the cemetery at Diego Garcia where our forefathers, brothers, sisters, mothers and fathers are buried, and to enable us to take care of the Diego Church where we were baptised" (Saminaden et al. 1975).

Jeannette Alexis, who was forced to leave Diego Garcia for the Seychelles as an adolescent, said she can see in her elders the pain of not going to the graves of their ancestors. Being barred from visiting their graves and bringing them flowers, she said, being separated from one's ancestors is yet another blow to their entire way of life. As Nayak writes of the Kisan, "In essence, they suffer from profound cultural and landscape bereavement for their lost origins" (Nayak 2000:96).

"I Am Alone on the Earth"

I am very unhappy
There's no one anymore
To console me.

The bird sings for me
The bird cries for me

The bird sings for me
The bird cries for me.

I left my country
I left my little island
I left my family
I also left my heart.

—Song composed and sung by Mimose Bancoult Furcy, posted on the office wall of the Chagos Refugees Group, 2004. Translation by author.

"Stress and depression trickle up and down the generations, affecting people almost irrespective of age or gender," writes Nayak. "The children can narrate the expulsion and resettlement experience in minute detail as if they had themselves experienced the process" (Nayak 2000:96).

Even among Chagossians born in exile, there is this kind of intimate, experiential, almost *bodily* awareness of and about life in Chagos and the expulsion. Many born after the final removals narrate stories of the islands and the *derasinman* just as one who was born there. Ivo Bancoult is the only one of Rita and Julien's children to be born in Mauritius. He described for me how pained he is at not having been born in the islands and being unable to live there now. Often Ivo asks himself and God why he was not born in Chagos.

And yet in many ways he spoke as if he had been born there too: "It's a very different thing to come to Mauritius by force," he said about his life, "compared to coming by choice. It's much harder to adapt when you come by force." "My father came by force!" Ivo said emphatically. "By *force* he came." By this he meant to indicate that many understand the experience of having been barred from Chagos to be as much a matter of "force" as of deportation.

Sitting behind the Chagossian community center in Pointe aux Sables, I asked Ivo if he, like others, distinguishes himself as being a *zanfan Chagossien*—a second-generation child of a *Chagossian* born in Chagos—as opposed to being a Chagossian proper. "I, truly, I am *Chagossian*," he replied. "I am Chagossian because my mother was born in Chagos. My father was born in Chagos. All my family was born in Chagos. I am a Chagossian. On paper perhaps" it says he was born in Mauritius, he continued, "but I am a Chagossian. Honestly. I am proud to be Chagossian."

Sagren, Latristes, Mizer

Sandrine Alexis, now in her early thirties, came to Mauritius as a young child with her parents and six siblings on one of the last voyages of the *Nordvær*. Sandrine explained that her family had to leave everything in Chagos. When they first arrived, the family lived on the streets of Port Louis's largest slum, Roche Bois. Often they had no food or water. When they came to Mauritius, her parents were healthy, she said. But once in Mauritius, her parents "*tombe malad*" with *sagren* and *latristes* (they fell ill with profound sorrow and sadness). They "*tombe dan mizer*" (they fell into miserable abject poverty), she continued. Over time, three of her siblings died in Mauritius.

When Joseph Vindasamy told me how his father died of *sagren* in 1970 after he was prevented from returning to Diego Garcia, I asked him to define *sagren*. Joseph replied, *sagren* is "not having work." It's "lacking" food, water, education for yourself and your children. It's not becoming "*abitye*"—being unable to adjust—to life in Mauritius.

We notice here how Joseph made no mention of sorrow or sadness in his description of *sagren*. For Joseph and others, the sorrow connoted by *sagren* is so obvious that it needs no mention. When Chagossians talk about *sagren*, we can see, they are talking about more than their deep sorrow. They are also talking about their experiences with what Sandrine and others call *mizer* (miserable abject poverty). Equally we can see, when people talk about *mizer*, they are referring to more than their experiences of deep impoverishment in exile. They are also talking about their feelings of *sagren* and *latristes* (their feelings of profound sorrow and sadness).

Sagren, *latristes*, and *mizer* have become three intertwined ways for Chagossians to talk about their suffering. In using any one of these words, people immediately refer to their common experience of having been *derasine* (deracinated, forcibly uprooted and torn from their birthplace) and the myriad ways (physical, economic, social, cultural, and psychological) that they have suffered as individuals and as a community as a result of their *derasinman* (their forced uprooting). *Sagren*, *latristes*, and *mizer* have come to represent the inseparable combination of Chagossians' profound sorrow over their expulsion and the profound material suffering the expulsion has caused.

Understanding Displacement

It is difficult to understand fully the pain of having been *derasine*, of having been uprooted from one's homeland. Most readers, like me, probably live far more transient lives than the Chagossians once did. Most probably expect to move several, perhaps many times in a lifetime, choosing to move from place to place following employment opportunities, education, family members, and even romance. "We have great difficulty grasping the full horror of the situation in which the Crow found themselves," the philosopher Charles Taylor (2007) has commented about Native American lives radically overturned by displacement, death, and the destruction of their way of life. Outsiders can only struggle to comprehend the lives of the Chagossians, the Crow, and too many others, to empathically understand, to comprehend the horror. We can only imagine what being forcibly uprooted and torn from Chagos felt like for the Chagossians who had been living there for generations, some never having left the islands.

I asked Rita what she felt that day when she heard she couldn't return to her islands. "Enormous anguish. Enormous problems for me. . . . How can I explain it—you know, there was a child that I breastfed. She grew all the way up to seventeen months. And despite it all, she died. It left me with enormous grief. The same grief. The same as when I lost Alette, when I lost . . . Eddy. The same suffering, David."

"The same suffering," I repeated.

"The same suffering. And how can I say it? When I have that suffering—there's a time when I remember, there's a time when I forget. But that moment, I turn it over. I turn it over in my mind. Because I've had so many problems, David. If my children and grandchildren were born there, it would be something different. They would have had a different house. They would have had a different everything. The same as I had."

Root Shock and Social Suffering

"Imagine the victim of an earthquake, a hurricane, a flood, or a terrorist attack," urges Mindy Fullilove (2004:12) in her discussion of root shock. "He suffers from root shock as he looks at the twisted remains of the known universe, searching for the road to the supermarket, which used to be there, but is now a pile of rubble. Imagining such a person—and knowing that these tragedies can happen to any of us—we open our hearts and our wallets to the Red Cross and other relief organizations that show up immediately to be . . . the transfusion of an environment to those who are naked to the elements." However, she adds, "The experience of root shock . . . does not end with emergency treatment, but will stay with the individual for a lifetime," potentially affecting "generations and generations."

This experience of root shock and the way it affects not just individuals but whole communities across generations is an example of what medical anthropologists mean by "social suffering" (Kleinman et al. 1997). The concept is useful for the way the word *social* helps identify a distinct kind of suffering whose causation resides in the social world rather than within individuals. "Social suffering," three prominent medical anthropologists explain, "results from what political, economic, and institutional power does to people." The phenomenon is also social because it affects specific populations as a result of their (vulnerable) positioning in the world—for example, Jews and other minorities in the Holocaust, Native Americans growing up on impoverished reservations, African Americans and Latinos consigned to urban poverty in the United States, and Iraqi refugees fleeing their homes. Further, the phenomenon is social because it is a kind of suffering that is fundamentally experienced not just as an individual but also socially, among a group or community of sufferers. This kind of suffering is so "profoundly social that it helps constitute the social world" (Kleinman et al. 1997:xxi–xxiv).

Yet unlike *nervos*, which is a form of social suffering that tends to obscure its own social, political, and economic sources, in Chagossians' use of the words *sagren*, *latristes*, and *mizer*, the islanders are implicitly identifying the source of their suffering. They are placing the blame for their afflictions squarely on their expulsion and the actions of the responsible governments. As a popular Chagossian song says, "The English arrived, Mr. Englishman arrived in Chagos. The English arrived, the English uprooted us, cut off our food supply." (In a classic example of an "oppression illness" [Baer et al. 2003; Singer 2004:17], some, however, also tend to blame themselves for their exile, internalizing their treatment as justly deserved.[9])

And so "social suffering" captures important elements of the Chagossian experience: as indicated by their common use of the words *sagren*, *latristes*, and *mizer* to describe their lives, Chagossians' suffering has been experienced not just individually but socially as well. With their lives utterly transformed by exile, they have suffered as a community, sharing common experiences that have shaped a common social world (see Jeffery 2006). *Sagren*, *latristes*, and *mizer* reflect this shared social reality; together they have come to serve as a kind of shorthand, among Chagossians and with outsiders, for the totality of their suffering and for the shared experience of having been *derasine*.[10] Likewise, their suffering was (and is still) caused by the force and power of the U.S. and U.K. governments, by individuals within those governments who targeted the Chagossians as a vulnerable group, and by the United States empire.

Health, Empire, and Militarization

Contrary to popular belief, the United States has been an empire since independence; George Washington, among other "founding fathers," referred to the United States as the "rising American Empire." The nation conquered lands and peoples in North America and islands outside the continent throughout the nineteenth and twentieth centuries. Since 1898 and after World War II, the United States has become a new kind of empire, depending less on seizing and controlling foreign lands or colonies and more on less visible forms of economic, political, and military power. Among these tools used to exert dominance in the world, the nation has maintained a massive collection of what are now around 1,000 military bases outside the 50 states and Washington, D.C.

During the creation of this overseas base network, the U.S. military has repeatedly displaced local peoples as part of the creation of military facilities. In addition to the systematic displacement of native peoples in North America in the nineteenth century, I have documented at least 16 cases of "base displacement" in addition to the Chagossians. These include Guam, Panama, the Philippines, Hawai'i, Alaska, Okinawa in Japan, Vieques and Culebra in Puerto Rico, Guantanamo in Cuba, South Korea, and at least five cases in the Marshall Islands, including the Bikini Atoll nuclear test site (Vine 2006, 2009).

"The fact is that nobody cared very much about these populations," said former Defense Department official Gary Sick, who testified to Congress in 1975 about the Chagossians' removal. "It was more of a nineteenth-century decision—thought process—than a twentieth- or twenty-first-century thought process. And I think that was the bind they got caught in. That this was sort of colonial thinking after the fact, about what you could do." And U.S. officials, Sick said, "were pleased to let the British do their dirty work for them."

With the British doing the dirty work on Diego Garcia, the United States has turned the island into what has become a major pivot point for its military dominance of Middle East oil transit routes. Diego Garcia was the base for the first large-scale U.S. military presence in the region following the Iranian Revolution and the Soviet invasion of Afghanistan in 1979. Diego Garcia is fully utilized for the U.S. wars in Iraq and Afghanistan. Indeed, the base was one of the first major steps by the United States to deploy its military power to the region. The island has thus been central to a more than half-century-long period during which, as Chalmers Johnson (2004:253) says, "the United States has been inexorably acquiring permanent military enclaves whose sole purpose appears to be the domination of one of the most strategically important areas of the world."

Given the centrality of oil to the U.S. economy, the connections between the suffering of the Chagossians, the militarization of Diego Garcia, and U.S. economic power are made clear. In the Chagossians' lives in exile, the security of the United State is built on the insecurity of others. *Sagren* is the hidden underside of the empire that the United States has become, and the source of the sorrow is the base that the U.S. military calls "The Footprint of Freedom."

Notes

1. We are not and have never been employed or paid for the work. The U.S. legal team reimbursed most research expenses during August 2001–December 2002 and some research expenses during 2004.

2. The Chagossian-run support group, which has brought suits against the U.S. and British governments, represents the vast majority of Chagossians in Mauritius and elsewhere in exile.

3. Rita Bancoult's surname has changed to Isou, but for the sake of clarity, I will use her previous name. In accordance with confidentiality agreements, all of the Chagossians quoted are pseudonyms, with the exception of the Bancoult family and Jeannette Alexis (now Esparon).

4. All quotations from Chagossians are my translations from Mauritian Kreol, Seselwa, or Chagos Kreol, with the exception of Jeannette Alexis, who spoke in English, and where otherwise noted.

5. Parts of this chapter are drawn from Vine (2009), courtesy of Princeton University Press.

6. For more on the broader patterns, see Vine (2009) and Vine et al. (2005).

7. The Comité Ilois Organisation Fraternelle, or Ilois Committee Fraternal Organization, was a group created by Mauritians in the 1970s to support the exiled Chagossians. The group helped to document the people's conditions in exile and helped to advocate on their behalf. Chagossians later founded their own organizations in the 1980s after many began to feel used and manipulated by some Mauritian supporters.

8. In future research and analysis, I will explore how the concept of "idioms of distress" may help in understanding Chagossians' experiences (see, e.g., Butzen 2003; Good 1977; Nichter 1981).

9. Like other victimized peoples and individuals, many have internalized blame for the expulsion, questioning how they could have allowed themselves to be exiled. Many in both the first and the second generation still wonder why the expulsion happened, why they were victimized, why they cannot live in their homeland, and why they did not resist. Jeanette Alexis remembers Chagossians on Diego Garcia being scared of U.S. military forces arriving on the island with their boats, planes, and heavy equipment, she remembers fearing that they might be bombed if they did resist, she remembers her father protesting the removals. Still, she wonders why the Chagossians let it happen to them.

10. These words point to a common narrative of the expulsion and to the injuries experienced in exile. Among other purposes that the shorthand serves is to allow people to allude to the expulsion and other painful experiences of suffering without having to recite the entirety of the narrative or the specifics of their own painful injuries (including rape, hunger, and crime) (see Jeffery 2006).

Works Cited

Archival Sources
  MA = Mauritius Archives, Cormandel, Mauritius
  NARA = National Archives and Records Administration II, College Park, MD

PRO = National Archives, Public Records Office, Kew Gardens, England
SNA = Seychelles National Archives, Victoria, Mahé, Seychelles
UKTB = U.K. Trial Bundle, Sheridans Solicitors, London

African Research Group
2000   BIOT: Health & Mortality in the Chagos Islands. Report, Foreign & Commonwealth Office, London, October.

Aust, Anthony
1970   Immigration legislation for BIOT. Memorandum, UKTB, January 16.

Baer, Hans, Merrill Singer, and John Johnsen
1986   Introduction: Toward a critical medical anthropology. *Social Science and Medicine* 23(2):95–98.

Baer, Hans, Merrill Singer, and Ida Susser
2003   *Medical Anthropology and the World System.* 2nd ed. Westport, CT: Greenwood.

Bandjunis, Vytautas B.
2001   *Diego Garcia: Creation of the Indian Ocean Base.* San Jose, CA: Writer's Showcase.

B.I.O.T. Death Peros-Banhos, Solomon Island, Diego-Garcia 1965–1971
N.d.   Death records. SNA.

Butzen, Fred
2003   Idioms of distress: Psychosomatic disorders in medical and imaginative literature. *Journal of the American Medical Association* 290:538–539.

Cernea, Michael M.
1993   Anthropological and sociological research for policy development on population resettlement. In *Anthropological Approaches to Resettlement: Policy, Practice, and Theory,* edited by Michael M. Cernea and Scott E. Guggenheim, 13–38. Boulder, CO: Westview Press.
1997   The risks and reconstruction model for resettling displaced populations. *World Development* 25(10):1569–1587.

Chagos Refugees Group
2001   Index of deceased Chagossians. Unpublished document, Port Louis, Mauritius.

Chalfont, Alun A. G. J.
1966 Letter to David K. E. Bruce, December 30, 1966, NARA II, RG 59/150/64-65, Subject-Numeric Files 1964–1966, Box 1552.

Cochrane, E. L., Jr.
1971 Memorandum for the Deputy Chief of Naval Operations (Plans and Policy), March 24. NHC, 00 Files, 1971, Box 174, 11000.

Comité Ilois Organisation Fraternelle
N.d. Paper Prepared by the Comité Ilois Organisation Fraternelle, Port Louis, Mauritius.

Draebel, Tania
1997 Evaluation des besoins sociaux de la communauté déplacée de l'Archipel de Chagos, volet un: Santé et education. Report, Le Ministère de la Sécurité Sociale et de la Solidarité Nationale, Mauritius, December.

Fadiman, Anne
1997 *The Spirit Catches You and You Fall Down: A Hmong Child, Her American Doctors, and the Collision of Two Cultures.* New York: The Noonday Press.

Farmer, Paul
1997 On suffering and structural violence: A view from below. In *Social Suffering,* edited by Arthur Kleinman, Veena Das, and Margaret Lock, 261–283. Berkeley: University of California Press.

Fullilove, Mindy Thompson
2004 *Root Shock: How Tearing Up City Neighborhoods Hurts America, and What We Can Do about It.* New York: One World.

Good, Byron J.
1977 The heart of what's the matter: The semantics of illness in Iran. *Culture, Medicine, and Psychiatry* 1:25–28.

Jeffery, Laura
2006 The politics of victimhood among displaced Chagossians in Mauritius. PhD diss., University of Cambridge.

Johnson, Chalmers
2004 *The Sorrows of Empire: Militarism, Secrecy, and the End of the Republic.* New York: Metropolitan Books.

Kirmayer, Laurence J., and Allan Young
1998 Culture and somaticization: Clinical, epidemiological, and ethnographic perspectives. *Psychosomatic Medicine* 60(4):420–430.

Kleinman, Arthur, Veena Das, and Margaret Lock, eds.
1997 *Social Suffering*. Berkeley: University of California Press.

Madeley, John
1985 *Diego Garcia: A Contrast to the Falklands*. The Minority Rights Group Report 54. London: Minority Rights Group.

Moulinie, M.
1999 Statement of Marcel Moulinie. Application for judicial review, Queen v. The Secretary of State for the Foreign and Commonwealth Office, ex parte Bancoult.

Naipaul, V. S.
1984 *The Overcrowded Barracoon*. New York: Vintage.

Nayak, Ranjit
2000 Risks associated with landlessness: An exploration toward socially friendly displacement and resettlement. In *Risks and Reconstruction: Experiences of Resettlers and Refugees*, edited by Michael Cernea and Christopher McDowell, 79–107. Washington, DC: World Bank.

Nichter, Mark
1981 Idioms of distress: Alternatives in the expression of psychosocial distress: A case study from South India. *Culture, Medicine and Psychiatry* 5(4):379–408.

Ottaway, David
1975 Islanders were evicted for U.S. base. *Washington Post*, September 9, A1.

Prosser, A. R. G.
1976 Visit to Mauritius, from 24 January to 2 February: Mauritius—Resettlement of persons transferred from Chagos Archipelago. Report, Port Louis, Mauritius, September.

Saminaden, Rosemond, Fleury Vencatassen, and Christian Ramdass
1975 Petition to British government. English translation. Port Louis, Mauritius.

Scheper-Hughes, Nancy
1992 *Death without Weeping: The Violence of Everyday Life in Brazil.* Berkeley: University of California Press.

Scudder, Thayer
1973 The human ecology of big projects: River basin development and resettlement. *Annual Review of Anthropology* 12:44–55.

Scudder, Thayer, and Elizabeth Colson
1982 From welfare to development: A conceptual framework for the analysis of dislocated people. In *Involuntary Migration and Resettlement: The Problems and Responses of Dislocated Peoples*, edited by A. Hansen and A. Oliver-Smith, 267–287. Boulder, CO: Westview Press.

Selvon, Sydney
2001 *A comprehensive history of Mauritius.* Mauritius: Mauritius Printing Specialists.

Sharsky, Scott W., et al.
2005 Acute and reversible cardiomyopathy provoked by stress in women from the United States. *Circulation* 111:472–479.

Singer, Merrill
1986 The emergence of a critical medical anthropology. *Medical Anthropology* 17(5):128–129.
2004 The social origins and expression of illness. *British Medical Bulletin* 69(1):9–19.

Singer, Merrill, and Hans Baer
1995 *Critical Medical Anthropology.* Amityville, NY: Baywood Publishing.

Sunday Times (London)
1975 The islanders that Britain sold. September 21.

Taylor, Charles
2007 A different kind of courage. Review of Jonathan Lear, *Radical Hope: Ethics in the Face of Cultural Devastation. New York Review of Books* 54(7), 4–8.

Titmuss, Richard M., and Brian Abel-Smith
1968 *Social Policies and Population Growth in Mauritius.* London: Frank Cass.

U.S. Congress, House of Representatives
1975   *Diego Garcia, 1975: The debate over the base and the island's former inhabitants.* Special Subcommittee on Investigations, Committee on International Relations, June 5 and November 4, 94th Cong., 1st sess. Washington, DC: U.S. Government Printing Office.

U.S. Embassy London
1964   Telegram to secretary of state, February 27, NHC: 00 Files, 1964, Box 20, 11000/1B, 1-2.

Vine, David
2003   The former inhabitants of the Chagos Archipelago as an indigenous people: Analyzing the evidence. Expert report for the Washington College of Law, American University, Washington, DC, July 9.
2004   War and forced migration in the Indian Ocean: The U.S. military base at Diego Garcia. *International Migration* 42(3):111–143.
2006   Empire's footprint: Expulsion and the U.S. military base on Diego Garcia. PhD diss., City University of New York.
2009   *Island of Shame: The Secret History of the U.S. Military Base on Diego Garcia.* Princeton, NJ: Princeton University Press.

Vine, David, Philip Harvey, and S. Wojciech Sokolowski
2008   "We all must have the same treatment": Calculating the damages of human rights abuses for the people of Diego Garcia. In *Waging War, Making Peace—Reparations and Human Rights*, edited by Barbara Rose Johnston and Susan Slyomovics, 132–151. Walnut Creek, CA: Left Coast Press.

Vine, David, S. Wojciech Sokolowski, and Philip Harvey
2005   Dérasiné: The expulsion and impoverishment of the Chagossian People [Diego Garcia]. Expert report prepared for the American University Law School, Washington, DC, and Sheridans Solicitors, London, April 11.

Walker, Iain B.
1986   *Zaffer Pe Sanze: Ethnic Identity and Social Change among the Ilois in Mauritius.* Vacoas, Mauritius: KMLI.

Walker, Martin
1975   Price on islanders' birthright. *Manchester Guardian*, November 4.

Wittstein, Ilan S., et al.
2005   Neurohumoral features of myocardial stunning due to sudden emotional stress. *New England Journal of Medicine* 352(6):539–548.

PART THREE

THE WAR MACHINE AND THE MACHINERY OF HUMAN SOCIAL LIFE

CHAPTER SEVEN

HASBARA, HEALTH CARE, AND THE ISRAELI-OCCUPIED PALESTINIAN TERRITORIES

Avram Bornstein

In the West Bank Palestinian town of Tulkarem, the chronic under-development of health care and well-being infrastructure—compared to its western neighbors in Israel or eastern neighbors in Jordan—was quickly evident to me when I began fieldwork is the early 1990s. It was visible in the dilapidated condition of the Tulkarem public hospital, the open and putrid cesspool downhill from the town, and the municipal trash burning in open fires that created a permanent cloud of choking and probably toxic smoke on the town's southern outskirts. Having seen these things firsthand, I have learned to be suspicious of the frequent claims made by the Occupation authorities of the benefits they brought to Palestinian health. For example, in a presentation to a Palestinian delegation in Washington, D.C., in 1992, Israel's chief medical officer described how Israel built sewage treatment facilities across the West Bank, including the town of Tulkarem in 1972, and organized and "modernized" garbage disposal. "Improved facilities for solid waste collection and disposal have contributed to improved sanitation in [the West Bank] & Gaza. A master-plan for garbage disposal in [the West Bank] was finalized and approved" (Israel Ministry of Foreign Affairs 1992). Having seen and smelled the Occupation at that time, I can only conclude that such statements about the Occupation's contributions to Palestinian health and well-being are what Israeli authorities call *hasbara*, or public relations.

The importance of public relations, a term often associated with big business or politicians, is also well known to military officers working in counterinsurgency. British and U.S. forces call it "winning the hearts and

Figure 7.1. October 2002, Tulkarem, West Bank. This sign in front of Tulkarem Hospital was erected in the mid-1990s to announce new construction funded by Japan and co-implemented by the United Nations Development Program and the Palestinian Authority's Ministry of Health. With the outbreak of the al Aqsa Intifada in 2000, the sign became plastered over, like many vertical surfaces in Palestinian towns, with posters of combatant and noncombatant "martyrs" for the liberation of Palestine.

minds" of the population under military siege. This strategy is evident in the Israeli army–issued "Operational Principles for the Administered Territories," published in October 1967, in which it described five "fundamental" (or strategic) guidelines: 1) ensure efficient military control; 2) encourage the departure and prevent the return of residents; 3) encourage the "evacuation" of Gaza Strip, especially the refugee camps; 4) integrate the infrastructure and lives of the remaining inhabitants into Israel; and 5) "have the local populace cooperate with and be dependent on the military government . . . as a means to thwart subversion intentions and attempts" (Gazit 1995:300). The document also describes 11 "operational" (or tactical) guidelines for dealing with everything from violence and civil disobedience to social services and the economy. The first operational guideline is public relations (*hasbara*): "Hasbara activity directed at the population of the administered territories is of the utmost importance. Emphasis must be put on: a) Fostering recognition and belief in Israel's intention to administer the territories for a long time. b) Persuading the populace that cooperation with the administrative authorities is worthwhile, whereas subversion and terrorism are not" (Gazit 1995:300–301).

The importance of so-called public relations for domination is well-trodden ground in the social sciences. Max Weber (1968) argued many years ago that states must create legitimacy, through charismatic leaders, tradition, or rational planning, because while the power of violence is sometimes necessary, ruling by force alone can become very costly. Antonio Gramsci (1988:194) explained that dominant groups must motivate compliance and cultivate collusion by organizing alliances in diversified spheres of power, such as political parties, social clubs, intellectual circles, professional associations, the arts or popular fashion, with the goal of fostering their own "moral and cultural leadership." There are many examples of how such a cultural hegemony of dominant groups is cultivated through ritual (Bloch 1986), literature (Said 1978, 1992; Williams 1977), urban landscapes (Mitchell 1989), social welfare (Piven and Cloward 1971), television (Herman and Chomsky 1988), and health care (Baer et al. 2003).

One of the pillars of Israel's struggle for cultural and ideological hegemony and the focus of this chapter is health care for Palestinians in the Occupied Territories. Providing better medical care to the "natives" has been a standard theme of European colonialism. Europeans' nineteenth-century scramble for empire was often accompanied by medical missionaries, like David Livingstone in Africa, whose work—as sincere and dedicated as it may have been—became an ideological and ethical cover for savage campaigns of imperialism. Similarly, in Palestine, the Zionist movement has done its best to maintain an image of an "enlightened" occupation (Gazit 1995; Segev 2007), and the claim of concern for Palestinians' health and well-being care have played a key role (see also chapter 9 in this volume).

Kanaaneh (2002) broke important ground investigating how health care and narratives of modernity were entwined in the Palestinian struggle. Her study describes how Israeli family planning policy inside 1948 Israel encouraged women who are Palestinian citizens of Israel in the Galilee to have smaller, "modern" families while encouraging Jewish mothers to have larger families; Palestinian women made a variety of choices but often explained them in terms of the national struggle and

modernity. Public health has played a role in the ideological and institutional expansion of the Zionist movement at least since the British
Mandate of 1918–1948. Sufian (2007) describes how antimalaria projects
and the draining of swamps in the Jezreel and Huleh valleys were health
and welfare campaigns that expanded the acquisition of land, organized
Zionist agencies, and became a metaphor for the nationalist project.
This official discourse of modernity was also used by Zionist leaders in
the 1950s and 1960s to subordinately incorporate Jews emigrating from
Muslim majority countries, like Moroccans, Yemenis, Iraqis, Egyptians,
Syrians, and Iranians, into the new state. Sa'di (1997:25) argues that
the "self-presentation of Israel as an agent of modernization vis-a-vis
the Palestinians dates back to the first encounters between Zionism and
the Palestinians at the end of the nineteenth century. Since 1948 it has
been the official discourse in explaining the relations between the Jewish
majority and the Palestinian minority inside Israel. With the signing of
the [Declaration of Principles in 1993] the evolvement of this discourse
has completed a full cycle; Zionism once again proclaims to fulfil the
role of modernizing agent in relation to all Palestinians who reside in
Palestine."

Kanaaneh's and Sufian's examples also show that hegemonic ideas
and practices surrounding health and well-being are not fixed by colonial
forces but can be partly appropriated and transformed by oppressed people
into counterhegemonic vehicles of resistance (see also Comaroff 1985;
Peteet 1994; Scott 1985). Israel failed to create collusion among Palestinians in the Occupied Territories largely because Palestinians experienced
firsthand the hardships caused by "fundamental guidelines" 1, 2, and 3,
which ensure military security and encourage Palestinian departure and
evacuation. These experiential lessons of dispossession counteract any
attempts by Israel to teach Palestinians, as instructed in guideline 5, to
"cooperate with and be dependent on the military government." Consequently, Palestinians organized grassroots independence movements,
and the Israeli military increased violence to suppress these aspirations.
Because of this increasing reliance on violence, Israeli *hasbara* has been all
the more necessary to shape public opinion, legitimize the Occupation,
and maintain alliances, not with those under the Occupation but with a
majority of Israelis, key international governing bodies, and popular con-
stituencies in Europe and North America.

This chapter describes the development of health care in the Occupied Territories, especially where it has become an active zone of the political struggle. The Israeli military's overall approach is described here in two overlapping phases: 1) 1967–1993, in which Israel tried to integrate and subordinate Palestinian health care systems despite Palestinian health care professionals' organized grassroots resistance to that subordination; and 2) 1993–2008, in which limited Palestinian autonomy was sown, but incrementally increasing closures, bombardment, and siege kept health care in a state of continual crisis. During the first phase, Israel may have hoped to win over Palestinians with notions of modernity. But by the second phase, health care public relations aimed mainly to counter Palestinian claims before international audiences of human rights abuses by Israelis. In this context, images of Palestinian health workers as terrorists and Israeli health workers as humanists were promoted. This chapter describes these two historical phases and then examines the struggle over the two national constructs of "Palestinian medic" versus "Israeli doctor" used to construct the mythical dichotomy between Arab and Jew. This dichotomy serves nationalist tendencies in Israel to marginalize Palestinian citizens of Israel, dispossess Palestinians in the Occupied Territories, delegitimize non-Zionist voices among Israeli Jews, and challenge human rights claims by international organizations and activists.

Occupation 1967–1993: Colonization as Open Bridges

The state of Israel established independence in 1948, largely under the hand of European Jewish refugees and émigrés, on about three-fourths of the British Mandate of Palestine (1918–1948), which was formerly part of the Ottoman Empire. The remaining one-fourth of the British Mandate was annexed by Jordan (East Jerusalem and the West Bank) and occupied by Egypt (the Gaza Strip). In Israel's independence war with surrounding Arab states, about 750,000 Palestinians became refugees, and the capital was divided into Israeli West Jerusalem and Palestinian East Jerusalem. Continuing conflict led to an Israeli army attack on Egypt in June 1967, that drew Jordan and Syria into the Six Days war, in which Israeli forces captured the Gaza Strip and Sinai Peninsula from Egypt, the Golan Heights from Syria, and the West Bank (including East Jerusalem) from Jordan. The Sinai was returned to Egypt as part of a treaty in 1978, and the Golan Heights were annexed in 1981, but for over 40 years, the West Bank and the Gaza Strip have remained Occupied Territories.

There has been military repression of Palestinian nationalist activists from the start (in the form of arrests, exiles, house destruction, and assassination), and large-scale control during the first 20 years of the Occupation was sought, as the army guidelines suggest, through the subordinate integration of Palestinians into Israel. This initial approach to ruling civilians in the Occupied Territories was called "Open Bridges" (Gazit 1995). By the mid-1980s, about 120,000 Palestinian workers from the Occupied Territories went to work in Israel every day, largely in agriculture, construction, manufacturing, and cleaning (Semyonov and Lewin-Epstein 1987). The roads, electrical and telephone lines, and water systems of the Occupied Territories were linked into the Israeli networks (Gazit 1995:169; Tamari 1980, 1981).

Although the Open Bridges policy was advanced by Israeli authorities as good publicity for their enlightened occupation, the systems created by this unequal integration were widely characterized as relations of colonial dependency (Owen 1989; Roy 1991; Samara 1989, 2001; Sayigh 1986; Tamari 1980, 1981, 1990). This colonial relationship became even more explicit and obvious when a new right-wing government came to power in Israel in 1977 that supported building Israeli settlements in the West Bank and Gaza. The number of settlers in the West Bank went from 3,176 in 1976 to 57,000 in 1987. Some Israeli parties, like Mayer Kahane's Kach Party, even advocated the ethnic cleansing or "transfer" of Palestinians from the Occupied Territories.

Improved health care for Palestinians became a common narrative used by Israeli authorities to make the Occupation seem like something good for Palestinians. For example, in a letter to the United Nations, Israel's ambassador Yehuda Blum (1984) paints a picture of Israel coming to the rescue of Palestinians by introducing medical technology and training facilities, establishing new hospitals and medical centers, expanding immunization programs, collecting information on contagious diseases, and improving sanitation and water systems (Blum 1984). Similarly, in 1992, an Israeli official told a Palestinian delegation that "since 1967, we have succeeded to improve, to develop and to strengthen the infrastructure of public health and preventive medicine. We have accomplished the building of a modern and stabile infrastructure" (Israel Ministry of Foreign Affairs 1992).

Among Israel's accomplishments, government health insurance became available in the West Bank in 1973 and in Gaza in 1976, and many Palestinians bought into it (Israel Ministry of Foreign Affairs 1992). Israel extended its own plan for immunization against infectious diseases into the Occupied Territories, which was necessary to protect Israel's population because of their physical proximity and frequent interaction with Palestinians. The Israeli Occupation claimed to have established over 50 new general clinics and over 100 mother and child health centers (Israel Ministry of Foreign Affairs 1992, 1994). A close reading of their counting, however, reveals that such a claim takes credit for development efforts made by the United Nations Relief and Works Agency (UNRWA) and independent nongovernmental organizations (NGOs) that military authorities merely allowed under its rule. Perhaps Israel's most prominent and truly significant claim to an enlightened occupation has been that "since 1967 Palestinian patients have been referred to Israeli hospitals for hospitalization and ambulatory care in cases that deserve specialized sophisticated departments that do not exist in Judea-Samaria and Gaza, or in cases that are in need of clinical specialists for diagnosis and treatment. All complementary services are continuously given to Palestinian patients from the autonomous areas" (Israel Ministry of Foreign Affairs 1994).

While many Palestinians benefited from cutting-edge care inside Israel unavailable in the Occupied Territories, these stories of enlightened development of Palestinian health care systems are contradicted by Palestinian health care professionals and by foreign visiting medical professionals. Palestinian professionals say that under Occupation authorities working for the Ministry of Defense—not the Ministry of Health—the governmental health care system was "stunted and underdeveloped, with severe budget restrictions, referral to Israeli hospitals for tertiary care, and restrictions on licenses for new medical and health care projects, thus creating a total dependence on the Israeli health system" (Giacaman et al. 2003:61). A fact-finding group of Swedish doctors described health care in the Occupied Territories as being in a state of deterioration because of an extremely small budget, a decrease in the number of government hospitals from 11 to nine, and antiquated facilities (Henley et al. 1986:135–136).

Similarly, an Anglo-Dutch team of physicians reported that the military occupation "fostered neglect and dependency on the Israeli health system" (Johannes Wier Foundation and Physicians for Human Rights 1998). The retardation of health services in the Occupied Territories of Palestine led some Palestinians to take matters into their own hands. The Union of Palestinian Medical Relief Committees (UPMRC), later the Palestinian Medical Relief Society (PMRS), which has grown to be one of the largest health NGOs in Palestine, was founded in 1979 to provide grassroots, community-based health care throughout the West Bank and Gaza Strip (PMRS n.d.). The Institute of Community and Public Health (ICPH) at Birzeit University was established in 1978 to provide "independent and informed health human resource development, research and planning, model building and implementation of health care services locally" (ICPH n.d.). These organizations—among others like the Health Services Committees, established in 1984, and the Union of Health Care Committees, formally created in 1985—not only provided services for an underserved population but also played a critical role, alongside agricultural relief committees, in recruiting the population into national-ist ideologies (Nasser and Heacock 1990; Robinson 1993). While many organizers were secular nationalists and leftists, following the Muslim Brothers examples elsewhere, the Islamic movement also became active in building health care charities in peripheral areas (Challand 2008).

This movement, not just in health care and agriculture but also among lawyers, teachers, laborers, and women's organizations, mobilized the population. In December 1987, a series of clashes in Jabalya Refugee Camp in Gaza spread across Gaza and the West Bank and became the first intifada. Children throwing stones and burning tires created me-dia spectacles. While uplifting for Palestinian dignity, the uprising was painful. Over 1,100 Palestinians and 160 Israelis were killed. To break the organized resistance, the Israeli army arrested and savagely beat over 100,000 Palestinians between December 1987 and July 1993 (Human Rights Watch 1994:3).

Occupation 1993–2008: Closures as Autonomy

After almost six years of the intifada uprising and suffering through the first Gulf War, the Israeli government and the Palestine Liberation Organization (PLO) signed a series of agreements (Oslo I, Oslo II, and Wye River) in the mid-1990s that allowed the PLO to return to Palestinian towns in the Occupied Territories. They also established a Palestinian Authority (PA), with limited civilian and security control, while Israel began a phased withdrawal from those towns. Under the PA, the Palestinian Ministry of Health (MoH) took responsibility for health services for Palestinians in the Occupied Territories.

It is difficult to compare numbers collected by different agencies with different methods. In the West Bank and Gaza health employees went from 1,549 in 1967 to 3,849 in 1992 (Israel Ministry of Foreign Affairs 1992) and to over 10,000 employed by the MoH by 2005 (World Health Organization [WHO] 2006b:10). The number of general hospitals grew from 23 with approximately 2,200 beds under Israel (Israel Ministry of Foreign Affairs 1992, 1994) to 77 hospitals in 2005 with 4,824 beds (25 MoH, 31 NGO, one UNRWA, and 23 private hospitals). The number of clinics grew from 198 under Israel (Israel Ministry of Foreign Affairs 1992) to over 700 clinics in 2005 (WHO 2006b:11). Under the PA, visits to general practitioners per person per year increased 15.4 percent in Gaza and 26.1 percent in the West Bank (Abu Mourad et al. 2008:128), and the maternal mortality ratio decreased by 66.0 percent (Abu Mourad et al. 2008:134).

This enormous growth was made possible largely by international aid for the Palestinians that has been described by the World Bank as one of the largest mobilization of donors in absolute terms and per capita ($175 per person). "Between 1994 and mid-1999, donors committed some US$353 million to the health sector and disbursed approximately half of that amount in actual assistance" (Giacaman et al. 2003:61). This flood of money and donors brought problems, however. According to the World Bank, more than forty donors, over two dozen multilateral organizations and UN agencies, and hundreds of local and international NGOs have in many cases "mobilized excessive human resources and created more fragmentation than cooperation" (Giacaman et al. 2003:64). Further, Giacaman et al. (2003:65) argue that the "limited political analysis on the part of the donors in relation to the major obstacles to health and well-being, and their proven incapacity to influence change in the political arena as a prerequisite to reforming the health system, have often resulted in the non-sustainability and ineffectiveness of projects" (see also Giacaman 1989).

The PA takeover of security and civilian affairs in the Occupied Territories might have led to further steps toward peace, but the process in the 1990s was undermined at almost every turn: checkpoint-enforced closures shut down Palestinians' ability to travel (Bornstein 2002); Israeli settlements in the West Bank ballooned to house 180,000 residents and an additional 200,000 in East Jerusalem by 1999 (Aronson 1999:128); the Israeli military and armed settlers confiscated and vandalized Palestinian property and assaulted, detained, and sometimes murdered Palestinians; Hamas sent three or four suicide bus bombers a year starting in April 1994; and in the summer of 2000, the Israeli prime minister made a "final offer" that was unacceptable to most Palestinians and made the so-called peace process seem fruitless. A new al-Aqsa Intifada uprising ignited in September 2000, escalating the killing of Palestinians to two, three, four, or more a day and the number of suicide bombers sent into Israel to two, three, four, or more a month.

The Israeli army imposed continuous closures, extensive curfews, and large and small military assaults to quell the uprising. On March 29, 2002, the Israeli army launched an invasion of five West Bank towns, bombing homes and businesses, shooting militants and noncombatants, arresting hundreds of men, and enforcing continuous curfews for weeks. The damage was extensive (Giacaman et al. 2004). In June 2006, Israel launched an invasion of Gaza and made over 260 air strikes, killing over 240, of whom 155 were civilian noncombatants, including 57 children; there were around 1,000 injuries, including over 300 wounded children; over 120 structures were destroyed, including the Gaza Power Plant, leaving Gazans with about six to eight hours of electricity a day; thousands fled their homes (Bandel and Habib 2006; Filc 2006). Urban areas in northern Gaza and Rafah had only about two or three hours of water per day, and lack of clean water caused diarrhea (United Nations Office for the Coordination of Humanitarian Affairs 2006; WHO 2006a:1). A second major invasion of Gaza occurred in December 2008–January 2009. By the end of January, the Palestinian MoH reported that the invasion had killed 1,380 Palestinians, including 431 children and 112 women, and injured approximately 5,380 people, including 1,872 children and 800 women; 15 of Gaza's 27 hospitals suffered damage, 41 (out of 55) PHC clinics were partially damaged, and two were destroyed (WHO 2009).

In addition to those directly killed or injured by the violence, the destruction and closures have led to other health and health care problems. Hospitals suffered blackouts for 8 to 12 hours (Amnesty International et al. 2008:5). There was a lack of laboratory supplies and X-ray films, drugs, and spare parts (WHO 2006a:2). Fuel, flour, baby milk, and rice became scarce and increasingly expensive for people who had less money (Amnesty International et al. 2008:4). Gazan families relying on humanitarian aid went from 63 percent in 2006 to 80 percent in 2008. "In less than ten years, the number of families depending on UNRWA food aid has increased ten-fold" (Amnesty International et al. 2008:4). By 2003, chronic malnutrition among children 6 to 59 months of age was 12.7 percent in the Gaza Strip and 9.2 percent in the West Bank (Abdeen 2005:8). In Gaza, coliform contamination of water increased from 15.5 percent in 1999 to 20.4 percent in 2003 (Abu Mourad et al. 2008:135).

Palestinian Medics as Terrorists

As the previous citations from UN agencies, human rights groups, and Palestinian grassroots intellectuals make abundantly clear, protest against Israeli violence in the Occupied Territories comes from a handful of sources. Stories about innocent civilians being unnecessarily prevented from receiving health care by Occupation authorities, a violation of the Geneva Convention relative to the Protection of Civilian Persons in Time of War of 1949 (Articles 54–57), have appeared in a variety of places, most notably in the British medical journals *Lancet* and the *British Medical Journal*. For example, over a decade ago:

> On March 15, 1996, a woman in labour who was trying to reach the Al-Ahli hospital in the Palestinian town of Hebron, had to give birth in a village clinic without medical assistance. Her baby died at birth or shortly afterwards. Had she been allowed to cross an Israeli checkpoint her baby, as the necropsy later revealed, might have survived. Israel's policy of internal closures had claimed another victim. (Pourgourides 1999:420)

B'tselem, a leading Israeli human rights organization, reports that in 2007 there were 58 permanent checkpoints within the West Bank, an additional 15 checkpoints in Hebron alone, 35 checkpoints between the West Bank and Israel, a weekly average of 200 temporary checkpoints inside the West Bank, and over 400 physical obstructions (concrete blocks, dirt piles, and trenches) that make roads impassable (B'tselem 2008b).

Israeli army spokespersons defend the checkpoints inside the West Bank and on the Green Line as security necessities: "Almost on a daily basis, the Israel Defense Forces have captured Islamic terrorists at Israeli Army security checkpoints in both the West Bank and Gaza attempting to smuggle both weapons and explosives into Israel" (Israel News Agency 2007). The Israeli army's official procedures for Palestinians who seek to cross checkpoints for medical treatment fall into two categories: emergencies and nonemergencies. According to the "Procedure for the Handling of Residents of Judea and Samaria Who Arrive at a Checkpoint in an Emergency Medical Situation" (translation from Swisa 2003:5),

> As a rule, the checkpoint commander will allow a person to cross the checkpoint (including to enter into Israel) to obtain medical treatment, even if the individual does not have the requisite approval, if an urgent medical emergency is involved. An example of a case of urgent medical emergency is if a woman about to give birth, a person suffering from massive bleeding, or a person with a serious burn injury arrives at the checkpoint.
>
> Whether a situation is an urgent medical emergency is left to the discretion of the checkpoint commander. The checkpoint commander will consult with a medical official, where time permits.
>
> In the event of doubt whether an urgent medical emergency is involved, the resident shall be given the benefit of the doubt.

In the army's "Procedure for the Handling of Requests of Residents of the Areas to Receive Medical Treatment," which is applied to Palestinians who are crossing to visit medical facilities without emergencies, the patient must get a permit from the local District Coordination Office.

Getting a one-day, one-visit permit requires a doctor to provide a medical report. Permits to Jerusalem are particularly difficult to get even though the six major specialized hospitals for the West Bank, including the main public referral hospital Makased, are in East Jerusalem. The number of approved permits to exit Gaza for medical reasons decreased from 89.3 percent of permit applications in January 2007 to 64.3 percent in December 2007. Even those patients who are granted permits are sometimes denied access by soldiers at the crossing itself; 27 such cases were reported in the month of October alone, and during the period October–December 2007, 20 patients—including 5 children—died because they were denied passage for medical treatment (Amnesty International et al. 2008:5). In many cases, Israeli soldiers and checkpoints ignore their own procedures, delay ambulances unnecessarily for extended periods, fail to consult with medical officials, do not give the benefit of the doubt to the sick person, or completely refuse to allow ambulances or anything else to pass (B'tselem 2008a; Swisa 2003:6). During the first three years of the al-Aqsa Intifada, Physicians for Human Rights, B'Tselem, HaMoked: Center for the Defence of the Individual, and the Palestinian Red Crescent received 185 complaints of delays caused by soldiers, most of which were in the Nablus area (B'tselem 2008a; Swisa 2003).

Checkpoints are only part of the obstacle to receiving health care. In many locations, roads in and out of villages are permanently blocked by physical obstacles such as concrete barriers, large boulders, deep trenches, or piles of dirt and rubble. To get around these obstacles, some patients must be driven on off-road paths or carried over hills or through ditches. At some of the locations, as I observed in Tulkarem, 12-year-old boys with donkeys and carts transport those who need help about 100 meters from one vehicle stopped at a barrier to another vehicle stopped at the next barrier. Similarly, at the Surda checkpoint north of Ramallah, two barriers a kilometer away from each other block the road, and the UPMRC has had to employ staff with wheelchairs and stretchers to assist patients (Swisa 2003:3). According to the Palestinian Red Crescent, ambulances reach the sick or wounded only 30 percent of the time because of such roadblocks. The consequence is that people are less likely to receive emergency care, and the percentage of women in the West Bank who gave birth in the hospital dropped from 95 percent before the al-Aqsa Intifada to less than 50 percent by September 2002 (Swisa 2003:3).

There have also been several reports of attacks made by the Israel Defense Forces (IDF) against ambulances and their staff. One ambulance driver explains,

> It is humiliating. My colleagues went to collect a body, and they were asked to hold up their hands. They are a medical team with a clear

medical symbol. A year ago, a tank shell hit a house in Beit Lahiya. We headed toward the house. Many Israeli soldiers were shooting. We were very surprised when they started shooting toward our vehicle. Two bullets were aimed my chest. I was lucky that I was driving and lying low to avoid the bullets, but I still have shrapnel in my head. (El Khodary 2005:33)

The situation became especially bad as suicide bombing in Israel began to climb in early 2002. In the first years of the al-Aqsa Intifada, the Palestinian Red Crescent and human rights organizations received reports of at least 28 cases in which soldiers and border police humiliated and beat medical personnel, sometimes deliberately damaging ambulances or medical equipment; in the first two years, about 118 ambulances were damaged, and 28 of which were rendered inoperable (Swisa 2003:11).

On March 4, 2002, the IDF opened fire on a Red Crescent ambulance in a Jenin refugee camp, and it exploded, burning the physician to death and injuring three crew members. The IDF first said that the explosion was caused by Israeli bullets hitting hidden explosives, but they later admitted that it was probably an oxygen tank (Ziv 2002:2). Four days later, on March 8, 2002, the IDF opened fire on a UNRWA ambulance in the Tulkarem area, killing the driver and injuring two crew members, and then on a Red Crescent ambulance, killing the driver and injuring two crew members. In all three of these cases, the ambulances had been coordinated in advance with Israeli authorities. Israeli Physicians for Human Rights said that the "apologies offered by the security forces are shameful and place the blame on the alleged use of ambulances to carry wanted persons and ammunition. No evidence has been offered for this sweeping allegation" (Ziv 2002:3). Similarly, two weeks after Israel began its December 2008 invasion of Gaza, the International Committee of the Red Cross stopped escorting Palestinian ambulances in Gaza because even they came under fire, even though Israel had anounced a pause to allow aid work (Associated Press 2009).

The Israeli government has attempted to justify the delays and attacks on ambulances, like all its violent actions, as necessary security measures. In February 2002, the Israeli army claimed that the Palestine Red Crescent Society (PRCS) participated in terrorism when the first woman suicide bomber, Wafa Idris, turned out to have once volunteered for them as a medic (Hockstader 2002). The Israel Ministry of Foreign Affairs website explains,

> Israeli security officials do not yet have a clear picture of how Idris made her way from Ramallah to Jerusalem. However, investigators believe that Red Crescent documentation held by the suicide bomber and her accomplices, and perhaps even a Red Crescent vehicle, helped them through IDF roadblocks and eased the checks they had to undergo.
>
> This is not the first incident in which ambulances have been used by terrorist organizations. Last October, Israeli security forces arrested Nidal Nazal, a Hamas operative from Kalkilya, brother of Natzar Nazal, one of the leaders of the Hamas in the city. Nidal Nazal worked as an ambulance driver for the Palestinian Red Crescent and there is information indicating that Nazal exploited his relatively easy movement around the West Bank towns as an ambulance driver to serve as a messenger between Hamas headquarters in the various towns (Israel Ministry of Foreign Affairs 2002b).

These accusations were repeated by the Israeli ambassador to the United Nations: "Evidence suggests that Idris used her medical accreditation, and possibly even a Red Crescent vehicle, to gain access to Israel" (Lancry 2002). Israel did finally admit that they did not have a "clear picture" and by the words "perhaps even" and "possibly," largely because they were without specific evidence. But a few days later, only a few weeks after the killing of the physician and drivers, the Israeli Army proclaimed that it had found its "smoking gun." The Israel Ministry of Foreign Affairs announced on March 27, 2002, at approximately 10:00 A.M., that a driver of a Red Crescent ambulance was arrested at an IDF roadblock near Ramallah with an explosives belt and other explosive charges concealed under the mattress of a stretcher bearing a sick child accompanied by two other children and their mother; they claim that the driver admitted that these were given to him by senior militants (Israel Ministry of Foreign Affairs 2002a). The PRCS leadership responded with a statement accusing the Israeli Army of fabricating the event.

> Our initial investigation leads us to believe that this was a staged event in which the Israeli army was involved to taint the Red Crescent ambulances. We have debriefed the passengers of the vehicle, examined

the timeline and other eyewitness accounts, and are amazed at how the Israeli army managed within the span of 20 minutes to invite the media and press corps in the area before even confirming the presence of the explosive device. If this was a routine and random search, one wonders why the occupants of the vehicle were so quickly released, except for the Red Crescent Medic? One also wonders as to the perfect timing [approximately 10 a.m.] and location of the incident so close for the media to get to? And one wonders about the Israeli reserve TV actor onsite participating in briefing the media? And of the army's initial claims that they had arrested a militant on their "most wanted list"? (PRCS 2002)

After having four ambulance personnel killed, 170 injured, 28 ambulances destroyed, and four cases in which medics were dragged from their ambulances and used as human shields by Israeli soldiers, Canadian doctor Hossam Sharkawi, the director of national disaster and emergency services for the PRCS, argued that the device was planted by the Israeli army. He defended his organization, saying,

Lies are powerful weapons of war, and the Red Crescent does not have the resources or the network to continuously counter the prevailing media spin. The Israeli army has banned the media from most areas in Palestine, and even when respected organizations such as the Red Cross, Amnesty International, and Human Rights Watch speak out, they are quickly dismissed as anti-Israeli.

... It is true that Wafa Idris, a Red Crescent volunteer first-aider, was the suicide bomber who carried out the tragic Jan. 27 attack in Jerusalem. But this was an isolated incident that does not reflect on the Red Crescent's work or its workers . . . any more than Baruch Goldstein, an Israeli army doctor who murdered 29 Palestinians in Hebron in 1994, is reflective of Israeli medical services. (Sharkawi 2002:19).

Soon after, repeated accusations in the media that UNRWA was supporting Hamas pushed the U.S. Congress to order an investigation by the Government Accountability Office (GAO). The GAO investigation approved of UNRWA's operating procedures regarding screening for terrorists (U.S. Government Accountability Office 2003).

International news media habitually carry stories of possible abuse of medical status by Palestinian groups. In May 2004, Reuters carried a story based only on an Israeli police spokesman's accusations that terrorists use fake ambulances for smuggling operations: "police are investigating the possibility the ambulances brought potential suicide bombers or explosive belts into Israel. Israel has said it has had to limit passage for ambulances— some of which are stolen vehicles painted to look like ambulances—to prevent terrorists using emergency vehicles to bypass security checks" (Reuters 2004). In October 2004, the Israeli army released grainy black-and-white footage video shot by an Israeli spy drone that, according to them, shows an ambulance and "a Palestinian terrorist carrying one of the homemade missiles used to bombard Israeli towns and Jewish settlements. It said the footage proved its frequent claims that the UN often helped terrorists in the occupied territories" (O'Loughlin 2004:12). The Israeli ambassador to the United Nations demanded the resignation of the head of the UNRWA, Peter Hansen, but it soon became clear that the object in question was a rolled-up stretcher, and the footage was quickly pulled from the Israeli government website. Nevertheless, with the help of lazy and passive news media organizations and ideologically motivated bloggers and grassroots groups, these stories are repeated as known facts and liberally distorted (Bard n.d.; Malkin 2004; McCann 2004; Miller 2004).

Bornstein (2002), Hammami (2004), Brown (2004), and Kelly (2006) show that despite the military's security explanation, checkpoints are widely perceived as collective punishment and an attempt to encourage Palestinian obedience or emigration. Hass (2002) argues that in the 1990s, the checkpoints and the phenomenon that became known as "closure" were intended to push the PLO to accept Israel's "final offer." But the strategy proved a failure when the PLO rejected Israeli demands in the summer of 2000. In the fall of 2000, although it added "fuel to the fire of the frustration and wrath," the closures in the West Bank were intensified to stop the al-Aqsa Intifada (Hass 2002:20). This political imperative, however, is illegal and cannot be used to justify closures to the outside world, nor should it encourage Israeli soldiers to ignore their duty, especially when it comes to medical personnel and patients. To create complicity and collusion with this policy the Israeli government has persistently attempted to smear Palestinian medical workers and their organizations by repeatedly holding up the case of Wafa Idris, a second disputed case of a bomb-belt discovery, and numerous other accusations without evidence except, perhaps, for confessions made under torture. For these two cases, all Palestinian emergency workers are suspected of being terrorists.

Israeli Doctors as Bearers of Enlightenment

On Thursday, January 15, 2009, the first morning of the cease-fire after more than three weeks of military assaults on Gaza that caused over 1,000 Palestinian deaths and far more injuries, the Israeli government decided to open a Magen David Adom (the Israeli version of the Red Cross) medical center at the Erez Crossing for wounded Gazans; by Sunday, the Israeli minister of social services, the minister of health, and the chief executive officer of Magen David Adom held an opening ceremony for the press on the Israeli side of border (Neiman 2009). This illustrates a long pattern in which Israeli doctors' assistance to Palestinians is used as *hasbara* for colonization and destruction.

For example, a BBC 2002 broadcast titled "Jerusalem Hospital Where There Is No Distinction between Arabs and Jews" maintaining that, in this hospital funded by a Jewish women's charity, "Jew and Muslim nestle side by side under state-of-the-art medical observation":

> In the current atmosphere of violence, there is rather too much ideology eddying around this hospital in the Judean hills. Its ideals remain intact, though, and a reminder to both communities that common bonds of humanity can still prove stronger than those of nationality or religion. That's what Avi Rivkind discovered when he was asked to save the life of a man responsible for two horrific bus bombs.
>
> Rivkind: Hassan Salame was responsible for the explosion of two buses. He was captured by our soldiers and they called me because he was severely injured. I operated, and then he was in a special room in the department, and I want to tell you a secret—one of our intelligence guys was hospitalised for elective surgery. I couldn't give him a place because Hassan Salame was in a room. So we gave him another place, not even in our department, and he was there because he was guarded, etc. I'm telling you, it can be only in Israel. Crazy people.

For Zionists, places like the Hadassah Hospital (described previously) represent extraordinary Israeli humanitarianism. An online *Time* magazine article reads, "At Hadassah, Jews save Arabs and Arabs save Jews" (Rees 2003). "Though Hadassah Ein Kerem has handled more victims of terrorist attacks than any other Israeli hospital, it stands as a model of integration in the conflict between Israelis and Palestinians. As politicians continually fail to find compromises for peace that will stick, Hadassah's mixed staff—operating under terrible pressure—manages to make coexistence work. 'I've seen our Palestinian victims, and I've seen Israelis after suicide bombs,' [a doctor] Ratrout says. 'I don't differentiate between them. Each time, I think, how can this happen?'" (Rees 2003).

The Israeli Ministry of Foreign Affairs website describes an arts education experience for Arab pediatric cancer patients in Hadassah: "Due to their better-established oncology facilities, Hadassah treats Arab children from beyond the Jerusalem area, including some who come from the Palestinian Authority" (Israel Ministry of Foreign Affairs 2005). A Web blogger passes on the message and explains that it should represent to all the real truth of the historical conflict:

> It's a pity that all the lying bashers of Israel (and they are not all limited to the Arab world or to Islamic countries) haven't visited Hadassah Hospital in Jerusalem to see just how malicious the Jews really are. Hadassah Hospital is a major medical center set up a few generations ago by Jewish American women. Immediately on entering, one is struck by the multi-racial nature of the place. Ostensibly a Jewish hospital, it seems that almost half its patients are nevertheless Arabs—not only from within Israel but from Judea, Samaria and other parts of the Arab world. (Dobrin 2008)

Stories of the magnanimity of Israeli doctors at Hadassah are sometimes contrasted with the story of how a medical convoy to Hadassah Mount Scopus was attacked on April 13, 1948, during the 1948 Israeli-Arab War, and 78 Jewish medical personnel were killed.

While doctors and staff in these hospitals undoubtedly give earnest and skilled care to all their patients, these stories are used to obfuscate or deny many other stories of occupation, including the fact that getting to Israel's hospitals is often impossible because of the closures and now, the wall. These stories about Israeli doctors also stand in sharp contrast to those told by Physicians for Human Rights-Israel (PHR-I). PHR-I, founded in 1988, has run a mobile clinic in cooperation with Palestinian organizations; has sent hundreds of medical professionals, both Jewish and Arab, into the Occupied Territories to examine and treat thousands of patients in isolated villages; and conducted specialist clinics in medical centers.

But more than providers of technical care, PHR-I advocates professional solidarity against the Occupation. A key area of their work during the first intifada was, along with other Israeli human rights organizations like B'Tselem, to expose the participation of physicians in the torture of Palestinians by the Israeli General Security Services (Gordon and Marton 1995). By questioning military officials, PHR-I gained a public admission when officials explained that the purpose of doctors' participation was to protect the health of the detainee from complications caused by interrogation, or to determine if a detainee can withstand particular methods (Ziv 1999:3–4). PHR-I exposed these gross violations of internationally codified medical ethics[2] and demanded that doctors who become aware of torture should provide necessary treatment, if authorized by the prisoner, and then "categorically prevent, by means of a doctor's order, the prisoner's return to the interrogation or to the place where he was held; and . . . must inform an authorised body within the system and outside it" (Ziv 1999:21).

PHR-I also criticized the silence of Israeli medical associations to the professional struggles of their Palestinian colleagues. They criticized Magen David Adom when the organization remained silent as Israeli soldiers attacked ambulances and then "broke its silence by issuing a condemnation of the Red Crescent, which it accused of the illegal use of ambulances. Magen David Adom accepted all the claims of the IDF. Moreover, after the president of the Palestinian Red Crescent was beaten and detained for hours by the security forces, the president of Magen David Adom, Dr. Moshe Malloul, made no effort to express solidarity with his Palestinian counterpart":

Medical crews are gravely injured; physicians are prevented from working safely to help their patients; hospitals are shelled; and medical personnel are killed while performing their duties, yet the Israel Medical Association [IMA] remains silent. Recently, after numerous calls by PHR-Israel, a forum was convened to discuss the position of the IMA in the face of the attacks on health services in the Territories. After almost two years of conflict, including worsening infringements in the health sphere, the IMA failed to express even once its solidarity with its colleagues. (Ziv 2002: 10)

The PHR-I has demanded that the IMA adopt an unequivocal position, as representatives of the medical establishment in Israel, that criticizes the actions of the Israeli security forces against Palestinian health and emergency personnel and facilities: "To adopt any other position would be to betray the IMA's mission, and would jeopardize the IMA's membership of the World Medical Association" (Ziv 2002:10).

The international community has approached the Israeli medical community more gingerly in an effort to create solidarity and mutual understanding with their Palestinian colleagues. Rather than try to shame them as PHR-I has done, the WHO has encouraged dialogue between medical professionals in what they call Health as a Bridge for Peace. Health as a Bridge for Peace began as a program of the Pan American Health Organization in 1984 to expand polio immunization in Central American conflict zones (Manenti 2004:3):

> Health as a Bridge for Peace (HBP) is a multidimensional policy and planning framework which supports health workers in delivering health programmes in conflict and post-conflict situations and at the same time contributes to peace-building. It is defined as the integration of peace-building concerns, concepts, principles, strategies and practices into health relief and health sector development. (WHO 2008)

To this end, *Bridges, the Israeli-Palestinian Public Health Magazine* was created as a publication produced by Palestinian and Israeli academics and health professionals under the sponsorship of the WHO to cover topics of interest to both populations. "In both structure and content bridges is a cooperative endeavor between Israeli and Palestinian health care professionals seeking to build relationships, links and common understanding" (Bridges 2004:2).

Conclusion

The case of the health and well-being infrastructure in the Occupied Territories illustrates in dramatic terms that such operations are not just biomedical, but social and political as well. Building or undermining health care systems—or claiming to build health care—is often tied up with modern states' efforts to dominate or mobilize. This is evident in Israeli attempts to disguise colonialism, in the international community's attempts to encourage Palestinians to accept the Oslo arrangements, and in Palestinian efforts to resist displacement, organize resistance, and build a state. Decades ago, Israeli authorities hoped they could colonize the West Bank and Gaza with the cooperation of Palestinians. They told themselves, the world, and Palestinians that the Occupation was enlightened and that "Open Bridges" would bring better health care to a backward people. Superior military power was combined with media work to attempt cultural hegemony. Israel failed to extend its hegemony over Palestinians and the Arab world, however, because repeated experiences of dispossession taught Palestinians not to cooperate but rather to organize grassroots resistance committees and to develop counterhegemonic ideologies and practices.

In response to this refusal to submit to dispossession, since 1993 the former policy to integrate Palestinian residents of the Occupied Territories has been replaced with a policy of isolation and encystation locking them behind checkpoints and walls (Bornstein 2008; Bowman 2007). The suffering of civilians following this change, especially of the sick and injured dying at checkpoints, was not completely invisible, and its appearance threatened to undermine the cooperation of Palestinians and the international community in their project of Israeli suppression. The target of health care propaganda shifted from the population to be ruled (winning their hearts and minds) to winning the hearts and minds of an international audience and coalition of dominators. Israeli public relations have attempted to cement alliances of collusion and complicity by demonizing Palestinian medical workers and painting the PRCS and UNRWA as organizations that provide material support to terrorists. In contrast to this, Israeli medical professionals are repeatedly portrayed as great humanitarians who even treat the terrorists who seek to kill them. These images are challenged by Palestinian health professionals who, with the occasional help of sympathetic Israeli and foreign colleagues, document the brutality of occupation and the complicity of Israeli physicians. Health care public relations is a common way in which the military occupation of Palestinians has been framed as enlightened Israelis and barbaric Palestinians.

Some will read these criticisms of Israeli *hasbara* about Palestinian health care and well-being and dismiss them as politically biased and agenda-driven scholarship that "inflames hatred of Israel, spreads anti-

Semitism, incites anti-Israeli militancy, and serves to excuse or tolerate terrorist attacks and genocidal threats against Israel" (Scholars for Peace in the Middle East n.d.). But ethnographers who work among those dominated by military rule have an ethical obligation to document the consequences of that domination, especially if documentation provides a balance to commonly accepted myths. The goal is not to demonize Israelis but to encourage skepticism of claims justifying war and military occupation. In all parts of the globe, we must be wary of attempts to use doctors and medical technology as a legitimization of military conquest.

Notes

1. "Occupation" is a term of international law. The Hague Convention IV (1907) says, "Territory is considered occupied when it is actually placed under the authority of the hostile army" (Sec. III, Art. 42). Furthermore, "The authority of the legitimate power having in fact passed into the hands of the occupant, the latter shall take all the measures in his power to restore, and ensure, as far as possible, public order and safety, while respecting, unless absolutely prevented, the laws in force in the country" (Sec. III, Art. 43). The laws pertaining to occupation are further elaborated in the Fourth Geneva Convention of 1949, Part III: Status and Treatment of Protected Persons, especially Section III on Occupied Territories.

2. United Nations Principles of Medical Ethics (1982) unambiguously states, "It is a gross contravention of medical ethics, as well as an offence under applicable international instruments, for health personnel, particularly physicians, to engage, actively or passively, in acts which constitute participation in, complicity in, incitement to or attempts to commit torture or other cruel, inhuman or degrading treatment or punishment." Principle 4 forbids health personnel, particularly physicians, from assisting in the interrogation, even if it is only "to certify, or to participate in the certification of, the fitness of prisoners or detainees for any form of treatment or punishment that may adversely affect their physical or mental health and which is not in accordance with the relevant international instruments." Principle 6 states that "there may be no derogation from the foregoing principles on any grounds whatsoever, including public emergency" (Ziv 1999:13).

Works Cited

Abdeen, Ziad
   2005   Armed conflict and food security: A nutrition profile of the West
          Bank and Gaza Strip. *Bridges* 1(3):8–12.

Abu Mourad, Tayser, Samir Radi, Suzanne Shashaa, Christos Lionis, and Anastas Philalithis
2008   Palestinian primary health care in light of the National Strategic Health Plan 1999–2003. *Public Health* 122(2):125–139.

Amnesty International UK, CARE International UK, Christian Aid, CAFOD, Medecins du Monde UK, Oxfam, Save the Children UK, and Trocaire
2008, March   *The Gaza Strip: A humanitarian implosion.* Online: http://www.oxfam.org.uk/resources/policy/conflict_disasters/downloads/gaza_implosion.pdf. Accessed July 2, 2008.

Aronson, Geoffrey
1999   Settlement monitor. *Journal of Palestine Studies* 28(3):128–138.

Associated Press
2009, January   *Red Cross will no longer escort Palestinian ambulances in Gaza.* Online: http://www.haaretz.com/hasen/spages/1054492.html.

Baer, Hans, Merrill Singer, and Ida Susser
2003   *Medical Anthropology and the World System.* 2nd ed. Westport, CT: Praeger.

Bandel, Maskit, and Ibrahim Habib
2006   Report: Harm to children in Gaza. Online: http://www.phr.org.il/phr/article.asp?articleid=395&catid=54&pcat=45&lang=ENG. Accessed July 2, 2008.

Bard, Mitchell
N.d.   *Transporting sick and injured Palestinians to hospitals.* Online: http://www.ujc.org/page.aspx?id=54765

BBC
2002, February 21   *Jerusalem hospital where there is no distinction between Arabs and Jews.* Online: http://news.bbc.co.uk/1/hi/events/newsnight/1836591.stm. Accessed June 25, 2008.

Bloch, Maurice
1986   *From Blessing to Violence.* Cambridge: Cambridge University Press.

Blum, Yehuda
1984   *Letter dated 8 June 1984 from the permanent representative of Israel to the United Nations addressed to the secretary-general.* Online: http://domino.un.org/unispal.nsf/2ee9468747556b2d85256cf60060d2a6/

31a418e3b52912cb052567fa00681035!OpenDocument. Accessed July 15, 2008.

Bornstein, Avram
    2002   *Crossing the Green Line between the West Bank and Israel.* Philadelphia: University of Pennsylvania Press.
    2008   Military occupation as carceral society: Prisons, checkpoints and walls in the Israeli-Palestinian struggle. *Social Analysis* 52(2):106–130.

Bowman, Glenn
    2007   Israel's wall and the logic of encystations: Sovereign exception or wild sovereignty. *Focaal* 50:127–135.

Bridges
    2004   Mission statement. 1(1):2.

Brown, Alison
    2004   The immobile mass: Movement restrictions in the West Bank. *Social and Legal Studies* 13(4):501–521.

B'tselem
    2008a *Infringement of the right to medical treatment in the West Bank.* Online: http://www.btselem.org/english/Medical_Treatment/Index.asp. Accessed February 5, 2009.
    2008b *Restrictions of movement: Information on checkpoints and roadblocks.* Online: http://www.btselem.org/english/Freedom_of_Movement/ Statistics.asp.

Challand, Benoît
    2008   A Nahda of charitable organizations? Health service provision and the politics of aid in Palestine. *International Journal of Middle East Studies* 40:227–247.

Comaroff, Jean
    1985   *Body of Power, Spirit of Resistance: The Culture and History of a South African People.* Chicago: University of Chicago Press.

Dobrin, Ralph
    2008, January 29   *Racism in Israeli hospitals.* Online: http://truthandsurvival .wordpress.com/2008/01/29/racism-in-israeli-hospitals.

El Khodary, Taghreed
    2005   An ambulance driver in the Gaza Strip talks about his work. *Bridges* 1(1):32–33.

Filc, Dani
2006, September   The Gaza Strip—State of disaster. Report. Cambridge, MA: Physicians for Human Rights.

Gazit, Shlomo
1995   *The Carrot and the Stick: Israel's Policy in Judea and Sameria, 1967–68.* Washington, DC: B'nai B'rith Books.

Giacaman, Rita
1989   Health as a social construction: The debate in the Occupied Territories. *Middle East Report* 161:16–20.

Giacaman, Rita, Hanan Abdul-Rahim, and Laura Wick
2003   Health sector reform in the Occupied Palestinian Territories (OPT): Targeting the forest or the trees? *Health Policy Plan* 18(1):59–67.

Giacaman, R, A. Husseini, N. H. Gordon, and F. Awartani
2004   Imprints on the consciousness: The impact on Palestinian civilians of the Israeli Army invasion of West Bank towns. *European Journal of Public Health* 14(3):286–290.

Gordon, Neve, and Ruchama Marton, eds.
1995   *Torture—Human Rights, Medical Ethics and the Case of Israel.* London: Zed Books.

Gramsci, Antonio
1988   *Selected Writings.* Edited by David Forgacs. New York: Schocken Books.

Hague Convention IV
1907   *Convention Respecting the Laws and Customs of War on Land.* Online: http://www.yale.edu/lawweb/avalon/lawofwar/hague04.htm#art41.

Hammami, Rima
2004   On the importance of thugs: The moral economy of a checkpoint. *Middle East Report* 231:26–34.

Hass, Amira
2002   Israel's closure policy: An ineffective strategy of containment and repression. *Journal of Palestine Studies* 31(3)5–20.

Henley, David, Eva Bergholtz, and Gunnar Olofsson
1986   Health and health care for the Palestinians of the West Bank and Gaza. *Journal of Palestine Studies* 15(2):132–140.

Herman, Edward, and Noam Chomsky
1988   *Manufacturing Consent*. New York: Pantheon Books.

Hockstader, Lee
2002, January 31   Palestinians hail a heroine: Israelis see rising threat; suicide bomber elicits pride and fear. *Washington Post*, 20.

Human Rights Watch
1994   *Torture and Ill-Treatment: Israel's Interrogation of Palestinians from the Occupied Territories*. New York: Human Rights Watch.

Institute of Community and Public Health
N.d.   *About ICPH*. Online: http://icph.birzeit.edu. Accessed June 18, 2008.

Israel Ministry of Foreign Affairs
1992   *Health services in the areas of Judea-Samaria and Gaza since 1967*. Online: http://www.israel-mfa.gov.il/MFA/Archive/Peace+Process/1992/Health+Services+in+the+Areas+of+Judea-Samaria+and.htm. Accessed July 23, 2008.
1994   *Health services development in Judea-Samaria and Gaza 1967–1994: 31 Dec 1994*. Online: http://www.mfa.gov.il/MFA/Archive/Peace+Process/1994/health%20services%20develoment%20in%20judea-samaria%20and%20G.
2002a, March 27   *Apprehension of ambulance harboring a wanted terrorist and weapons at a checkpoint near Ramallah*. Online: http://www.mfa.gov.il/MFA/Government/Communiques/2002/Apprehension+of+ambulance+harboring+a+wanted+terro.htm.
2002b, February 14   *Use of ambulances and medical vehicles by terrorist organizations*. Online: http://www.israel-mfa.gov.il/MFA/Government/Communiques/2002/Use%20of%20ambulances%20and%20medical%20vehicles%20by%20Palestin.
2005, June 26   *Israeli project empowers young Arab cancer patients*. Online: http://www.mfa.gov.il/MFA/Israel+beyond+politics/Israeli%20project%20empowers%20young%20Arab%20cancer%20patients%2026-Jun-2005. Accessed June 25, 2008.

Israel News Agency
2007, January 1   *Israel Defense Forces ease restrictions in West Bank*. January 1. Online: http://www.israelnewsagency.com/palestineisraelsecurity idfhumanitarian48990107.html. Accessed August 17, 2007.

Johannes Wier Foundation and Physicians for Human Rights
  1998   *A False Dawn: Palestinian Health and Human Rights under Siege in the Peace Process*. Amersfoort: Johannes Wier Foundation and Physicians for Human Rights.

Kanaaneh, Rhoda
  2002   *Birthing the Nation: Strategies of Palestinian Women in Israel*. Berkeley: University of California Press.

Kelly, Tobias
  2006   *Law, Violence and Sovereignty among West Bank Palestinians*. New York: Cambridge University Press.

Lancry, Yehuda
  2002   *Letter dated 5 April 2002 from the permanent representative of Israel to the United Nations addressed to the secretary-general*. Online: http://domino.un.org/unispal.nsf/eed216406b50bf6485256ce10072f637/5d197bc5a8ebd6cc85256b960050b9ab!OpenDocument.

Malkin, Michelle
  2004   *The ambulances for terrorists scandal*. Online: http://www.jewishworldreview.com/michelle/malkin_ambulances_for_terrorists.php3. Accessed July 18, 2008.

Manenti, Ambrogio
  2004   Why bridges. *Bridges* 1(1):3.

McCann, Paul
  2004, June 9   Threatened at gunpoint. *Washington Times*, 18.

Miller, Sarah
  2004, June 11   U.N. at gunpoint? *Washington Times*, 26.

Mitchell, Timothy
  1989   *Colonizing Egypt*. Berkeley: University of California Press.

Nasser, Jamal, and Roger Heacock, eds.
  1990   *Intifada: Palestine at the Crossroads*. New York: Praeger.

Neiman, Rachel
  2009   *Israeli medical center for Gazans opens as ceasefire begins*. Online: http://www.israel21c.org/bin/en.jsp?enDispWho=Articles%5E12425&enPage=BlankPage&enDisplay=view&enDispWhat=object&enVersion=0&enZone=Health&.

O'Loughlin, Ed
2004, October 8   Truth becomes the casualty in tale of missile in UN ambulance. *Sydney Morning Herald*, 12.

Owen, Roger
1989   The West Bank now: Economic development. In *Palestine under Occupation: Prospects for the Future*, edited by Peter Krogh and Mary McDavid, 43–56. Washington: Georgetown University Press.

Palestine Red Crescent Society
2002   *Statement.* Online: http://www.palestinercs.org/modules/content/?id=6.

Palestinian Medical Relief Society
N.d.   *About us.* Online: http://www.pmrs.ps/last/etemplate.php?id=56. Accessed July 15, 2008.

Peteet, Julie
1994   Male gender and rituals of resistance in the Palestinian Intifada: A cultural politics of violence. *American Ethnologist* 2(1):31–49.

Piven, Frances Fox, and Richard Cloward
1971   *Regulating the Poor.* New York: Vintage Books.

Pourgourides, Christina
1999   Palestinian health care under siege. *Lancet* 354:420–421.

Rees, Matt
2003, June 15   *Amid the killing, E.R. is an oasis.* Online: http://www.time.com/time/magazine/article/0,9171,1101030623-458754,00.html. Accessed June 25, 2008.

Reuters
2004, May 26   Israel accuses Palestinians of misusing ambulances. *National Post* (Canada), 16.

Robinson, Glenn
1993   The role of the professional middle class in the mobilization of Palestinian society: The medical and agricultural committees. *International Journal of Middle East Studies* 25:301–326.

Roy, Sara
1991   The political economy of despair: Changing political and economic realities in the Gaza Strip. *Journal of Palestine Studies* 20(3):58–69.

AVRAM BORNSTEIN

Sa'di, Ahmad
1997 Modernization as an explanatory discourse of Zionist-Palestinian relations. *British Journal of Middle Eastern Studies* 24(1):25–48.

Said, Edward
1978 *Orientalism.* New York: Random House.
1992 *Culture and Imperialism.* New York: Random House.

Samara, Adel
1989 The political economy of the West Bank 1967–1987: From peripheralization of development." In *Palestine: Profile of an Occupation.* Atlantic Highlands, NJ: Zed Press.
2001 *Epidemic of Globalization: Ventures in World Order, Arab Nation and Zionism.* Glendale, CA: Palestine Research and Publishing Foundation.

Sayigh, Yusif
1986 The Palestinian economy under occupation: Dependency and pauperization. *Journal of Palestine Studies* 15(4):46–67.

Scholars for Peace in the Middle East
n.d. SPME Mission. Online: http://spme.net. Accessed 29 September 2009.

Scott, James
1985 *Weapons of the Weak.* New Haven, CT: Yale University Press.

Segev, Tom
2007 *1967: Israel, the War, and the Year That Transformed the Middle East.* New York: Metropolitan Books.

Semyonov, Moshe, and Noah Lewin-Epstein
1987 *Hewers of Wood and Drawers of Water: Noncitizen Arabs in the Israeli Labor Market.* Ithaca, NY: International Labor Organization Press, Cornell University.

Sharkawi, Hossam
2002, May 14 Who you calling terrorist? The Palestine Red Crescent Society has gotten a bad rap in the current conflict. *The Globe and Mail* (Canada), 19.

Sufian, Sandra
2007 *Healing the Land and the Nation: Malaria and the Zionist Project in Palestine.* Chicago: University of Chicago Press.

Swisa, Shlomi
   2003   *Harm to medical personnel: The delay, abuse and humiliation of medical personnel by the Israeli Security Forces.* Online: http://www.phr.org.il/ phr/article.asp?articleid=90&catid=54&pcat=45&lang=eng. Accessed July 2, 2008.

Tamari, Salim
   1980   The Palestinians in the West Bank and Gaza: The sociology of dependency. In *The Sociology of the Palestinians*, edited by Khalil Nakhleh and Elia Zureik. New York: St. Martin's Press.
   1981   Building others people's homes: The Palestinian peasant's household and work in Israel. *Journal of Palestine Studies* 11:(1)31–66.
   1990   Revolt of the petit bourgeoisie. In *Intifada: Palestine at the Crossroads*, edited by Jamal Nassar and Roger Heacock. New York: Praeger.

United Nations Office for the Coordination of Humanitarian Affairs
   2006, August 24   Situation Report Gaza Strip, 7–24 August. Jerusalem: UNOCHA-oPt.

U.S. Government Accountability Office
   2003   *Department of State (State) and United Nations Relief and Works Agency (UNRWA) Actions to Implement Section 301(c) of the Foreign Assistance Act of 1961, November 17, 2003.* Online: http://www.gao.gov/htext/ d04276r.html. Accessed July 26, 2008.

Weber, Max
   1968   *Economy and Society.* New York: Bedminster Press.

Williams, Raymond
   1977   *Marxism and Literature.* Oxford: Oxford University Press.

World Health Organization
   2006a   *Health sector surveillance indicators: Monitoring health and health sector in the oPt: September 5, 2006.* Online: http://www.healthinforum.net/ modules.php?name=Downloads&d_op=viewdownload&cid=120.
   2006b   *WHO-AIMS report on mental health systems in West Bank and Gaza.* Online: http://www.healthinforum.net/files/mental/who_aims_ Mental.pdf.
   2008   *What is health as a bridge for peace?* Online: http://www.who.int/hac/ techguidance/hbp/about/en/index.html.
   2009   *Health situation in Gaza—4 February 2009.* Online: http://www.who .int/hac/crises/international/wbgs/sitreps/gaza_4feb2009/en.

Ziv, Hadas
    1999   *Physicians and torture—The case of Israel.* Online: http://www.phr
        .org.il/phr/article.asp?articleid=385&catid=67&pcat=50&lang=eng.
        Accessed July 2, 2008.
    2002   *Medicine under attack: Critical damage inflicted on medical services in the*
        Occupied Territories: An interim report. Online: http://www.phr.org
        .il/phr/article.asp?articleid=383&catid=54&pcat=45&lang=eng. Ac-
        cessed July 2, 2008.

CHAPTER EIGHT

WAGING WAR ON THE WAGELESS
Extrajudicial Killings, Private Armies, and the Poor of Honduras
Adrienne Pine

War Is the Health of the State

In his unpublished 1918 essay widely referred to as "War Is the Health of the State," Randolph Bourne argued that in war, "the State becomes what in peacetimes it has vainly struggled to become—the inexorable arbiter and determinant of men's business and attitudes and opinions" (Bourne 1918). The health of the state, as Bourne describes it, is in wartime inversely proportional to the health of the majority of the people living within its borders. In Honduras, the machinations of the international war machine with the full compliance of the state—a state with far less power than Bourne imagined but perhaps the same aims— has led to a devastating picture of human health in that country today.

Outside of Honduras, few people consider the country to be engaged in a war. That assessment is a grave mistake. I argue, following Hardt and Negri's (2005) analysis of metaphorical war, that we must take seriously claims of Honduran politicians and members of the private sector to be engaged variously in wars on crime, drugs, and terror. More than metaphors (e.g., Hartmann-Mahmud 2002), these combined wars are in reality a full-scale war on the public, the poor, and the structurally vulnerable. For though it is not internationally recognized as such, state violence and neoliberalism is experienced *as war* by those Hondurans who live with it. This chapter explores the confluence in Honduras of the war machine and the "infernal machine" (Bourdieu 1998) of neoliberalism—the "Washington Consensus" package of structural adjustments imposed on indebted countries around the globe by the International Monetary Fund (IMF) and the World Bank, in which public resources are privatized; regressive taxation and "free trade" policies are implemented; and industrial deregulation is coupled with a significant weakening of labor, environmental, and health care protections—all in the name of "development."

As described in the introduction and conclusion to this volume, I use the phrase "war machine" to refer to a series of processes that are diverse yet related to the extent that they emerge from and serve the same capitalist imperative to accumulate. My reading of the war machine is also informed by Deleuze and Guattari's (1987) work, in which they argue that the war machine is exterior to the state apparatus but that the state can appropriate it to serve its own ends. The infernal machine (neoliberalism), according to Bourdieu (1998), entails "not only the poverty of an increasingly large segment of the most economically advanced societies, the extraordinary growth in income differences, the progressive disappearance of autonomous universes of cultural production . . . through the intrusive imposition of commercial values, but also . . . the destruction of all the collective institutions capable of counteracting the effects of the infernal machine, primarily those of the state, repository of all of the universal values associated with the idea of the public realm" (see also Hodge and Singer, this volume).

The War Machine in Honduras: A Brief Overview

The state violence in Honduras is extreme by any measure. On September 11, 2008, the national human rights commissioner, Ramón Custodio, reported that Honduran homicide rates were 2.4 times greater than the average for the rest of the Americas (Redacción 2008f). According to the statistics of the United Nations Development Program (UNDP) Violence Observatory, the homicide rate for the entire country in 2007 was 49.9 per 100,000, placing Honduras among the most dangerous countries in the world. By comparison, the 2006 rate in Canada was 1.85 (Statistics Canada 2007), and the 2006 rate in the United States was 5.7—although the rate in the city of Detroit that year was 47.26, underscoring both the tendency of extreme structural violence to effect exceptionally high mortality rates (Federal Bureau of Investigation 2007a, 2007b), and the extremely uneven distribution of violence in the United States.

The victims are particularly concentrated among the youth. Since January 1998, the nonprofit organization Casa Alianza (Covenant House) has carefully tracked each murdered child. In July 2008, the number of murders tracked was 4,268 youths under 23, the vast majority of them male (Casa Alianza 2008). If the United States had had a similar youth homicide rate (around 100 per 100,000) over the past 10 years, that would represent an equivalent of roughly 100,000 slaughtered children (based on population calculations using data from the U.S. Census Bureau 2008). In addition, between 2003 and 2008, 450 deaths occurred in prisons in Honduras, 96 percent of them violent (Almendares 2007).

The idea that Honduras is at war pervades everyday discourse. On June 12, 2008, right-wing members of the state legislature claimed that police job protections were excessive. Legislator Silvia Ayala of the leftist UD (Democratic Union) Party took the floor to argue that the police needed more protection than other workers, not less. One hundred and forty police are killed yearly, she pointed out, and they officially earn only 5,000 lempiras per month (around U.S.$250). Her colleague Doris Gutierrez added, "The police are at war every day." In March 2006, the Security Minister Álvaro Romero claimed that the majority of police officers paid protection money, popularly called "war taxes," to gangs (Associated Press 2006). Self-identified gang members I have spoken with, however, claim that the opposite is true; indeed, my interviews with numerous and diverse Honduran informants paint a picture of war taxes paid in many directions.

As a result of this state of war, Honduran subjectivities are dominated by a sense of bodily terror. This fear constitutes in discourse what Linda Green (1999) refers to (in Guatemala) as a "metanarrative" for all members of society. Even in "safer" neighborhoods, very few people walk outside after dusk, perhaps for fear of attack, and Hondurans' warnings to be careful are incessant—not just to me, the naïve gringa anthropologist, but to each other. "It's not like when I grew up," a nurse told me on her way to visit her childhood neighborhood in Puerto Cortes on June 6, 2008. "Then, we knew all our neighbors, we helped each other, we left our doors unlocked. Now, my sister drops my niece off at school, and she picks her up, and she doesn't let her leave the house. You can't live like that, with so much fear." The woman sitting next to me on a bus later the same day echoed that sentiment: "They say every single place is dangerous, but you can't flee every single place."

This ever-present fear is embodied, that is, experienced at the level of habitus. Wacquant (2006, 318) (following Bourdieu) describes habitus as "the way society becomes deposited in persons in the form of lasting *dispositions*, or trained capacities and structured propensities to think, feel, and act in determinate ways, which then guide them in their creative responses to the constraints and solicitations of their extant milieu." Contributing to the sense of *embodied insecurity* existing at the level of habitus is the genre of reporting that I call *death porn*, following José Alaniz (2005). On mainstream Honduran television shows, cameras zoom in, sometimes for minutes at a time, on bodies lying in pools of their own blood. Bloated drowning victims, decapitated victims of extrajudicial assassinations, corpses of infants killed in shootouts, and in-ambulance interviews with the horrifically injured and with shocked, grieving family members are all regular lunchtime fare. Full-color images of the same sort grace the covers of mainstream Honduran newspapers nearly every day. Thus, in death, commodified bodies of the poor attain a value they did not have in life (Moodie 2006).

In contrast to the violence experienced by wealthy Hondurans, much of the bodily violence experienced by the poor is portrayed only impersonally in the media. Deeply sympathetic stories of society women and men kidnapped for ransom remain on the front pages for months, whereas violence done to the poor is shown in gory color images of dehumanized bodies, reported on but not individualized or remembered except by relatives and neighbors. In war photography, as Susan Sontag (2004, 70–73) has noted, there is an interdiction against showing the naked face of *our* dead, whereas it is natural to do so for *theirs*. This dichotomy is significant, for it fits with the logic of the infernal machine, which destroys collectivities, promoting in their absence an ideology of individual responsibility. Ruling-class "individuals" can practice this ideal much more easily than can the poor, rendered as faceless masses and stripped by neoliberalism of customary mechanisms of solidarity.

Stratified bodily worth, internalized as habitus, is reinforced at death and in illness, with bourgeois notions of bodily ownership keeping anyone who can afford it out of public hospitals. Hospital Mario Catarino Rivas, the largest such facility in San Pedro Sula, is locally nicknamed "*el matarino*" from the verb *matar*, "to kill." This reflects the fears of Hondurans that a stay in the overcrowded and underfunded hospital could leave them sick, mutilated, or dead. These fears are well founded: the rate of nosocomial infection in the intensive care unit at the country's premier public hospital, Hospital Escuela, was 17.4 percent in 2006, compared with a worldwide average of 5 to 10 percent (López-Maldonado, Galo, and López-Maldonado 2007). The director of medical services at Hospital Escuela stated in an interview, "We're just like a war hospital" (Redacción 2008e). Hospital Escuela nurses I spoke with echoed this assessment. In 2008, nationwide drug supply shortages—in this case a result of misappropriation rather than lack of public funds—meant that people unable to pay simply went without (Sauceda 2008). But more telling than the statistics are the stories. Everyone has at least one. For example, in the summer of 1999 while my friend Lesly Rodriguez was living with me, her beloved father-in-law went to *el matarino* for an injured finger. After Lesly and her husband spent a week desperately searching for and not being able to locate him within the hospital, he was returned to them—without a hand.

According to Deleuze and Guattari (1987: 425–426), mutilation at the hands of the state is not accidental:

> It is true that war kills, and hideously mutilates. But it is especially true after the State has appropriated the war machine. Above all, the State apparatus makes the mutilation, and even death, come first. It needs [its subjects] preaccomplished, for people to be born that way, crippled and zombie-like. The myth of the zombie, of the living dead, is a work myth and not a war myth. . . . The State apparatus needs, at its summit as at its base, pre-disabled people, preexisting amputees, the still-born, the congenitally infirm.

The creation of a physically and psychically mutilated population through the war machine to serve the interest of capital is thus essential to the health of the state. A self-sufficiently healthy populace has no need for a state that ultimately has nothing to offer but crutches for the mutilated. Even hospitals become complicit in this war mutilation when the infernal machine of neoliberalism deprives doctors and nurses of their ability to heal.

Iatrogenesis (illness resulting from medical treatment) happens on a much larger scale in Honduras as well. Several cases of medical equipment that have become highly radioactive "orphan sources" are known to the authorities: "We may not have nuclear weapons, but we still use radioactive material," a frustrated Honduran nuclear scientist employed by the government told me over drinks on June 13, 2008. Ironically, despite the dangers and costs of technology in a context where the most basic preventive medicine would go much further toward curing "forgotten" diseases and maintaining basic health, health care technology—often developed with military funding in the United States—is touted as a panacea. "Come see the medical advances in our hospital for the benefit of the Honduran population," announced a brief article in *El Heraldo* newspaper, advertising a technological open house alongside an investigative series on the disintegration of basic hospital services (Redacción 2008g).

The neoconservative strategy of promoting and/or taking advantage of wars and other crises to eliminate the public sector through skeletal social spending and privatization is what Bourne wrote about in 1918 and what journalist Naomi Klein (2007) more recently has brought into the public lexicon as "the shock doctrine." The gutting of public services enacted over recent decades during which public and political discourse has focused on war has meant that health care, for many people, is not an option. The media coverage surrounding the fortieth anniversary of Hospital Escuela in June 2008 highlights this. Headlines read, "40th Anniversary: Shortages Slowly Consume the Hospital Escuela," "Doctors without Pay," "Nobly Resisting," "[Hospital] Escuela in Intensive Care for Lack of Beds," and "Garbage Piles Up outside the Hospital Escuela" (El Tiempo 2008a; Redacción 2008d, 2008i, 2008j, 2008k). Pictures from the first article show the ceiling, which "little by little is disappearing"; the water heaters, which have collapsed; and the old rusted-out water tubes that no longer work. The second article discusses the many doctors who, like head orthopedic surgeon Octavio Alvarenga, work without pay. (This, of course, is somewhat misleading. As is common in the United States, many of these doctors have private practices to which they refer patients who *can* pay.) As the final article notes, garbage, including medical waste, does indeed lie in piles outside the hospital, as municipal spending is diverted away from public services like health care and trash removal and toward private security for the privileged (Redacción 2008l).

The solution presented by the hospital? A fundraising drive. "With the marathon on June 20th they hope to at least solve the hydro-sanitary problems of the premier health facility in the country," reads the subtitle of the first headline mentioned in the previous paragraph (Redacción 2008d). A later article about the same marathon noted that its sponsors were hoping to raise 15 million lempiras to be able to rebuild the failed hydrosanitary system not updated since the hospital's original construction 40 years earlier (Gonzales 2008). A marathon, needless to say, is not a viable long-term solution to the hospital's economic woes. Another marathon for kids with cancer was ironically sponsored by the Banco Central de Honduras, whose policies in compliance with the conditionalities of the IMF's Poverty Reduction and Growth Facility (PGRF) and those of PGRF predecessors have been responsible for so much of the poverty and environmental destruction tied to illnesses, including the one for which the race was organized (Redacción 2008h).

On June 18, 2008, I asked Julieta Castellanos, coordinator of the UNDP Violence Observatory and professor of sociology at UNAH (the National Autonomous University of Honduras), whether in her perception Honduras was in a state of war. "Objectively that's what it is," she said, after a thoughtful pause. "But war among whom? That is the question." For many Hondurans, that is indeed the question. In talking with numerous people in a ten-year period, I have found there to be a consensus that the country has indeed been at war. But how does one begin to analyze the health impact of a war that feels, as my friend Elena put it, "generalized"? In Honduras, identities like "gang member" and "delinquent" are externally imposed, often postmortem, fail to conform to subjectivities, and link victims to each other in popular discourse. Meanwhile, their killers remain unidentified, referred to only as other "gang members," "street cleaners," or "hit-men" (*sicarios*) and occasionally lumped into the category of "terrorist." Everyone is afraid.

A Bloody Legacy: Continuities in the Honduran War Machine

So what is the cultural logic of the war machine in Honduras? It is not difficult to trace structures of violence in what is now Honduras back to at least the Spanish conquest, but to avoid imposing false continuity or a narrative of historical inevitability, let us begin with the most recent period during which Honduras was entangled (albeit unofficially) in a recognized war: the 1980s. To prevent the communist shibbolith from entering the

United States through the "back door," United States president Reagan invested heavily and illegally (using the profits from arms sales to Iran and elsewhere when he failed to get approval from the Congress) in the Honduras-based Contra forces that he and his allies created to fight the popular Sandinistas in Nicaragua. American-funded counterinsurgents fighting the Salvadoran FMLN were also based in Honduras. In 1981, U.S. military aid to Honduras, a small country with a population of 4.2 million that was not at war, was U.S.$8.9 million. By 1984, U.S. military aid leveled off at U.S.$77.4 million, earning the country the nickname "USS Honduras" (Espetia 1984; LaFeber 1993).

With wars being fought across all its borders, the Honduran state began implementing a domestic counterinsurgency project. On the legal front, this included the so-called Anti-Terrorist Law, part of the National Security Doctrine promoted by the United States; it stipulated that security forces were to focus not on external threats but on potential internal subversion. As Ismael Moreno, Jesuit priest and director of Radio Progreso has argued, the Anti-Terrorist Law "justified the 'militarization' of society, with the military leading the fight against 'communism' and 'revolution'" (Moreno 2008). This law represented a preemptive strike at a phantom since the insurgent threat to the Honduran state was minimal compared to the large movements afoot in neighboring countries.

On the military front, Battalion 316 was created. Battalion 316 was a death squad led by General Gustavo Álvarez Martinez and overseen by then-U.S. ambassador John Dmitri Negroponte, a man characterized by Larry Birn, director of the Council on Hemispheric Affairs, as "a rogue, a jackanape, a bounder of the worst type" (Haygood 2004). Battalion 316 had the explicit sanction of the U.S. government, including training by the Central Intelligence Agency (CIA) and courses for several of its officers at the School of the Americas (for more on the role of the School of the Americas throughout the hemisphere, see Gill 2004). Suspected subversives—including students, journalists, and union activists—were captured by disguised Battalion 316 agents in unmarked vehicles, often in broad daylight. They were then taken to secret jails, interrogated, tortured, and sometimes visited by CIA agents. The majority of the disappeared, at least 180 people, were never seen again (Cohn and Thompson 1995). The 1980s campaign of state terror successfully quashed the small Honduran left but, more important for the purposes of the state in conjunction with the war profiteers of the infernal machine, kept the population in fear (if not exactly "zombie-like") and the threat of democratic involvement—"collective structures which may impede the pure market logic"—at bay (Bourdieu 1998).

As Hondurans fixated on the immediate threats of bodily harm from "communists" or the military (despite the fact that only the latter was engaged in torture and disappearances in Honduras), something else was happening. The economic policies that accompanied Reagan's Cold War rhetoric in the United States—the infernal machine, "starving the beast" of "big government" through privatization and cutting corporate taxes—were beginning to take hold there. Private schools expanded, increasing the educational gap between rich and poor, and private medical clinics started appearing around the country, while underfunded public hospitals began their rapid decline. Meanwhile, Reagan's Caribbean Basin Initiative, an economic incentive package originally intended as a way to channel funding to the Contras (LeoGrande 1998: 151), was bolstering the tax-free international maquiladora industry. Like the banana industry before it, which had sponsored numerous wars, coups, and Honduran governments (see, e.g., Langley and Schoonover 1995), the maquiladoras promised to bring progress, peace, and development to the people of Honduras. In reality it offered only exploitative low-wage jobs with significant health risks, and exported most of its profits along with its products. The Honduran poet Divina Alvarenga put it succinctly to me in a Tegucigalpa café on June 12, 2008: "What they have in the United States is not development, if you ask me. And if what they have isn't development, how can we be underdeveloped? We've used our resources for their development."

The End of the Cold War and the Creation of Gangs

With the end of the Cold War and communism no longer a credible threat to capitalists in Honduras, the war machine required a new foil. In the 1990s, as Hondurans loudly demanded justice and accountability for the military crimes of the previous decade, that foil began to appear in the persons of gang members. Youth street gangs were at least in part the waste products of the war machine, initially formed in Honduras by refugees from U.S.-sponsored wars in Central America (and the regional

249

economic devastation that accompanied them) who had fled to and been deported from Los Angeles and other U.S. cities. As suspected criminals, deportees (gang members or not) in Honduras were kept from jobs at the same time that the maquiladora industry was feminizing the labor force, thus limiting the number of jobs available to young men.

With gangs, the war machine had an ideal new "enemy." In the late 1990s and early 2000s, gang members employed cultural and symbolic capital that marked them as partly (though not entirely) distinct from other Hondurans; they wore "cholo" clothing, they used hand signals, and they spoke in slang that drew on U.S.–Mexico border vernacular and at times even Hollywood-derived Spanglish (Pine 2008: 36–47). Many of them— shut out from meaningful employment—committed crimes, did drugs, and lived precariously. Meanwhile, non–gang-related *organized* crime was flourishing on a much larger scale in Honduras. As the 1988 "Senate Committee Report on Drugs, Law Enforcement and Foreign Policy" (chaired by Senator John Kerry) demonstrated in its examination of the financing of the Contra War, large sums of money from the U.S.-based "War on Drugs" were actually used instead to fund military elites—many of them involved in drug trafficking themselves—in Central American countries, including Honduras (U.S. Congress 1988). Numerous scholars and investigative reporters have shown that the War on Drugs continues to function as a war machine throughout Latin America in ways that ultimately defeat its stated goals by benefiting large-scale drug traffickers (even within the military). Although at times the War on Drugs does succeed in decreasing access to some drugs, it also increases access to others, which are an easy sell to people mutilated by war (Carlsen 2009; Cockburn and St. Clair 1998; Gill 2004; Scott and Marshall 1998; Singer 2008).

It is worth stressing here, along the lines of Deleuze and Guattari, that the war machine is external to the state. The "War on Drugs" (and the [erroneously] discursively separated "Drug Wars" that have directly resulted in countless deaths of Latin Americans over the past four decades) was originally an appropriation of the war machine by the U.S. state, which continues to be its primary sponsor. In 2008, the War on Drugs claimed approximately 7,000 bodies (a figure that does not include the health effects of drug use or nonlethal war injuries) in Mexico alone. As the number of brutally slain mayors, police captains, and politicians increases through the War on Drugs, it becomes increasingly evident that stopping this war has proved to be outside the control of any involved state—if indeed stopping it is a state goal, which should not be assumed (see, e.g., Carlsen 2009).

Drug use and crime became an increasing obsession of Hondurans in the late 1990s. Drug users, described interchangeably as drug addicts, delinquents, and gang members, were depicted in the media as violent and crazed. In some cases, they were. But the prevalence and availability of dangerous drugs was driven largely by corporate and war-related profiteering. In addition to the example of cocaine made available to Hondurans (primarily in the form of crack) by the War on Drugs, the case of Resistol is instructive. Resistol, the brand name for H. B. Fuller's toluene-based shoe glue, has been used by millions of street children and others as a cheap intoxicant throughout Latin America for decades. In 1989, the Honduran Congress passed a law mandating that mustard oil, a nontoxic and inexpensive substance that had been previously shown to reduce abuse, be added to toluene-based products. Fearing lost sales, H. B. Fuller responded with a lobbying campaign, convincing shoemakers that mustard oil was in fact toxic, ultimately convincing lawmakers to pick other battles (Jeffrey 1995). In this way, the company succeeded in reversing the mandate, thus enabling tens of thousands more Honduran children—without opportunities for schooling or jobs and in many cases without shelter—to become addicted to their product, which causes myriad neurological, cardiac, gastrointestinal, liver, kidney, blood, and skeletal muscle ailments (Byrne et al. 1991; Caravati and Bjerk 1997).

At breakfast in a Tegucigalpa Super Donuts, the well-known physician and human rights activist Dr. Juan Almendares recounted to me how limits on the sale of alcohol have been similarly stymied by the alcohol industry's lobbying efforts within Honduras. In addition to the profit motive of the alcohol industry, corporations like H. B. Fuller, and organized crime, there is a history of business explicitly promoting drunkenness among poor Hondurans so as to keep them politically docile as laborers (Laínez and Meza 1973). Following Singer, I find deep underlying similarities in the ways that both legal and illegal "drug corporations" in Honduras function to maintain a profoundly stratified and unjust society (Singer 2007a; see also Hunt and Barker 2001).

Public druggedness/drunkenness is concentrated among the poor for two primary reasons: first, there are more of them than any other group, and, second, the poor do not have access to private distributing venues. Although there is no evidence that poor Hondurans abuse drugs (including alcohol) in higher proportions than the wealthy, drug use, which is popularly associated with criminality, is thought of in Honduras as an intrinsic trait of the poor (Pine 2008, 93–96). Despite the fact that capitalists and (other) organized criminals are those who most benefit from (and are partly responsible for) drug use, in Honduras drug and alcohol use is seen as the *cause* of violence rather than its *result*.

Meanwhile, in the Honduran workplace, neoliberalism completes the mutilation of subjects whom Deleuze and Guattari argue the state apparatus has prepared, "predisabled," on behalf of capital. As work is "flexibilized," insecure workers enjoy fewer protections in physically harmful jobs and decreased access to health care. Ailments and injuries could be prevented by workplace safety gear, humane working hours, bathroom breaks, and proper ventilation in the factory. Throughout the country, the structural vulnerability of the poor to capitalism and its war machines has facilitated the return of "forgotten" diseases like Chagas, tuberculosis, and malaria.

To say that the poor drink, do drugs, suffer increased violence, or become ill as a result of their poverty is a case of inverted causality: violence, illness, and insecurity are a result largely of what Singer (2007b) has referred to as the "culture of wealth." If not for the profit motive and neoliberalism clearing the path of regulations and protections, it is hard to imagine that so many people would be sick and dying in Honduras's current war. After all, who benefits from all this mutilation and death? H. B. Fuller stockholders; elite families involved in the maquiladoras, energy industry, telecoms, tourism, banking, finance, and cement industries; private security company owners; corrupt government officials; private health clinics; and media owners (a category overlapping with almost all the above in Honduras), to name a few.

Although in large part an outcome of the structural violence of capitalism, the existence of drunks, gangs, and so-called delinquents is interpreted in Honduras in psychological and epidemiological terms. The individualized cures promoted (but not funded) by the state in hospitals and jails, evangelical church, and gang rehabilitation programs teach people to frame their common problems as individual, moral, and medicalized failings and to understand them as a part of a culture of poverty (Pine 2008: 14). Sectors of the poor are collectively medicalized in public discourse as well, a fact facilitated by the culturalist tendency to blame high rates of "forgotten" illnesses among the poor on their "traditional" practices (Briggs and Mantini-Briggs 2003). As in the United States, it is also common to hear gang members and delinquents described as a cancer or a malignant growth that must be excised in order for society to be healthy again. Despite well-documented evidence of extrajudicial assassinations targeting poor boys and carried out with the approval of the state, from the late 1990s to the mid-2000s, *only* gangs were demonized for the high Honduran homicide rates by the Honduran and U.S. states alike (Jahangir and United Nations 2002; U.S. Department of State 2008). Just as the U.S.-based "War on Terror" assumes that by getting rid of certain people who are labeled "terrorists," terror can be eliminated, an ideology that attributes all of society's problems to criminals—identified as poor young men rather than wealthy beneficiaries of war—assumes that removing criminals will bring peace.

Medical discourse reinforces this logic. Violence against human bodies can be used within a medicalized framework to craft the case for a private security state. A study in the journal *Injury* titled "Violence Related Injuries, Deaths and Disabilities in the Capital of Honduras" provides an example. Looking at primarily 2001 epidemiological data from Hospital Escuela, the article's only attempt to isolate protagonists is the following unsupported statement: "Young people involved in juvenile gangs are thought to account for a large proportion of this violence" (Yacoub et al. 2006: 429). The article's conclusion is as follows:

> In summary this study has highlighted the enormous burden of deaths, injuries and disabilities from violence on the youth of Tegucigalpa. Violence against the young could have far reaching consequences not only at an individual level but also for the society and the economy of the country. It disables the workforce, discourages tourism and foreign investment, which perpetuates a vicious cycle of low economic growth and high prevalence of violence. It is hoped that the provision of these data will increase awareness of this problem and lead to better-targeted control programs, which may eventually put an end to these crimes against humanity. (Yacoub et al. 2006: 434)

The tendency of medical analysis to blind itself to violent political-economic structure provides expert credibility to dangerously flawed conclusions. Ignoring the infernal and war machines effecting the violence destroying Honduran bodies, the authors prescribe solutions only exacerbate the problem. The "vicious cycle" of low economic growth is not a result of violence. Rather, violence is part and parcel of the concentration of economic wealth. As one of my informants once told me of violence, "It just comes along with progress." Misidentification of the cause results in useless solutions like "awareness" and "better-targeted control programs" as well as in more deadly "penal common sense" criminalizing the poor (Wacquant 2004). As a starting point, any attempt to end illness and suffering borne of violence must address both the infernal machine of neoliberalism and the war machine that together harm bodies and deprive them of the resources necessary to heal.

Penal Truth Comes to Tegucigalpa

After the son of wealthy banker Ricardo Maduro was kidnapped for ransom and murdered, he became the presidential candidate for the neoconservative National Party. He harnessed the empathy of so many Hondurans who themselves had similarly lost family members and, calling for a war on crime, won handily in 2001. Maduro's prescription for ending violence came from former New York City mayor Rudolph Giuliani, who employed a zero-tolerance crime control policy in New York in order to "fix broken windows" and increase investment through the criminalization of acts and states of being associated with poverty (Kelling 1996). It became criminal to bodily engage in the public sphere in ways that offended investor sensibilities, such as being publicly drunk, urinating, being homeless, and engaging in "informal" labor. President Maduro's "war on crime," using Giuliani's methods, was likewise part of what Farmer (2005) calls "the new war on the poor" and what Neil Smith (1998), writing about "Giuliani Time," referred to as revanchism, "[blending] revenge with reaction." Maduro's 2003 Anti-Gang Law, for example, criminalized loitering, affiliating oneself with a gang, and having a tattoo, at the time a common gang practice. The Honduran Anti-Gang Law also bore a striking resemblance to the 1980s Honduran Anti-Terrorist law, once again justifying the militarization of society; only now, rather than communists and revolutionaries, the enemy of the state had become unemployed young men and boys (Moreno 2008).

Although extrajudicial assassinations of youths had been increasing for several years, Maduro's version of zero tolerance led to a spike in such killings, allowing their perpetrators to act with impunity. To my urban Honduran informants, zero tolerance was synonymous with "street cleaning," which to them meant the governmentally sanctioned liquidation of "delinquents," in what I have elsewhere termed (following Scheper-Hughes 1982) an invisible genocide (Pine 2008, 61). Even in 2008, Julieta Castellanos told me, 8 to 11 percent of extrajudicial murders were committed by the police. Many other young people are killed by employees of private security companies who outnumber both the police and the Honduran army. Most of my informants initially approved of Maduro's policy, even when the same death squads were shooting at their own children, just as many U.S. citizens initially approved of the Patriot Act, though it curtailed their own civil liberties, or support the death penalty, though it has shown to be ineffective as a deterrent to crime and in many cases has been applied to people innocent of the crime of which they were accused.

The twisted logic of the infernal machine of neoliberalism, as Caldeira (2002) has shown in Brazil, is that the removal of liberties and imposition of a police state becomes the appropriate answer to "insecurity." Wacquant (2004: 162) refers to such thinking as "'penal common sense'—a new configuration of self-evident 'truths' about crime and punishment aiming to criminalise poverty and thereby normalise precarious wage labour [which] has incubated in [the United States of] America and is being internationalised alongside the neoliberal economic ideology that it translates and complements in the realm of 'justice.'" As my friend Alba Mejía said to me one night, "People think of young poor men and gang members as killing machines. And who cares about killing a machine?"

Mercenaries, Health, and Plunder

From a diachronic perspective, the Honduran war on crime is an outgrowth of the wars of the 1980s. Synchronically, the war on crime that was officially waged during the Maduro campaign had global currency because it fit so neatly into ideology of the post–September 11 international war machine. The links between Central American wars of the 1980s, the current state of war in Honduras, and wars being fought abroad are numerous and at times border on the absurd. In a speech at the Heritage Foundation on October 31, 2002, Otto Reich, U.S. special envoy to the Western Hemisphere for the secretary of state, board member of the School of the Americas, and formerly a central player in Reagan's war against the Sandinistas, applauded President Maduro for his work implementing the "rule of law" (Reich 2002). This is a concept that Mattei and Nader have convincingly argued has consistently been little more than a justification for *plunder* from colonial times to the present neoliberal period (Mattei and Nader 2008). On November 4, 2003, U.S. Secretary of State Colin Powell echoed those remarks while on a visit to Tegucigalpa to thank the Honduran president for sending troops to Iraq and to advocate for the passage of the Central American Free Trade Agreement (a key part of neoliberal strategy in the region), commending Maduro also on his crime-fighting efforts at home (U.S. Department of State 2003). At that point, 370 Honduran soldiers were in Iraq despite wide Honduran opposition to that deployment. The troops were recalled by Maduro in deference to popular sentiment on April 19, 2004, the same day U.S. President Bush nominated John Negroponte as the U.S. ambassador to Iraq.

Meanwhile, Maduro's minister of public security, Oscar Álvarez, nephew of Battalion 316 leader General Álvarez Martinez, claimed that Central American gang members were helping al-Qaeda terrorists infiltrate the United States—despite a complete lack of evidence (Associated Press 2004). In 2005, agents from the FBI went to Honduras and other Central American countries "to find out how they have been able to successfully combat the dangerous and feared youth gangs or 'maras' that terrorize Central America" (Associated Press 2005b). In San Pedro Sula, a gang member with the street name Osama Bin Laden (née José Geovanny Savilla López) was killed by three unknown men in a hail of bullets (Anonymous 2003).

In late 2003, my good friend Teto e-mailed me, excited, to tell me about a great opportunity: the U.S. embassy in Tegucigalpa was facilitating the recruitment of Honduran laborers by private contractors to aid in Iraq's "reconstruction." Much to my relief, I was able to talk him out of it over his initial protests that anything would be better than living in Tegucigalpa, jobless and in fear. But this was the tip of the iceberg; in a context of structural violence, mercenary and related war work (the "economic draft") becomes one of the few economic opportunities available to the structurally vulnerable. In December 2006, days before Negroponte announced he would leave his post as director of national intelligence to become deputy secretary of state, the U.S. Army was considering setting up recruiting stations overseas, offering citizenship as an incentive to potential recruits (Bender 2006). But the army had nothing on its private counterparts. United Nations reports show that international mercenary organizations like the private security firm Triple Canopy, in addition to recruiting in Honduras, had been using Lepaterique, the former training ground for the Contras and Battalion 316, as a training ground for security agents being sent to Iraq and Afghanistan (Stoner 2008). In 2005, as Honduras faced a 30 percent unemployment rate, Assistant Labor Minister Africo Madrid publicly advertised 2,000 job openings for Triple Canopy's subsidiary Your Solutions in Iraq (Associated Press 2005a). Later that year, after an exposé in the Honduran newspaper *La Tribuna*, the embarrassed Honduran government ordered the expulsion of all foreign mercenaries training with Your Solutions in Lepaterique (Bermúdez 2005; Stoner 2008).

Mercenaries, true foot soldiers of the war machine, have unhealthy jobs. A UN report focusing on Honduran recruits to Iraq found "irregularities of contracts, harsh working conditions with excessive working hours, partial or non payment of remuneration, ill-treatment and isolation, and lack of basic necessities such as medical treatment and sanitation" (United Nations 2006). When mercenaries return with physical injuries or posttraumatic stress disorder, the monetary value of their bodies to the war machine is exposed. The irony of the United States employing Honduran bodies in war (as tax dollars fund private security firms) without being officially at war against Honduras means that most victims of war there get no compensation; their body parts are worth more if blown off in Iraq (McDonnell 2008). And domestically, those who fight for the health and labor rights of private security guards do so at the risk of losing their lives: in 2006, lawyer Dionisio Díaz García (at the time representing hundreds of private security guards in complaints against 13 private security companies) was killed, shot at close range by two masked men in front of the Supreme Court of Justice.

In Honduras, Billy Joya Améndola, a key player in Battalion 316 in the 1980s, is currently the head of one of the country's largest domestic private security companies. In 2004, as security adviser for the former mayor of Tegucigalpa, Miguel Pastor, Joya was accused of issuing death threats to Pastor's political opponents, including journalists, as well as overseeing death squads in Maduro's war on crime (International Press Institute 2004). In an interview with Father Ismael Moreno at the offices of Radio Progreso on June 23, 2008, he pointed out to me that additionally, in San Pedro Sula, a former Battalion 316 colonel and the head of another private security company named Eric Sanchez was in charge of security for mayor Oscar Kilgore. American-trained torturers of the 1980s thus profit from the embodied insecurity—the habitus of fear—they helped to create. As Father Moreno put it, "All these people were deeply involved with 316. Private security *defines* security [here], and it's in the hands of those who are most directly responsible for the insecurity in this country—organized crime . . . because insecurity is a business. When there's more fear among the population there's more demand for the services of private security and when there's more mistrust in public security, there's more demand for the [services of] private security companies."

The methods of the protagonists of the war on crime are nearly identical to the methods of the protagonists of the counterinsurgency war of the 1980s, which is not at all surprising given the fact that in many cases said protagonists are the same people. Although the victims are identified today as gang members and delinquents, like the accused insurgents of the 1980s they are discursively positioned as enemies of capital and the state. In the 1980s, the army decried them as communists, whereas today, in line with the broken-windows theory, they are painted by the media and many government/corporate actors as threats to foreign investment and thus development.

"Development" is highly contested by scholars who point to the development industry's social Darwinist assumptions, imperialist agenda, and flawed teleological assumptions of progress in a world system that requires "underdevelopment" (Escobar 1995; Gunder Frank 1975; Rahnema and Bawtree 1997; Wallerstein 1984). Quality of life does not improve with economic investment in low-wage jobs that bring nothing in the way of infrastructural investment on a societal level; indeed, it may well decline. Rather than a threat to *development,* the dangerous bodies of poor young men are a threat to the unimpeded hegemony of neoliberal ideology. They are the infernal machine's waste product and the state's pretext for war.

The dead of the Honduran war, in the 1980s and today, are the victims and potential opponents of capital. Young people are rendered redundant and targeted for "cleansing" by a job market that has no room for them and a public sector that offers vastly inadequate health care and education. The "reserve army of employees rendered docile by [the] social processes that make their situations precarious" (Bourdieu 1998) created by neoliberalism—much like Deleuze and Guattari's zombies—is *actually a reserve army* from the perspective of the war machine. It is poor young unemployed men who become underpaid police, military, private security agents, and hit men, who either join the anarchic and apolitical armies of gangs, or who become their casualties. Meanwhile, Hondurans who expose the logic of the war machine and the infernal machine and who challenge their beneficiaries—people like Dionisio Díaz García, labor leader Altagracia Fuentes, and journalist Carlos Salgado—are murdered as examples to those who might follow (La Tribuna 2008).

The administration that took control after Maduro's was of the opposing Liberal Party. President Manuel Zelaya promised a more humane approach to law enforcement. However, though zero tolerance was no longer official state policy, the war on crime had escaped state control. In an attempt to rein in the violence and appear tough on crime, in 2006 Zelaya further privatized the war by granting private security guards the authority to act as police officers (Starkman 2006; T. Mejía 2006). In 2009, he signed the Merida initiative (also called Plan Mexico), agreeing to receive millions of dollars to intensify the war on the poor (Anonymous 2009). On his earlier agreement to do so, the U.S. State Department had boasted, "The Presidents of Central America have clearly expressed the political resolve to join forces to strengthen regional security and seek additional tools and capacity to execute such will" (U.S. Department of State 2007). And in a stunningly frank admission of state incompetence, Zelaya instructed community groups organizing around issues of social justice to bring their demands not to him but to the "groups of power," presumably meaning the Honduran power elite (Mills 1959), including organized crime. With these actions, Zelaya appears to recognize that in a very practical sense, the war machine is indeed exterior to the state apparatus (Deleuze and Guattari 1987: 351). Although it can never fully control the war machine, the state and, more importantly, the corporate entities it represents can benefit from war (as Bourne noted), particularly when the ideology of the state-appropriated war machine reinforces the idea that democracy and civil liberties are incompatible with security.

Ironically, the human devastation wrought by the war machine and neoliberalism serves as an excuse to both further militarize and further privatize. In recent years, Honduran politicians have called for public funds to be used for a new high-security prison to be built by the Noa Group, an Israeli consortium run by former Mossad agents. As a justification, they have pointed to the numerous prison massacres in recent years. This logic is flawed, given the fact that agents of the state have been implicated in a majority of these massacres. For example, in June 2008, a Honduran court found 22 soldiers and police guilty of charges related to a prison massacre that took place in El Porvenir prison in La Ceiba in 2003, in which 68 people were killed. There is ample evidence that the massacre was planned well in advance by higher authorities (El Tiempo 2008b; Estrada 2008).

Another case blamed on gangs, the 2004 massacre of 28 people on a public bus in Choloma (Anonymous 2004), is widely suspected to have been orchestrated by members of the National Party as an election ploy to reinforce the public's sense of insecurity and desire for a security state. Bus travel is terrifying to many Hondurans, underscoring the vulnerability of public (i.e., poor) Honduran bodies in war. While being driven one day by my young friend Vanesa, her mother, Rebeca, mentioned to me that she didn't drive. I told her I don't either, explaining that I had quit two years earlier after a fender bender and decided to only use my bicycle and public transit because it was safer. Vanesa set me straight: "Maybe [in the United States] it's safer to take public transportation but not here. Here they assault you. There are massacres on the buses, especially in the poor areas like Choloma." Bus services for the poor stand in marked contrast to luxury lines like Hedman Alas, whose employees demand a national ID or passport for each ticket purchase, inspect all luggage, and take a digital picture of each passenger as they board.

In the midst of Hospital Escuela's anniversary, a front-page headline read, "Canadians recommend that Hospital Escuela be demolished" (alongside a death porn photo on another topic) (Redacción 2008c). The infernal machine, through its creation of a reserve army, joins the war machine in bringing about the failure of the public sector by turning public investments like hospitals, prisons, roads, buses, schools, and "streets" into spaces of death (Taussig 1984). Amidst calls for the demolition of the dangerous public sector, neoliberalism offers the solution in the form of private clinics, private schools, the development of a prison-industrial complex, expensive private transportation, and toll roads.

Hospital "Security"

As described earlier, hospitals are considered spaces of death, even to the extent that Hondurans refer to them by nicknames like "el matarino," because of the prevalence of iatrogenesis in them. The sickening nature of hospitals during wartime is part and parcel of a mercenary logic. In line with Giulianian zero tolerance, security has overtaken health care as a priority even within hospitals, and basic resource allocation (given a limited funding pool) has contributed to a dearth of preventive care; much of hospitals' resources are diverted to crises in the attempt to repair bodies torn apart by guns, knives, machetes, and years or even decades of failing health. Below is an excerpt from a 2007 report on the impact of externally caused injuries on Hospital Escuela, issued by Hospital Escuela and the Pan-American Health Organization (regional office of the World Health Organization):

> Hospitals in these countries, night and day mainly focus on repairing injuries generated in and by citizens of increasingly violent societies. The packed operating rooms, with patients affected by injuries of external cause [referred to here by the Spanish initials "LCE"], relegate regularly-scheduled patients to an immense queue. Increasingly, there are dire shortages of medicines and surgical supplies, in the context of the growing demands presented by victims of traffic accidents, firearms, etc.
>
> The contribution of LCEs to the loss of quality and care of normal services in public health institutions is, in large part, product of the slow but increasing quasi-monopoly of hospital beds by LCE; by the same token, the presence of police watching over individuals accused of various criminal acts in their hospital rooms is common. Public hospitals are not free from the insecurity and violence that prevail on the streets.
>
> The transition from the view of violence as an emerging health problem, to its consideration as a problem of public health that can be prevented in addition to being treated, is not one that has clearly taken

place in Latin America. Rather, as a product of the success of repressive police measures implemented in countries like United States of North America, the implementation of policies like "zero tolerance" has become increasingly common, leaving institutions like public health out in the cold and elevating the position and importance of the police and military institutions. The virtual "reduction" of public health institutions to "citizen repair workshops" presupposes a marked deterioration in the explicit function of said institutions as being guided by universally accepted ideas about treating health not as the absence of illness but as the permanent attainment of a state of integral well-being of the citizens. (Kafati et al. 2007: 10–11, translation my own)

The dangers of hospital insecurity, above and beyond iatrogenesis, were highlighted in a newspaper article about a 2008 hospital kidnapping that began, "They walk the halls of Hospital Escuela disguised as 'Good Samaritans,' but in reality they're nothing more than delinquents who take advantage of the humility of the patients who come from the interior [rural areas] of the country, to rob them of the little money they have, and in some cases, they even kidnap their victims" (Redacción 2008b).

The hospital itself is also a victim of crime, quite likely with the assistance of underpaid hospital staff. A 2008 Honduran listserv discussion on hospital theft included the following commentary: "theft is out of control . . . it reminds me of when they stole washers and dryers that had been donated by an organization to the Hospital de Occidente. Nobody knows how they disappeared; in one night 5 commercial washers and dryers, nobody saw and nobody noticed when they took them out the front door. The same thing happened with one of those cameras in an office in the same hospital and bam! it disappeared. You can't leave anything out . . . that's why [in the United States] they prefer to live inside high walls and fill the prisons with so many innocents rather than working and avoiding common delinquency." Another member added, "They also swiped EVERYTHING from the hospital of Puerto Cortés . . . and they left it practically without the ability to accept patients."

Another example of the blatant deprioritization of health care as a public good in Honduras's war economy is in the treatment of health care workers. In 2008, public-sector nurses earned a monthly salary of 3,299 lempiras, around US$170. By contrast, the average maquiladora worker earned around 6,000 lempiras monthly. The basic cost of living was declared by the minister of industry and commerce in May 2008 to be 7,000 lempiras per month (Agencia P.L. 2008; Redacción 2007). As noted earlier, low-ranking police officers themselves earn a paltry 5,000 lempiras per month, a fact that speaks more to the hypocrisy of "security" talk than anything else, as vast amounts of money earmarked for public projects are ferreted away by corrupt politicians while massacres occur in prisons. In addition to inadequate salaries, health care providers face impossible scenarios at work. In Hospital Escuela, according to numerous nurses I interviewed, the normal daytime nurse-to-patient ratio on a medical/surgery unit is about 1 to 17. By comparison, the legally mandated *minimum* safe standard for ratios in California on medical/surgery units is one to five. At night, it is not uncommon for one Hospital Escuela nurse to be in charge of 60 patients.

Even with the miserable salary nurses make (without benefits of health insurance, life insurance, or pensions, they point out), they could be making less. "Every little thing we have," a hospital nurse named Liliana from Olancho told me during a June 18, 2008, conversation with several Honduran nurses, "we have because we went out in the streets for it. All our tiny little raises [*aumentitos*], our uniforms, because we went out in the street. They gave us one pair of shoes per year at 300 lempiras, and we had to go out and fight for it." This labor militancy was evident in August 2008, when nurses in the capital took to the streets for nine days (elsewhere, even longer) demanding that salary increases promised them the previous year be fulfilled (L. Mejía 2008; Proceso Digital 2008). Indeed, the nurses' union is one of the more active unions in Honduras. On the wall of the union hall hang photographs of recent rallies. On the day I spoke with Liliana, nurses there showed me pictures of themselves carrying signs declaring, "No to the demands of the IMF, World Bank, and Interamerican Development Bank" and "No to the privatization of public services."

Conclusion

The public sector nurses with whom I spoke justified many of their demands in terms of their own patients' health, expressing horror at the poor allocation of inadequate funds, which left patients unattended, without privacy (sometimes even naked for lack of hospital gowns), and unsafe.

But health care workers themselves are not immune to the penal common sense that makes "street cleaning" seem a favorable option. A seasoned Hospital Escuela nurse named Victoria told me that in 2006, when the gang presence was more pronounced, things had been worse in her unit. Then, if a gang member was dying, "the others would be behind you, shouting at you to not let him die, using bad words." As she said this to me, I overheard a nurse named Eva saying to Liliana, "It'd be better just to leave them in the room and wait outside for them to die."

Gang members have even come into the hospital to kill their rivals, they told me. "Now not as many gang members come," Victoria said, "and in those years they were very *identificados* [identified; tattooed]. Not now." Until 2006, the group told me, the gangs had been a serious problem in hospitals. When I asked why gangs were not around anymore, Victoria responded in a hushed voice, "Because they killed most of them." I heard this explanation for the visible absence of gangs numerous times in 2008, but it was not entirely true. Many young people at risk of being identified as gang members were living in virtual house arrest, given the fact that a visible tattoo can amount to a death sentence. Many others had migrated toward the United States. And the new participants in groups of young people at risk of being identified as "gangs" simply had learned to look like everyone else.

I asked nurses about the proliferation of private clinics, something that I had noticed in the past 10 years. "There are more," one told me. "In my *pueblo* there was just one [government] health center and now there are five private clinics." Victoria added, "Privatization worries us because it hurts the poorest." One way that privatization of hospitals hurts is in worker strength ("collective structures that impede the pure market logic"). Private-sector nurses are not legally eligible to join the national nurse union, and even public hospitals are union busting through the increasing practice of hiring nurses as "contract workers" (called travelers in the United States) who are likewise ineligible to join their peers in effectively advocating for workers' rights and patient safety. Even in the public sector, a male nurse named Hector pointed out, health care is semiprivatized; patients have to pay a fee at public facilities. Beforehand, patients paid an amount that was, he said, "mostly symbolic." But since around 1990, fees have been increasing. "It's not like in other countries, like Cuba," he added, asserting that in the constitution of the republic, it says that health care should be free. There are people who are so poor, I was told, that they cannot even pay five lempiras (around a quarter of a dollar) for a checkup. In a separate conversation, Alicia Reyes, reporter for Radio Progreso, put it succinctly: "You're sick and you don't have money? Die."

Corruption plays an important role in maintaining the health of the war machine and the infernal machine of neoliberalism and illness of Hondurans. As Singer (2008) has noted, this is not inconsistent with the implementation of Millennium Development Goals worldwide, which—rather than fostering democracy and economic parity—have furthered the neoliberal model of structural adjustments leading to mutually reinforcing increases in corruption, drug abuse, and social suffering in the so-called developing world. In April and May 2008, a number of Honduran prosecutors highlighted the connection between violence, corruption, and health in a 38-day hunger strike. Camped outside the Congress building, they demanded the dismissal of the attorney general and his deputy for failure to investigate cases of corruption involving high-level government officials of both major parties (T. Mejía 2008). The 22 cases described a variety of frauds, including mysteriously ownerless luxury airplanes, hush payments to journalists, and vast quantities of illegally untaxed gasoline.

Some of the most egregious cases were health related. The case called Caso PRAF-SALUD, for example, was brought against Elias Lizardo, minister of health under President Maduro, and Elizabeth de Mazariegos, director of the Family Allocation Program (Programa de Asignación Familiar). Lizardo and de Mazariegos held a conference on the topic of covering health care for temporary contract workers. The money distributed at the conference amounted to around 525 million lempiras of public funds (approximately U.S.$29 million at the time) and was given to people who did not, technically, exist. The projects were never carried out, but the checks were cashed (Redacción 2008a; Fernández Guzmán et al. 2008). On June 7, 2008, my friends Elena and Suyapa spoke excitedly about the hunger strike, at the same time expressing deep cynicism about its potential effectiveness. "You can't martyr yourself here because death doesn't matter," said Suyapa.

As health care becomes more expensive, life becomes cheaper. Repairing the bodies of poor citizens is not worth five lempiras to an infernal machine that has already devalued them as laborers. And as health care is privatized and citizens are rendered commodities, maintaining the bodies of the poor becomes a matter of private charity (e.g., marathons) rather than the public duty of the state. It also falls into the hands of numerous nongovernmental organizations (NGOs), staffed by poorly paid, nonunionized locals and well-paid foreigners, and run without any semblance of democratic involvement on the part of Hondurans. Anthropologist Ibrahim Sajid Malick argues that NGOs are bureaucracies that "[legitimize] corrupt leaders, oppressive governments, and imperialist structure" (Sajid Malick 2007). During our June 7, 2008, conversation, Elena expressed a similar assessment: "NGOs are central to privatization, they are part of the violence. They have overtaken the government. They are part of a democratic farce. Now there are donors like never before, and they know what they're doing. They are helping to destroy the country by furthering the neoliberal agenda."

I again visited my friend Rebeca in 2008 and discovered that she had had two ovarian operations the previous year at a total cost of 42,000 lempiras (around U.S.$2,225). These surgeries, which were done at a private clinic (she did not consider going to el Matarino, the closest public hospital), cost well over any amount she had ever made in a year. She was able to afford them only because her 20-year-old son Omar had traveled to take advantage of the economic opportunities afforded in another war zone: New Orleans. There he had worked alongside private contractors hired in lieu of public workers for "reconstruction," organized in some cases by the same mercenary firms hiring Latin Americans to carry out "security" work without civilian oversight or accountability in Iraq.

War is the health of the state, and at times it is directed inward and unleashed against the state's citizens. Since the function of the state is the protection of private profits of the ruling class and its corporations, the citizens' very bodies, when inconvenient to capital accumulation, are declared enemies of the state, and the full force of nationalist rhetoric and state violence is used to destroy them. In this way, the health of the people becomes an impediment to the health of the ruling class (the state). As Divina Alvarenga said to me during a June 12, 2008, conversation, "Capital says that if you think differently, you're a terrorist, or an ecological radical." Like nurses, many other Hondurans have been willing to risk incurring the wrath of the war machine to protest the infernal machine, though community health organizers complain to me is that it is hard to mobilize for fights about health risks like radiation from neighborhood cell phone towers, when a more immediate struggle is to find enough rice to eat from one day to the next. War in Honduras from the 1980s to the present has been fought in defense of an economic model that has left millions sick in Honduras and the United States and countless more around the world. To improve our health and, indeed, to save our lives, we must address the true causes of our illness. We must create collectivities in the face of neoliberalism's attempts to destroy them. We must disallow the infernal machine from creating the world in its own image—an economic model with little room for human health. And we must reject the penal truth that comes with the state's appropriation of the war machine so that it may implement neoliberal policy over the dead bodies of its citizens. It is time that we sacrifice the health of the state in order to ensure our own.

Works Cited

Agencia, P. L.
2008　Sube el costo de la canasta básica en Honduras. *Radio La Primerísima, La Gente,* May 28. Online: http://www.radiolaprimerisima.com/noticias/resumen/30445. Accessed September 14, 2008.

Alaniz, José
2005　Death porn: Modes of mortality in post-Soviet Russian cinema. In *Interpretation of Culture Codes: Madness and Death.* Vol. 3. Edited by Vadim Mikhailin, 185–211. Saratov: Saratov State University Laboratory of Historical, Social and Cultural Anthropology.

Almendares, Juan
2007　Torture as an international crime. In *Presentation of the Book "Universal Justice for International Crimes" by Spanish Jurist Manuel Ollé Sesé.* Tegucigalpa: House of the United Nations.

Anonymous
2003　"Osama bin Laden" muere acribillado. *La Tribuna,* June 30
2004　*Gang linked to Honduras massacre.* Online: http://news.bbc.co.uk/2/hi/americas/4124133.stm. Accessed September 14, 2008.

2009   *EE UU y Honduras firman convenio de cooperación en seguridad: La Iniciativa Mérida pretende combatir las maras, narcotráfico y trata de personas.* Online: http://www.latribuna.hn/news/45/ARTICLE/ 53350/2009-01-09.html. Accessed March 19, 2009.

Associated Press
  2004   *Al-Qaida recruiting Central American gangs? Honduran official insists, but U.S., other Latin leaders skeptical.* Online: http://www.msnbc.msn. com/id/6300888. Accessed March 14, 2008.
  2005a *Una empresa estadounidense busca hondureños trabajar como guardaespaldas en Irak y Afganistán.* Online: http://www.lukor.com/not-mun/ america/0505/18065111.htm. Accessed September 14, 2008.
  2005b *FBI Conocerá Cómo Centroamérica Combate las Pandillas.* Online: http:// www.bohemionews.com/news.php?nid=1379. Accessed March 14, 2009.
  2006   Security minister: Even Honduran police pay gang extortion. Associated Press Worldstream, March 30.

Bender, Bryan
  2006   *Military considers recruiting foreigners.* Online: http://www.boston. com/news/nation/articles/2006/12/26/military_considers_recruiting_foreigners. Accessed September 10, 2008.

Bermúdez, Darío
  2005   *Pistoleros a sueldo (mínimo).* Online: http://www.lanacion.cl/prontus_ noticias/site/artic/20050924/pags/20050924155052.htm. Accessed September 14, 2008.

Bourdieu, Pierre
  1998   The essence of neoliberalism. Online: http://mondediplo.com/1998/ 12/08bourdieu. Accessed September 12, 2008.

Bourne, Randolph
  1918   *The state.* Online: http://flag.blackened.net/revolt/hist_texts/war healthstate1918.html. Accessed September 12, 2008.

Briggs, C. L., and C. Mantini-Briggs
  2003. *Stories in the Time of Cholera: Racial Profiling during a Medical Nightmare.* Berkeley: University of California Press.

Byrne, A., B. Kirby, T. Zibin, and S. Ensminger
  1991   Psychiatric and neurological effects of chronic solvent abuse. *Canadian Journal of Psychiatry* 36(10):735–738.

Caldeira, Teresa P. R.
　2002　The paradox of police violence in democratic Brazil. *Ethnography* 3(3):235–263.

Caravati, E. M., and P. J. Bjerk
　1997　Acute toluene ingestion toxicity. *Annals of Emergency Medicine* 30(6):838–839.

Carlsen, Laura
　2009　*Drug war doublespeak*. Online: http://americas.irc-online.org/am/5935. Accessed March 18, 2009.

Casa Alianza
　2008, July　*Análisis sobre ejecuciones y/o muertes violentas de niños/as y jóvenes en Honduras, Mayo–Junio 2008*. Tegucigalpa, Honduras.

Cockburn, Alexander, and Jeffrey St. Clair
　1998　*Whiteout: The CIA, Drugs and the Press*. London: Verso.

Cohn, Gary, and Ginger Thompson
　1995　Unearthed: Fatal secrets. When a wave of torture and murder staggered a small U.S. ally, truth was a casualty. Was the CIA involved? Did Washington know? Was the public deceived? Now we know: Yes, yes and yes. *Baltimore Sun*, June 11, A1.

Deleuze, Gilles, and Félix Guattari
　1987　*A Thousand Plateaus: Capitalism and Schizophrenia*. Minneapolis: University of Minnesota Press.

El Tiempo
　2008　Emergencia hospitalaria: En cuidados intensivos el Escuela por falta de camas. *El Tiempo*, June 15, Nacionales section, 4.
　2008　June 18　Estado podría pagar por masacre ocurrida en gobierno de Maduro. *El Tiempo*, June 18, Nacionales section, 16.

Escobar, Arturo
　1995　*Encountering development: The making and unmaking of the Third World*. Princeton, NJ: Princeton University Press.

Espetia, Tony
　1984, April 7　Honduran military purge no threat to U.S. United Press International.

Estrada, Oscar
　2008　*El Porvenir*. DVD. Marabunta Films.

Farmer, Paul
2005 *Pathologies of Power: Health, Human Rights, and the New War on the Poor: With a New Preface by the Author.* Berkeley: University of California Press.

Federal Bureau of Investigation
2007a Table 1—Crime in the United States 2006. In *2006: Crime in the United States.* Online: http://www.fbi.gov/ucr/cius2006/data/table_01.html. Accessed September 11, 2008.
2007b Table 8 (Michigan)—Crime in the United States 2006. In *2006: Crime in the United States.* Online: http://www.fbi.gov/ucr/cius2006/data/table_08_mi.html. Accessed September 11, 2008.

Fernández Guzmán, Victor Antonio, Foad Alejandro Castillo, Jari Dixon Herrera, et al.
2008 Casos presentados ante el CN por los fiscales en huelga de hambre. Online: http://radioprogresohn.net/index.php?option=com_content&task=view&id=95&Itemid=1. Accessed September 14, 2008.

Gill, Lesley
2004 *The School of the Americas: Military training and political violence in the Americas.* Durham, NC: Duke University Press.

Gonzales, Enma
2008 Hospital Escuela celebra 4 décadas con maratón. *El Tiempo,* June 23, Nacionales section, 16.

Green, Linda
1999 *Fear as a Way of Life: Mayan Widows in Rural Guatemala.* New York: Columbia University Press.

Gunder Frank, Andre
1975 Development and underdevelopment in the New World: Smith and Marx vs. the Weberians. *Theory and Society* 2(4):431–466.

Hardt, Michael, and Antonio Negri
2005 *Multitude: War and Democracy in the Age of Empire.* New York: Penguin.

Hartmann-Mahmud, L.
2002 War as metaphor. *Peace Review* 14(4):427–432.

Haygood, Will
2004 Ambassador with big portfolio; John Negroponte goes to Baghdad with a record of competence, and controversy. *Washington Post,* June 21, Style section, C01.

Hunt, Geoffrey, and J. C. Barker
2001   Socio-cultural anthropology and alcohol and drug research: Towards a unified theory. *Social Science and Medicine* 53(2):165–188.

International Press Institute
2004   *World Press Freedom Review: Honduras.* Online: http://www.free media.at/cms/ipi/freedom_detail.html?country=/kw0001/kw0002/kw0023/&year=2004. Accessed September 14, 2008.

Jahangir, Asma, and United Nations
2002   *Civil and Political Rights, Including the Question of Disappearances and Summary Executions.* June 14, Geneva: Economic and Social Council, United Nations.

Jeffrey, Paul
1995   *Glue maker's image won't stick.* Online: http://www.multination almonitor.org/hyper/issues/1995/12/mm1295_05.html. Accessed September 13, 2008.

Kafati, Rosa, Karla Díaz, Alberto Concha-Eastman, and Rodulio Perdomo
2007   *Impacto económico y financiero de las lesiones de causas externa en el Hospital Escuela.* Tegucigalpa: Panamerican Health Organization.

Kelling, George L.
1996   *Fixing Broken Windows: Restoring Order and Reducing Crime in Our Communities.* New York: Martin Kessler Books.

Klein, Naomi
2007   *The Shock Doctrine: The Rise of Disaster Capitalism.* New York: Metropolitan Books/Henry Holt.

LaFeber, Walter
1993   *Inevitable Revolutions: The United States in Central America.* 2nd ed. New York: Norton.

Laínez, V., and V. Meza
1973   El enclave bananero en Honduras. *Nueva Sociedad* 6:21–43.

Langley, Lester D., and Thomas David Schoonover
1995   *The Banana Men: American Mercenaries and Entrepreneurs in Central America, 1880–1930.* Lexington: University Press of Kentucky.

La Tribuna
2008   *Fue muerte por "encargo."* Online: http://www.latribuna.hn/news/45/article/32513/2008-04-24.html. Accessed September 11, 2008.

LeoGrande, William M.
  1998   *Our Own Backyard: The United States in Central America, 1977–1992.*
         Chapel Hill: University of North Carolina Press.

López-Maldonado, Wilmer, Carlos Meza Galo, and Mebis López-Maldonado
  2007   Enfermedades Nosocomiales en los Pacientes Ingresados en la Uni-
         dad de Cuidados Intensivos del Hospital Escuela. *Revista Médica de
         los Postgrados de Medicina UNAH* 10(1):82–83.

Mattei, Ugo, and Laura Nader
  2008   *Plunder: When the Rule of Law Is Illegal.* London: Blackwell.

McDonnell, Patrick J.
  2008   *Iraq contractors tap Latin America's needy.* Online: http://www.latimes
         .com. Accessed September 15, 2008.

Mejía, Lilian
  2008   *Enfermeras finalizan paro.* Online: http://www.laprensahn.com/index
         .php/Ediciones/2008/09/02/Noticias/Enfermeras-finalizan-paro.
         Accessed September 14, 2008.

Mejía, Thelma
  2006   *A violent death every two hours.* Online: http://ipsnews.net/news
         .asp?idnews=35275. Accessed September 10, 2008.
  2008   *Honduras: Prosecutors on hunger strike against corruption.* Online:
         http://ipsnews.net/news.asp?idnews=42263. Accessed September 14,
         2008.

Mills, C. Wright
  1959   *The Power Elite.* New York: Oxford University Press.

Moodie, Ellen
  2006   Microbus crashes and Coca-Cola cash. *American Ethnologist*
         33(1):63–80.

Moreno, Ismael
  2008   *Honduras' prison massacres reflect a social and political crisis.* Online:
         http://www.envio.org.ni/articulo/3201. Accessed September 13,
         2008.

Pine, Adrienne
  2008   *Working Hard, Drinking Hard: On Violence and Survival in Honduras.*
         Berkeley: University of California Press.

Proceso Digital

2008   *Enfermeras suspenden paro.* Online: http://www.proceso.hn/2008/
08/27/Nacionales/Enfermeras.suspenden.paro/7998.html. Accessed
September 14, 2008.

Rahnema, Majid, and Victoria Bawtree, eds.

1997   *The Post-Development Reader.* London: Zed Books.

Redacción

2007   *Gobierno fija 11.1%: 3428 lempiras es el salario mínimo.* Online: http://
www.elheraldo.hn/clicks.php?nid=90640&nfecha=2007-12-27&sec
=8&k=2&url2=12&url=nota. Accessed August 22, 2008.

2008a *Apela sobreseimiento a favor de Elías Lizard.* Online:http://latribuna
.hn/news/45/article/41744/2008-08-24.html. Accessed September
14, 2008.

2008b *Asaltan y raptan una paciente en hospital.* Online: http://www
.elheraldo.hn/ez/index.php/plain_site_user/ediciones/2008/07/28/
asaltans_y_raptan_una_paciente_en_hospital. Accessed July 30,
2008.

2008   Canadienses sugieren demoler Hospital Escuela. *Diario El Heraldo,*
June 11, 1.

2008   Las carencias consumen lentamente el Hospital Escuela. *Diario El
Heraldo,* June 11, 30.

2008   Doctores con vocación. Hospital Escuela, un espacio solo para "gla-
diadores." *Diario El Heraldo,* Metro section, June 12, 26.

2008   *Homicidios lideran tasa de muertes violentas en Honduras: Custodio.* Sep-
tember 11, Online: http://www.elheraldo.hn/Ediciones/2008/09/11/
Noticias/Homicidios-lideran-tasa-de-muertes-violentas-en-Honduras-
Custodio. Accessed September 11, 2008.

2008g Jornada científica en aniversario de hospital. *Diario El Heraldo,* June
11, p. 32.

2008h Maratón en beneficio de niños con cancer. *Diario El Heraldo,* June
12, 28.

2008i Médicos ad honoren. *El Heraldo,* Metro section, June 12, 25.

2008j Un promontorio de basura ocupa una acera del Hospital Escuela.
Diario El Heraldo, June 12, 32.

2008k Resistiendo con hidalguía. *Diario El Heraldo,* June 11, 29.

2008l Servicios de seguridad y limpieza podrían contratarse. *El Heraldo,* June
12, Salud section, 12.

Reich, Otto
2002   Remarks by Otto Reich, assistant secretary of state for Western
        Hemisphere affairs at the Heritage Foundation. October 31, State
        Department Briefing. Washington, DC.

Sajid Malick, Ibrahim
2007   *Global politician–NGOs–bureaucracies legitimizing oppression and cor-
        ruption.* Online: http://www.globalpolitician.com/22700-ngo. Ac-
        cessed March 9, 2009.

Sauceda, Juan
2008   *Compra directa benefició a farmacéuticas descalificadas.* Online: http://
        www.tiempo.hn/mostrar_noticia.php?id=64566&seccion=1. Acces-
        sed September 13, 2008.

Scheper-Hughes, Nancy
1982   Small wars and invisible genocides. *Social Science and Medicine*
        43(5):889–900.

Scott, Peter Dale, and Jonathan Marshall
1998   *Cocaine Politics: Drugs, Armies, and the CIA in Central America.* Berke-
        ley: University of California Press.

Singer, Merrill
2007a   *Drugging the Poor: Legal and Illegal Drugs and Social Inequality.* Pros-
        pect Heights, IL: Waveland Press.
2007b   Poverty, welfare reform and the "culture of wealth." *Practicing An-
        thropology* 29(4):43–45.
2008   *Drugs and Development: The Global Impact on Sustainable Growth and
        Human Rights.* Itasca, IL: Waveland Press.

Smith, N.
1998.   Giuliani time: The revanchist 1990s. *Social Text 57* 16(4):1–20.

Sontag, Susan
2004   *Regarding the Pain of Others.* New York: Picador.

Starkman, Eytan
2006   *Honduras' Operación Trueno: An audacious proposal that must be
        reformed and renovated.* Online: http://www.coha.org/2006/10/
        honduras%E2%80%99-operacion-trueno-an-audacious-proposal-
        that-must-be-reformed-and-renovated. Accessed March 14, 2009.

Statistics Canada
2007   *Crime Statistics 2006.* Online: http://www.statcan.ca/Daily/English/
        070718/d070718b.htm. Accessed September 11, 2008.

Stoner, Eric
  2008   *Outsourcing the Iraq War: Mercenary recruiters turn to Latin America.*
          Online: http://nacla.org/node/4805. Accessed September 14, 2008.

Taussig, M.
  1984   Culture of terror—space of death. Roger Casement's Putumayo Re-
          port and its explanation of terror. *Comparative Studies in Society and
          History* 26(3):467–497.

United Nations
  2006   Press release: UN working group on the use of mercenaries con-
          cludes visit to Honduras. Online: http://www.unhchr.ch/huricane/
          huricane.nsf/view01/29396527AAC62B20C12571D80035A42C?
          opendocument. Accessed September 14, 2008.

U.S. Census Bureau
  2008   *Tables by country.* Online: http://www.census.gov/ipc/www/idb/
          idbsprd.html. Accessed September 11, 2008.

U.S. Congress
  1988   *Report on Drugs, Law Enforcement, and Foreign Policy.* Senate Com-
          mittee on Foreign Relations, Subcommittee on Terrorism, Narcotics,
          and International Operations. 100th Cong., 2nd sess., 36–39.

U.S. Department of State
  2003   *Remarks with Honduran President Ricardo Maduro after Their Working
          Lunch: Secretary Colin L. Powell, Casa Presidencial, Tegucigalpa, Hon-
          duras.* Washington, DC: U.S. Department of State.
  2007   *The Merida Initiative: United States–Mexico–Central America se-
          curity cooperation.* Online: http://www.state.gov/r/pa/prs/ps/2007/
          oct/93800.htm. Accessed September 14, 2008.
  2008   *Central America and the Merida Initiative.* Online: http://www.state.
          gov/p/wha/rls/rm/2008/q2/104479.htm. Accessed September 15,
          2008.

Wacquant, Loïc.
  2004   Penal truth comes to Europe: Think tanks and the Washington
          consensus on crime and punishment. In *Truth and Justice: Official
          Inquiry, Discourse, Knowledge.* Edited by George Gilligan and John
          Pratt, 161–180. Portland, OR: Willan Publishing.
  2006   Habitus. In *International Encyclopedia of Economic Sociology.* Edited
          by J. Beckert and M. Zafirovski, 317–321. New York: Routledge.

Wallerstein, Immanuel
    1984   The development of the concept of development. *Sociological Theory*
            2:102–116.

Yacoub, S., S. Arellano, and D. Padgett-Moncada
    2006   Violence related injuries, deaths and disabilities in the capital of
            Honduras. *Injury* 37(5):428–434

CHAPTER NINE

OLIVE DRAB AND WHITE COATS
U.S. Military Medical Teams
Interoperating with Guatemala
Abigail E. Adams

The sun sets in Guatemala, a computer screen illuminates, and a uniformed man types a description of the day's events: "Hundreds of patients have stood in line for care, some having traveled over four hours by foot. Including dental and optometry, the clinic is seeing approximately 600 patients a day. . . . The number of prescriptions filled at the pharmacy set up by the [USS] *Boxer* team went from approximately 500 the first two days in Escuintla to over 1,000 per day the next two days" (U.S. Southern Command 2008b).

Similar scenes and blogs by U.S. Southern Command public relations officer Commodore Peter Dallman play over several days in several countries: similar scenes but with interchangeable characters—long lines of men, women, and children, including the elderly and entire families. Sometimes the people speak Spanish, sometimes Creole, sometimes an indigenous language. Some are dressed in locally produced indigenous clothing, while others are dressed in cheap mass-produced Western-styled garb. Ahead of them is the blur of bustling "green people": men and women in military uniforms (U.S. and other), green hospital scrubs, and a few white coats here and there. It is the close of another day of the U.S. military short-term missions known as MEDRETES: Medical and Dental Readiness Training Exercises.

The U.S. military now delivers a significant portion of U.S. overseas development assistance (ODA)—including medical, public health, and education aid—while foreign aid delivered by U.S. civilian agencies has dropped precipitously. The Department of Defense provided some 20 percent of total ODA by 2007, though overall aid levels dropped 22 percent from 2005 to 2007, according to the Center for Global Development (Radelet et al. 2008). The major reason for this increase is that the military delivers much of its aid to Afghanistan and Iraq, countries in which violence precludes the work of civilian aid agencies.

The U.S. military is also providing an increasing share of U.S. ODA in countries not at war, particularly in Central America. The military's role in delivering aid in "peaceful" regions is still directly a result of wartime commitments: because of its proximity and economic dependencies, Central America provides the ideal staging ground for the military deployment exercises that prepare the National Guard and military reserves for active duty. The need for such deployment training has intensified with U.S. military involvement in Afghanistan and Iraq.

Deployment training includes the MEDRETES, which evolved as a part of the U.S. military's Humanitarian Civic Assistance programs (HCA). The HCA programs have their roots in the 1960s and the Vietnam War, during which the Medical Corps ran Medical Civic Programs, known as MEDCAPs, initially for the Vietnamese military and later for Vietnamese civilians. At that time, the primary objective was to win the "hearts and minds" of the Vietnamese people (Jenkins 1988). MEDCAPs are the predecessors of today's MEDRETES, which were introduced to Latin America in 1989, when the U.S. Southern Commander, Army General Maxwell Thurman, saw a need to engage partner nations through humanitarian projects (Wimbish 2007).

By law the U.S. military cannot make humanitarian aid the first priority of the HCA programs. Instead, HCA's primary purpose must be the training of U.S. forces in deployment, readiness exercises, or military operations, and the promotion of "interoperability."[1] "Interoperability" refers to building compatibility between U.S. and foreign military hardware and personnel.

> Overseas deployments are an integral aspect of maintaining a forward U.S. military presence, ensuring operational readiness to respond to crises, and preparing National Guard and Reserve Forces to perform their wartime missions. These exercises enhance U.S. military operational readiness by providing unique training opportunities in remote and austere environments. (U.S. Department of Defense 2002)

As we will see, MEDRETES deliver a great deal of medical aid in Central America and make a significant impact in other regions in which they are staged. In a country such as Guatemala, with poor health care and a low standard-of-living profile, free medical care and pharmaceuticals are very appealing to local populations. As President George W. Bush pointed out after a March 2007 visit to one MEDRETE in Guatemala, more than 160,000 Guatemalans since 2001 have received services in these "missions of compassion . . . [that are] making a difference in peoples' lives" (Wimbish 2007). The MEDRETES also enjoy the strong support of the U.S. Departments of Defense and State. The current U.S. Southern Commander, Admiral James Stavridis, pointed out,

> Even though each [MEDRETE] has a small footprint, they have a huge impact. Imagine if you were suffering from a painful skin rash or an eye injury and did not have the means to get treatment. Then, a team of uniformed U.S. military doctors come in and offer free medical care. This is what the MEDRETES do—provide potentially life-changing experiences and show that Americans care. . . . I can think of few better ways to spread U.S. goodwill. . . . The MEDRETES are a fundamental part of our mission to engage with the region. (Wimbish 2007)

Indeed, the MEDRETES are a runaway success from the perspective of "interoperability," in which the U.S. and Guatemalan militaries benefit from the power and prestige of the United States, its military, and the health services provided to the population.

But others are not so bullish on the MEDRETES or other HCA joint exercises. Scholars, religious and peace groups, and members of Guatemala's civil society are concerned about the impact of the collaborative military exercises on that country's peace process. Guatemala's 1996 Peace Accords require that the Guatemalan military downsize and relinquish control of the country's government (Republic of Guatemala 1996a, 1996b). Yet the MEDRETES and other HCA programs elevate the Guatemalan military's status and engage it for civilian functions—while the appropriate national civilian agencies are bypassed. In this way, ME-DRETES undermine a host country's public health commitment and infrastructural investment. Other problems are common to any form of U.S. short-term medical foreign assistance—whether civilian, military, or missionary—such as their contribution to evolving antibiotic-resistant bacteria, and problems associated with the massive medical material transfer usually accompanying these medical missions.

MEDRETES both undermine local, regional, and national public health and reinforce U.S. global military and market dominance. Achieving these objectives through a system of medical care delivery affirms the often subtle complexities of the war machine around the world. In this instance, health care itself is mobilized in the service of the war machine, through the MEDRETES' offer of short-term palliative health gains in developing countries.

Ethnographic data were gathered during the period from 1992 to 1994 in Alta Verapaz, where I conducted dissertation fieldwork. I was recruited to serve as a volunteer translator with several short-term medical missions carried out by U.S. religious, professional, and military organizations. The U.S. military medical team came to my field site during the 1993 *Fuertes Caminos* ("Strong Roads") exercises. I also draw on other firsthand accounts of the MEDRETES. These accounts include that of Joyce, a bilingual 62-year-old Texan nurse-midwife who had extensive experience working with Hispanic patients; she was a volunteer with Project HOPE and kept a weblog of her experiences serving in the U.S. military's 2008 "Continuing Promise" exercises.[2] Another source is the reports of the U.S. military public relations office and Commodore Peter K. Dallman (2008), who maintained a lively blog throughout Continuing Promise. Finally, I incorporate the observations and analysis of Dr. Laura Montgomery, a medical anthropologist who has studied short-term medical missions since the early 1990s.

From "Strong Roads" to "Continuing Promise": How the MEDRETES Work

The U.S. Southern Command describes each MEDRETE as a series of clinics promoted, delivered, and staffed by small medical teams of U.S. military personnel visiting rural, underdeveloped areas for roughly two weeks (U.S. Air Force Southern Command 2008):

> The MEDRETE format includes two-week clinics of general multi-medical specialties, such as preventive medicine education, pediatrics, primary medical care, immunizations, pharmacy services

and dental activities including fluoridation, dental extractions, and oral hygiene education; two-week specialty surgery team clinics in the following specialties: ophthalmology, otolaryngology, orthopedics, hand reconstruction, plastic surgery for cleft lip and palate and burned patients, and urology; and, two to three day dental clinics.

Some MEDRETES also provide veterinary care, examining and vaccinating livestock and giving advice to local farmers. In 2007, U.S. military veterinarians treated more than 75,000 animals. The MEDRETES are often carried out with other HCA programs, such as road and school construction and well digging. These are staffed primarily by National Guard or reserve units. The personnel that make up the U.S. military medical teams are from all regions of the United States and from all branches of the armed services; MEDRETES also draw personnel from the U.S. embassy country teams, U.S. nongovernmental organizations (NGOs), and, most important, the host nation's military, government agencies, and local civilian organizations.

Since September 11, 2001, momentum for the deployment training that includes the MEDRETES has intensified. In 2008, two naval MEDRETES worked in nine Latin American and Caribbean nations. The first of these, dubbed "Continuing Promise," deployed from the Pacific and visited El Salvador, Guatemala, and Peru; it worked with more than 150 military medical professionals as well as those of U.S. NGOs. The Continuing Promise MEDRETES also worked with volunteers from Project HOPE, "the pioneer in medical diplomacy,"[3] treating 14,000 patients as well as 2,900 animals. In 2007, the U.S. Southern Command carried out a series of MEDRETES in 13 Central American, South American, and Caribbean nations, dubbed "New Horizons," treating 200,000 patients and conducting 3,000 surgeries. In 2006, MEDRETES saw 275,000 patients in 14 countries and in 2005 saw 203,000 patients in 18 countries (U.S. Southern Command 2008a; Wimbish 2007).

Ethnographic Encounter with Militarized Medicine

My direct experience with the MEDRETES began on January 19, 1993, when a U.S. military medical team from "Fuertes Caminos" came to the northern Guatemalan town of San Juan Chamelco, accompanied by the

Guatemalan military. The U.S. military team operated out of the region's army base, which had taken the slogan, "Home of the *Tzuultaq'a*" (The *Tzuultaq'a* are the region's earth deities; see Adams 2001a, 2001b, 2004; Wilson 1995.[4] The time frame of this particular mission was six days before the first group of Guatemalan refugees arrived in the region's capital on its return from Mexico through Guatemala City. The return was highly politicized, negotiations between the government and the refugees over the conditions of the return having been tense. On January 15, the refugees announced that they would return by the end of the month, and the next day the Strong Roads exercise was announced. During the week before the U.S. military medical clinic, Guatemalan soldiers from the region's base walked daily through town and then out to rural areas. Rumors of "guerrilla" sightings spread around town, creating an atmosphere of anxiety and militarization.

On the day of the medical mission, the U.S. military set up a clinic on the school grounds of a rural village, about a 10-minute drive from town over an unpaved road. It opened early in the morning, but the lines had already formed. I volunteered in the morning as a translator along with schoolteachers from the town who had been recruited for translation (Mayan and Spanish) and crowd control. Other community leaders were present as well: the town's mayor, some church elders, and local committee heads. The U.S. forces included some bilingual members (Spanish and English).

We were not the only townspeople present; family members of my hosts were among the many townspeople who attended the one-day "remote" clinic. My host family and friends were fairly well-to-do and bilingual Mayan townspeople, but the majority of the clients were monolingual Mayan farmers. For this reason the clinic visits usually required trilingual translation. Few of the medical mission team members spoke Spanish fluently, and almost none spoke Mayan. The interviews went from English to Spanish to Mayan and then back again from Mayan to Spanish to English. I was the only person who spoke at least some of all three languages, but this did not avert communication problems. At one point, I asked (I thought) a woman if her three sons had been dewormed yet. She gasped and held her boys close; someone intervened and explained that the word for "worm" was *lukum*, not *kum* ("penis").

Ability to seek services at the clinic had less to do with medical necessity than with access to the community leaders and schoolteachers who were charged with controlling the waiting clients and establishing priority. Everyone waiting in line surely looked "poor" to the U.S. military personnel, but there were very different levels of urgency and poverty present among the potential patients. The locals were impressed that the U.S. military kept order in the section of the line closest to the actual intake desk; all "cutting" in line happened out of their sight.

We volunteers were impressed with the sheer amount of material aid that people were carrying as they exited the clinic. My friends returned home with a large jar of generic skin lotion that the mother of the family reported had been given to her for her *manchas* (Spanish: "stains," or patchy skin problems) and with a nearly full clinic-size container of ibuprofen, 400 milligrams each, for her youngest daughter's menstrual cramps. Other families received antifungal soaps, delousing products such as Quell shampoo, and courses of wide-spectrum, low-toxicity antibiotics.

As the one-day clinic came to a close, people who were still waiting in line went home empty-handed. This was similar to the other medical missions on which I served as a translator. In one mission, sponsored by the Assemblies of God denomination, some 200 people were seen in two days. More than 50 people, however, had to be sent away, and the supply of medications was inadequate. Those of us who had volunteered for that clinic counted ourselves lucky when we learned a few months later of a violent incident at a different religious medical mission held in the same region; local residents had stoned the volunteers when they almost immediately ran out of supplies after opening.

In town the next day, I encountered a cobbler friend whose face had been transformed by new eyeglasses. Over the next few months, I spotted other pairs of the generic reading glasses as well as people wearing newly acquired spectacles, donated glasses from the United States. As noted, the military MEDRETES integrate civilian medical missionaries, NGOs, and transnational service networks. The 1990s Strong Roads exercises, for example, distributed "recycled" eyeglasses and new readers that were collected by the Lion's Club International Sight Foundation, saving the Lion's Club shipping and distribution costs. In 2008's Continuing Promise exercises, the military distributed about 3,500 pairs of eyeglasses collected through the Lion's Club.

"I'm in the Navy Now":
Serving with 2008's Continuing Promise

The Internet makes possible a firsthand glimpse into 2008's Continuing Promise. Joyce, a volunteer with Project HOPE, served from May 3 to 19 in 2008. She wrote on May 3, 2008: "'I'm in the Navy Now': I was invited to go on this trip by Project HOPE, at their expense. This is not tourism. The whole operation is being subsidized by the U.S. Navy. And boy, can you tell." Joyce served as part of the education team, whose director stated that they would offer "trainings specific to the desires of the host nation (or HN). . . . This is normally a *fantastic* experience—you will be able to work side by side with people and do interactive training. My experience the last few years is that this is so much fun that nobody realizes how much information is shared!" Joyce prepared very seriously for her assigned role as an educator, yet during her entire service, only one formal education session was arranged for the education team and its clients. She wrote, "The Centro de Salud was hot (108 degrees), and there were few people there for our 'training.' Yolanda spoke about STDs, and I gave a talk on normal labor and delivery including active management of [the] third stage. Lunch was Meals Ready to Eat, or MREs, where the entree gets heated up chemically, in its own bag. In the afternoon Yolanda spoke about diabetes, and I spoke about OB emergencies. I picked out those things that the people might see in their clinic, like hemorrhage, or shoulder dystocia, or prolapsed cord. If they have complications there, they transfer to a hospital."

After that workshop, the educators were not assigned to a specific training and found that their days at clinics were less structured. They were instructed "to find opportunities for informal teaching." Joyce reported the next day, "It was even hotter than the day before (109 degrees), and people were standing in line for hours. I found my little niche at the pharmacy, handing out the medications prescribed by the providers. That counted as 'education' because I could talk about how to take the pills and what to avoid, also what other things the people could do to alleviate their conditions."

For the rest of the clinic days, Joyce searched out other niches. For example, one day she traveled with the maternal/child educator back to a school: "Monday was kids' day, and the plan was to see the students at the school, beginning with the youngest (kindergarten or prekindergarten) and work up through the high school. There were the same stations—medical, dental, deworming, eye care. The weather was even hotter than the day before, with a heat index at 109 degrees." That did not stop the long lines of locals who came to get help or reassurance for their children. Joyce's "informal teaching" consisted of translating for the doctors and then returning to the pharmacy to hand out medications.

"What I learned from those two tasks was how almost every patient has the same complaints. Mostly it was the moms who spoke for the little kids, and the moms had the same concerns each time—the child isn't eating properly, maybe he has lost weight, he always has belly aches, headaches, knee and leg pain, sometimes dysuria [painful urination], sometimes upper respiratory infection, with an occasional case of head lice thrown in. I think a lot of these visits were simply to seek reassurance and to obtain some relief for these symptoms by getting vitamins or analgesics or antacids or an occasional round of antibiotics. The deworming station probably did the most direct good. I'm sure there will be relief from belly pain after the kids are worm free."

She then spent the next half of the day "in the exit area. . . . We had lots of handouts to give. From donations, there were toothbrushes and toothpaste and floss; feminine hygiene products like antifungal vaginal creams, sanitary napkins, and nursing pads; lots of sample medicines like Tylenol, cough syrup, antacids; and first-aid items like band-aids, antibiotic spray, and gauze pads with medicine to stop bleeding fast. All those give-aways needed instructions on how to use properly. Everyone seemed very appreciative. One of the teachers said that this was the first time any aid had come their way."

Joyce was unable to use the PowerPoint presentations that she had prepared because of a lack of electricity, so she improvised poster presentations. For example, she quickly prepared a poster session "on vaginitis, a topic which I thought deserved attention after seeing how we handed out Clotrimazole the other day." She presented the posters to the schoolteachers who were at the clinic to take care of crowd control. These teachers were among many community celebrities making appearances at the clinics. The U.S. military told the Project Hope volunteers that local Guatemalan civilians, "to make sustainable changes," were also participating; "The mayor of Aldea Linares makes daily visits to the site there. Yesterday the vice president of Guatemala came for lunch. (He is a thoracic surgeon who worked for about 20 years in Houston.)"

Halfway through her trip, Joyce paused from writing descriptions of the work to try to communicate the scale of the mission. "The scope of this operation is awesome, that is, inspiring awe. The projected cost is about $22,000,000. And so many groups have come together to make this work. It is hard to convey the scope of this whole operation with mere snapshots." The U.S. Navy provided the Guatemalan community with ample opportunities for awe: "This Continuing Promise operation is making all sorts of headlines here and in the military papers. . . . ComRel (Community Relations) report that about 400 people toured the ship. And there was a very impressive luncheon for dignitaries, including the U.S. ambassador to Guatemala. The Ward Room was transformed into a very attractive formal dining room. We got great leftovers."

The Guatemalan military also made an impression on Joyce: "Ah, a word about 'force protection.' We are not allowed to go anywhere without force protection. And since the [U.S.] Navy isn't supposed to bear arms on this mission, we have to depend upon the Guatemalan military for force protection. To every unit from the boat that moves on land, there are assigned armed Guatemalan military to accompany us. These are kids about 13 or 14, armed with automatic weapons. Makes you feel so very secure. But I guess they are necessary because I learned today that about $14,000 worth of an unescorted lumber shipment for a construction site for the Construction Battalion (SeaBees) was hijacked yesterday. Security is a big deal."

When Joyce's service was cut short by a knee injury, she prepared the PowerPoint presentations to leave with the navy medics by writing translations because "they are happy to use my presentations but cannot understand them (since I did them in Spanish). . . . Then I hope they pass them on to the next guys, for use in the future. I'd like to think I left them with something useful."

Analysis of the Biomedical Aspects

Joyce's and my experience share much in common, although the two are separated by fifteen years, and illustrate some issues that apply to short-term medical missions generally—whether these be military, civilian, or religious. The primary sets of issues are caused by the lack of preparation for the cross-cultural setting and the scale of the sudden influx of bio-medical and hygiene material aid, what I call a "pharmaceutical dump." Other concerns are applicable specifically to U.S. military humanitarian work. In this section, I examine the biomedical and public health impact on individuals and populations of the U.S. military's host nations as well as the health care delivery consequences.

Some biomedical good does result from the short-term medical missions. Very poor individuals do receive quality diagnoses for conditions that can be followed up locally. The deworming medications routinely (and cheaply) provided for most children at the clinics probably do some longer-term good. Despite the fact that the children will return to the same conditions and may be reinfected with the same worms, they will remain worm free for up to six weeks and will benefit developmentally from that parasite-free window. The medications have fairly low toxicity, and the children make health gains that persist even after reinfection.

Short-term medical missions, however, seldom promote a more enduring public health care structural outcome. Medical anthropologist Laura Montgomery, in her long-term work with civilian short-term medical missions, has concluded that "these missions . . . have insignificant and even negative consequences" (Montgomery 2000). She clarified that the quality of the medical and dental care was "not what is at issue" since clinic practitioners were all fully trained and certified medical personnel. My observations in the civilian clinical settings confirm this. However, I also observed considerable overstepping of the expertise line by nonmedi-cal personnel who offered diagnosis and prescriptive advice to patients, particularly in the pharmacy where nonmedical personnel were often filling prescriptions. Civilian short-term medical mission teams, religious and secular, include many nonmedical members who paid their own way, made additional monetary and material sacrifices and donations, and were longing to make a personal hands-on "difference." I did not observe this same problem in the military clinic setting, leading me to speculate that that particular problem may not exist in the military clinics, given the hierarchical nature of the military and the low tolerance for unskilled, undisciplined do-gooders.

It would be difficult to underestimate the scale of the pharmaceutical dump accomplished with each short-term clinic. The material impact of the missions, in the form of over-the-counter items and prescription medications, is considerable and is highlighted in every day's 2008 weblog accounts by military public relations officers. In the first series of the 2008 exercises, for example, the U.S. military dispensed 40,000 medications; it is not clear whether over-the-counter remedies are included in this count (U.S. Southern Command 2008a). At all the medical missions with which I served, many of the supplies were samples, overstock, and sometimes soon-to-expire materials that reflect what the donors need to give away rather than what the local community really needs.

Prescriptions and care instructions are often unclear because of problems of language, which can involve three languages and two non-medical interpreters. For example, the young woman in my household who attended the 1993 Fuertes Caminos MEDRETES had been given several hundred ibuprofen pills (a potentially risky medicine) at twice the strength offered in U.S. off-the-shelf bottles, but she had no idea of the appropriate dosage. I could not find instructions on the bottle in any language, and I learned that she had not been instructed to drink lots of water with the ibuprofen. Her mother, who had received the skin lotion, was told that it would help with her skin patches, some caused by a treatable fungal infection and others permanent damage caused by nutritional deficiencies during pregnancy. I noticed that there was no antifungal ingredient in the lotion, nor had my friend received any information about the difference between the permanent patches and the treatable ones.

A far greater problem is the development of antibiotic-resistant bacteria as a result of the lack of follow-up that is inherent in short-term medical missions. I have seen time and again what happens when an individual patient receives a course of antibiotics at these clinics: as soon as the symptoms, such as coughing or an ear infection, start to improve, the antibiotics are shared with other affected family members. When the full course of prescribed antibiotics is not finished, this encourages the evolution of antibiotic-resistant bacteria. Public health workers around the globe face this particular dynamic of antibiotics misuse: those workers who must live in the same communities where the antibiotic-resistant pathogens quickly evolve then suffer the consequences. In a short-term medical mission, such feedback and accountability are lost. Montgomery observed a similar dynamic in the faith-based short-term medical missions that she studied: postclinic effects of the antibiotics and other prescriptions and document were not taken as instructed, increasing morbidity as a result (Montgomery 2006).

The lack of necessary oversight or education for the use of medications is compounded by the cross-cultural and transient frame of the short-term medical missions. The clinics do not have adequate diagnostic time or resources to handle the patient load, which is similar to the frustrating reality for many "free" clinics or clinics for low-income clients in the United States. Both Joyce and I saw long lines of people. In the 1993 Fuertes Caminos clinic, people were turned away. The U.S. military's own blog about the MEDRETES states that "hundreds of patients have stood in line for care, some having traveled over four hours by foot." Indeed, the patient load is overwhelming.

While the military describes the MEDRETES as "small" medical missions set in rural, undeveloped, and "remote" locations, Joyce's adjective "awesome" is more accurate. None of the locations at which Joyce or I served were "remote." In fact, in both of the first-person accounts presented here (from 1993 and 2008), services were delivered within a half-hour drive or less from a paved road and major urban area. News of the missions spread through media channels and word of mouth, increasing the numbers of attendees and onlookers as well as the magnitude of the impression made. Finally, in the civilian missions at which I assisted and those that Montgomery studied, medical personnel were concerned that some individuals had waited for the mission's free care rather than get to a local clinic earlier, consequently undermining their health status and arriving in more critical stages of illness or with fewer and only more costly treatment options useful.

The need for translation is enormous. In 1993, when I was recruited as a translator, my availability was a complete windfall, not planned at all. In 2008, Joyce described the intentional presence of many more translators for the Guatemalan stage of the Continuing Promise exercises. Yet she, the education team member, is a bilingual medical practitioner who on her own finds her "niche" for most of her time with the MEDRETES in the pharmacy, handing out medications and giving verbal instructions. She remarks on the pressing need for what she is doing; otherwise, the patients would have received the drugs without any instruction. Verbal instruction has several shortcomings, as it is unclear how well the patient understands the instructions, will remember later, or is even listening. Given the unorganized nature of translation services in these cases, it seems likely that often effective translation is absent.

The missions dedicate little or no time for the systematic evaluation required to assess their actual impact on local health status and health care delivery systems, despite the sizable investments of material and professional resources involved (Montgomery 2000, 2006). I would add that these foreign medical missions also do not provide their clientele with adequate postclinic follow-up or any legal recourse for malpractice. The clinics were not established in local health centers, but patients received instructions to follow up locally, as if the regional health care providers would provide free follow-up care to very large numbers of patients.

In my experience, in Joyce's experience, and according to Montgomery's observations, U.S. medical mission personnel and volunteers receive little (or no) cultural orientation; they are generally unaware of nonbiomedical health values or care practices. They receive little or no orientation regarding the socioeconomic context of their clients' health care conditions. In Montgomery's words, "Teams are not challenged to confront the question of why the people they treat do not have access to medical services or sanitary conditions (or sufficient nutrition) in the first place," including the allocation of resources into the war machine rather than health care infrastructure (Montgomery 2000). Among the civilian volunteers and the military personnel with whom I worked, advice or education directed to the patients was often given from the condescending assumption that the problem was the patient's ignorance or lack of willpower rather than grinding poverty. In Joyce's description of the work carried out by the USS *Boxer*'s prevention teams, their suggestions were technical fixes—as if these had not already occurred to local populations, who were constrained by lack of public resources and political will.

Rather than contributing to the long-term goals of raising public health standards in severely underserved, underresourced areas, medical missions can reinforce the myth that health problems will be solved with more efficient delivery of better pills from elite foreign sources. The foreign military medical missions further erode the host nations' public health frame and structure. The military's deployment culture and structure reinforce the kind of hierarchy that erases the "public" as stakeholder, resource, and advocate; the clinics separate deliverers of public health from those who are subject to the public health conditions. The so-called public participation relegated local volunteers to crowd control and to carrying items, a fact frankly admitted by the U.S. military (U.S. Air Force Southern Command 2008). The MEDRETES reinforced the local patterns of patron–client channels of access. The people who were tasked with triaging the "public" were local power brokers—teachers, pastors, priests, and mayors—whose power benefited from serving as the access point for those who could prove useful to them later. At the top of the patron–client ladder at the time was President George W. Bush, in whose name as commander in chief the troops were acting.

The U.S. military has made a point of emphasizing prevention and education, public health concerns, and "partnerships" with host nations. But while the military had created some intentional education, translation, and prevention teams by 2008, Joyce's recent experience indicates that her ability to educate was almost accidental. The education that she did was involved primarily in clinical distribution of the medications. The classes that were explicitly set up were poorly attended or attended by schoolteachers who were drafted to help with crowd control. The U.S. military blog spun the circumstances this way: mission volunteers "took time to educate patients standing in line for medical treatments" (U.S. Southern Command 2008a). "The main goal of preventative medicine is to educate them on how to better care for themselves, versus us having to come back here every year," said Technical Sergeant Mary Preolette, the noncommissioned officer in charge for a July 2007 MEDRETE mission in Honduras (Wimbish 2007). Despite this official rhetoric, some military personnel and employees themselves have spoken with me about the shortcomings of the MEDRETES. They are aware that their mission and training are not in international development. For that reason, they regard the most successful MEDRETES missions as those that provide dental and veterinary services, which, in their view, involve a minimum of cross-cultural contact and maximum short-term benefit. Nevertheless, medical missions continue to operate in Central America and keep making Continuing Promises.

ABIGAIL E. ADAMS

"Nobody really knows how much information is shared": The Transnational Cultural Setting of Interoperability

Recall that MEDRETES are military exercises, not medical training, and that, by law, their first priority must be military readiness for U.S. troops and U.S. national security. The MEDRETES fact sheet states:

> The most valuable part of MEDRETES for units deploying is that it gives them real deployment and readiness experience, as well as experience operating in austere environments. For the host nation, MEDRETES provide health education, disease prevention training, and personal and professional exchanges. (U.S. Air Force Southern Command 2008)

While the second sentence in this statement may seem somewhat hollow—duplicitous in light of the previous discussion concerning the haphazard means of delivering health education and prevention training—a more ample exploration of the U.S. military's goal of interoperability will demonstrate how integral the health aspects are. Joyce's 2008 Continuing Promises education team leader's statement that "nobody really knows how much information is shared" suggests how well the medical missions work, although perhaps inadvertently, within the strategy of interoperability.

The priority of the programs, according to the State Department, is "to enhance interoperability with Guatemalan units" (U.S. Department of State 2009). "Interoperability" is a term that the Department of Defense uses primarily regarding weapons technology and support equipment such as construction and transportation vehicles. If different nations were to use U.S. military products, then in the case of a conflict the different sets of technologies will work together, or "interoperate." The U.S. military's plan for building "interoperability" is not just based on joint maneuvers, HCA, and military, but primarily on U.S. arms sales abroad (see Hartung 1996; Hartung and Berrigan 2008). The United States reaffirmed in 2007 its leadership in world arms trade, having cornered nearly 42 percent of the market as the wars in Iraq and Afghanistan prompted a weapons shopping spree among neighboring nations (Grimmett 2007). Perhaps even more important in the strategy of interoperability is that the different sets of equipment are interchangeable and therefore substitutable. Personnel make up the other context that is slated to be "interoperable." "Fuertes Caminos" promotes "interoperability" of Latin American and U.S. troops in that they learn to work together and follow the same protocols and drills, presumably those developed and used by the United States. The term also carries the sense of "interchangeable," in which Latin American troops could be used with—and perhaps in place of—U.S. troops.

The military medical missions promote the "interoperability" of multiple groups of local people: U.S. reserve and National Guard members, defense industry workers, U.S. church and charity volunteers who run associated or similar activities, and the Guatemalan medical clinic clients, local authorities, and vendors. Within the strategy of interoperability, people need not achieve uniformity in areas such as human rights standards, language, culture, and local economies or even share the same ideas about bodies or families or race. Instead, interoperability is achieved through uniformity and mutual dependence only in areas such as technology, work protocols, and appetites.

Montgomery identifies the meta-U.S. cultural assumption implicit in the short-term medical mission frame as the emphasis on short-term quick-fix solutions rather than longer-term or preventive approaches. Mission members feel a need for immediate tangible results, a need to see that they have made a difference; hence, intervention is more valued, and distributing material aid is prioritized (Montgomery 2000). Joyce's and the U.S. military's recounting illustrate this mentality clearly: from the official "blog" descriptions of the Guatemala stage of Continuing Promise to the reports to sponsors from civilian medical groups, the focus is on quantity: how many people lined up every day, the quantity of patients seen, teeth extracted, children inoculated, and prescriptions filled. Even prevention and education should be quantified:

> HCA says USS *Boxer* crew also provided valuable training, such as CPR, nutrition, basic sanitation techniques, and first aid to 18,000 students in 123 classes. . . . The *Boxer's* environmental-health team conducted 12 different assessments . . . the education team taught 80 midwives basic CR and conducted classes on hand washing, universal precautions, and neonatal resuscitation. They also taught dental health for approximately 300 people.

This focus on numbers is exacerbated by another cultural characteristic that Montgomery identifies: the naive and ethnocentric belief that approaches suitable in one setting are appropriate in another. Therefore, no special planning or specialized knowledge for medical practice abroad is needed (Montgomery 2000). Delivery of services and supplies from the outside medicalizes and individualizes the effects of poverty, unclean water, malnutrition, poor sanitation, and other structural and infrastructural problems.

But here is where the "locals" and foreigners coincide. The medications, the "stuff," Joyce's "handouts"—these are what the clinic clients want at the end of their long wait in line. American military and economic foreign aid has promoted U.S. exports, in the name of achieving national security, since the Truman administration. Today, U.S. medical foreign aid reinforces a post–Central American Free Trade Agreement campaign promoting U.S. health products over locally or nationally produced remedies that are consistently and fairly cheaply available. In this way, MEDRETES build on long-standing U.S. commercial and cultural imperialism that entangles local Guatemalan civilians and ties them to the United States, its prestige, and its products.

Throughout Guatemala and elsewhere in Latin America, people seek articulation with the United States through language, education, dress, travel, friendships, popular culture, and technology. One rather "skin-deep" example that I encountered during the medical missions was skin treatments. Lotions and topical medications were in high demand among both indigenous and nonindigenous (Ladino) clients. For many Ladino Guatemalans, self-improvement means adopting and immersing oneself in Eurocentric U.S.-centric standards, standards of dress, language, tastes, and "white" skin color. Generally, I found that Ladino patients sought an upgrading associated with the United States: the requests for diet pills, for lotions that "whitened," and for "better" pills and vitamins, many of which people requested so that they could "concentrate" or "think" better.

Until recently, Maya people avoided the westernizing effect of certain substances. Eating too much bread is said to weaken people, as compared with eating corn; the same was true of milk powder. Three decades ago, rumors spread in Alta Verapaz and in other regions that the milk powder that U.S. voluntary agencies were distributing was actually ground up babies' bones. But now, Maya people are increasingly interested in Western medicine and products; today powdered milk is an inventory staple in most stores. During the medical mission clinics, many Mayan women requested lotions to remove *manchas* (skin patches), such as the dark facial blotches that my friend Rosa had from nutritional deficiencies during pregnancy and from a tropical fungus. I first wondered if part of her motivation were deracializing of the skin, but it seems that the issue was more related to class. People described the permanent marks left after pregnancy as signs of poverty that revealed that a family was too poor to feed their mothers well. Rosa and her husband were now prosperous tailors and merchants who had worked their way up from very humble beginnings; she did not want the class-based stigma of dark spots.

In 1994, Guatemalans launched a series of attacks on visiting North American women, after rumors moved rapidly around the country that "outsiders" were stealing babies and harvesting their body organs (Adams 1998). After those rumors and attacks, I thought often about the Q'eqchi' woman medical mission client who gasped when I mistranslated the request to deworm her sons as a suggestion to castrate them. In fact, her response seemed more logical in many ways than that of the clients who sought and did not question the intrusions of the poorly or unexplained clinical process.

Yet that same year, 1994, the U.S. military successfully ran ME-DRETES in the countryside, in which hundreds of Guatemalans allowed the *gringos* to pull their teeth, palpitate their abdomens, and prescribe hundreds of pills. Later that year, a year in which the U.S. State Department issued travel advisories and warnings to its citizens to not photograph, touch, or even point at Guatemalan children, former president George H. W. Bush traveled the country, kissing Guatemalan babies and posing for photos with those babies thrust at him by admiring Guatemalan citizens (New York Times 1994). Thirteen years later, President George W. Bush and wife, Laura Bush, visited one MEDRETE in Guatemala during his March 2007 tour of five Latin America nations. Later, during a press conference held with then Guatemalan President Oscar Berger, Bush stated, "The American people would have been incredibly proud of watching our military folks dispense with basic health care needs to people who needed help. And the people of Guatemala would be especially proud to have seen your military working side by side with our troops to do the same thing" (Wimbish 2007).

From Genocide to Healing? The Guatemalan Military

As one political scientist pointed out, it would be hard to find a Latin American political institution more widely condemned than the Guatemalan military (Ruhl 2005). Guatemala's two truth commission reports, one sponsored by the United Nations and the other by the archbishop of Guatemala, concluded that the Guatemalan military carried the responsibility for the genocidal and indiscriminate violence against civilians during the 36-year-plus civil war and counterinsurgency, particularly during the early 1980s (Comisión para el Esclaracimiento Histórico 1999; REMHI 1998).

The Peace Accords require that the Guatemalan military downsize, relinquish control of the country's government, and retreat to matters of security from external threat rather than internal control (Republic of Guatemala 1996a, 1996b). Guatemala's civilian leaders have struggled to enforce the military elements of the accords. The first post–Peace Accords president, Alvaro Arzu, did manage to establish civilian dominance over the military, slash its numbers from 46,900 to 31,423 and its budget by 33 percent, and vastly curtail its control over rural areas and peoples. But the next president, Alfonso Portillo, increased both budget and personnel, brought back corrupt officers purged by Arzu from the military ranks, blocked prosecution of the military, and increased the military's internal security and other roles ("protecting prison perimeters, delivering fertilizer and library books, and vaccinating children and improving school nutrition"), especially in dealing with street crime. Two amendments to Guatemala's constitution—to provide for a civilian minister of defense and to end the military's control over internal security—were defeated in May 1999 and not reintroduced (Hartmann 2002; Ruhl 2005). The president who departed office in January 2008, Oscar Berger, managed again to cut the military's size and budget by 33 percent and to get the military out of the rural areas (Waiser 2008). Nevertheless, the Guatemalan military maintains nearly opaque budget management, and while the civilian budget has faced drastic cuts (particularly in the wake of ex-President Portillo's corruption), the military budget has ballooned (Ruhl 2005).

The Guatemalan army's presence at the U.S. joint military exercises powerfully reintroduces them into the countryside. The Guatemalan military is displayed, promoted, and highly valued during the exercises, as demonstrated during both the 1993 and the 2008 medical missions. The exercises reinforce the military's role in nation-building and undermine the legitimacy of the appropriate civilian ministries. Despite the fact that Guatemala's Ministry of Public Works is charged with roads and civil engineering projects, in 2008 the U.S. military reported that "throughout the entire operation, the Seabees were working side-by-side with Guatemalan military civil engineers who provided their own experience and skills to the work at hand" (Wimbish 2007). The U.S. government reinforces the status quo, the military's control of critical infrastructure, and its expertise at the expense of the civilian ministry.

Health care delivery is a particularly powerful arena for establishing relations of patronage and manipulation. Power accrues to all actors in the arena: credentialed doctors, the state, local healers, and missionaries. Two of the medical missions for which I translated were religious-sponsored missions that, like the military exercises, distributed quite a bit of medicine and vitamins. One such team, from the U.S. Assemblies of God, would hand patients a prescription, ask if they were "Christians," pray over them, fill the prescription, and say the medicine would work if it was God's will. A different group did not connect the power of pharmaceuticals with the power of God and proselytizing, but the team members did hold the clinic in the local church, a common location for the ME-DRETE teams as well. They placed the pharmacy shelves and dispensary on the altar platform, the elevated focal point that caught the attention of the more than 1,000 patients seen during their visit. Each patient would enter the doorway, register his or her name, get a number, and then pass through the aisles to a doctor or diagnostician, and eventually to the altar to receive medication.

In Joyce's 2008 experience with Continuing Promises, the U.S. military held the clinics not in churches but in schools and community centers. However, the Seabees that accompanied them rebuilt, reroofed, and repainted several churches. In one village, when the church was finished, the "chaplain from the ship celebrated mass with the local priest. The folks were very moved by that."

In northern Guatemala, the deities responsible for healing are the Q'eqchi' Maya mountain spirits, the *Tzuultaq'a*, which are the embodiment of power. It is not clear how the region's military base received the slogan "Home of the *Tzuultaq'a*," but in this naming the Guatemalan military claimed its power over both humans and the spiritual landscape of Verapaz. The U.S. military's medical programs provided the Guatemalan army with yet another means of controlling civilian bodies.

Conclusion

Guided by the principle of interoperability, the United States is export-ing protocols, personnel, and equipment that promote national security through uniformity and dependence in certain areas, such as technology, work, and bodies. The MEDRETES promote interoperability of the U.S. reserves and National Guard and civilians both abroad and at home, drawing on people who give annual service but lead civilian lives in civilian economies, on people who work for the defense industry, and on people who volunteer their time for the peripheral activities, such as the eyeglass donation projects and the Project HOPE education teams. The need for deployment training has intensified with the Iraq War and the drawdown of "reserve" troops into cycle after cycle of active duty.

When President George W. Bush toured Guatemala in 2007 and visited the MEDRETE, he finished with a press conference in the capi-tal city. The bulk of that press conference was not about the problems of Guatemala but concerned "illegal" Guatemalan immigrants in the United States and the accelerating deportations of such Guatemalans following U.S. factory raids, in many cases leaving children in the United States. Guatemala's economy depends on remittances from its 13 million compatriots now residing in the United States who contribute over $3 billion a year, and are the top economic contributor to Guatemala's GNP (Cheikhrouhou et al 2006).

This speech was before the failure of the comprehensive immigra-tion bill in 2007, when he said, "We want there to be a rational way for people to come and do jobs Americans aren't doing" (White House 2007). Notably, in this light, the first soldier in the U.S. military to die in Iraq, the immigrant Jose Gutierrez, was an orphaned Guatemalan who at the time of his death was not even an American citizen (he was naturalized posthumously). Several weeks after his death, the U.S. military changed its story about how he died, finally admitting that he fell to "friendly fire." He has been dubbed the "green-card soldier," one of many who may have responded to a 2002 executive order by President Bush expediting naturalization for aliens and noncitizen nationals who serve in active-duty status during the War on Terror. The order, effective for all military personnel who enlisted after the terrorist attacks of September 11, 2001, allows noncitizens to apply for citizenship immediately on arrival at their first military base rather than having to wait the usual three to four years. According to Bush, persons "serving honorably in active-duty status in the Armed Forces" do a service to their new country, so they should be granted citizenship more quickly than via regular channels.

As this example affirms, whatever the short-term health benefits of military-based health aid, the ultimate goal of such programs is enhancement of the war machine. In the case of soldier Gutierrez, the war machine creates another interoperable "body" of military recruits, of "people to come and do jobs Americans aren't doing." Health care delivery, in short, is mobilized as one more strategy for this ultimate objective of interoperability. Moreover, short-term health care gains are contradicted by longer-term health costs in terms of the diversion of funding into the military and away from health care infrastructural needs, the contribution to the development of drug-resistant pathogenic strains of bacteria, the undercutting of local health care providers, the potential for the misuse of widely distributed pharmaceutical products, and the enhanced power and legitimacy of Guatemala's own local war machine.

Notes

1. Section 401, Title 10 of the U.S. Code, which authorizes the Humanitarian and Civic Assistance program. See also Latin American Working Group (2005).

2. This and all following quotes from Joyce appear on her blog at http://joyceinguatemala.blogspot.com.

3. Project Hope's mission is as follows: "To achieve sustainable advances in health care around the world by implementing health education programs and providing humanitarian assistance in areas of need." See http://www.projecthope.org.

4. The *Tzuultaq'a* are local "mountain-valley" supernatural beings who control agricultural and human health and who are renowned for their mercurial nature.

Works Cited

Adams, Abigail E.
   1998   Gringas, ghouls and Guatemala: Hypogamy and transnational kinship in the post-NAFTA world. *Journal of Latin American Anthropology* 4(1).
   2001a "Making one our word": Evangelical Q'eqchi' Mayans in Highland Guatemala. In *Holy Saints and Fiery Preachers: The Anthropology of Protestantism in Mexico and Central America.* Edited by James W. Dow and Alan R. Sandstrom. Westport, CT: Praeger.
   2001b The transformation of the *Tzuultaq'a*: Jorge Ubico, Protestants and other Verapaz Maya at the crossroads of community, national and transnational interests. *Journal of Latin American Anthropology* (special edited volume).
   2004   Ethnographic notes in Q'eqchi' cave rites: Implications for archaeological interpretation. Coauthored with James Brady. In *In the Maw of the Earth Monster: Studies of Mesoamerican Cave Use.* Edited by James A. Brady and Keith Prufer. Austin: University of Texas Press.

Cheikhrouhou, Hela, Rodrigo Jarque, Raúl Hernandez-Coss, and Radwa El-Swaify
   2006   *The U.S.-Guatemala Remittance Corridor: Understanding Better the Drivers of Remittances Intermediation.* World Bank Working Paper No. 86, Washington, DC: World Bank.

Comisión para el Esclarecimiento Histórico
   1999   *Guatemala: Memoria del Silencio.* Online: http://shr.aaas.org/guatemala/ceh/mds/spanish/toc.html.

Dallman, Commodore Peter K.
   2008   Online: http://www.southcom.mil/AppsSC/news.php?storyId=1141.

Grimmett, Richard F.
   2007   *U.S. Army Sales: Agreements with and Deliveries to Major Clients: 1999–2006.* Washington, DC: Congressional Research Service, Library of Congress.

Hartmann, Scott
   2002   MINUGUA critiques new government budget. New York: United Nations Foundation, November 22.

Hartung, William D.
   1996   *Welfare for Weapons Dealers: The Hidden Costs of the Arms Trade.* Washington, DC: World Policy Institute.

Hartung, William D., and Frida Berrigan
    2008   *U.S. Weapons at War 2008: Beyond the Bush Legacy.* Washington, DC: New America Foundation.

Jenkins, Elray
    1988   *Medical Civic Action Programs (MEDCAPS) and Medical Readiness Training Exercises (MEDRETES) as Instruments of Foreign Policy.* Carlisle, PA: Army War College.

Latin American Working Group
    2005   *Just the Facts: A Civilian's Guide to U.S. Defense and Security Assistance to Latin America and the Caribbean.* Washington, DC: Latin American Working Group.

Montgomery, Laura M.
    2000   Short-term medical missions: Enhancing or eroding health. *Missiology*, January–February.
    2006   Paper delivered for the invited panel "Short-Term Religious Missions in Latin America." American Anthropological Association, San Jose, CA, November.

New York Times
    1994   Bush discovers, and enjoys, a life after politics. *New York Times*, October 4, A15.

Radelet, Steve, Rebecca Schutte, and Paolo Abarcar
    2008   *What's Behind the Recent Decline in U.S. Foreign Assistance?* Washington, DC: Center for Global Development.

REMHI/Guatemalan Interdiocesan Project to Recover the Historic Memory
    1998   *Nunca Mas (Never Again).* Guatemala: REMHI.

Republic of Guatemala and the Guatemalan National Revolutionary Unity
    1996a Agreement on a firm and lasting peace in Guatemala.
    1996b Agreement on the strengthening of civilian power and the role of the armed forces in a democratic society. UN ref. no. A/51/410-S/1996/853.

Ruhl, J. Mark
    2005   The Guatemalan military since the Peace Accords: The fate of reform under Arzú and Portillo. *Latin American Politics and Society* 47(1):55–85.

U.S. Air Force Southern Command, 12th Air Force
  2008   *Fact sheet: Medical readiness training exercises (MEDRETES)*. Online:
          http://www.12af.acc.af.mil/library/factsheets/factsheet.asp?id=7694.

U.S. Department of Defense, Defense Security Cooperation Agency
  2002   *Humanitarian and Civic Assistance Program of the Department of*
          Defense, Fiscal Year 2001. Washington, DC: U.S. Department of
          Defense.

U.S. Department of State
  2009   *FY 2010 Congressional Budget Justification for Foreign Operations*.
          Washington, DC: U.S. Department of State.

U.S. Southern Command
  2008a   *Continuing Promise, May to December 2008*. Online: http://www
          .southcom.mil/AppsSC/factFiles.php?id=53.
  2008b   *HHS Commissioned Corps officers join Operation Continuing Promise*. On-
          line: http://www.southcom.mil/AppsSC/news.php?storyId=1141.

Waiser, Ray
  2008   *Alvaro Colom Takes Charge of Guatemala; New Optimism for a Troubled*
          Neighbor. Washington, DC: Heritage Foundation.

White House
  2007   President Bush and President Berger of Guatemala participate in
          joint press availability. Washington, DC: Office of the Press Secre-
          tary, White House, March 12.

Wilson, Richard
  1995   *Maya Resurgence in Guatemala*. Norman: University of Oklahoma
          Press.

Wimbish, Michael
  2007   *18th year of MEDRETES completed*. Online: http://www.southcom
          .mil/AppsSC/news.php?storyId=804.

CONCLUSION
The Political Economy and Critical Geography of the War Machine
G. Derrick Hodge and Merrill Singer

Everywhere today,
every aspect of our lives
is being violently reorganized.
Everywhere there is war.
A war without a battlefield.
A war without an enemy.
A war that is everywhere.
A thousand civil wars.
A war without end.
The Fourth World War.[1]

The preceding chapters have cataloged the disastrous health consequences of war in its many forms: active warfare, military bases scattered across the globe, war economies, war-related global warming, the psychosocial trauma of child soldiers, neocolonial and internal colonial genocide, the "war on crime" and the "war on terror," postwar malnutrition, decimated public health budgets, devastated global and local ecologies, a ruling class that declares war on its poor, and a ruling ethnicity that declares genocidal war on its Others. In collecting the data and analyzing these wars, the contributors to this book have responded to the moral imperative to report, analyze, and confront the violence of our contemporary world, a world dramatically more militarized than it was in 1981. The scholars whose words are recorded here have not shied away from telling the truth of war, from naming the aggressors, or from taking a political stance in opposition to war and its costs in the realms of health and well-being. Despite this political commitment, our goal in assembling this book is not solely to catalog the health consequences of war and to call for peace, for such a project would be platitudinous and of little scientific value. Rather, we seek to move beyond mere denunciation of that which even most conservatives would bemoan. The primary goal of this volume has been to demonstrate how war and war machines destroy human life and well-being across time and space, leaving carnage seldom reported by the corporate media.

The preceding chapters have accomplished this task well, using the framework of critical medical anthropology (CMA) (Baer et al. 1997, 2003; Singer 1986; Singer and Baer 1995). As a theoretical perspective within medical anthropology, CMA focuses attention on the social origins of health, illness, and mortality, including the mechanisms through which discrimination, poverty, violence, and fear of violence influence the health and well-being of a community and its members. While especially concerned with issues of power and inequality (because these are seen as playing central roles in shaping human events and activities), CMA does not take a "top-down" approach that views political and economic structures as narrowly determining what happens in people's lives.

Rather, critical medical anthropologists argue that experience and "agency," that is, individual and group decision making and action, are "constructed and reconstructed in the action arena between socially constituted categories of meaning and the political-economic forces that shape the context [and texture] of daily life" (Baer et al. 2003:44). In other words, people develop individual and collective understandings and responses to illness and other threats to their well-being, such as violence and armed conflict, but they do so in a world that is "not of their own making," a world in which a hierarchical structure of social statuses and relations locally, nationally, and globally plays a significant role in constraining options.

Our final task, reserved for this conclusion, will be to demonstrate that war and its disastrous health consequences are neither random nor unfortunate accidents but rather follow a political-economic logic that propels them. We posit, following many others, that war and the terror it unleashes are inevitable results—and even sometimes intentional tools—of capitalism's insatiable drive to accumulate wealth. In this way, the war machine in all its manifestations is a series of rational processes, produced and unleashed according to the laws of capital accumulation, even if its consequences are chaotic and unpredictable. The collateral damage to human life and health, even when spatially and temporally displaced, becomes an unfortunate but acceptable cost of the profits that "creative destruction" produce.

What remains, then, is to connect three related processes that have been described throughout this volume: the war machine and the destruction of human life and health, the neoconservative and territorial logics of power that produce war, and the micro- and macroprocesses of capital accumulation that propel the dialectic of war and wealth. Accomplishing this task will require an examination of the work of two eminent critical geographers—David Harvey and Neil Smith—who have insightfully and convincingly demonstrated the connections between space, war, power, and capitalism. The various chapters in this volume illustrate what Harvey and Smith have forcefully articulated: the inextricable connections between rapacious capital and territorially based state power—even under a supposedly deterritorialized globalization—and the series of processes and relationships we have called the war machine. An examination of the political-economic logic that drives the war machine indicates that war is not merely brutal and unthinkable madness—though it can appear to be just that—but instead is madness with a purpose. While "war as madness" is condemnable, it is ultimately not stoppable, since it has neither order nor reason. "War as purposeful madness," by contrast, creates space for not merely denouncing the ugly horrors of armed conflict but also for identifying alternative, less conflicted, political-economic contexts for human societies. In the end, we return to the specific cases presented in this volume, uniting our theory of causation with real-world accounts of consequences.

Dialectics of the War Machine

The analytical project of this concluding chapter will require attention to dialectics both as a method of inquiry and as a description of the historical interactions of divergent material processes. This methodological commitment emerges from our framework of CMA, which encourages an analysis that engages distant political-economic processes with the microscale of individual bodies. Three aspects of dialectics will guide our analysis. First, there is no such thing as a *thing*; rather, we are interested in *processes*. Objects of scientific investigation that appear to be things are in fact series of processes that may—for a time—congeal into apparently stable things. But such "things" are in fact always in motion, shifting and never stable. Rather than stable things, we see fluid sets of processes working with and against each other to produce a complex social reality. Second, all processes and sets of processes are plagued by internal contradictions. There is no object of investigation that is internally homogeneous; it would be an error to examine a "thing" without due attention to its inconsistencies and internal contradictions. Such a claim does not mean that, as with temporal stability, sets of processes do not from time to time serve the same goals or function according to similar logics. But coherence in this way is not intrinsic to any processes and will always degrade over time.[2]

A third way in which a dialectical methodology will be useful for our purposes emerges from the concept of geographic scale. Inspired by Marxist dialectics, critical geographers have shown that any process occurs at various geographic scales simultaneously. For instance, globalization is a set of processes that occurs between states, between regions and cities, within a subnational region, in a neighborhood, and within a household. "Globalization" at the level of the neighborhood within a city (say, Ciudad Juarez along the Mexican–U.S. border) is not merely *related* to globalization as it occurs in the state or globe but in fact the exact *same* process that happens at both sites and on both scales at the same time. David Harvey argues convincingly that even the individual human body, as discussed here, is a geographic scale that reflects processes at the regional, national, or global scales.

Fourth, the body behaves (both analytically and historically) like any other dialectical process in several ways. It is produced through the interaction of multiple processes. It is not stable but in flux (e.g., it ages and gets sick and well again) and not homogeneous but comprised of multiple processes that are sometimes internally contradicted: "The body is not a closed and sealed entity, but a relational 'thing' that is created, bounded, sustained, and ultimately dissolved in a spatio-temporal flux of multiple processes" (Harvey 2000:98). Following Marx ("A being which does not have its nature outside itself is not a natural being"), Harvey (2000:120) concludes that "no body exists outside of its external relations with other bodies and the exercise of powers and counterpowers among bodies is a central constitutive aspect of social life." Finally, bodies are "porous"; that is, they are not bounded entities but are interactive with external processes: "The body . . . is itself a site of contestation for the forces that create it. The body (like the person and self) is an internal relation and therefore open and porous to the world" (Harvey 2000:130).

The relevance of these ideas for our purposes is not difficult to discern. We resist a political tendency to imagine that the "war machine" (even if used in the singular) is in fact a unitary and bounded entity. It is of course not true—Cheney, Wolfowitz, Rumsfeld, and the contemporary neoconservative think tanks notwithstanding—that there are proverbially dark and smoke-filled rooms in which iniquitous corporate executives and right-wing politicians dream up new ways to go to war, beef up military budgets, deprive citizens of health care, and the like. Our chapters amply demonstrate that there are a variety of logics that operate, sometimes in an apparently coordinated way but at other times in quite different ways across both time and space. Geography matters, and despite the enthusiastic claims of globalization boosters, the globe has not yet been entirely leveled. Differences in aims and method make it obvious that the "war machine" is not a tight thing but rather a collection of different logics whose cohesion is tenuous at best. These processes sometimes work in collaboration, but just as often are at cross-purposes. That is, civil war in Sudan might in fact *not* be consistent with the best interests of the oil industry that encourages warfare elsewhere. Divergences reveal just as much as do the similarities about how war machines work.

If a dialectical analysis reveals that war machines are diverse and differentiated and serve divergent purposes, it also reveals two important consistencies. First, following Harvey's conception of geographic scales, *all* war machines operate on all scales, including the body. In fact, one objective of this volume has been to demonstrate how global, national, and regional processes of warfare are inflected differentially on individual and community bodies. The contributors to this volume have sought to draw attention to the body, as uniquely formulated in a specific time-space, as a site on which operate global and national social processes.

The second important consistency revealed by a dialectical analysis is the highly implicated (if not determinate) machinations of global and local political economies. This is, after all, a central claim of the CMA framework: we cannot understand the workings of the war machine, or indeed of any process that impacts on health, without considering the po-litical-economic contexts in which they occur. While this supposition has united the literature of CMA investigation since the development of the framework, we now add a further elaboration that an enhanced dialectical analysis reveals: not only must we consider the *context* in which bodies live and die, as if those contexts were stable things that either contribute to or ameliorate poor health outcomes. Additionally, we must consider the *logic* that produces the shifting contexts that harm the bodies that inhabit them. That is, we cannot take the contexts themselves as preexisting givens that deserve no analytical attention. If the preceding chapters have demonstrated how poor health outcomes are produced by contexts of war and violence, we seek now to delve one step deeper to demonstrate how war itself is produced by the economic exigencies of the accumulation of wealth. *The full relation is thus exposed: if war destroys health in multiple seen and unseen ways, then what is it that produces war in multiple seen and unseen ways?* It is to this question that we now turn.

Political Economies and War Machines

War, warfare, war machinery, war economies, war rhetoric, war prepara-tion, war justification, war ideologies—none of these appear ex nihilum, nor do they emerge "naturally" from some imagined evolutionary instinct to compete, to overcome, to destroy. Something other than human nature or human folly causes war and constructs war machines, and war machines serve a logic that is external to them. To explain the source of this logic we turn to the foundational work of critical geographers Neil Smith and David Harvey, elaborating on it in light of the insights provided by the preceding chapters.

Territorial Power

Much popular condemnation of the blatant imperialism of the neoconservative movement conflates territorial power with economic power; wars are seen as a ruling-class quest to expand wealth using the violence machinery of nation-states. This is accomplished through territorial expansion in either a neocolonial or an imperialist manner in a search of new markets, new raw material, cheap labor to exploit, or a combination of these. It is true that those who possess the power of nation-states and thus control their machinery of violence are also often the same as those who rule capital and who profit most from its endless expansion. We need look no further than Enron and Halliburton as evidence of this fact. It is also true that nation-states use myriad powers of consent and coercion, control over labor contracts, police forces and prison systems, powers of eminent domain, monetary and credit system control, and the like to facilitate capital accumulation. Nation-states are, indeed, active agents of rapacious accumulation on behalf of their ruling classes.

One way in which this congruence of interests occurs is through the state's power of destruction, particularly that which can be properly called the war machine: systems of weaponry, military bases, a militaristic ideology in the body politic, and the like. Harvey's summary of these processes is suggestive of their relevance for understanding the various elements of the war machine. Despite the state's need for order and stability to ensure effective management and control of labor,

> capitalism perpetually seeks to create a geographical landscape to facilitate its activities at one point in time only to have to destroy it and build a wholly different landscape at a later point in time to accommodate its perpetual thirst for endless capital accumulation. Thus is the history of creative destruction written into the landscape of the actual historical geography of capital accumulation. (Harvey 2003:101)

This creative destruction is one source of accumulation in which the war-making powers of the state have historically and recently been quite useful; we refer, for example, to the Iraq War, in which the destruction of infrastructure was quite convenient for Halliburton, which then was assigned, at significant profit, to rebuild it. The fact that so may thousands of bodies on both sides had to be destroyed in the process is of little consequences from the perspective of the accumulation of wealth.

Molecular Accumulation

Yet a simple conflation of the local machinations of capital accumulation (i.e., "molecular accumulation") with territorial (state) power would be an analytical error. Harvey (2003) explains in detail that the two logics are neither analytically nor politically collapsible into each other, even though current configurations of power in Britain and the United States might recommend just such a conclusion.[3] Nation-states are comparatively fixed in time and space, and at times the power of the nation-state is inconsistent with the power of the local logics of capital accumulation within them. We need not look far to find examples to illustrate Harvey's ideas: the embargo of Cuba that robs U.S. capital of the opportunity to profit from the island's resources; the Cold War, in which the isolation of the Soviet Union and its aligned states meant that entire regions of the globe could not be mined as sources of profit; the British colonial practice of enforcing underdevelopment, thus rendering vast territories unable to absorb surplus capital in the form of commodities or investment; and the monumental destruction of the Vietnam War that rendered the region worthless for many years to come as a source of capital investment and accumulation.

War, does, of course, enrich the arms industry, which in fact finds it very profitable to convince the public that a perpetual war economy is necessary. Indeed, filmmaker Eugene Jarecki's (2005) film *Why We Fight* argues convincingly that Dwight Eisenhower's dire prediction has become reality: political power and military-industrial power have fused. Democratic decision-making is not possible when the profit of many corporations, located in every state of the United States, are entirely dependent on selling weapons, for which new wars are so useful. Says Charles Lewis of the Center for Public Integrity, "Our attempt at democracy [in the United States] is a constant struggle between capitalism and democracy. . . . The fundamental reality is that most of the government's decisions today are substantially dictated by powerful corporate interests. Clearly, capitalism is winning." Chalmers Johnson, analyst for the Central Intelligence Agency (CIA) from 1967 until 1973, adds, "The defense budget is three quarters of a trillion dollars. Profits went up last year [2004] well over 25%. When war becomes that profitable, you're going to see more of it."

But then again, other capitalist groupings find violent conflict to be rather inconvenient indeed. Losses of profitable opportunities because of territorial conflicts lead to conflicts that are profitable for some but ultimately not in the best interests of accumulation in general. The same tension between territorial logics and capital accumulation could be seen today in the energetic debates over the question of Mexican immigration to the United States. Irrational patriotism and territorial hypernationalism are very useful to ruling classes for the purpose of internal social control, but when such sentiment threatens to reduce the flow of very cheap and exploitable labor to agribusiness, the construction industry, meatpacking, and the restaurant and hotel trades, the logics of territory and of accumulation are at loggerheads.

All this is to reiterate that these two logics of power are neither conflatable nor necessarily structurally opposed, but rather interact dialectically. Although the rapaciousness of capital will always ultimately seek expansion to solve its recurrent crises, and although the state's mechanisms of coercion are useful instruments in this regard, the state itself also at times finds its interests contradicted by the desire for flexible accumulation through financial and geographic mobility. Although Harvey is quite correct to stress the dialectical relation between them, the preceding chapters suggest that the capital logic of power is the side of the dialectic that seems to be more aggressive, more energetic, more flexible, and more demanding of a periodic reconfiguration of territorial logics. That is, when push comes to shove, the capitalist demand for accumulation overpowers territorial logics of states. In this regard Harvey would seem to concur:

> The evident corollary of all this is that geopolitical conflicts would almost certainly arise out of the molecular processes of capital accumulation no matter what the state powers thought they were about, that these molecular movements (particularly of finance capital) can easily undermine state powers, and that the political state, in advanced capitalism, has to spend a good deal of effort and consideration on how to manage the molecular flows to its own advantage both internally and externally. (Harvey 2003:108)

Spatial barriers defined by nation-states must be destroyed so that they can be reformulated according to the needs of capital: "The production of space, the organization of wholly new territorial divisions of labour, the opening up of new and cheaper sources for the extraction of natural resources, of new regions as dynamic spaces of capital accumulation, and the penetration of pre-existing social formations by capitalist social relations and institutional arrangements . . . provide important ways to absorb capital and labor surpluses" (Harvey 2003:116). Recent history is replete with examples of territorial boundaries being ignored or violently reformulated by multinational corporations in search of profits. Royal Dutch Shell and its war-making history in Africa comes immediately to mind. The fact that Shell's profiteering has sometimes been consistent with the "national interests" of Britain and the Netherlands does not mean that its violence in Africa is an outcome of territorial logics of power. Indeed, since Shell is more powerful than most states of the region, it has been able to manipulate and even exacerbate subnational divisions. In this regard, multinational corporations may even find civil wars and disputed borders to be quite useful. Global capital accumulation finds the territorial logics of power based in nation-states to be only instrumentally and occasionally useful; capital is ready and willing to energetically undermine state power when it becomes a barrier to profit.

This is particularly true when capitalists based in different states or regional configurations finds themselves in competition with each other and need military power to be triumphant, or when national capital exhausts local resources and needs to expand to prevent the recurrent crises of overaccumulation. Harvey explains (2003:132–133):

> It is at this point that the territorialized politics of state and empire re-enter to claim a leading role in the continuing drama of endless capital accumulation and overaccumulation. The state . . . is the political entity, the body politic, that is best able to orchestrate institutional arrangements and manipulate the molecular forces of capital accumulation to preserve that pattern of asymmetries in exchange that are most advantageous to the dominant capitalist interest working within its frame.

The quest for accumulation—which during the Clinton years found expression in the neoliberal free-for-all—now finds itself in need of the violence of the war machine to continue its project. This is how Harvey understands the war in Iraq. It was not merely, as some on the left insist, the need to secure access to oil that motivated the invasion. Nor was it merely the creative destruction and the vast opportunities for accumulation afforded to Halliburton and the like. Rather, however important these specific aims, it was a much larger project based on the territorial logic of power that was determinant. It was a desperate gamble on the part of the United States to save its hegemonic position in relation to the global economy.

Geographic Logics and the American War Machine

The preceding discussion identifies a disturbingly confusing array of logics of power: nation-state, subnational capital, supranational and transnational fixed capital, financial (necessarily global), regional-political (such as the European Union), global manufacturing capital, and global credit (such as the World Bank and the International Monetary Fund). Various combinations and alliances do sometimes coalesce around a particular imperial project, but just as often these alliances fall apart when—like a band of thieves stealing from each other—each connives to grasp more than its share of the stolen loot. The result is lived experience of chaos and conflict of the sort that can only promote violence. This is the context of competing logics of power and competing geographic scales that produces the variety of war machines documented in the preceding chapters. The violence and chaos of global political economy, working furiously to avoid systemic crises, is manifest even on the geographic scale of the individual body—mutilated, disfigured, and often dead, scarred physically and emotionally, cannon fodder in the creative destruction of rapacious capital accumulation.

Although various war machines appear to be very different and may serve competing logics of accumulation or territory, they nonetheless emerge from a common frantic effort to avoid the inevitable crises of over-accumulation under late capitalism. The logics behind the "spatial fix" (see Harvey 1982) are just that—logical, rational, and intentional. The presence of social chaos and violence does not mean that an economic logic is not working itself out in a methodical way. Neither are the contemporary clashes of ruling classes and working classes—which may appear to be about ethnicity, religion, or internecine power struggles—anything new; all manner of contemporary conflict around the globe, not least U.S. imperialism, is consistent in two ways: first, within a particular spatial configuration, the past is consistent with the present, and within the present, the logics of warfare in one space are consistent with those of another. Consider the forceful argument of Neil Smith (2005:26):

> Viewing empire thorough geographic lenses help to crystallize that continuity: although the location of imperial power may have switched from London to New York and Washington, and although a territorially defined colonialism may have given way to an imperialism of markets and missiles, and although the national definition of capitals may have given way to a new globalism, the reality of exploitation and domination of the poorest parts of the world by the richest and most powerful has not changed at all.

It is not merely that oppression and exploitation are consistent with the past and consistent across space. Nor is it merely that the various forms of war and violence documented in the preceding chapters are different manifestations of political-economic oppression, made unique in a particular time and place. Nor even is it merely that the logics of the war machines emerge from similar political-economic exigencies. Rather, and even more, our claim is that *it is the same logic*, working differentially through geohistoric specificity.

If this is true, then the "new imperialism" announced by David Harvey in 2003 is not really new at all, as his own volume argues. In this regard, Harvey's City University of New York colleague Neil Smith has demonstrated in more detail how the apparent newness of U.S. imperialism is instead continuous with both the distant and the most recent American past. What has changed is its unfettered and unmasked arrogance. Smith convincingly argues that the neoliberal and the neoconservative agendas have the same goal of global economic control and the maintenance of U.S. hegemony. Working through diplomacy, enforcement of "free trade," and even, if needed, economic terrorism (see Perkins 2005, 2008), the policies of the Clinton administration served the same territorial and accumulative logics of Reagan's saber-rattling program, but at a measured pace and under the guise of global prosperity. The "new imperialism" is simply an impatient continuation of this process. Although economic arm-twisting did work gradually, the neoconservative movement—best articulated by the Project for a New American Century—was dissatisfied. It seemed to want more, faster, and was willing to militarily pry open unwilling economies for plunder: "Neoliberal incrementalism and global compromise, a certain penchant for reconciling global conflicts diplomatically rather than militarily . . . are all eschewed in this unbridled ambition for a forceful American globalism" (Smith 2005:20). Both Smith and Harvey point out that Paul Bremer's main task as the "provisional" leader of Iraq was to force open national assets to foreign control. This he did by changing the constitution to allow for foreign ownership of formerly national resources, the privatization of nearly all formerly public ventures, and the export of profit. In short, the riches of the Iraqi economy were to be open for looting by U.S. and British corporations, long after fortunes wrought from the destruction and reconstruction of infrastructure were over.

It is true, as we have seen, that more than a few U.S. corporations—Bechtel, Blackwater, Halliburton (and its subsidiary Kellogg Brown & Root), and not least the manufacturers of tons of weaponry used against the Iraqi people—became very wealthy indeed as a result of the second U.S. invasion of Iraq. But it was not the direct and immediate profiteering by these corporations or even the forced liberalization of the Iraqi economy, says Harvey (2003), that was the real motivation for that particular war. Rather, the second invasion of Iraq should be seen as an anxious scramble to secure another century of U.S. economic dominance. The United States is no longer the global leader in production, and its wildly irresponsible borrowing (nationally and on the part of its citizens) is costing it global dominance even in finance. Further, even its formerly preeminent status as a receiver of rents (through technology, software, and pharmaceuticals) is, as Harvey (2003) convincingly argues, a perilous basis for economic hegemony.

The only source of power remaining, then, is the control of someone else's oil that is urgently needed by the newly dominant economies of the European Union and China. The war was not about acquiring enough oil to feed the domestic U.S. demand but rather about the ability to manipulate and even starve the two economies that are now outperforming that of the United States. Harvey (2003:25) sees in the Iraq War the need to maintain economic control despite the dismal economic future of the United States:

> What better way for the United States to ward off that competition [from Europe and Asia] and secure its own hegemonic position than to control the price, conditions, and distribution of the key economic

resource upon which those competitors rely? And what better way to do that than to use the one line of force where the U.S. still remains all-powerful—military might?

Smith (2004:24, 26) states this argument succinctly:

[While] the war in Iraq has to do with oil, . . . it is not simply a war for oil but a larger war to control the global economic infrastructure, practices and relations that orchestrate the global economy (of which oil is a significant part). In short, it's about the endgame of globalization.

Although Smith agrees with Harvey that control of the oil spigot is indeed a central goal of U.S. aggression in the region, the matter is not so simple. In this regard, Smith provides a complication to Harvey's chapter "It's All about Oil." Rather, Smith (2005:189) argues that it's all about oil *and* geography *and* the dangers of oppositional coalitions:

Having lost its grip in the region, and recognizing the power of the emerging and antagonistic Islamism, Washington's major fear in the 1990s was that some sort of working coalition might emerge between Saudi Arabia, Iraq, and possibly other states. Such a coalition would fill the void left by lost U.S. influence in the region, . . . leaving the U.S. government (but not necessarily the embedded oil companies) out in the cold. The multinationalism of the oil companies and their increased independence from specific governments further weakened the hand of the U.S.

Smith's word "endgame" is well chosen and communicates exactly what is at stake. The "new" imperialism is the Hail Mary pass in which the United States has gambled it all, hoping to maintain is obscene consumption habits and its rentier profits well beyond its own real economic capacity. The "'endgame global America' [is] the culmination of a U.S.-centered (but *not exclusively American*) political and economic globalization" (Smith 2005:12). This is the third and final moment of American global dominance, and in this regard, Smith and Harvey again agree. Following Arrighi (1994), Smith argues that the beginning of the end of British dominance was marked by a movement away from productive economic control in favor of financial control. When Britain became "the world's bank—a rentier state—its financial hegemony actually marked the zenith of its imperialism; competitors, especially the U.S. and Germany, supplanted its economic power. . . . As one theorist of imperialism put it at the time, a "rentier state is a state of parasitic, decaying capitalism" (Smith 2005:23, quoting Lenin).

If a rentier economy is actually one in decay, then how much more unstable and on the verge of collapse is an economy that grasps at the straw of a reterritorialization of power through control of someone else's wealth? The inevitable—according to Smith, Harvey, and Arrighi—collapse of U.S. domination is likely to lead to global economic and military chaos unless the United States gently retreats from its coercive leadership history, an unlikely event. Harvey quotes Arrighi and Silver: "If the [global capitalist] system eventually breaks down, it will be primarily because of U.S. resistance to adjustment and accommodation. And conversely, U.S. adjustment and accommodation to the rising economic power of the East Asian region is an essential condition for a non-catastrophic transition to a new world order" (Arrighi et al. 1999:288–289 in Harvey 2003:75).

It is this slipping away of U.S. dominance and its increasingly desperate efforts to reverse that loss that accounts for the particular virulence of state-sponsored violence (including, of course, war in its various manifestations) documented herein. *One* of the logics of the war machines discussed in this volume—though as we have argued there is certainly more than one logic and more than one war machine—is not merely the United States using its strength to bully its way to economic control. Moreover, the increasingly vociferous U.S. bluster is a sign of weakness in the face of an inevitable loss of economic *and* military hegemony. It is true that the volume of this rhetoric has diminished somewhat since the election of President Barack Obama, but this fact will likely only delay or mitigate—not eradicate altogether—the military conflicts that changes in economic regimes almost inevitably bring.

Based on the preceding discussion, we posit the following: First, the war machine is not a unified and coherent "thing" but rather a series of processes that take many different shapes and forms in various times and places. Second, whatever the differential natures of war and war-like processes, they all emerge from some convergence of the logics of territorial-based state power and/or molecular capital accumulation. Third, these logics are in dialectical relation and thus often oppose each other even as at other times they interact creatively. Fourth, and despite this interaction, given the contemporary configurations of capital and state, it seems that the power of capital accumulation is the engine that most energetically propels the dialectic toward its next violent "resolution." Fifth, since ruling classes the world over are not likely to voluntarily relinquish even a small portion of their privilege, more entrenched, energetic, and autonomous war machines are surely on the way, bringing with them more of the catastrophic health consequences described in detail in the preceding chapters. Sixth, the configuration and reconfiguration of space is essential to the continuing cycles of accumulation.

These theses provide coherence to the confusing military-related violence we witness in the world today. The accumulation of wealth through the production of space is a violence process. No fine-tuning of the most well-intentioned economists or political leaders can change this fact. Nor even is a well-intentioned peace movement, absent a wholesale transformation of the logic of capital accumulation, likely to have much positive effect in the bigger picture. The price of stable processes of accumulation is the health and lives of massive numbers of people, combatants and (more often) noncombatants alike, with territorial logics of power and—as the mechanism of its enforcement—war and war machines. And when the pile of dead and dying bodies becomes too inconvenient, space is reconfigured again elsewhere to permit another cycle of capital accumulation. *The production of space, the production of war, and the production of wealth cannot be separated analytically or politically.*

Ethnographies of War and Health

Our task at this point is to apply these findings of economic geography to the ethnographic data of the preceding chapters. Each of the specific accounts offered by contributors to this volume reflects a somewhat different face of the torturous encounter of war and health, while reflecting different configurations of the operating logics of state and capital. Apparent convergence and temporary coherence should not mask the quite different faces of war and war machinery, even if the same logics of capital accumulation propel them all forward. It has been the argument throughout this conclusion that the various manifestations of national and global war machines do not represent a unified body of actors or social sectors, but this does not mean that there is not a singular logic that provides at least an analytical—if not also political—cohesion to the multiplicity of violences described here.

In the introduction, we cited a large number of studies that document the many ways in which war machines produce health crises for many years after hostilities have ceased or even in the absence of a hot war, such as with war budgets that steal from public health. A great number of studies have documented injuries and deaths of civilians, lifelong psychological trauma, late-onset problems, undocumented casualties (such as the "disappeared"), decimation of health and social infrastructures, environmental damage of war and its production, intergenerational transmission of war-related illness, and the health consequences of bloated war budgets. The chapters that followed offered an in-depth analyses of one or more of these manifestations of war-related damage to human lives.

Patrick Clarkin's contribution began the volume with an excellent and erudite analysis and synthesis of the work of more than 100 scholars, regarding war-related food insecurity and the consequences of poor nutrition on fetal and early childhood development. He arrived at two very important conclusions. First, as we might expect, food insecurity as a result of war seriously impacts even the adult health of the following generation. Thus, even a generation that has not known war directly experiences its consequences in the bodies of its constituents. Living bodies, then, become the parchment on which are inscribed previous generations of conflict. It is in this regard that Clarkin makes his second important contribution. He insists that the multiple analytical tools of anthropology must be harnessed in an analysis of war-related health and illness. His own subfield of biological anthropology, by itself, provides an inadequate understanding of war and health. But CMA, the guiding framework of this volume, also could benefit from the insights of biological/evolutionary/paleontological anthropology (Goodman and Leatherman 1999). As a field that already incorporates culture, political economy, and public health, CMA is already well disposed, as seen in recent work in the field, to this sort of multidisciplinary analytical interaction (Baer and Singer 2009; Singer 2009).

Clarkin's analysis begins with the fact of war and describes its health consequences, saving the causes of war for other analysts. His findings emerge from a broad analysis of many studies of different wars rather than from a single ethnographic context. Hans Baer similarly explores the health consequences of the war machine as a single undifferentiated series of processes, operating across ethnographic contexts. He documents the massive use of oil by military vehicles as one of the multiple causes of global warming resulting from carbon emissions, a serious threat to global health: "As a result of these factors, it is appropriate to speak of the *diseases of global warming* (Baer and Singer 2009). This includes any 'tropical disease' that spreads to new places and peoples but also includes failing nutrition and freshwater supplies because of desertification of pastoral areas or flooding of agricultural areas and other diseases as well, such as heat stroke." Baer's chapter also reviews literature regarding "petro-imperialism," the matter explored in depth by Smith and Harvey. A particularly insightful contribution is his identification of a powerful dialectic of the war machine and health: "The war machine generates a considerable level of greenhouse gas emission, which, in turn, contributes to global warming and resulting impacts on health. At the same time, global warming contributes to armed conflict, creating a vicious cycle for the planet and its inhabitants" (see also Baer and Singer 2009). Baer is clear throughout his chapter that war does not appear on the global scene sui generis; rather, as argued above, war and the war machines are inevitable (if not intentional or coordinated) consequences of global economic structures that produce inequality and scarcity.

The seven subsequent ethnographic chapters also document war and war machines that can be traced to economic processes. The political-economic basis of the U.S. military aggression in the Middle East is perhaps the most obvious example of this. Hills reports that "Iraqi health is worse today than at any other time in history," and Harding and Libel declare that the catastrophe in Iraq is a "man-made disaster," calling to mind the Marxist concept of "creative destruction": a temporary solution to recurrent crises of overaccumulation. Whether it was purely for access to the oil wealth, control of the oil spigot to contest the growing economic power of China and the European Union (Harvey 2003), or to prevent a pan-Arab coalition (Smith 2005), the economic motivations are clear. We would argue, in fact, that many conflicts that appear to be about strategic (military) concerns are ultimately about economics. If some form of direct or indirect control of the Middle Eastern oil supply and transport is an economic and strategic exigency of the United States, then the military machinations in the area are also motivated by economic self-interest. Movements in this regard began as early as the 1960s, when U.S. economic domination was still secure.

In this regard, David Vine's chapter documents the astonishingly rapid deterioration of the health of the Chagossians and the sudden increase in death by sadness after they were forcibly relocated from their island home of Diego Garcia to the slums of Mauritius and the Seychelles. A geographical gymnastics was required to circumvent international law so as to secure for the United States a strategically located military base should any intervention in the Middle East someday become convenient: "The U.S. government convinced the British government to give it permission to build a military base on Diego Garcia. . . . U.S. officials insisted on receiving Diego Garcia and, as the bureaucratically worded expulsion order put it, 'exclusive control (without local inhabitants).'" The ruling class of the United States apparently imagined a day when its economic hegemony would slip away and military force be required to secure the obedience of the globe. The lives of a few thousand Chagossians was judged to be insignificant when compared with the need to sustain otherwise unsustainable profits and consumption 17,000 kilometers away. As we have argued, and despite Harvey's warning of the need to keep the dialectic in mind, territorial logics such as that explained by Vine are propelled by an economic engine: the need to ensure the continuation of unsustainable profits through military aggression.

It is not at first glance evident that an economic logic lies behind the territorial conflict in Palestine and Israel. In his chapter, Avram Bornstein documents the catastrophic consequences to Palestinian morbidity and mortality of the continued and intensifying Israeli military aggression. While medical care—or, rather, claims about it and even the idea of it—have been used as one of the justifications of the Israeli invasions, Bornstein "challenges the hegemonic assertion that an extended military occupation is 'enlightened.'" Any glance at life in occupied Palestine makes it quite clear that the situation is not conducive to human life, and in fact this may be one of the goals: to make life so unpleasant that the redundant population simply goes away, leaving the entirety of biblical Israel and Judah ripe for the taking. The territorial logic behind Zionism is obvious. Yet most Israelis, even ardent supporters of the colonization of Palestine, are not in fact Zionists. What, then, is the logic behind the geographic manipulation of Palestinian land and the brutal devaluation of Palestinian life? Bornstein's description elsewhere (2002:69–81) of economic life in the West Bank seems hauntingly familiar: a redundant population, undocumented migrant workers, unregulated labor markets, free trade zones, and underdevelopment—in a word, neoliberalism *par excellence*. Uneven geographic development of just this sort, as a strategy for capital accumulation and for the temporary "spatial fix" to recurrent crises, has been explained with great detail and insight by both Neil Smith (1984, 2003, 2005, 2008) and David Harvey (1982, 2000, 2003, 2006, 2007). The production and reconfiguration of space in just this way might appear to be territorial but, in the end, is thoroughly economic (see also Henri Lefebvre 1991). From the perspective of the United States, of course, Israel is like a Diego Garcia, with benefits. While the United States provides much of the war material, Israelis do the fighting. The end result of geographic control of a economically strategic region formerly under the thumb of the English (and the French) is the same.

Adrienne Pine finds that Honduras is similar in this regard. At first blush, state violence in and around San Pedro Sula appears to be a purely domestic matter. The Honduran ruling class, she tells us, has engaged in multiple synergetic ideological manipulations to produce an internal Other, a favorite of most nation-states: poor teenage men. Control of the media enables the ruling class to naturalize violence and provides a weapon of symbolic violence used to convince working-class Hondurans that they are naturally violent and need to be controlled by a strong state. Having bought into this hegemonic notion, many citizens welcome the "mano dura" of state and paramilitary death squads that drive about assassinating entire groups of young people who have the misfortunate of having a tattoo. All the problems of the national economy and of crime—both real and imagined—are the evil workings of young "gangs" whose numbers are surely inflated. The bodies of poor young men become the container of all the inadequacies of Honduran character.

This would all seem to stem from a standard mechanism of the territorial logic of power in which the ruling class attempts to solve a crisis of legitimacy by distraction and internal othering. It would be, that is, if Honduras had not already been ravished by neoliberalism. The analysis changes entirely if we consider the fact that San Pedro Sula happens to host a USAID-established free trade zone in which Gap clothing is manufactured by teenage girls. The production of a redundant population—displaced agricultural workers and their unemployed children—should thus be seen not only as a matter of internal power relations but, rather, also as the necessary condition for the export of profit through offshore sweatshops. That is, the devaluation of labor hugely increases profitability. What might otherwise be called a matter of internal "security" or a local elite exercising its exclusive right to use violent force is in fact an economic process involving the spatial fix of "free trade."

Both Honduras and neighboring Guatemala are hardly new targets of imperial and neocolonial power plays. Guatemala was also an early recipient of special Cold War attentions when the CIA, under the influence of the infamous United Fruit Company (now Chiquita Brands International), planned and facilitated the military coup that ousted reformer president Árbenz in 1954. And both Honduras and Guatemala were staging grounds for the Reagan wars of the 1980s against progressive-thinking governments in El Salvador and Nicaragua. Thus, there is quite a bit of historical precedent that the internal security of both Central American states has been organized around the needs of external capital, according to both its territorial (e.g., military launch pads) and its economic (i.e., Chiquita et al.) logics.

The chapter in which Adams documents and analyzes the significant military operations in Guatemala today describes but the most recent manifestation of this neocolonial presence. Considering the enormous amount of death and suffering inflicted on Central Americans throughout the Cold War, it is ironic that the provision of health services is so much a part of U.S. military operations in the region today. Although originally conceived as a public relations ploy, a way to "engage partner nations through humanitarian projects," Adams in this volume tells us that the provision of medical services to civilian populations is now only a side effect of the main training mission of the Medical and Dental Readiness Training Exercises (MEDRETES): "because of its proximity and economic dependencies, Central America provides the ideal staging ground for the military [training] exercises that prepare the National Guard and military reserves for active duty [in Afghanistan and Iraq]." It would seem that even Central America is once again the victim of territorial struggles on the other side of the globe. (This time around, though, despite the many problems that Adams documents, at least the presence of the MEDRETES is a less violent intervention than the state terrorism of the Reagan years.)

Yet even the MEDRETES in Guatemala do not primarily serve a territorial logic of military strategy, readiness, training, and the like.

Adams reports that there is a blatant economic interest even in this apparently military strategy: "American military and economic foreign aid has
promoted U.S. exports, in the name of achieving national security, since
the Truman administration. Today, U.S. medical foreign aid reinforces
a post–Central American Free Trade Agreement campaign promoting
U.S. health products. . . . The medical missions reproduce an historic
U.S. commercial and cultural imperialism." In this way, the story of the
MEDRETES could be read as yet another instance of an apparently geopolitical process that in fact is a geoeconomic one.

The Maoist insurgency in Nepal analyzed by Kohrt, Tol, Pettigrew,
and Karki presents another version altogether of how territorially based
war machines are intertwined with the machinations of capital accumulation. The insurgency does indeed reflect a territorial logic of power in
that one set of social actors wished to replace the ruling elite of the state
or, in their words, to "smash the reactionary state and establish a new
democratic state." But the conflict was more than a mere contest over
control of the state apparatus. The insurgents' program included, at least
rhetorically, a plan to overturn existing power relations that depended on
unequal distribution of wealth by "rectifying economic and social injustice, abolishing monarchy, and establishing a constituent assembly." Thus,
economic justice was one motivation behind the civil unrest.

A second way in which the Maoist and state war machines are products of economic disparity has to do with the child soldiers Khort and his
colleagues studied. They tell us that there are various reasons that a young
person would choose to join the insurgency: "Poverty, gender and ethnic
discrimination, and legacies of state-sponsored violence create circumstances in which children voluntarily join armed groups." Girls, especially,
sometimes choose to join the insurgency as a way to escape gender-based
oppression. Thus, a desire to escape poverty was not the only motivation.
It would seem, then, that in this case our general thesis—that war machines of various sorts follow a logic that has to do with capital accumulation—does not hold. Nevertheless, Khort and his colleagues tell us, the
history of unequal power relations cannot be divorced from any social process in Nepal: "The macrosocial-level push factors involved in these cases
include discrimination and marginalization resulting from a feudal legacy
that concentrated wealth and political power among local elites based in
Kathmandu." The source of conflict in Nepal, therefore—even when it is

expressed through gender inequality—is not contemporary global capitalism per se but rather a history of unequal local distribution of wealth and
power. A highly stratified social structure thrives on conflict and nurtures
increasing material inequality—fertile ground for the implantation of
the logics of capital accumulation. And, as David Harvey (2003) points
out, primitive accumulation did not end with the modern era in Europe;
rather, it continues unabated in the form of what he calls "accumulation
by dispossession." "Dispossession" is an apt word to describe the displacement of children from their homes, incorporation into an insurgent army,
and the resulting psychological and social damage that Khort and his colleagues so skillfully document. We conclude, therefore, that even absent
the avowedly neoliberal imperative of Honduras or Guatemala, Iraq or
Palestine, deregulated and privatized capital accumulation is behind an
enormous amount of war and violence around the globe—even in Nepal.

The Fourth World War

In every place the war looked different.
In some places it killed with bullets and bombs,
in others with hunger and neglect.
In some places it worked through global institutions and agencies,
in others through local thugs and profiteers.
Corporate globalization. Neoliberalism. Empire.
The logic that this violence served was called different things in different places.
But everywhere it was the same:
It was fragmentation. Isolation. Fear.
It was the rule of money and the market
extending itself over every inch of the planet
and every aspect of our lives.

In every place, as the documentary film *The Fourth World War* tells us,
the war does indeed look different. It kills differently. Different actors on
either side struggle for different goals: wealth, power, borders, survival,
cultural purity. But all these faces of war seem to be traceable, if not to
the same war machine, then to the same set of processes of territorial
power and molecular accumulation. Bodies die of differing immediate
causes, but what every body and every soul—be it a child soldier in Nepal, an Iraqi civilian, a Honduran teenager, an imprisoned Palestinian, a

homesick Chagossian, or a malnourished newborn—has in common are fragmentation, isolation, and fear. And in the words of the film and in the analyses we have presented, the cause of all this suffering is "the rule of money and the market extending itself over every inch of the planet and every aspect of our lives."

The creation of wealth leads necessarily to the creation of suffering, capitalism irrevocably destroys the earth's resources, human life becomes increasingly difficult to sustain, and long-term global environmental integrity is sacrificed for short-term private profit—such processes make war and its attendant morbidity and mortality inevitable. This would suggest that the site of transformative intervention should not be limited to the scale of the individual bodies that bear the scars of war (although medically these must be attended), nor to the level of national territorial struggles or state violence, nor even to the level of war machines. In addition to these sites, intervention must occur at the *causal* level, that is, with political-economic systems whose insatiable drive for profit perpetuates inequality and suffering.

Interventions at this scale have been occurring at increasing frequency and with some success, as the moving frames of *The Fourth World War* document. Massive and well-coordinated movements against evictions and water privatization in South Africa, land displacement in Chiapas, genocide in Palestine, and neoliberalism in South Korea, Italy, and Canada are all depicted in the film. But there is always a response. States' apparatus of violence are servants of more powerful masters. The narrator continues:

And then the Empire spoke again.
And it tried to drown our voices in the deafening violence of war.
The illusions of stability, economic efficiency, and representative democracy were replaced with crisis, war, and terror.
With war *as* terror.
Wherever our movements won victories, the system's response was war.
War that cannot be won.
War that they have no intention of ending.
War that is irrational and inefficient.
War that does not end, that is an end in itself.

If indeed war is an end in itself, then we cannot be content with any formulation, political or scientific, that posits war as the unfortunate consequence of occasional madmen whose damage must be minimized. For the maintenance of ruling class power within states as well as the search for sources of accumulation across states, war and war machines are in fact rather convenient. This will not change until the very configuration of ruling classes is overturned. Understanding the full toll of wars and the war machines as well as the ultimate source of their grinding destruction is, we believe, only a starting point for achieving this (ultimately) public health objective.

Notes

1. From *The Fourth World War*, directed by Richard Rowley (2004).

2. For a discussion of the logical and historical development of this understanding of dialectics and the relation between the dialectics of Marx versus that of Hegel, see Bhaskar (1996).

3. The fact that President Obama does not embrace the neoconservative military agenda does not mean that the basis of class relations has been challenged.

Works Cited

Arrighi, Giovanni
    1994   *The Long Twentieth Century: Money, Power, and the Origins of Our Time*. New York: Verso.

Arrighi, Giovanni, Beverly J. Silver, and Iftikhar Ahmad
    1999   *Chaos and Governance in the Modern World System*. Minneapolis: University of Minnesota Press.

Baer, Hans A., and Merrill Singer
    1992   *African-American Religion in the Twentieth Century: Varieties of Protest and Accommodation*. Knoxville: University of Tennessee Press.
    2009   *Global Warming and the Political Ecology of Health: Emerging Crises and Systemic Solutions*. Walnut Creek, CA: Left Coast Press.

Baer, Hans, Merrill Singer, and John Johnsen
    1986   Introduction: Toward a critical medical anthropology. *Social Science and Medicine* 23(2):95–98.

Baer, Hans A., Merrill Singer, and Ida Susser
  1997 *Medical Anthropology and the World System: A Critical Perspective.* Westport, CT: Bergin & Garvey.
  2003 *Medical Anthropology and the World System.* Westport, CT: Praeger.

Bhaskar, Roy
  1996 Dialectics. In *A Dictionary of Marxist Thought.* Edited by T. Bottmore, Laurence Harris, V. G. Kiernan, and Ralph Miliband, 143–150. Oxford: Blackwell.

Bornstein, Avram S.
  2002 *Crossing the Green Line between the West Bank and Israel.* Philadelphia: University of Pennsylvania Press.

Goodman, Alan H., and Thomas L. Leatherman
  1999 *Building a New Biocultural Synthesis: Political-Economic Perspectives on Human Biology.* Ann Arbor: University of Michigan Press.

Harvey, David
  1982 *The Limits to Capital.* Chicago: University of Chicago Press.
  2000 *Spaces of Hope.* Berkeley: University of California Press.
  2003 *The New Imperialism.* Oxford: Oxford University Press.
  2006 *Spaces of Global Capitalism: Towards a Theory of Uneven Geographical Development.* London: Verso.
  2007 *A Brief History of Neoliberalism.* Oxford: Oxford University Press.

Jarecki, Eugene
  2005 *Why We Fight.* Video documentary. 108 minutes. United States: Charlotte Street Films and BBC Storyville.

Lefebvre, Henri
  1991 *The Production of Space.* Oxford: Blackwell.

Perkins, John
  2005 *Confessions of an Economic Hit Man.* New York: Plume.
  2008 *The Secret History of the American Empire: The Truth about Economic Hit Men, Jackals, and How to Change the World.* New York: Plume.

Rowley, Richard
  2004 *The Fourth World War.* 75 minutes. Big Noise Films. Produced by Jacqueline Soohen and Richard Rowley.

Singer, Merrill
  1986 The emergence of a critical medical anthropology. *Medical Anthropology* 17(5):128–129.

2009   *Introduction to Syndemics: A Critical Systems Approach to Public and Community Health*. San Francisco: Jossey-Bass.

Singer, Merrill, and Hans Baer
    1995   *Critical Medical Anthropology*. Amityville, NY: Baywood.

Smith, Neil
    1984   *Uneven Development: Nature, Capital, and the Production of Space*. New York: Blackwell.
    2003   *American Empire: Roosevelt's Geographer and the Prelude to Globalization*. Berkeley: University of California Press.
    2005   *The Endgame of Globalization*. New York: Routledge.
    2008   *Uneven Development: Nature, Capital, and the Production of Space*. Athens: University of Georgia Press.

Smith, Neil, and Peter Williams
    1986   *Gentrification of the City*. Boston: Allen & Unwin.

INDEX

ABOUT THE CONTRIBUTORS

Abigail E. Adams, Ph.D., is a sociocultural anthropologist, professor at Central Connecticut State University, and former journalist. She did her doctoral work at the University of Virginia, researching the role of U.S. and Mayan evangelical Christians during Guatemala's 36 years of civil war and counterinsurgency. She earned her master's degree in Latin American studies from Stanford University and her undergraduate degree from Haverford College in biology and anthropology. She has worked in Central America since studying Spanish in Guatemala as an undergraduate, during the first years of the acute genocidal violence. She continues research and publishing on Mayan cultural revitalization, U.S.–Central American relations, and postviolence political culture.

Hans Baer, Ph.D., is senior lecturer in the School of Philosophy, Anthropology, and Social Inquiry and the Centre for Health and Society at the University of Melbourne. He has conducted research on the Hutterites in South Dakota; the Levites (a Mormon sect in Utah); African American Spiritual churches; alternative medicine in the United States, the United Kingdom, and Australia; sociopolitical and religious life in East Germany; conventional and alternative HIV clinics in a western U.S. city; and the climate justice movement in Australia. He has published 16 books, coedited several special journal issues, and published some 150 book chapters and journal articles. Some of his books include *Recreating Utopia in the Desert*, *African American Religion* (with Merrill Singer), *Encounters with Biomedicine: Case Studies in Medical Anthropology*, *Critical Medical* (with

Merrill Singer), *Medical Anthropology and the World System: A Critical Perspective* (with Merrill Singer and Ida Susser), *Biomedicine and Alternative Healing Systems in America: Issues of Class, Race, Ethnicity, and Gender, Toward an Integrative Medicine,* and *Introducing Medical Anthropology* (with Merrill Singer).

Avram Bornstein, Ph.D., is an associate professor in the Department of Anthropology at John Jay College of Criminal Justice and at the Graduate Center of the City University of New York. He is the author of numerous articles and reviews concerning borders, state violence, and the Middle East, as well as the book *Crossing the Green Line between the West Bank and Israel* (2002), which focuses on the impact of checkpoints on Palestinians living under the Israeli Occupation in the West Bank.

Patrick F. Clarkin, Ph.D., earned his doctorate at Binghamton University in 2004. He is an assistant professor of anthropology at the University of Massachusetts, Boston. He has conducted research in the field of biological anthropology with Hmong and Lao refugees in the United States and French Guiana, looking at the long-term effects of the wars in Southeast Asia on health and physical growth. He has published research in the *American Journal of Human Biology* and the *Hmong Studies Journal.*

Scott Harding, Ph.D., received his doctorate from the University of Washington School of Social Work. He is assistant professor of community organization in the University of Connecticut School of Social Work. He is associate editor of the *Journal of Community Practice.* Since late 2006, he has been involved in a research project on the politics of humanitarian assistance for Iraqi refugees in the wake of the U.S.-led war in 2003.

Elaine A. Hills is an epidemiologist and a lecturer in the Department of Anthropology at the State University of New York (SUNY) at Albany. She has a varied background in public health, international studies, biological and medical anthropology, and social epidemiology. She holds a master's degree in anthropology. She served as a Rotary Ambassadorial Scholar at the University of Durham, England and is currently a Ph.D. candidate in epidemiology at the SUNY School of Public Health.

G. Derrick Hodge is an economic anthropologist who currently teaches at the University of Missouri Kansas City. His research specialty is political-economy and youth in Cuba. He is also the course director of medical anthropology in the MD/MPH program at the Mount Sinai School of Medicine in New York.

Rohit Karki received his bachelor's degree in social work from Saint Xaviers in Kathmandu, Nepal. He is a master's candidate in the Department of Sociology and Anthropology at Tribhuvan University in Kathmandu. His research focus is on developing participatory approaches for children's involvement in peace and conflict interventions. Karki, along with Save the Children—Sweden, developed the Child Led Indicator approach as a tool kit for child participatory programming. He is the project coordinator for the Transcultural Psychosocial Organization Nepal's Children Associated with Armed Forces and Armed Groups Program.

Brandon A. Kohrt, M.D., Ph.D. (Department of Anthropology, Emory University, Atlanta) is a resident in the Department of Psychiatry at Emory University School of Medicine. His research focus is on the mental health impact of political violence. He is a research adviser to the Transcultural Psychosocial Organization Nepal, and the founding director of the Atlanta Asylum Network for Survivors of Torture. In 2005 he received the Physicians for Human Rights Navin Narayan Award for leadership in health and human rights. He is the cowriter of the documentary *Returned: Child Soldiers of Nepal's Maoist Army.*

Kathryn Libal, Ph.D., received her doctoral degree in anthropology at the University of Washington. She is assistant professor in the University of Connecticut School of Social Work. Her research focuses on human rights, humanitarianism, and social welfare in Turkey and the Middle East. Since late 2006, she has researched the politics of humanitarian assistance for Iraqi refugees in the wake of the U.S.-led war.

Judith Pettigrew, Ph.D. (University of Cambridge), is an anthropologist and a member of the Faculty of Education and Health at the University of Limerick, Ireland. She has conducted long-term anthropological research in Nepal since 1990 and is the coauthor of the edited volume *Windows* *into a Revolution: Ethnographies of Maoism in South Asia*. She is currently writing a monograph on the impact of the Maoist insurgency on rural civilians. Her work has appeared in numerous journals, including *Anthropology Today*, and edited books, including *Resistance and the State: Nepalese Experiences, Himalayan People's War*, and *Nepalis inside and outside Nepal: Political and Social Transformations*. Pettigrew has been trained in occupational therapy and psychotherapy.

Adrienne Pine, Ph.D. is a medical anthropologist and author of *Working Hard, Drinking Hard, on Violence and Survival in Honduras* (2008). She has conducted research in Honduras since 1997, exploring the intersections of violence and subjectivity in a wide variety of sites, and serves frequently as an expert witness on Honduras in U.S. federal court. After receiving her doctorate from the University of California at Berkeley, she spent three years fighting market-based health care as lead political educator for the California Nurses Association. She has taught anthropology at the American University in Cairo and is currently assistant professor of anthropology at American University in Washington.

Merrill Singer, Ph.D., is the former director of the Center for Community Health Research at the Hispanic Health Council. He is currently a senior research scientist at the Center for Health, Intervention and Prevention and a professor in the Department of Anthropology at the University of Connecticut. He also is a research affiliate of the Center for Interdisciplinary Research on AIDS at Yale University. He has published over 200 articles and chapters in health and social science journals and books and has authored or edited 21 books, including *The Political Economy of AIDS* (edited), *Medical Anthropology and the World System* (with Hans Baer and Ida Susser), *Introducing Medical Anthropology* (with Hans Baer), *Unhealthy Health Policy* (edited with Arachu Castro), *Something Dangerous, Drugging the Poor, Killer Commodities: Public Health and the Corporate Production of Harm* (with Hans Baer), *Global Warming and the Political Economy of Health* (with Hans Baer), and *Introduction to Syndemics: A Systems Approach to Public and Community Health*. He is the recipient of the Rudolph Virchow Prize, the AIDS and Anthropology Paper Prize, the George Foster Memorial Award for Practicing Anthropology from the Society for Medical Anthropology, and the Prize for Distinguished

Achievement in the Critical Study of North America from the Society for the Anthropology of North America.

Wietse A. Tol, Ph.D., received a master's degree in clinical and health psychology from Leiden University and a Ph.D. at the Vrije University of Amsterdam. He is a technical adviser with HealthNet TPO for the Transcultural Psychosocial Organization Nepal. His intervention and research interests concern the design, implementation, and evaluation of psychosocial and mental health projects for populations exposed to organized violence and other complex emergencies in low-income settings. He has published research on the efficacy of programs for torture survivors in Nepal and school-based programs for war-affected children in Burundi, Indonesia, and Sri Lanka and has consulted for a variety of organizations, including UNICEF, Save the Children, and the World Health Organization.

David Vine, Ph.D., is assistant professor of anthropology at American University in Washington, D.C., and the author of *Island of Shame: The Secret History of the U.S. Military Base on Diego Garcia* (2009). His writing has appeared in the *New York Times*, the *Washington Post*, *Mother Jones* online, the *Chronicle of Higher Education*, *International Migration*, and *Human Rights Brief*, among others. He is a contributor to Foreign Policy in Focus, a project of the Institute for Policy Studies, and a founding member of the Project on Foreign Military Bases and the Network of Concerned Anthropologists.

Dahlia S. Wasfi, M.D., is an internationally known speaker and activist. Born in New York to an American Jewish mother and an Iraqi Muslim father, she lived in Iraq as a child, returning to the United States at age five. After graduating from Swarthmore College with a BA in biology in 1993, she earned her medical degree from the University of Pennsylvania in 1997. She has made two trips to Iraq since the 2003 "Shock and Awe" invasion, including a three-month stay in Basrah in the spring of 2006.